LISTEN TO HIP HOP!

Recent Titles in
Exploring Musical Genres

Listen to New Wave Rock! Exploring a Musical Genre
James E. Perone

Listen to Pop! Exploring a Musical Genre
James E. Perone

Listen to the Blues! Exploring a Musical Genre
James E. Perone

Listen to Rap! Exploring a Musical Genre
Anthony J. Fonseca

Listen to Classic Rock! Exploring a Musical Genre
Melissa Ursula Dawn Goldsmith

Listen to Movie Musicals! Exploring a Musical Genre
James E. Perone

Listen to Psychedelic Rock! Exploring a Musical Genre
Christian Matijas-Mecca

Listen to Soul! Exploring a Musical Genre
James E. Perone

Listen to Punk Rock! Exploring a Musical Genre
June Michele Pulliam

LISTEN TO HIP HOP!

Exploring a Musical Genre

ANTHONY J. FONSECA AND
MELISSA URSULA DAWN GOLDSMITH

Exploring Musical Genres
James E. Perone, Series Editor

BLOOMSBURY ACADEMIC
NEW YORK • LONDON • OXFORD • NEW DELHI • SYDNEY

BLOOMSBURY ACADEMIC
Bloomsbury Publishing Inc
1385 Broadway, New York, NY 10018, USA
50 Bedford Square, London, WC1B 3DP, UK
29 Earlsfort Terrace, Dublin 2, Ireland

BLOOMSBURY, BLOOMSBURY ACADEMIC and the Diana
logo are trademarks of Bloomsbury Publishing Plc

First published in the United States of America by ABC-CLIO 2021
Paperback edition published by Bloomsbury Academic 2025

Copyright © Bloomsbury Publishing Inc, 2025

For legal purposes the Acknowledgments on p. xvii constitute
an extension of this copyright page.

Cover Photo: Mathangi Maya Arulpragasam, better known as M.I.A.,
performing at The Danforth Music Hall, Toronto, Canada, July 18, 2013.
(EXImages/Alamy Live News)

All rights reserved. No part of this publication may be reproduced or transmitted
in any form or by any means, electronic or mechanical, including photocopying,
recording, or any information storage or retrieval system, without prior permission
in writing from the publishers.

Bloomsbury Publishing Inc does not have any control over, or responsibility for,
any third-party websites referred to or in this book. All internet addresses given
in this book were correct at the time of going to press. The author and publisher
regret any inconvenience caused if addresses have changed or sites have
ceased to exist, but can accept no responsibility for any such changes.

Library of Congress Cataloging-in-Publication Data
Names: Fonseca, Anthony J., author. | Goldsmith, Melissa Ursula Dawn, author.
Title: Listen to hip hop! : exploring a musical genre / Anthony J. Fonseca
and Melissa Ursula Dawn Goldsmith.
Description: [1.] | Santa Barbara : Greenwood, 2021. | Series: Exploring
musical genres | Includes bibliographical references and index.
Identifiers: LCCN 2021001379 (print) | LCCN 2021001380 (ebook) |
ISBN 9781440874871 (cloth) | ISBN 9781440874888 (epub)
Subjects: LCSH: Rap (Music)—History and criticism.
Classification: LCC ML3531 .F65 2021 (print) | LCC ML3531 (ebook) |
DDC 782.421649—dc23
LC record available at https://lccn.loc.gov/2021001379
LC ebook record available at https://lccn.loc.gov/2021001380

ISBN: HB: 978-1-4408-7487-1
PB: 979-8-2162-7004-1
ePDF: 978-1-4408-7488-8
eBook: 979-8-2161-1194-8

Series: Exploring Musical Genres

To find out more about our authors and books visit www.bloomsbury.com
and sign up for our newsletters.

Contents

Series Foreword	ix
Preface	xiii
Acknowledgments	xvii
1 Background	1
2 Must-Hear Music	13
Aaliyah (featuring DMX) and Rihanna (featuring Jay-Z): "Come Back in One Piece" and "Umbrella"	13
Paula Abdul and Tony! Toni! Toné!: "Straight Up" and "Feels Good"	19
Afrika Bambaataa & the Soulsonic Force (Music by Planet Patrol): "Planet Rock"	24
Afroman: "Because I Got High"	30
Akon: "Beautiful"	33
Die Antwoord: "Ugly Boy"	36
A$AP Rocky: "Sundress" and "Kids Turned Out Fine"	39
Babyface: "It's No Crime" and "There She Goes"	43
Beyoncé: "Run the World (Girls)"	46
Black Eyed Peas: "Boom Boom Pow"	51
Boyz II Men (featuring Michael Bivins): "Motownphilly"	54

Brett Domino (The Brett Domino Trio): "Pinocchio"	57
BTS: "Idol"	61
Cee-Lo Green (featuring Timbaland): "I'll Be Around"	65
Childish Gambino: "This Is America"	68
Chinese Man: "I've Got That Tune"	73
George Clinton: "Atomic Dog"	76
DJ APS: "Tabba"	81
Donatan/Cleo: "My Słowianie"	85
Fifth Harmony (featuring Kid Ink): "Worth It"	89
Dominic Fike: "3 Nights"	93
Fugees: "Nappy Heads" (remix)	97
Gorillaz: "Clint Eastwood"	101
Great Big Sea: "Beggar Dude"	104
Hamilton (Cast): "Ten Duel Commandments"	106
Herbie Hancock (featuring DXT): "Rockit"	109
Janet Jackson: "Rhythm Nation"	114
Jessie J (featuring Ariana Grande and Nicki Minaj): "Bang Bang"	119
Mateo Kingman: "Sendero Del Monte"	122
K'Naan: "Take a Minute" (album version)	126
Little Big: "Skibidi"	130
M.I.A.: "Paper Planes"	132
M.I.A.: "P.O.W.A."	136
Mix Master Mike (featuring DJ QBert): "Cosmic Assassins"	141
Nicki Minaj: "Roman Holiday"	145
NKOTBSB: "Don't Turn Out the Lights (D.T.O.T.L.)"	149
Frank Ocean: "Swim Good"	152
Plastician: "Windwalker" and "Tainted"	157

Contents **vii**

Psy: "Gangnam Style" (album and music video single)   161

Punjabi by Nature (featuring Offlicence and Charanjit Chani) and Yo Yo Honey Singh (featuring TDO, Singhsta, and Neha Kakkar): "Jaan Punjabi" and "Makhna"   165

Mark Ronson (featuring Bruno Mars): "Uptown Funk!"   170

Shaggy (featuring Rikrok): "It Wasn't Me"   175

Sukshinder Shinda (featuring Cheshire Cat and Tenashus): "Balle"   179

Ana Tijoux: "1977"   183

Timbaland (featuring Nelly Furtado and Justin Timberlake): "Give It to Me" and "Carry Out"   187

Justin Timberlake (featuring Timbaland) and La Materialista: "Sexyback" and "Los Pantaloncitos"   191

Time Zone (featuring John Lydon): "World Destruction"   197

Tricky: "Ghetto Stars"   203

Tumi and Chinese Man (featuring Taiwan MC): "Better That Way"   206

Pharrell Williams: "Freedom"   210

3 Impact on Popular Culture   215

4 Legacy   231

Further Reading   245

Index   253

Series Foreword

Ask some music fans, and they will tell you that genre labels are rubbish and that imposing them on artists and pieces of music diminishes the diversity of the work of performers, songwriters, instrumental composers, and so on. Still, in the record stores of old, in descriptions of radio-station formats (on-air and Internet), and at various streaming audio and download sites today, we have seen and continue to see music categorized by genre. Indeed, some genre boundaries are at least somewhat artificial, and it is true that some artists and some pieces of music transcend boundaries. But categorizing music by genre is a convenient way of keeping track of the thousands upon thousands of musical works available for listeners' enjoyment; it's analogous to the difference between having all your documents on your computer's home screen versus organizing them into folders. So, Greenwood's Exploring Musical Genres series is a genre- and performance group–based collection of books and e-books. The publications in this series will provide listeners with background information on the genre; critical analysis of important examples of musical pieces, artists, and events from the genre; discussion of must-hear music from the genre; analysis of the genre's impact on the popular culture of its time and on later popular-culture trends; and analysis of the enduring legacy of the genre today and its impact on later musicians and their songs, instrumental works, and recordings. Each volume will also contain a bibliography of references for further reading.

We view the volumes in the Exploring Musical Genres series as a go-to resource for serious music fans, the more casual listener, and everyone in between. The authors in the series are scholars, who probe into the details of the genre and its practitioners: the singers, instrumentalists, composers, and lyricists of the pieces of music that we love. Although the authors' scholarship brings a high degree of insight and perceptive analysis to the reader's understanding of the various musical genres, the authors approach their subjects with the idea of appealing to the lay reader, the music nonspecialist. As a result, the authors may provide critical analysis using some high-level scholarly tools; however, they avoid any unnecessary and unexplained jargon or technical terms or concepts. These are scholarly volumes written for the enjoyment of virtually any music fan.

Every volume has its length parameters, and an author cannot include every piece of music from within a particular genre. Part of the challenge, but also part of the fun, is that readers might agree with some of the choices of "must-hear music" and disagree with others. So while your favorite example of, say, grunge music might not be included, the author's choices might help you to open up your ears to new, exciting, and ultimately intriguing possibilities.

By and large, these studies focus on music from the sound-recording era: roughly the 20th century through the present. American guitarist, composer, and singer-songwriter Frank Zappa once wrote,

> On a record, the overall timbre of the piece (determined by equalization of individual parts and their proportions in the mix) tells you, in a subtle way, *WHAT* the song is about. The orchestration provides *important information* about what the composition *IS* and, in some instances, assumes a greater importance than *the composition itself*. (Zappa with Occhiogrosso 1989, 188; italics and capitalization from the original)

The gist of Zappa's argument is that *everything* that the listener experiences (to use Zappa's system of emphasizing words)—including the arrangement, recording mix and balance, lyrics, melodies, harmonies, instrumentation, and so on—makes up a musical composition. To put it another way, during the sound-recording era, and especially after the middle of the 20th century, we have tended to understand the idea of a piece of music—particularly in the realm of popular music—as being the same as the most definitive recording of that piece of music. And this is where Zappa's emphasis on the arrangement and recording's production comes into play. As a result, a writer delving into, say, new wave rock will examine and analyze the B-52's' version of "Rock Lobster" and not just the words, melodies, and chords that any band could sing and play and still label the result "Rock Lobster." To use Zappa's graphic way of highlighting particular words, the B-52's' recording *IS* the piece. Although they have expressed it in other ways, other writers such as Theodore Gracyk (1996, 18) and Albin J. Zak III (2001) concur with Zappa's equating of the piece with the studio recording of the piece.

In the case of musical genres not as susceptible to being tied to a particular recording—generally because of the fact that they are genres often experienced live, such as classical music or Broadway musicals—the authors will still make recommendations of particular recordings (we don't all have ready access to a live performance of Wolfgang Amadeus Mozart's *Symphony No. 40* any time we'd like to experience the piece), but they will focus their analyses on the more general, the notes-on-the-page, the expected general aural experience that one is likely to find in any good performance or recorded version.

Maybe you think that all you really want to do is just listen to the music. Won't reading about a genre decrease your enjoyment of it? My hope is that you'll find that reading this book opens up new possibilities for understanding your favorite musical genre and that by knowing a little more about it, you'll be able to listen with proverbial new ears and gain even more pleasure from your listening experience. Yes, the authors in the series will bring you biographical detail, the history of the genres, and critical analysis on various musical works that they consider to be the best, the most representative, and the most influential pieces in the genre; however, ultimately, the goal is to enhance the listening experience. That, by the way, is why these volumes have an exclamation mark in their titles. So please enjoy both reading and listening!

—*James E. Perone, Series Editor*

REFERENCES

Gracyk, Theodore. 1996. *Rhythm and Noise: An Aesthetics of Rock*. Durham, NC: Duke University Press.

Zak, Albin J., III. 2001. *The Poetics of Rock: Cutting Tracks, Making Records*. Berkeley: University of California Press.

Zappa, Frank, with Peter Occhiogrosso. 1989. *The Real Frank Zappa Book*. New York: Poseidon Press.

Preface

This book explores non-rap hip hop music, and as such serves as a complement to *Listen to Rap! Exploring a Musical Genre* (Anthony J. Fonseca, 2019), which discussed at length fifty Must-Hear rap artists, albums, and songs. Readers interested in more detail about rap music should consult Fonseca's text. Although the words "rap" and "hip hop" were at one time synonymous, in this book we consider rap to be a subset of hip hop music, along with boy and girl band hip hop-infused music, dance-based hip hop, trance, new jack swing, and hip hop-infused pop music, among others. Even though some of the songs included here have rapped verses or sections, they have only isolated elements in common with rap songs. And while contemporary rap lyrics are typically sociopolitical and economic statements, the hip hop songs here are more concerned with partying, uplifting messages, sex, and bragging rights (old-school rap often had these same themes).

Like Motown, the rap music scene gave African American musicians, music studio entrepreneurs, and producers (both financiers and music engineers) a chance to make their mark in the predominantly white music business. More importantly, rap gave African Americans, and to a lesser extent Latinx Americans, a chance to become multimillionaires who could establish and run their own record labels. Ultimately, rap (and later non-rap hip hop, the main topic of this book) redefined the music industry, replacing rock-and-roll as the top moneymaker. Today, *Rolling Stone* magazine, originally focused on rock music, devotes its covers and most of its pages to rappers, dance-based hip hop singers, and hip hop producers.

Looking back, it seems a long shot that the DIY (do-it-yourself) efforts of rap music and hip hop dance music would make such a strong artistic, cultural, and sociopolitical impact. Most early labels got their start when rappers and producers used glorified home studios to record music audiocassettes and CDs, which were then sold out of their car trunks. No Limit (New Orleans), one of the biggest early rap labels, started this way. Sugar Hill Records (Englewood, New Jersey) found its rappers in places like pizzerias, where they were working at the time. Ruthless Records (Compton, California, and later Los Angeles) found its rappers, music engineers, and executives selling drugs on street corners. Death Row Records (Los Angeles) strong-armed its rivals into breaking contracts so that it could hire rappers from other labels. Despite these humble and troubled beginnings, and despite subsequent attempts at censorship, rap music caught on—not just with the African American community, but in white suburban households as well. Today rap is a multibillion-dollar industry that has interests in music, fashion, and the performance arts. Rap music has become part of the mainstream, with rappers performing at the Kennedy Center and on Broadway and being inducted into the Rock and Roll Hall of Fame, the Smithsonian, and the Library of Congress.

Listen to Hip Hop! provides close listening and reading of a diverse set of non-rap hip hop songs and their lyric concerns, by a variety of artists—not just from the United States and the U.K. but also from other countries (for example, Canada, Chile, Ecuador, France, Poland, Russia, Somalia, South Africa, and South Korea). A few entries pair songs together to highlight significant connections in style or treatment. While each Must-Hear Music entry's main focus is the song itself, each also includes information about the singers, bands, songwriters, and producers, and how they use hip hop elements and conventions. Most of these conventions were established with various subgenres (or styles) of rap: alternative, chopper, gangsta, g-funk, horrorcore, mobb, snap, and trap, to name a few. These are subgenres that usually differ mainly in either specific lyrical content (e.g., gangsta, g-funk, and trap create portraits of inner-city lifestyles; horrorcore basks in violence and gore; mobb uses mafia imagery and icons to tell inner-city stories) and/or by using different choices in instrumentation, production, and/or vocal delivery (e.g., snap uses the sounds of either finger snaps or hand claps to create its beat, g-funk samples 1970s funk, chopper emphasizes the rapper's speed).

For the most part, this book's Must-Hear Music entries focus on songs and not albums, mainly because most artists who use hip hop conventions do so occasionally, incorporating these elements into their usual music genre. For example, Tony! Toni! Toné! and Boyz II Men, groups known mainly for R&B, use hip hop elements on occasion, as does M.I.A., an artist known mainly for her techno and electronic music style. In each entry, we will identify both the artist's usual genre and the hip hop elements the artist uses, both in general and in the particular song example. Also, we will carefully analyze and deconstruct each song's musical elements, discussing the sound and paying close attention to instrumentation and production values, including the use of sampling, which is a staple of rap. Song structures, keys, meters, and other technical elements of music are provided to appeal to readers with some musical background. Explanations of music terminology are given for readers with less musical experience who nevertheless wish to delve deeply to learn more about music and the sounds of hip hop. Entries also provide historical and sociocultural context, where appropriate.

Overall, these songs were selected for one of three reasons: influence, representation of a musical style, or creativity in their use of musical elements. Artists included in this book are often associated with other music genres and many use hip hop elements sparingly—the most conspicuous example being Great Big Sea, a traditional Irish music and rock quartet out of Newfoundland, Canada, that has used hip hop elements in just one song during its twenty-year run. That song, "Beggar Dude," is included here for that reason as well as for its creativity. Concerning influence, most of the artists included here have achieved iconic status. Many have been extremely successful commercially, selling tens of millions of singles and albums and receiving invitations to play the world's largest venues, including the Super Bowl Halftime Show.

Acknowledgments

Listen to Hip Hop! Exploring a Musical Genre is our second book in ABC-CLIO's Exploring Musical Genres Series, and we were delighted to work again with the series editor, James E. Perone, and acquisitions editor, Catherine M. Lafuente. We are grateful for their guidance, support, and suggestions as well as for the opportunity to engage in such fascinating music through close listening and analysis. We would also like to thank our friends Amy Baker, Jessica Barker, Steve Berlin, Kathleen Chapman, Jaqueline M. DeMaio, Jim and Pat Gallant, Valerie Lavender, Latisha Rocke, and David Ruddeforth, in addition to our Elms College and Westfield State University colleagues, who have shown genuine interest in the book and its progress. More than half of this book was written at Mosaic Café in Northampton, Massachusetts, which serves delicious Mediterranean cuisine. There, we enjoyed a wonderful writing atmosphere as well as many rounds of Moroccan mint tea, vegetarian stews, salads, and namoura. We thank the Mosaic Café staff for their hospitality, good food, kindness, and interest in the book as well.

The final writing stages of this book took place during the COVID-19 pandemic and the 2020 murders of Ahmaud Arbery, Breonna Taylor, and George Floyd, who represent just three of many Black victims of police brutality. Not only hip hop music, but also the larger culture of hip hop, has been crucial to the elevation of Black voices and the empowerment of Black people. We support efforts to demand justice for these murders as well as to confront and end systemic racism that exists in the United States and worldwide.

CHAPTER 1

Background

IN THE BEGINNING WERE THE WORDS, AND THEY WERE RAPPED

A celebration of urban, ethnic culture and art, hip hop culture produced a new musical genre called rap (a.k.a. MCing, spitting, or rhyming). Rap involves spoken vocals that typically feature rhyme, alliteration, assonance, wordplay, and imagery, all used to express an idea, message, or other kinds of content musically. It uses street slang and/or urban idioms. Also called MCs, rappers were known for their urban slang and their preference for replacing singing with a rhythmic version of rhymed talking that can best be described as a high-energy, jazzy (including jazz's improvisation element), aggressive version of talk-singing or patter song, both of which can be traced back for many centuries.

The earliest precursors to rap are West African griot traditions in which rhythmic chanters reported news, praised kingdoms, or kept genealogical records of families, all while usually accompanying themselves on a string instrument (a chordophone played like a harp) called the *kora*. Griots were travelling poets who employed talk-singing, without adding criticism to their lyrical content. Their lesser known West African contemporaries, who played *bolon* (also a chordophone but with a lower register than the kora and played like an upright bass), performed talk-singing that was allowed to be critical and came closer to prefiguring the sociopolitical rap that emerged much later in the United States. Other examples of talk-singing were used in blues, jazz, and American stage and film musicals (e.g., the patter song dialogue in Glenn Miller's "The Lady's in Love with You" and "The Little Man Who Wasn't There," both from 1939 and about romance, and Meredith

Willson's song "Rock Island" from *The Music Man*, from 1957, which used street slang and vocables to warn about the troubled youth who hung out at pool halls).

The most direct antecedent to rap used in hip hop, which was concerned with African American history and Black issues, is jazz poetry. Serious, socially conscious jazz poetry was made famous by Gil Scott-Heron (1949–2011) in songs like his 1971 single "The Revolution Will Not Be Televised." Heavyweight champion Muhammad Ali's "trash talk" of his opponent parodied jazz poetry to comic effect but was also influential. Scott-Heron and early MCs cited the band The Last Poets (1968–) as another strong influence, bridging jazz poetry to early rap. By 1971, the word "rap" was used to describe the rhythmic talking on albums, such as Isaac Hayes's funk song "Ike's Rap" from his studio album *Black Moses*. In 1975, Manhattan DJ Hollywood (Anthony Holloway, 1954–) became the first radio DJ to rap against a track of an album, played on a turntable, for an entire minute. Adapting and reworking the lyrics of Hayes's "Good Love 6-9969" (also 1975) and rapping them to MFSB's disco and funk song "Love Is the Message" (1974), DJ Hollywood not only rapped to the downbeat but also employed syncopation (shifting accents from the most expected beats such as the downbeat to unexpected beats; in other words, shifting from emphasis on beat one, also known as the downbeat, to beats two or four in a four-beat measure in quadruple meter). In 1978, he also became the first DJ to perform with turntables and a mixer at the Apollo Theater.

Early rappers were masters of both freestyle and recorded rap, and many participated in rap battles, where they were judged on their style and delivery. The pace at which rap is delivered, along with the force with which it is delivered, contributes to its flow. There are about as many kinds of rap deliveries as there are rappers; they can range from fast-paced and aggressive to laid-back and chant-like. Other kinds of flow range from the sing-song rhythms of schoolyard chants, childhood taunts, jump-rope rhymes, and clapping games to complex melodic lines with varying cadences and surprising uses of *enjambment* (instead of ending a lyrical line at the end of a complete thought or sentence, breaking the line up so that the meaning cannot be understood until the subsequent line is delivered, in essence leaving the listener hanging). The ability to create complex rhymes within a rap song's typical quadruple meter or 4/4 beat time signature (four beats per measure) also factors into a rapper's skill; an MC who can incorporate multiple end (exterior) rhymes and interior rhymes (and near rhymes), in addition to shifting flow and syncopation, is considered more skilled than one who simply uses end rhymes, the same flow, and raps on the beat only.

Early rap, sometimes called old-school rap, typically followed the example of the party DJ, keeping the rhymes simple and dealing with themes like romance, sex, money, and partying. Around the mid-1980s, rappers began experimenting more with rhyme and melodic line, and lyrics started dealing with sociopolitical issues like drugs, violence, activism, and police brutality. Rakim (William Michael Griffin Jr., 1968–), of Eric B. & Rakim (1986–1993; 2016–), is credited with changing the sound of rap: in contrast to his contemporaries, his focus was on a less predictable flow. In addition, as gangsta rap (which both attacked and embraced the urban lifestyle choices of drugs, sex, and murder) emerged, lyrics started to emphasize urban issues such as crime. Gangster life was glamorized by some artists, so materialism—the accumulation of what was nicknamed "bling"—also became popular in songs. The rap music we hear today owes a great debt to gangsta rap and g-funk.

Another influence on rap's development, still heard today, is the sound of the Jamaican deejay. His main function was delivering what were called "toasts," set to music. These toasts were done in a monotone voice with a microphone and set against a beat. Toasting included rhymed introductions of people (including the deejay) and calls to dance. At times toasts incorporated tales of heroism, simple boasting (braggadocio), and taunts aimed at specific people, all to get the audience to engage in dancing and thus to liven up the party atmosphere. From the Jamaican deejay developed the MC, the hype man (the rapper's sidekick who performs vocalized boosting, supporting commentaries, or response tags), and the DJ (eventually a turntablist). Public Enemy's (1985–) Flavor Flav (William Jonathan Drayton Jr., 1959–) is the quintessential hype man. As technology improved and music production software replaced turntables, the DJ evolved into today's producer/mixer. Toasting found its way into the United States in the 1970s when DJ Kool Herc introduced not only the idea of short rap stanzas and toasts at his block parties but also elaborate sound systems and samples of previously released songs.

When rap first became popular in the United States, it was localized, on both the East and West Coasts, in several New York City boroughs and in South Central Los Angeles. It made its way across the country only when major African American–owned labels emerged in New Orleans and Atlanta. African Americans then began to create, maintain, and control label-associated rap scenes in urban cities such as Oakland, Newark, Philadelphia, Miami, and Houston.

Arguably, gangsta rap began in the Northeast, with Philadelphia's Schoolly D (Jesse Bonds Weaver Jr., 1962–), the Bronx's BDP (Boogie Down Productions, 1986–1992), and Newark's Ice-T (Tracy Lauren Marrow, 1958–), who drew on gangsta themes. Nonetheless, the West Coast can lay a legitimate claim to its origins because of the Compton, California–based crew N.W.A. (1986–1991), a Ruthless Records rap crew that redefined gangsta and, more importantly, made it extremely successful commercially. Surprisingly, N.W.A.'s urban and ethnic themes appealed to suburban America, which fell in love with the music. Gangsta rap evolved into various styles, the most popular being g-funk (a.k.a. gangsta funk), which sampled funk albums of the 1970s and used a less aggressive tone both instrumentally and vocally, as it was informed by a laid-back ethos. Co-founded by N.W.A.'s Dr. Dre (Andre Romelle Young, 1965–) and The D.O.C. (Tracy Lynn Curry, 1968–), working with director of operations Suge Knight (Marion Hugh Knight Jr., 1965–), Death Row Records (1991–2008) dominated the rap charts with g-funk acts such as Dr. Dre, Tupac Shakur (Lesane Parish Crooks, 1971–1996), and Snoop Dogg (Calvin Cordozar Broadus Jr., 1971–).

G-funk was certainly not the first hip hop musical subgenre to popularize rap in the mainstream. Before g-funk and gangsta took hip hop into the suburbs, Kurtis Blow (Kurtis Walker, 1959–) worked toward catapulting rap music into the mainstream with his 1980 certified-gold rap single, "The Breaks." Because of the efforts of Kurtis Blow, N.W.A., and Public Enemy, rap would ultimately go viral. Gangsta rapper Coolio (Artis Leon Ivey Jr., 1963–) had a 1996 megahit single with "Gangsta's Paradise." It sold five million units, rose to No. 1 on the charts in fifteen countries, and won a Grammy. The song's video is considered a benchmark moment in rap music history.

LOCATION IS EVERYTHING

By 1990, two New York rap icons, Puff Daddy (a.k.a. P. Diddy, Sean John Combs, 1969–) and Tupac Shakur, had emerged in Harlem. The former became a leading producer, performer, entrepreneur, celebrity, and founder of Bad Boy Records (a.k.a. Bad Boy Entertainment, 1993–); the latter tied social consciousness with the gangsta ethos and became the most notable victim of the East and West Coast rap wars. Harlem was also the home of an influential hip hop style called new jack swing, which fused hip hop elements with R&B, sometimes including funk and gospel. In Philadelphia, DJ Jazzy Jeff (Jeffrey Allen Townes, 1965–), a world turntablist champion, co-founded the rap duo DJ Jazzy Jeff &

the Fresh Prince (1985–1994) with Will Smith (Willard Carroll Smith, 1968–). The duo won two Grammy Awards, with the album *He's the DJ, I'm the Rapper* (1988) going triple platinum. Boston's early rap successes included Bahamadia (Antonia Reed, 1966–), a native of Philadelphia, who began her career by working with Boston- and Brooklyn-based Gang Starr (1986–2006, 2019–). Newark's Queen Latifah (Dana Elaine Owens, 1970–) was an early rapper who achieved icon status and is now known as the First Lady of Hip Hop. In 1995, she co-founded her own label and management company, Flavor Unit Records. South Orange–native Lauryn Hill (Lauryn Noelle Hill, 1975–) eventually earned five Grammy awards for her solo album, *The Miseducation of Lauryn Hill* (1998), a collection of songs that bridge the gap between rap, danceable hip hop, soul, and R&B.

Los Angeles was home to rap poetry, electronic dance rap, Chicano rap, and experimental turntablism. Rapper and poet Aceyalone (Edwin Maximilian Hayes Jr., 1970–) recorded poetry and alternative trip hop and mentored absurdist rappers like Busdriver (Regan Farquhar, 1978–), while Los Angeles's Black Eyed Peas (1995–) launched the era of hip hop and electronica rap. West Los Angeles's Cut Chemist (Lucas MacFadden, 1972–) became known for his sample-based turntablism that was influenced strongly by East Coast hip hop. Turntablism also became important in Northern California. In San Francisco, iconographic scratcher/producers DJ QBert (Richard Quitevis, 1969–) and Mix Master Mike (Michael Schwartz, 1970–) co-founded Invisibl Skratch Piklz (1994–2000; 2014–). As turntablism became more complex, DJs like Roc Raida (Anthony Williams, 1972–2009) and turntablist collaboratives like the X-Ecutioners (1989–) became popular.

Houston's main contribution to rap was the popularization of hardcore rap and horrorcore. A few years after the debut album of Detroit-based Esham's (Esham Attica Smith, 1973–) *Boomin Words from Hell 1990* (1989) introduced horrorcore lyrics, Houston-based Ganksta N-I-P (Lewayne Williams, 1969–) released his debut album *The South Park Psycho* (1992), preparing rap fans for the Geto Boys (1986–), a group which proved to be influential on both horrorcore and Dirty South, with its single "Mind Playing Tricks on Me" (1991) becoming a genre classic. Miami's contribution to rap music was a style called Miami bass, best represented by the band 2 Live Crew (1983–1998, 2009–2016) and its rapper/promoter Luke (a.k.a. Luke Skyywalker, Luther Roderick Campbell, 1960–), who created a heavy bass, synthesized melodic and drum sound. Atlanta is best known for the subgenres crunkcore and trap, the former a hybrid subgenre of electronica/dance/pop, screamo, and crunk, and the latter an extreme version of urban rap concerned with gritty portrayals of urban street life. Atlanta's other contribution, the 1990s Dirty South fad, was a rap style associated with regional slang and speech patterns, danceable beats, and pronounced bass. Snap and trap are subgenres that came out of Atlanta. Both spread from Atlanta to urban areas like Houston and Memphis. Chopper style rapper Ludacris (Christopher Brian Bridges, 1977–), originally from Champaign, Illinois, moved to Atlanta as a teen and worked with Timbaland (Timothy Zachary Mosley, 1972–) as a guest rapper. He later co-founded Disturbing Tha Peace Records. Atlanta is also the home of three influential hip hop artists: Bronx-born Swizz Beatz (Kasseem Dean, 1978–), hip hop trio TLC (1991–2002; 2015–), and Dirty South duo OutKast (1991–2006; 2014–).

HIP HOP CULTURE AND ITS MUSICAL CONVENTIONS

Although some of the earliest uses of the term *hip hop* were associated with music acts like Grandmaster Flash and the Furious Five (1978–1983, 1987) and The Sugarhill Gang (1979–1985, 1994–), hip hop can best be understood as a cultural (sociological, political, and artistic) movement created by African Americans, Latinx Americans, and Caribbean Americans in the Bronx (a New York City borough). While music is its most notable element, hip hop culture also includes dance (b-boying and b-girling, a.k.a. breakdancing), fashion, art (graffiti), African identity politics, religion, socio-politics, collectivity (rap groups and labels often form collectives), localization (rap songs are generally specific to locales), and self-actualization. All these elements of hip hop culture have spread to both urban and suburban communities throughout the United States and most nations (although some nations, due to religion, politics, and musical preference, have little to no hip hop scene). In every country where rap has taken hold, these elements have been adapted to fit local tastes and conventions, merging with local and traditional styles. Today, hip hop continues to expand globally and elementally, with new art forms such as hip hop theater and hip hop film and musical stage emerging; hence, the inclusion in this book of "Ten Duel Commandments" from *Hamilton*, which appears as a Must-Hear Music entry.

The main subject of this book, non-rap-based hip hop songs, share musical characteristics, or conventions if you will, with rap music. A vast majority of them employ the Roland TR-808 Rhythm Composer drum machine (a.k.a. 808 or 808 drums), their sound usually being produced by a synthesizer since Roland ceased manufacturing the TR-808 and pulled it off the market after a few years because it was a commercial failure. In addition, virtually every early rap song (recall that early rap was synonymous with hip hop) employed turntablism, and although it fell out of favor, the turntable scratch sound still manages to find its way into music. Aside from producing turntable sounds, early DJs heavily used sampling; however, copyright lawsuits led to the need to create original beats. Sampling is still used today, but much less frequently and on a much smaller level. MCing is of course a staple of rap music, although it has evolved to include not only rapping but also chanting and talk-singing (and a highly auto-tuned hybrid that is referred to as mumble rap). As of the last two decades, auto-tuning has become virtually universal in rap—although to be fair, it is used very often in other music genres as well. Even though it has all but disappeared due to the use of drum machines and synthesizers, beatboxing was ubiquitous in early rap music.

The element that sets rap apart from other popular music genres is the absolutely essential role of the producer. Although MCs and singers are usually placed in the foreground of hip hop hit songs, these songs' producers became highly sought after for their own musical talents. A discussion of MCs/rappers belongs in the following list; however, they were discussed earlier in this chapter.

MUSICAL CONVENTIONS OR ELEMENTS

Producers

It is impossible to overstate the importance of producers in rap. Like musicians in rock bands, their names are usually listed alongside those of rappers and singers in music credits. Of course, post-production plays a big role in all genres of music, but in hip hop, because beats are usually generated with digital equipment, usually through a drum machine, synthesizer, and/or sound board, the producer fills the role of the band in other music genres—or the DJ in old-school rap—creating virtually the entirety of a song's instrumentation. Typically, the instrumentation created by a hip hop producer will include a song's signature beats (a collection of drum set and other percussion instruments that may be real, virtual, or combined), samples (previously recorded album material that can be isolated, such as bass lines, as well as media files such as speeches or dialogue, and synth-based voices), turntablism (scratching), and original synthesizer melodies. Some producers also act as studio executives, recruiting rappers and DJs and often having them collaborate on songs, a method of producing music that highlights new rappers when they collaborate with established, commercially successful rappers.

Further, some producers arrange the recording session, coach the rappers, and, if they do not mix and master song tracks themselves, recruit

8   Listen to Hip Hop!

music engineers. Iconic producers include the aforementioned Timbaland and Dr. Dre, as well as J. Dilla (James Dewitt Yancey, 1974–2006), Kurtis Blow (Kurtis Walker, 1959–), and 9th Wonder (Patrick Denard Douthit, 1975–). Today's producers use digital audio workstations (DAWs), outfitted with software such as Ableton Live, Pro Tools, Fruity Loops, and Digital Performer. These tools allow them to multi-track a song's various voices (both vocal and instrumental), so that singers can harmonize with themselves or sing backup and countermelodies. The software also allows the correction of any mistakes made during recording, such as a singer's being off-pitch or an instrumentalist's incorrect notes. DAWs have made it possible for more people to become beat-makers and producers, as these systems are becoming affordable and can fit into a spare room (hip hop has many DIY [do-it-yourself] or home studio performers). Beats are such an integral part of hip hop that producers often make instrumental mixtapes or albums, inviting rappers to use their instrumentation, both freely, for exposure, and through licensing.

Auto-Tuning

Auto-Tune, an audio processor created in 1997 by Antares Audio Technologies, measures and alters pitch in vocal and instrumental music recording and performances. Auto-tuning devices plug directly into DAWs (and some can also be used in real time for live performances, working much like guitar effects pedals). Originally intended to alter off-pitch vocals to the nearest true, correct semitone, auto-tune is now used extensively to distort vocals, sometimes making them sound robotic. Auto-tune devices, such as the TC-Helicon Vocal Processor, the Behringer Virtualizer, the Roland Voice Transformer, the Tascam Vocal Producer, and the Boss Vocal Performer Multi-Effects Pedal, are now standard equipment in both professional and DIY recording studios. Hip hop and R&B recording artist T-Pain (Faheem Rasheed Najm, 1985–) actively and aggressively used auto-tune in his songs, to the point where the sound became associated with his style. Rap artists such as Kanye West (1977–), Future (Nayvadius DeMun Wilburn, 1983–), Travis Scott (Jacques Berman Webster II, 1992–), and Lil Uzi Vert (Symere Bysil Woods, 1994–), and rap groups such as Migos (2008–) use auto-tune as their signature sound.

808 Drums

The Roland TR-808 Rhythm Composer, one of the most ubiquitous instruments used in early rap music, allowed hip hop producers to program original beats by establishing tempo and time signature, as well as manipulating effects such as tuning and decay. Basically a drum machine, it became a cornerstone of electronic hip hop with the iconic song "Planet Rock," by Afrika Bambaataa & the Soulsonic Force (1980–). Through analog synthesis, not sampling, the 808 produced various drum sounds, including bass (kick), snare, tom, conga, claves, hand claps, maracas, cowbell, cymbal, and hi-hat. Though it was a commercial failure, its unique sound, once popularized in the early 1980s, has since been incorporated into various synthesizers. The 808 sound is so common in rap that Kanye West used it on every track on his 2008 album *808s & Heartbreak*. Today, the actual TR-808 Rhythm Composer is making a comeback. In 2014, Roland released the TR-8 drum machine, which recreates the 808 and 909, following it with the TR-08 (2017), a miniaturized 808 featuring MIDI and USB connections, making it more user-friendly.

Turntablism

Kingston-born DJ Kool Herc (Clive Campbell, 1955–), developed breakbeat deejaying in the Bronx by isolating and repeating the breaks of funk songs in music for the purpose of keeping dancers at all-night dance parties moving without interruption. DJ Kool Herc's announcements and exhortations to dancers would popularize the syncopated, rhymed spoken accompaniment to music known as *toasting*. He dubbed his dancers break-boys and break-girls, or simply b-boys and b-girls—and eventually they accepted the mainstream name for their movements, breakdancing. Subsequent DJs such as Grand Wizzard Theodore (Theodore Livingston, 1963–), Grandmaster Flash (Joseph Saddler, 1958–), and the aforementioned DJ Jazzy Jeff refined and developed the use of breakbeats, including scratching and cutting. These DJs, also called turntablists, used scratching techniques to manipulate sounds and create beats. They generally used two or more phonograph turntables, vinyl records, tapes, CDs, and digital audio files, which they mixed, often in real time. Turntable scratching became one of the most conventional sounds associated with early hip hop music. Turntablism developed through new techniques, such as beat-matching, and through new technologies, such as the Technics SL-1200 MK 2 (late 1970s), which also allowed for precise variable pitch control. A list of DJ pioneers includes Afrika Bambaataa (a.k.a. Afrika Bambaataa Aasim and Lance Taylor, Kevin Donovan, 1957–), DJ Jazzy Jeff, Grandmaster Flash, Jam Master Jay (Jason William Mizell, 1965–2002), and Mix Master Mike.

Sampling

Sampling owes its existence to musique concrète (which emerged in the 1940s with practical applications that trace back to the late 1920s), a kind of Western art music that consisted of making music by manipulating sounds that were captured by tape recorder. Early methods for manipulating these sounds include physically distorting the tape—stretching, crumpling, or splicing it—as well as looping it (often done by using a microphone stand). The looping technique also could be used as the basis for creating a tape delay by using, for example, two reel-to-reel machines—one playing a tape at regular speed while the other, with the tape looped around a mic stand, being delayed through the tape machine reader. The collection and use of these new sounds prefigured the use of pre-existing sound files, or samples, used in music from the mid-1980s on.

Typically, sampling involves the liberal use of pre-recorded music excerpts such as bass lines, drum beats, guitar riffs, sung and instrumental lines, and hooks that can be easily isolated; a musical gesture or passage surrounded by silence or rests, for example, would make an excellent sample. Since the mid-1980s, nonmusic audio files, which may include speeches and lines of film dialogue, have also been sampled. Samples can be incorporated in their original forms or can be manipulated through distortion, pitch-altering, hiccupping, clipping, and other musique concrète techniques to create new sounds.

Sampling is one of the building blocks of early rap music, as DJs and producers created new music by using samples of funk and soul tracks on vinyl albums, particularly their drum beats, to create breaks over which new material could be rapped. But once copyright lawsuits became a common occurrence, rap groups moved away from sampling. Landmark legal cases, such as *Grand Upright Music, Ltd. v. Warner Bros. Records Inc.* in 1991, resulted in the ruling that unlicensed sampling constituted copyright infringement. The two most commonly sampled songs are James Brown's "Funky Drummer" (1969) and Fab 5 Freddy's "Change the Beat" (1982).

Beatboxing

During the 1980s, rap also embraced the creation of original beats and rhythms by using the human body, via the vocal percussion technique of beatboxing. Pioneers such as Doug E. Fresh (Douglas Davis, 1966–), Darren Robinson (a.k.a. the Human Beat Box, 1967–1995) of The Fat Boys (1982–1991, 2008–), and Biz Markie (Marcel Theo Hall, 1964–) made beats, rhythm, and musical sounds using the mouth, lips, tongue, voice, and other body parts. By holding the microphone close to their mouths, these beatboxers were able to imitate all kinds of instrumentation, including bass lines and kick drums. Biz Markie was unique in his ability to hit what sounded like a sub-bass range. Beatboxing can be a simple beat or an elaborate combination of sounds. For example, in the Doug E. Fresh and the Get Fresh Crew 1985 old-school song "La Di Da Di," Doug E. Fresh begins with a minimalist simple beat, which slowly builds up to include three sounds—a plosive-based beat made with his mouth, a castanet sound he makes with his teeth, and a laser sound he makes by putting the mic up to his throat. He continues to combine these three as his MC, Slick Rick (Richard Martin Lloyd Walters, 1965–), leads into the rap. Slick Rick cues Doug E. Fresh, at which point the beatboxing becomes more frenetic and aggressive, concentrating more on the plosives, which are now voiced at a deeper register to give the song a sense of bass; at this point and throughout the song, the beatboxing becomes more regular and predictable so that Slick Rick can rap against it.

Other world-renown beatboxers include Bellatrix (Belle Ehresmann, 1989–), Eklips (Eddy Blondeau, 1980–), Kenny Muhammed (1968–), Nicole Paris (1992–), Rahzel (Rahzel Manely Brown, 1964–), SkilleR (Alexander Deyanov, 1988–), and Spencer X (Spencer Polanco Knight, 1992–). Bellatrix is known for her ability to reach notes in the bass vocal range. In 2007, she formed The Boxettes, an all-female beatboxing group. By 2009, she was crowned the Female World Beatbox Champion. French beatboxer Eklips began performing in the 1990s and is one of the most famous beatboxers today. Kenny Muhammed, the originator of what he called the "wind technique," the skill of audible breathing while seamlessly merging sounds, has performed with full orchestras and is nicknamed The Human Orchestra. Rahzel, formerly of The Roots (1987–), is known for his ability to beatbox, rap, and sing. SkilleR is Bulgaria's first national beatbox champion and is considered one of the world's fastest beatboxers. The two youngest of the elite group are Nicole Paris and Spencer X. The former, the daughter of beatboxer Ed Cage (1973–), has created an uptempo style that incorporates elements of electronic dance music (EDM). The latter, nicknamed The Mouth Music Man, has an impressive range of sounds and is considered one of the world's foremost up-and-coming beatboxers.

Although beatboxing has all but disappeared from hip hop music, these other elements continue to be used—some, such as rapped interludes and the use of other rhythmic talk-singing, along with the 808, quite liberally. Readers will note in this book's Must-Hear Music entries that one or more of these elements inform every song discussed.

CHAPTER 2

Must-Hear Music

AALIYAH (FEATURING DMX) AND RIHANNA (FEATURING JAY-Z): "COME BACK IN ONE PIECE" AND "UMBRELLA"
ALBUMS: *ROMEO MUST DIE: THE ALBUM* (2000, LATER REISSUED ON *ULTIMATE AALIYAH*, 2005) AND *GOOD GIRL GONE BAD* (2007)

Actresses, models, songwriters, and mezzo-sopranos Aaliyah (Aaliyah Dana Haughton, 1979–2001) and Rihanna (Robyn Rihanna Fenty, 1988–) became internationally known as primarily R&B and pop singers; however, their musical output often consists of hip hop elements—particularly rap, beats, and loops. Starting young, both found huge success recording albums. Saint Michael, Barbados, native Rihanna, who also performs and records reggae and electronic dance music, released hip hop songs on *Good Girl Gone Bad* (2007), *Rated R* (2009), and *Talk That Talk* (2011). Many of her Billboard Hot 100 hit singles, including "We Ride" (2006), "Umbrella" (2007), "Rockstar 101" (2009), "Talk That Talk" (2011), and "Nothing Is Promised" (2016) also contain hip hop elements. Brooklyn-born and Detroit-raised Aaliyah, who appeared as a child on *Star Search* in 1989, performing alongside Gladys Knight (ex-wife of her uncle, Barry Hankerson), released hip hop songs on her entire studio album output, which includes *Age Ain't Nothing But a Number* (1994), *One in a Million* (1996), and *Aaliyah* (2001). At the age of 12, Aaliyah signed with Jive Records under the mentorship of R. Kelly, who produced her debut album, which became RIAA-certified double platinum in the United States. Aaliyah then worked with producers Timbaland and Missy Elliott on a second album, which sold more than eight million copies worldwide, and again with Timbaland on her final eponymous album. Like Rihanna, Aaliyah had a solo artist recording career concurrently with a featured-artist one. In the latter role, both sing contrasting lyrical passages to featured rappers.

Aaliyah's "Come Back in One Piece" (2000) and Rihanna's "Umbrella" (2007) are both mid-tempo songs in quadruple meter (four beats per measure) and F-sharp major with easy-to-follow song structures. "Come Back in One Piece" (2000) was produced by rapper Lil Rob (Roberto L. Flores, 1975–) and Murder Inc. Records' (a.k.a., The Inc.) co-founder Irv Gotti (Irving Domingo Lorenzo, Jr., 1970–). It was the third single from the soundtrack to Andrzej Bartkowiak's film *Romeo Must Die*, a loose adaptation of William Shakespeare's *Romeo and Juliet*. Making her film acting debut with the significant Juliet-based role, Aaliyah was one of the executive producers of the *Romeo Must Die* soundtrack album, to which she contributed four songs. Rapper-songwriter DMX (Earl Simmons, 1970–2021), featured in "Come Back in One Piece," also starred in the film. *Romeo Must Die: The Album* was recorded in 1999 and 2000 at an undisclosed studio and released on the Blackground Entertainment label (founded in 1999 by Aaliyah's uncle in Delaware yet active in Santa Monica, California) and Virgin Records America, in association with Warner Bros. Records. Although "Come Back in One Piece" did not chart on the Billboard Hot 100, it was No. 36 on Billboard's Hot R&B/Hip-Hop Songs. Another song, Aaliyah's "Try Again," composed by Static Major and Timbaland, was the soundtrack's lead single and became No. 1 and 4, respectively, on the Billboard Hot 100 and Billboard's Hot R&B/Hip Hop Songs, earning Aaliyah a Grammy Award nomination for Best Female R&B Vocalist.

"Come Back in One Piece" is a funk-infused hip hop love song about a woman who worries nightly that her lover will be killed because of his gangsta lifestyle. The main funk element is a sample of Stanley Clarke's (1951–) melodic electric bass guitar line, doubled by electric guitar, which is almost entirely based on Parliament's "Sir Nose D'Voidoffunk" (1977). This melody serves as the song's *ostinato* (a persistently repeated melodic and/or rhythmic pattern throughout all or most of a song). Clarke's ostinato incorporates slap bass—his using the thumb to strike the strings hard against the fretboard to make a slapping or popping sound—and a lot of wah pedal effect. Because of the use of "Sir Nose D'Voidoffunk's" bass line as well as acoustic piano chords, composer credits for "Come Back in One Piece" include its own writers, Stephen Garret (Static Major), Earl Simmons (DMX), Irving Lorenzo (Irv Gotti), and Rob Meys, as well as "D'Voidoffunk's" George Clinton and

Parliament's Bernie Worrell and William Collins. Stylistically, "Come Back in One Piece" is also based on snap, once an Atlanta hip hop musical style that was derived from crunk and characterized by its use of finger snaps in its beats. Rather than using finger snaps, this song uses an actual drum kit instead and replaces the consistent snap sound with snare drum rim shots.

"Come Back in Once Piece" uses repetitive harmonic motion to reaffirm the home key by starting on G major and resolving to F-sharp major (or II-I in F-sharp major). Typically, the second scale step in a major scale is a whole step (two piano keys) above the home pitch (the next pitch up from F-sharp should be G-sharp) and serves as the root of a minor chord (called the supertonic or ii). But to add some listening interest, the chord is altered by lowering the G-sharp a half-step down to G and substituting G-sharp minor (ii) with G major (II). This II-I harmonic progression with the ostinato's ascending motion contribute to the song's funky sound: The guitars complete the pattern by moving upward chromatically (by half-step or one piano key) from E to F and then landing satisfyingly on F-sharp, the home key.

The song's structure is as follows: intro (trifurcated); verse 1 (A, quadfurcated); verse 2 (A′, bifurcated, truncated); refrain (four times); middle-eight (B, bifurcated); verse 3 (A″, bifurcated, truncated); refrain′ (eight times); instrumental interlude (bifurcated); refrain″ (about six times, bifurcated, and used as the outro). Prime markings, such as A′, A″, or refrain′, indicate changes to the original section or passage, which may range from slight to significant. For example, the first refrain is repeated four times while the second, labeled refrain′, is repeated eight times; the same music is used in verse 1 (A) as verse 2 (labeled A′), but the latter verse has a different text and a different structure, and is truncated. The first part of the intro begins with spoken-word male vocals, as DMX performs a mic check. In the second part, the kick drum and cymbals alternate with electric guitars, followed by a snare drum rim shot that establish the song's quadruple meter time signature. In the third part, the groove emerges and works like a vamp (cueing the singer to start). It consists of the guitars, acoustic piano chords, and beats—the latter includes kick drum (also called bass drum), snare drum rim shots, ride cymbals, and shakers. Folded into this accompaniment is a keyboard synth-generated melody that uses a lot of sine wave in order to sound smooth and high-pitched. DMX returns, uttering vocables and then rapping in the foreground. Male backing vocalists join him, adding tags (gestures that stand out at the end of lines or passages) and engaging in call-and-response with him. Here, DMX establishes that he is a "dog" who needs a "b****," a female version of himself, as only one dog can control another.

Verse 1 features DMX, rapping aggressively against the continuing groove. Although the synth sine wave and acoustic piano drop out in the first and second parts, additional snare drum, toms, and cymbal strikes are folded in. Throughout this verse DMX's flow is slow and steady. Other male voices supply vocables, reactions such as "uh huh," sound effects such as dog barks, and occasional harmonizing of sung lines. The synth sine wave and acoustic piano reappear in the third part. Aaliyah's singing voice emerges in the foreground in the second half (measure three of four) of the fourth part, a prefiguring of her singing verse 2 and the refrain.

Verse 2 features Aaliyah's sung vocals, which are not multi-tracked or processed much but rather kept thin and dry, which gives the overall impression that she is girlish. Sometimes she is backed by harmonizing female vocalists. Her verse prefigures the refrain melody. The verse is half the length of DMX's verse (a total of eight instead of sixteen measures), but because the same groove is used, it is also labeled here as an A-section verse. At the end of her melodic lines in verse 2 as well as in the refrain, her vocals double the catchy ascending chromatic part of guitars' ostinato. Her vocals are clipped as she lands on the home pitch (F-sharp), an articulation that parallels the guitars. The synth sine wave and acoustic piano drop out in verse 2 but return in the refrain. DMX punctuates Aaliyah's melody with vocables in the background as she sings the refrain's couplets four times.

The first part of the middle-eight employs the song's sparsest texture as the groove drops out and is replaced by kick and snare drums only. Aaliyah's singing voice is now multi-tracked and harmonized with a lot of added reverb. DMX's vocables punctuate her in both parts. Usually, middle-eight sections (also called *bridges*) consist of a new home key. At the beginning, Aaliyah starts her new melody on the pitch A, perhaps suggesting to some listeners that this section will be in a new key; however, with the reappearance of the guitars' ostinato and II-I chord progression in the second part and her constantly concluding her melody on F-sharp, the middle-eight's home key actually remains as F-sharp major.

DMX returns in verse 3 (also just eight measures), which sounds similar to verse 1 but with more studio production effects (for example, his "what" alternates quickly between speakers in the first part). The refrain' is a lengthy repetition of the previous one, repeating the melody eight times and lasting for sixteen measures. Listeners may expect that the song will fade out here, but the refrain' is followed by a funky instrumental interlude. The first part features the synth electric guitar playing the ostinato as a solo; the second part features Clarke's electric bass doing the same but an octave lower. The drums continue to accompany these solos, but the acoustic piano and synth sine wave have again dropped out. Cosmic-sounding synth-produced sound effects appear and are used with backing male and female vocables to punctuate the passage. A fade-out could happen here, too, but this is saved for the refrain". Its first part repeats the melody four times. As the second part attempts to repeat the melody four more times, the song fades out close to the sixth time.

Like "Come Back in One Piece," Rihanna's hit, "Umbrella," from *Good Girl Gone Bad* (2007), is also a "you and me against the world" love song. Stylistically, it differs from "Come Back in One Piece." "Umbrella" fuses more R&B elements with hip hop, as well as pop rock and soul. "Umbrella" features rapper-songwriter and producer Jay-Z (Shawn Corey Carter, 1969–), who co-wrote the song with its producers Tricky Stewart (Christopher Alan Stewart, 1974–) and Kuk Harrell (Thaddis Laphonia Harrell, n.d.), along with additional writing from The-Dream (Terius Youngdell Nash, 1977–). The song was recorded on the Def Jam and SRP labels at Westlake Recording Studios in West Hollywood, California. In 2008, "Umbrella" earned Rihanna and Jay-Z a Grammy Award for Best Rap/Sung Collaboration, in addition to receiving nominations for Record of the Year and Song of the Year. This No. 1 song on the Billboard Hot 100 attained six-times platinum certification in the United States and also topped charts internationally, selling more than 6.6 million copies worldwide. Though the music video adds a sexualized context to "Umbrella," the refrain stands alone well commercially, appealing to listeners attracted to the singer while at the same time containing an uplifting message that applies not only to romance but also to friendship.

The song structure of "Umbrella" is as follows: intro (quadfurcated); verse 1 (A, bifurcated); refrain (bifurcated); bridge (or postchorus); verse 2 (A', bifurcated); refrain' (bifurcated); bridge' (or postchorus'); middle-eight (B, bifurcated); refrain" (bifurcated); bridge" (or postchorus"); outro (bifurcated). The first part of the intro of "Umbrella" begins with an actual drum kit's kick and snare drums and closing hi-hat, which play beats against Jay-Z's spoken-word hype that introduces Rihanna and mentions the album's title. Several keyboard synths play in the background, which initiates the intro's second part. One prominent synth is an oscillating keyboard voice playing in a high register; within the context of the song's lyrics, it may be heard as evoking raindrops. Here, Jay-Z starts to rap. Rihanna appears for the first time in the third part, punctuating Jay-Z with clipped and hiccupped sung vocables ("eh"). These are processed with filters and added reverb to have an ethereal quality that contrasts with Jay-Z's low tenor-range rap in the foreground. A pause takes place, followed by a metatextual moment in which Jay-Z cues in Rihanna.

In verse 1, Rihanna's R&B style singing, with some vocal grinding (purposefully raspy), is multi-tracked with applied reverb to make it sound fuller. Some delay is also applied to her voice, which can be heard on the right speaker. The drums and synths continue as her accompaniment with a synth bass and electric bass guitar accentuate the kick drum's downbeat. Far into the background, fret noise is added for a light timbral effect.

The refrain, the most melodic part of the song, exhibits a catchy pop style that features Rihanna's very clear multi-tracked vocals that harmonize with her. The drums and synths continue (including the oscillating keyboard one), but a new synth-produced electric guitar chorus voice emerges and plays sustained pitches that accompany Rihanna, contributing to the song's densest texture at this point. Immediately following the refrain, Rihanna repeatedly sings the word "umbrella," reducing it to the vocables "ella" and "eh" (the last was foreshadowed in the intro's third part). This passage seems to have the sole purpose of travelling to another passage, as expected, with a bridge. But because it seems to wind down the energy of the refrain, it also serves as a postchorus. During this passage, the synth electric guitar chorus accentuates the kick drum's downbeat, reducing the texture while adding the same dramatic effect heard in verse 1.

Rihanna also sings verse 2, which uses the same accompaniment as the previous verse. A new high-pitched synth strings stinger emerges in the second part. At the end of the verse, the electric guitar chorus synth, doubled with synth strings, plays a tag and leads into the refrain" and bridge', which both have more synth strings and a denser texture than the first time they were used.

The previous drums, synth guitar chorus, and low synth strings drop off dramatically in the middle-eight, a gospel-inspired passage featuring Rihanna's no longer multi-tracked singing vocals accompanied by an acoustic piano. Here, her voice sounds thin and nasally, as the section begins in B major (IV of F-sharp major). As she reassures her partner to come to her while struggling (the rain is a metaphor for the harsh world), the first part is suddenly soft. The high synth strings continue to accompany her, and the previous drums are replaced by kick drum and drum-machine-produced hand claps. The second part remains soft, but at the end of the passage, the crash cymbal is struck dramatically and reintroduces the hi-hat, and the lower strings suddenly reappear as well and build up to the refrain on an E-sharp major chord (VII of F-sharp major, which serves as a large dominant or V substitution and indicates a return to the home key). The refrain″ and bridge″, in the home key, are heard one more time with a return to the full texture, adding higher synth strings in both passages.

Instead of just fading out on the refrain″, though, the song concludes on an outro that features a new melody in the home key. Rihanna's multi-tracked vocals, with applied delay, return one last time. The first part focuses on raining and is sung twice, whereas the last part focuses on pouring—it is also sung twice. In both parts, she reassures her baby that he can come to her, against the dramatic synth strings, oscillating keyboard synth, and drumming until the song fades out.

In 2001, Aaliyah began filming in the title role of Michael Rymer's *Queen of the Damned* (2002), an adaptation of Anne Rice's horror novel of the same title (1988), which was part of The Vampire Chronicles series. That same year, she was killed in a small-airplane crash in the Bahamas. The news of her untimely death at age 22 brought attention to her films and music. As of 2021, her music continues to achieve commercial success, with at least 24 million albums sold worldwide.

Rihanna has continued recording and collaborating with hip hop producers and artists, including Jay-Z, Kanye West, Drake, Eminem, Ne-Yo, Nicki Minaj, and Chris Brown. In 2009, her relationship with Brown made media headlines when he physically assaulted her in a domestic violence incident that took place in public. As of 2021, Rihanna is the youngest solo artist to have as many as twelve No. 1 singles on Billboard's Hot 100. She has also won nine Grammy Awards, and all eight of her studio albums have been certified at least platinum.

PAULA ABDUL AND TONY! TONI! TONÉ!: "STRAIGHT UP" AND "FEELS GOOD" ALBUMS: *FOREVER YOUR GIRL* (1988) AND *THE REVIVAL* (1990)

Dancer, choreographer, actress, and television personality Paula Abdul (1962–) was one of the main forces behind the popularity of new jack swing. An ex-Laker Girl, she was discovered by Janet Jackson (1966–), who hired her for video choreography (for the songs "Nasty" and "Control"). Abdul's debut album *Forever Your Girl* (1988) sold seven

Paula Abdul performs in July 2017 during The Total Package Tour at NYCB Live, located at Uniondale, New York's Nassau Veterans Memorial Coliseum. (Dwong19/Dreamstime.com)

million copies and produced four No. 1 singles: "Straight Up," "Forever Your Girl," "Cold Hearted," and "Opposites Attract." Like Abdul, Oakland's Tony! Toni! Toné! (1988–97, 2003–) recorded some of the most iconic new jack swing songs, although the trio is mainly known for its soul and R&B recordings. The most popular lineup for the band consisted of D'wayne Wiggins (1961–, lead vocals and guitar), his brother Raphael Saadiq (Charles Ray Wiggins, 1966–, lead vocals and bass), and their cousin Timothy Christian Riley (1965–, drums and keyboards). The band's debut album, *Who?* (1988) went gold. Its second album, *The Revival* (1990), produced by the band's members, reached platinum status and spawned several R&B chart toppers, including "Feels Good," which reached the Billboard Hot 100 Top Ten, peaking at No. 9. "Straight Up" (1988) and "Feels Good" (1990), both examples of new jack swing, fuse hip hop elements with R&B, sometimes including funk and gospel.

Especially popular from 1987 to 1993, new jack swing employs typical instruments found in hip hop, such as drum machines, synthesizers, and scratch tones and effects from turntablism. A funky bass line—played or sampled by either a synthesizer or bass guitar—is also added. Typical musical hardware used to create sampled beats were the E-mu

SP-1200 sampler and the programmable Roland TR-808. The usual synthesizer, if added, was either a Roland W30 or a Yamaha S30. Rhythm and meter are repetitive and consistent. Using 4/4 (quadruple meter, four beats to a measure) and a tempo typically between 100 (ballad) and 112 (dance) bpm (beats per minute), new jack swing musicians created repeated or looped core beats with kick drum beats on the first (heaviest) and third beats, combined with rapid snare drum beats that fall on the and-beats and on beats two and four. The latter results in the swing beat and syncopation. Sixteenth-note triplets with their first beats accented for each eighth-note value produces the swing beat shuffle heard in "Straight Up."

"Straight Up," the third single from *Forever Your Girl*, is a plea from a female narrator or protagonist to her love interest to be straightforward with her about where he sees the relationship headed so that she does not get hurt. Written and produced by Elliot Wolff (1956–2016), it was eventually RIAA-certified platinum and spent three weeks at No. 1 on the Billboard Hot 100, reaching the top position on the charts in Norway and Canada. The song's melodic instrumentation includes Wolff's own funk-inspired horn riff, a melody created on a Roland D50 synthesizer with a pre-set horn sound from the keyboard's sound bank, and a later melody created on a Yamaha DX7 synthesizer with a pre-set flute sound. Wolff's prominent bass line and occasional string stabs (used as tags) on a Yamaha DX7 synthesizer accompany these melodies. Both synthesizers were frequently used in late 1980s studio sound recordings. Other instruments, in addition to Abdul's mezzo-soprano lead vocals, include electric guitar, used both for an ostinato (a persistent melodic and rhythmic pattern used throughout the song) with a wah-wah pedal and whammy bar effect, as well as power chord tags and programmed drum beats; the latter includes a timbale and bass beat, with a snare tag at end of the bass phrases.

"Straight Up" is a mid-tempo dance song in quadruple meter (four beats per measure) and D minor. The recorded song's structure is as follows: instrumental intro; verse 1 (section A); prechorus; refrain; verse 2 (A'); prechorus; refrain; middle-eight (section B, also called the bridge); vocal and instrumental bridge; prechorus; instrumental bridge; refrain (extension); refrain (as outro). The intro begins with the horn riff as the main melody, along with electric guitar (right speaker), accompanied by bass (mainly left speaker), and drums, followed by synthesizer strings (left speaker). The intro, refrains, B section, and bridges are based on a four-chord progression in D minor: D minor-B-flat major-C major-D minor (D minor: i-VI-VII-i). Abdul's lead vocals take the main melody in verse 1, though the horns and bass continue as accompaniment. A string stab (left speaker) punctuates this first verse, and electric guitar continues (left speaker now) as well. The horns drop out in the prechorus, which starts in G minor (iv of D minor), as the bass becomes the prominent accompaniment. Building up energy, the prechorus ends on the home key, leading to the refrain. Backing voices, which are used sparingly in verse 1, are in the foreground by the first refrain. Here, electric guitar also returns, as well as another string stinger (now right speaker). Abdul's vocables ("oh–oh–oh") add a rhythmic point of interest in the refrain.

A horn tag at the end of the refrain cues verse 2. In this verse, the electric guitar is more prevalent, and a string stinger (center) serves as the tag. The next prechorus and refrain are the same but are followed by the middle-eight, with Abdul's voice doubled by backing vocals that are an octave below. In the vocal and instrumental bridge, Abdul's vocal repetitions of the phrase "do you love me" work like a hook and resemble a turntable scratching break or hiccup. In the second prechorus, synthesizers are more prominent, especially their playing a descending *glissando* (a downward scale). Generally, Abdul's vocals feature unexpected pausing and phrasing, with lengthy pauses sometimes in the middle of lines. In the repeat of the prechorus, her voice creates the tag that leads into a bubbly and higher pitched synthesizer voice on the Yamaha DX7, which resembles flutes. This voice becomes prominent in the instrumental bridge and following extension of the refrain. The last instance of the refrain repeats and is used as the song's outro, which fades out. A final string stinger (right speaker) is then heard, while Yamaha DX7 strings appear in a rhythmic role (left speaker), accompanied again by electric guitar and electric bass.

"Feels Good," the second single from *The Revival*, topped the Hot R&B/Hip-Hop Songs chart and reached No. 3 on the Dance Club Songs chart. It features a brief guest artist rapped verse by old-school rapper Mocedes (a.k.a. Wycked or Mopreme Shakur, Maurice Harding, 1967–). "Feels Good" is a typical romance/love song thematically, with verses that tell the story of a first-time sexual encounter that has the male narrator thinking that he has found his future wife. The song's refrain and its rapped verse are metatextual expressions of braggadocio, making the case that Tony! Toni! Toné! are expert songwriters, musicians, mixers, and producers. The two themes of sexual and musical dominance are equated by the idea of "rhythm" (musical and sexual) that causes women to moan in ecstasy. In fact, female vocalizations take the form of three women seductively saying "ooh, ooh, baby," each taking one word, and these vocalizations are repeated throughout. They move from the left speaker to the right speaker constantly.

The recorded song's structure is as follows: spoken-word intro; intro (bifurcated); refrain; bridge; verse 1; refrain; bridge; verse 2; refrain (extension); bridge; instrumental bridge; rap interlude; refrain (extension, twice); vocal bridge; refrain (as outro). The first part of the song's spoken-word intro is meant to sound like it is being read by a white newscaster, who prescribes the song as if it were medicinal. Overall, the bifurcated intro is divided between a vocal part and an instrumental part. Both contain the song's basic funk-disco groove, which includes two turntables—one which plays the break in reverse (left speaker), and the other which plays the break normally (right speaker). In addition, vibraslap (right speaker then left speaker), kick and snare drum (one beat on the kick followed by one on the snare, alternated every third and fourth phrase with two on the kick and one on the snare), and hi-hat strikes are combined with tambourine (beat three), shakers, and synth voices. These are all set against stinger strings that use B as a pitch center. The groove has two sets of alternating two-measure passages: the first ends with an ascending string tag; the second ends with descending backing vocals. The drums and vibraslap groove is sampled from Kid 'n Play's "Do This My Way" (1988), while the tambourine groove is sampled from Lyn Collins's "Think" (1972), recorded with James Brown's band The J.B.'s (1970–). Electric bass guitar is added against this groove in the refrain, which is also accompanied by soaring strings and backing vocals.

The refrain serves as the song's brightest passage, in D major (with the lead vocalist singing A to F-sharp or scale step 5 to scale step 3 in D major). The bridges and verses are in B minor and sound darker despite the song's prevalent sunshine mood. The bridge contains two vocal hooks, the first sung by male voices, and the second (the aforementioned "ooh, ooh, baby") by female voices. The second hook (on right, center, then left speakers, then in reverse) is a sample of Indeep's "When Boys Talk" (1983). The accompanying synthesizer horns used in the bridges' and verses' backgrounds are reminiscent of Collins's recording. After verse 2, a vocal countermelody is added to the refrain, which is also extended. The instrumental bridge with string stingers cues a contrasting rap section with vocals pitched lower than the singing parts. This section serves as a rhythmic break from the groove, where all accompaniment stops when the rapper declares that the trio has "done it again." Another extended version of the refrain, now including acoustic piano, and a vocal bridge, take the song to an outro that includes some brief scatting and fades out.

Into the early 1990s, Billboard's Hot 100 and/or Billboard Hot R&B/Hip-Hop Songs charts were topped by new jack swing songs, as well as songs that contained new jack swing elements. These hits were not limited to the United States. Global success stories include Bahamian singer Johnny Kemp's "Just Got Paid" (1988), Stockholm-born and England-raised Neneh Cherry's "Buffalo Stance" (1988), English R&B and soul band Soul II Soul's "Keep on Movin'" (1989), Canadian singer Jane Child's "Don't Wanna Fall in Love" (1990), and Australian singer Kylie Minogue's "Word Is Out" (1991). France/Zaire's Tribal Jam and South Korea's BtoB (Born to Beat) also employed the new jack swing sound.

AFRIKA BAMBAATAA & THE SOULSONIC FORCE (MUSIC BY PLANET PATROL): "PLANET ROCK" ALBUMS: *PLANET ROCK EP* (1982, LATER REISSUED ON *PLANET ROCK: THE ALBUM*, 1986)

The Bronx's Afrika Bambaataa (a.k.a. Afrika Bambaataa Aasim or Lance Taylor, Kevin Donovan, 1957–), the founder of the Universal Zulu Nation (1973–), was a towering figure in 1970s and 1980s New York City hip hop and African American cultures, as he was highly instrumental in channeling gang members into creative outlets, such as b-boying, beatboxing, and rapping. A former warlord for the gang the Black Spades (1968–), he enforced the 1971 ceasefire between the city's Black and Latino gangs. His adopted stage name, which translates loosely as "Chief Affection," was borrowed from a 19th-century Zulu chief, and his Universal Zulu Nation was inspired by the code of honor demonstrated in the English and American film *Zulu* (1964). He was also known as an American leader of Islam. His block parties were meeting places for DJs (turntablists), MCs (rappers), b-boys (breakdancers), and taggers/bombers (graffiti artists). By the early 1980s, he was himself a highly respected, accomplished DJ and had formed several well known DJ crews, including the Soulsonic Force (1980–).

In 1980, Afrika Bambaataa & the Soulsonic Force (under the name Cosmic Force) recorded the album *Death Mix*, as well as the song "Zulu Nation Throw Down" (Afrika Bambaataa was credited as Kevin Donovan) on the Paul Winley Records label in Harlem. Both fused funk, soul, and old-school hip hop. *Death Mix* was an unofficial release, whereas this version of "Zulu Nation Throw Down" became an official debut single. In 1981, Afrika Bambaataa & the Soulsonic Force began working with the New York City-based hip hop label Tommy Boy and was introduced to the label's producer, Arthur Baker. Together, they released Tommy Boy's first hip hop album, the 12-inch single "Jazzy Sensation"

(1981, composed by Kenton Nix), which featured Afrika Bambaataa & The Jazzy 5 (the latter a pioneering group of MCs that formed in the mid-1970s and became associated with the Zulu Nation). Interested in fusing funk and hip hop in more recordings, Baker and Afrika Bambaataa began working together, along with "Jazzy Sensation" keyboardist John Robie (n.d.) to create the groundbreaking hip hop recording "Planet Rock."

Many details are known about the preliminary planning and recording of "Planet Rock," a dance song that uses the metaphor of the Earth as a nightclub. Two useful sources are Robert Fink's 2005 article, "The Story of ORCH5, or, The Classical Ghost in the Hip Hop Machine" in *Popular Music* and Richard Buskin's 2008 article and interview of Baker, "Afrika Bambaataa & the Soulsonic Force: 'Planet Rock'," in *Sound on Sound*. "Planet Rock" is a pioneering work in the electronic (synthesizer-based) hip hop style. It builds upon the electronic sounds of Kraftwerk, while also being inspired by George Clinton, Gary Numan, and Yellow Magic Orchestra. For many, it marks the beginning of electrofunk as a musical genre (and it was an early techno recording as well). At the time, Afrika Bambaataa and Baker loved the title track of *Trans-Europa Express* (1977), the sixth studio album by the pioneering electronic band Kraftwerk (1970–). A continuation of their techno, robot synth-pop, and rock sound, *Trans-Europa Express* was No. 32 in Kraftwerk's native West Germany; Nos. 2 and 8, respectively, on album charts in France and Italy; and Nos. 49 and 119, respectively, in the U.K. and United States. Also charting internationally, the title track reached No. 67 on the Billboard Hot 100 and became Kraftwerk's second most successful single in the United States, following "Autobahn" (1974).

"Planet Rock" was recorded at Intergalactic Studios in New York City. In the early 1980s, the use of sampling and beat machines was new. Intergalactic Studios had on hand an extremely expensive Fairlight CMI (computer musical instrument), a very early digital synthesizer and digital audio workstation (DAW), introduced in 1979, with floppy disc files of previously sampled sounds. Afrika Bambaataa and Baker selected one of its orchestral files, the ORCH5, for "Planet Rock's" orchestral stingers or stabs. The ORCH5 contained a pitched sample of the opening chord of "Danse infernale de tous les sujets de Kachtcheï" ("Infernal Dance of All the Subjects of Kastchei"), toward the end of the First Tableau of Igor Stravinsky's ballet *L'Oiseau de feu* (*The Firebird*, 1910). Marked as *subito fortississimo* (*sfff*), the chord is played suddenly, with force, as loud as possible. According to Fink, though state of the art, the Fairlight CMI was unable to simulate actual instrument sounds—by current standards, the ORCH5 was a low-resolution glimpse of an orchestral sound played by piccolos, flutes, oboes, clarinets, bassoons, trumpets, French horns, trombones, timpani, concert bass drum, acoustic piano, violin, viola, cello, and bass, based on either the 1910 *Firebird Suite* or its 1919 reduction. Other recordings, such as Kate Bush's "The Dreaming" (1982), which was recorded close to the same time on the EMI Records label, used ORCH5, but as Fink notes, "Planet Rock"'s use of the ORCH5 for orchestral stingers became seminal to hip hop.

Afrika Bambaataa, Baker, and Robie also turned to music that they liked to create "Planet Rock"'s beats. Among their favorite initial ideas were the beats in Kraftwerk's "Trans-Europa Express" and the lengthy dance break that appears toward the middle (ca. 00:04:56) of Captain Sky's (Daryl L. Cameron, 1957–) psychedelic Afro-futurist funk song "Super Sporm" (1979). Baker rented a Roland TR-808 drum machine, which Buskin notes he found in the *Village Voice*. Because the beats on Kraftwerk's "Trans-Europa Express" were too slow, he paid the owner, who remained uncredited, to program the machine to copy (or sound as close as possible to) the beats heard on another Kraftwerk single, "Numbers" (1981), which bubbled under at No. 103 on the Billboard Hot 100. "Planet Rock" was no different from other early hip hop recordings for relying on at least one musician to create sounds that at a later time would be sampled. Robie played the Micromoog and Prophet-5 synthesizers, emulating, for example, the sonic laser zap effects (Micromoog) and the synth horns heard on Babe Ruth's "The Mexican" (1973), which was based on Italian film composer Ennio Morricone's melody "Per qualche dollar in più" ("For a Few Dollars More") from the 1965 spaghetti Western film of the same title. He also composed a keyboard melody for "Planet Rock" that was based on this melody.

Vocoders were also new and not so readily available. The robotic sounds and other vocal effects were created by using a Lexicon PCM41 digital delay processor and SONY DRE 2000 Digital Reverberator. Using electronic instruments only to accompany its vocals, "Planet Rock" features brief spoken-word, chant-rapping, and sung lyrical exchanges between Afrika Bambaataa and other vocalists. MC G.L.O.B.E. (John Miller, 1945–), a member of one of Afrika Bambaataa's Universal Zulu Nation rapping groups, wrote the verses. He also solved the issue they were having with rapping on the beat by suggesting that they rap to a track at half-time; according to Buskin, this syncopated rap style was called "MC popping."

"Planet Rock" is entirely in B minor, though other pitch centers and keys, most notably B major (the parallel major of B minor), are used, albeit rarely and very briefly. The song's structure is as follows: intro (bifurcated); verse 1; instrumental refrain; verse 2 (extended); instrumental bridge; robot interlude (contains hook); verse 3; instrumental refrain' (twice, contains robot hook); verse 4; verse 5 (truncated); vocal refrain (extended); call-and-response interlude 1; instrumental interlude 1; verse 6 (extended); instrumental interlude 2; vocal bridge; call-and-response interlude 2; instrumental bridge'; verse 7 (truncated); vocal bridge 2; verse 8 (extended); outro (bifurcated, consisting of vocal refrain' repeated twice and then vocal refrain" repeated four times). The first part of the song's intro begins with Afrika Bambaataa's unaccompanied, highly processed singing to nightclub partiers. His sustained "yeah" very briefly establishes G as a pitch center. His baritone voice, with a lot of applied reverb, receives cheers, then hand claps, followed by the first ORCH5 stinger, which initiates the beats and punctuates the second part. Here, B minor is established as the home key and B as the pitch center. These vocalizations continue against drum machine beats (snare and kick drums on both speakers with closed hi-hat ticks on the right) copied from "Numbers" over a funky Prophet-5 synth-produced bass. Micromoog synth-produced sonic laser gun shooting effects are also incorporated in the beats.

Verse 1, also in B minor, features Afrika Bambaataa with a group of male chant rappers against the continuing beats. The ORCH5 stingers, funky bass, and cosmic effects are placed further in the background. Initially, the voices alternate between the left and right speakers, creating a psychedelic production effect; their dry sound contrasts with the highly reverbed sound of Afrika Bambaataa's voice in the intro. The verse lasts for eight measures (or four-plus-four-measures, based on the vocalists' phrasing).

The instrumental refrain consists of "Planet Rock"'s most memorable melody, which was not its own but rather an ominous motive from "Trans-Europa Express," transposed from the original C minor just a half-step down to B minor (the pitches in "Planet Rock" are F-sharp-G-C-B, F-sharp-G-B-A, F-sharp-G-C-B-F-sharp-B). In "Planet Rock," Robie plays this synth strings melody on his Prophet-5. In his analysis, Fink calls this melody *Weltschmerz* (world pain or world weariness, a profoundly sad Romantic world outlook over the suffering human condition). Many examples of *Weltschmerz* exist in nineteenth- and twentieth-century German music, but the most prominent figure in this regard is Austrian composer Franz Schubert (1797–1828), who incorporated *Weltschmerz* in his entire compositional output. Examples include his *Lied* (German art song) "Gretchen am Spinnrade," D. 118

("Gretchen at the Spinning Wheel," composed in 1814); his song cycle (a collection of *Lieder* bound by a narrative) *Winterreise*, D. 911 (*Winter Journey*, 1823); and his Piano Trio No. 1 in B-flat major, D. 898 (1827). Kraftwerk's melody, composed by classically trained member Ralf Hütter (1946–), uses *Weltschmerz's* hallmark minor key and chromaticism. Within the Afro-futurist context of "Planet Rock," it sounds otherworldly yet catchy. The melody is played twice over the same beats, with additional shuffling snare beats added.

Verse 2 sounds similar to verse 1. The cosmic effects and synth bass drop out in the instrumental bridge, leaving the beats only. The robot interlude is a four-measure passage that contains the song's most popular hook, the line "rock, rock to the Planet Rock—don't stop," chanted in a robotic voice over the beats, with added shuffled snare beats. It ends with a Prophet-5 strings chord tag. Verse 3 also uses the same chant flow, instrumentation, and beats, but with less alternation between speakers than the previous verses. The instrumental refrain' returns, but this time it is punctuated with the robot hook during its repeat. It is followed by verses 4 and 5. The latter is truncated to just four measures and uses a quieter, lengthier flow than the previous verses.

Male voices sing the vocal refrain in R&B style. This melody stands out for its bluesy sound, momentarily in B major against the B-minor accompaniment. The group uses call-and-response interlude 1 to engage the fictional nightclub audience (and other listeners) in a simple sing-along, which also continues the song's party atmosphere. This ten-measure passage employs the same beats and cosmic effects of interlude 1, punctuated by the ORCH5. At the end of call-and-response interlude 1, the song reaches its climax. The group announces the Soulsonic Force. Here, the Prophet-5 horns emerge for the first time, and big ORCH5 stingers cease.

Instrumental interlude 1 is the song's lengthiest passage, lasting for sixteen measures. Over the nightclub screams, cheers, and hand claps, Robie's bold, ascending Prophet-5 synth strings melody in B minor plays, punctuated by Prophet-5 horns and accompanied by continuing beats with some new Micromoog cosmic effects at the end. This melody is inspired by, rather than borrowed directly from, "Trans-Europa Express."

Verse 6 uses less alternation between speakers than the previous verses, and it differs by being punctuated by Prophet-5 synth horns and other Micromoog cosmic sound effects (including those played during instrumental interlude 1). Instrumental interlude 2 employs a new Prophet-5 keyboard synth solo, with a melody inspired by Babe Ruth that was discussed earlier in this entry. A cosmic effect is added to the attack of each note of this melody. The same beats with the cosmic effects and funky bass, as well as shuffling snare drum, accompany it. The song's only vocal bridge follows, a stuttered word over beats for four measures without sonic effects, which return in the next passage, call-and-response interlude 2. Here, the song returns to engaging the audience in a sing-along while reinforcing the song itself (referencing its title) and borrowing vocally from "Numbers" by counting in Japanese. Bridge 1' returns for four (instead of two) measures. A timbale beat enters the foreground, with its cowbell hitting an A-flat pitch (left speaker). Verse 7, which is truncated, without voices alternating between speakers, follows. Bridge 2's lyrical content refers to funk, and it folds in a funk-sounding Prophet-5 electric guitar. Verse 8 uses a smooth flow, but with less alternation between speakers. The voices are eventually accompanied by a descending chime-like Micromoog sonic laser effect.

The outro uses the R&B style melody in vocal refrain', now sung twice in the first part. The vocal refrain" sung four times concludes the second part, which ends the song. Instead of starting on B, however, the voices start on C-sharp, a whole step higher. The song concludes by fading out on these vocals, which gradually get more reverb applied as they appear more prominently in the foreground.

"Planet Rock" started out as a popular underground recording in the United States, Canada, and the U.K., but it soon entered the mainstream at Nos. 48 and 53, respectively, on the Billboard Hot 100 in the United States and the U.K. Singles Chart. It eventually became the first 12-inch single that was RIAA-certified gold in the United States. Afrika Bambaataa's "Looking for the Perfect Beat" (1983) continued "Planet Rock"'s fusion of rap, funky bass, synthesized beats, and techno-rock electronica. This style, which he called electro-funk, was enormously influential on the development of rap and electronic dance music over subsequent decades. The song not only reached the top of R&B and dance charts in the United States, it also took the hip hop creative world by storm.

"Planet Rock" was later reissued on Afrika Bambaataa & the Soulsonic Force's *Planet Rock: The Album* (1986), which attained critical praise. In 2002, pianist-composer Jason Moran released his postmodern jazz homage to "Planet Rock" on his album *Modernistic*, using the same title, electronic musical instruments, psychedelic studio production techniques, and elements of the song, such as the synth bass line, verse melody, the instrumental refrain and interlude 1, and the vocal refrain. As of 2021, according to the *WhoSampled* website, which traces sampling, lyrics, and other musical elements in a large repertory of hip hop and other popular music genres, "Planet Rock" has been sampled in nearly 400 songs. The most famous sampling is still Public Enemy's "Fight the Power" (1989); however, "Planet Rock" has also been sampled in other popular songs that fuse hip hop with alternative indie music, R&B, and/or pop.

AFROMAN: "BECAUSE I GOT HIGH"
ALBUM: *THE GOOD TIMES* (2001)

In 1998, Afroman (Joseph Edgar Foreman, 1974–) released his first album, *My Fro-losophy*, and relocated to Hattiesburg, Mississippi, where he met producer Headfridge (Tim Ramenofsky, n.d.), who produced and released the album *Because I Got High*. Kevin Smith directed the song's popular music video, which stars Afroman and features a brief appearance of the two cannabis-selling fictional characters Jay and Silent Bob. In actuality, Afroman is not a drug addict; he is a Los Angeles-based West Coast comedic hip hop singer-songwriter, multi-instrumentalist, and rapper who made a name for himself with "Because I Got High" and "Crazy Rap (Colt 45 & 2 Zig Zags)." Both songs were released in 2000, off the albums *Because I Got High* and *Sell Your Dope*, and both were re-released on *The Good Times* (2001), a compilation of his first two albums, with some new tracks. *The Good Times* became a hit, reaching No. 10 on the Billboard 200. Also a hit, "Because I Got High" reached No. 13 on the Billboard Hot 100 and No. 6 on the Hot Rap Songs chart, resulting in Afroman's being nominated for a Grammy Award in 2002.

Similar to the lyrics of Shel Silverstein's "I Got Stoned and I Missed It" (*Freakin' at the Freakers Ball*, 1972), which had a cover version by Jim Stafford reach No. 37 on the Billboard Hot 100 in 1975, the lyrics of "Because I Got High" chronicle the various events that the song's narrator has missed out on because he was stoned. According to the narrator of "Because I Got High," his drug habit has caused him to forget to clean his room, fail his college class, lose his job, miss court dates and child support payments, lose his car, become injured in a police chase, become homeless, and (in a comic twist) perform the song "Because I Got High" incorrectly.

Instrumentally, the song incorporates hip hop elements into its reggae, downtempo funk, and soft rock conventions. Entirely in G major, it features Afroman's soft, laid-back baritone voice, and the song's structure is very simple: it consists of a trifurcated intro and then ten four-phrase verses, each turning the fourth and last phrase into the song's hook, which references the title of the song. These are followed by an eleventh, extended verse that leads into the outro. A closer look into the structure of the verses, however, reveals more complexity. Though the verses demonstrate the song's simple and predictable tonal harmonies, they use an ornamentation in the vocals that is called an *appoggiatura*: a non-chord pitch that creates a dissonance but quickly gets resolved.

Afroman's first sung phrase in these verses begins in the song's home key. G major (or I) and ends on a brief appoggiatura to get to C major (IV). In the vocal melody, the non-chord tone is F-sharp, against G major (its pitches are G-B-D, and the F-sharp is a dissonance against G). The F-sharp quickly resolves to E and moves to C major (IV). The second phrase begins in D major (V) and also uses an appoggiatura. To get back to the home key, Afroman sings an E against the G major chord (its pitches are again G-B-D, and the E is a dissonance against D). The E quickly resolves to D. The third phrase moves from G major (I) to D major (V). Because V is expected to return to I, the fourth phrase sounds like it answers the third one. The fourth phrase is also the song's hook, a melody based on a descending G-major scale that repeats the song's title three times. The phrase ends on a perfect authentic cadence (I-V-I) and consists of one more appoggiatura, an elongated A sung against G major. The hook is followed by the song's second most memorable element: a descending vocal tag ("la da-da, da, da-da-da") sung by both Afroman and the song's male chorus, creating a brief melody that ends the verse and cues the beginning of the next one.

While vocals are complex, instrumentation is sparse: it consists mainly of electric bass guitar and the drum set's snare, tom, and crash cymbals. The song is in quadruple meter (four beats per measure), and the snare hits on just beats two and four, creating syncopation that is usually heard in reggae. The electric bass guitar's pattern (riff) appears throughout the song. It emphasizes its pitches (G, C, D, and G—implying, in G major, I-IV-V-I). The timbre of these instruments suggests the reggae influence, especially since the laid-back bass guitar emphasizes tones; it sounds as though a thumb is hitting the strings (in reggae, this technique is commonly called "big finger"). Its note progression, along with a pitchy or slightly off-pitch C, combined with the song's dynamics and variation, helps create the idea of laziness, or the reality of being stoned. The snare drum, with its flat, dry timbre, resembles the sound of aluminum drums. These are often used in reggae music, with the wires having been disengaged by the drummer's either loosening them or muting them (with tape or another object).

The recording of the extended version opens with a trifurcated intro. Its first part consists of a snare count-off, followed by Afroman's speaking, and the snare's establishing its beats on two and four. The bass riff starts in the second part of the intro and is rhythmically punctuated by the snare and more spoken-word vocals, now a tongue-in-cheek exchange between Afroman and the chorus. This ends with an exhale. Here, Afroman tells listeners to light up, which he is also presumably doing. The third and most lyrical part of the intro features Afroman's singing with a choir of male singers, ending with their first expression of the phrase "la da-da" and the hook, followed by a tag of tom beats and a slightly off cymbal crash.

In verse 1, Afroman's voice is multi-tracked briefly, backed by male vocalizations. The vocals in this verse represent many that are heard in subsequent verses: a combination of lyrical singing that is first on-key, then slightly off-key, accompanied by the sound of laughing, boosting (punctuating the main melodic line with vocables, e.g., "uh, uh,"), the use of vocal sound effects, and a call-and-response between Afroman and the all-male backing chorus. Beyond the song's story about all the things that Afroman missed because he got stoned, vocal variation keeps the song both musically interesting and funny.

By verse 3, the backing vocals become energetic, as a tom and kick drum are briefly added to the beat. In this verse, the chorus begins boosting, through "whoops," laughs, and metatextual comments on the song's structure (e.g., "go to the next one"). This instrumentation and vocal interplay continue well into verse 9, when Afroman becomes metatextual, mentioning that he wants to stop singing the song because he is so high that he is singing it badly (he also comments on the song's lack of potential for record sales). Here, the tom and kick drum disappear, indicating that the song is winding down. At the end of this verse, the hook changes to the phrase "because I'm high," suggesting an arrival to the present time. The song continues winding down in verse 10, in which Afroman resorts to scatting, punctuated by the chorus's boosting and followed by the hook—and chicken clucks from one of the backing singers.

Verse 11, the final verse, is the song's signature verse. If the first part of the intro can be heard as Afroman's signing in and representing, this verse is Afroman's signing out. Here, he says his name and mentions that he is from East Palmdale (part of northern Los Angeles), using a device not only common in other popular songs such as hip hop or chansonnier pop songs but that also likely traces back to earlier than the days of troubadour singers in the Middle Ages. Instead of the expected hook, however, listeners get vocalists' laughter, and the extension of the current verse, now used as the song's outro. And it breaks down further into a seemingly improvised set of spoken-word comments, laughter, more scatting, and jokes. No more singing is heard. The outro then ends, with these vocals accompanied still by bass and snare beat, and Afroman offers a curiously provoking comment about not believing in Hitler and, later, a joke that the song won't sell any albums, as well as a statement against the corporate world.

After it was featured on *The Howard Stern Show*, "Because I Got High" rose from obscurity. It eventually reached the No. 1 spot in nine countries: Australia, Austria, Belgium, Denmark, Germany, Ireland, New Zealand, Norway, and the United Kingdom. It also reached No. 2 in France, Portugal, and Switzerland. In 2014, Afroman released a remix of the song, touting the positive effects of cannabis in support of national legalization of marijuana. Frequent parodies of this song, as well as unofficial videos, also exist. A recent example is Omar Xerach's "Corona Song" (2020), which was a response to the COVID-19 pandemic and shelter-in-place efforts.

AKON: "BEAUTIFUL"
ALBUM: *FREEDOM* (2008)

Although he calls St. Louis home, Akon (Aliaume Damala Badara Akon Thiam, 1973–) lived in Senegal until he was seven, when his parents relocated to the United States. Like his upbringing, his popularity is international. He became a star in Africa and Europe, where fans have been mesmerized by his mixture of hip hop and techno, combined with occasional reggae. His albums *Trouble* (2004), *Konvicted* (2006), and *Freedom* (2008) were all certified platinum and charted on the Billboard 200, at Nos. 18, 2, and 7, respectively. Having a troubled past, Akon got a second chance after being arrested several times. He was sentenced to three years' probation and served some jail time, but Wyclef Jean (Nel Ust Wyclef Jean, 1969–) gambled on him and produced *Trouble*, which went viral. Its first single, "Locked Up," foreshadowed Akon's thematic concerns. He developed a strong belief in personal responsibility, as well as in the power of hip hop to uplift others.

"Beautiful" (2009), which features singer Colby O'Donis (Colby O'Donis Colón, 1989–) and rapper Kardinal Offishall (Jason Drew Harrow, 1976–), was the third single from Akon's third studio album, *Freedom* (2008). It has been released as an official American single, as well as in three international versions (usually without the rap but with sung lyrics by various artists). Those versions are Portuguese, with Brazilian singer Negra Li (Liliane de Carvalho, 1979–); Dutch, with Dutch singer Brace (Eddy Brace Rashid MacDonald, 1986–); and Mexican, with singer Dulce María (Dulce María Espinosa Saviñón, 1985–). Nonetheless, the American version reached No. 19 on the Billboard Hot 100, making it one of 19 hits that as of 2021 have peaked inside the Top 20 for Akon, as either lead or featured singer. Fourteen of these have landed in the Top Ten, with two, "I Wanna Love You" and "Don't Matter," hitting No. 1 in 2006.

"Beautiful" stands out for its juxtaposition of seemingly oppositional elements: lyrically, it is a sex song mixed with metaphors of love (e.g., "I'mma spend them grands after you undress/not like a hooker, but more like a princess"), while musically it is beat-heavy but is basically a snap song, using echo-heavy hand claps instead of snaps. It also uses a catchy 1980s-style keyboard melodic line, accompanied by melodramatic synth strings and at times a synth bass. Overall, the instrumentation includes the synth voices as well as kick drum (with occasional snare tags), claps (on the second and fourth beats), and synth-based electric guitar. In C minor, the song is in quadruple meter (four beats per measure). Its harmonic structure is based on a constant repetition of a four-chord progression. There is usually a chord change per measure (every four beats): C minor-A-flat major-E-flat major-B-flat major. Sometimes the A-flat major chord enters two beats early and lasts for six beats. The B-flat major (as VII of C minor) leads back to C minor (the home key), which starts the pattern over again.

The structure of the song is as follows: intro (bifurcated); verse 1; prechorus 1; prechorus 2; refrain; bridge (or postchorus); verse 2; prechorus 3; prechorus 2; refrain; bridge' (or postchorus'); rap interlude (bifurcated); prechorus 2; refrain; bridge (or postchorus); verse 3; prechorus 3; prechorus 2; refrain; instrumental outro. The expected function of the prechoruses is to build up to the refrains. The song's bridges may also be heard as postchorus or winding-down extensions of the refrain, but they are labeled in this discussion as bridges because they function as such, by bridging or leading into subsequent verses or the rap interlude (the final refrain abruptly ends—and the instrumental outro begins—which supports this structural interpretation).

The bifurcated intro begins with a 1980s-style synth keyboard melody, accompanied by low strings on synth and bass (the latter is mostly on the left speaker). Hi-hat cymbal strikes mark the latter half of this intro. The beats, which consist of kick drum (with occasional snare tags) and hand claps, enter for the first time in verse 1 and continue. Akon, a low tenor, sings lead vocals on the first part of the song, from verse 1 until the first bridge following the first refrain. Though the keyboard melody and synth bass drop out in the verses, the synth strings continue as accompaniment. Vocals are highly processed, especially Akon's, which are obviously auto-tuned and multi-tracked for self-harmonies and reverberated echoes (the echoes usually appear at the end of his lines). The beats fill in more in prechorus 1, though the tempo remains constant throughout the song. During prechorus 2 and the refrains, the keyboard melody and synth bass return, still accompanied by synth strings. The keyboard melody also drops out in the bridges, as well as in the subsequent verses.

To fold the sound of his softer, Michael Jackson-sounding tenor voice into the song, O'Donis harmonizes with Akon during the bridge, before he takes over lead vocals on verse 2. O'Donis's vocals (also low tenor but with a muted timbre) are auto-tuned, though they are less processed, sounding more natural than Akon's. O'Donis continues with lead vocals in prechorus 3. Akon's lead vocals return as before in the repeat of prechorus 2. During his repeat of the refrain, Kardinal Offishall's deeper and more assertive sounding baritone vocalizations enter the background. These include toasting-inspired hollers, laughs, spoken-word sounds, and tongue-rolls, which continue into the repeat of the bridge, which also consist of O'Donis's earlier harmonies. Kardinal Offishall shines in his speed rap, during the bifurcated rap interlude where he is comfortable in his upper register. His baritone vocals are kept dry, with no auto-tuning. In the first part, the same low synth strings heard in the intro and bridges accompany him.

Akon doubles some of his words, such as "brute" in the first part, and "zone" in the second part. The synth-produced electric guitar heard previously in prechorus 3 marks the second half of the rap interlude. Akon returns to singing lead vocals in a repeat of prechorus 2 after this rap interlude. Here, Kardinal Offishall's toasting-inspired vocalizations accompany him. After a repeat of the refrain and bridge, Akon sings the final verse. O'Donis's lead vocals return on a repeat of prechorus 3, followed by harmonizing on the final prechorus 2, and the refrain. The song concludes with an instrumental outro that is related to the intro, again using the synth strings, accompanied by the beat and hand claps.

The phrasing of "Beautiful" is highly symmetrical, with a four-plus-four measure intro, as well as eight-measure verses, prechoruses, bridges, and outro. The rap interlude is also symmetrical, with eight-plus-eight measures (dancers may like to hear this section as four sets of four-measure passages). This predictable phrasing makes the song easy to dance to, even during Kardinal Offishall's rap. Other sounds include female vocalizations in the background. Overall, the song has an expansive atmosphere, with post-production techniques, including chamber reverb, that give it a sense of having been recorded in a cavernous enclosure.

An entrepreneur, Akon founded KonLive Distribution (2006–) and Konvict Clothing (2007–), which have both had major successes. As a singer, he has recorded hit songs with such icons as Snoop Dogg, Michael Jackson, Whitney Houston, Gwen Stefani, Lionel Richie, and Lady Gaga. His closest collaborator is Wyclef Jean, with whom he recorded the 2007 hit song "Sweetest Girl (Dollar Bill)." As a philanthropist, Akon created the Konfidence Foundation (2007), aimed at improving the lives of people in Africa and the United States, and Lighting Africa (2014), a project that seeks to provide electricity to millions. In 2007, he was embroiled in a controversy when he simulated (and had filmed and uploaded to YouTube) sex as part of a performance with a nightclub patron; he did not know that she was fifteen, as the club claimed to have a 21-years-and-over age requirement. The controversy found its way into his No. 7 hit "Sorry, Blame It on Me" (2007), co-written and produced by Boston-based DJ, producer, songwriter, recording artist, and radio and personality Clinton Sparks (1975–). The song was released by Universal Motown as a promotional single.

DIE ANTWOORD: "UGLY BOY"
ALBUM: *DONKER MAG* (2014)

Cape Town, South Africa's Die Antwoord (2008–) embraces South Africa's *zef* (an Afrikaans word used as a derogatory slang term for the suburban working class of Cape Town) counterculture. In fact, the band has not only embraced zef, but has turned it into a celebration of ugliness. Musically, Die Antwoord combines rave energy and pace (beats per minute) with hip hop beats and edgy rapping, with a flow that usually approaches chopper style. The group's three members, rapper Ninja (Watkin Tudor Jones, 1974–), from Johannesburg; rapper/singer Yolandi Vi$$er (a.k.a. Yolandi, Anri du Toit, 1984–), from Port Alfred; and DJ Hi-Tek (a.k.a. HITEK 5000, God, Justin de Nobrega, n.d.), of Cape Town, began as part of the hip hop group MaxNormal.TV (a.k.a. Max Normal, 2001–2002, 2005–2008). Die Antwoord's sound is unique, with Ninja's Eminem-style rapping contrasting starkly with Yolandi's eerie, shrill, childlike voice, with lyrics sung and rapped in both Afrikaans and English. Their recordings are frenetic, and their videos and live performances typically feature costumes that push the envelope of good taste, as well as odd contact lenses that make the band's members look inhuman.

Despite the fact that Ninja and Yolandi have consistently maintained public personae as wild, savage, and absurd parodies of zef stereotypes, Die Antwoord's debut album *O* (2009) led to a recording contract with the American label Interscope Records and the EPs *5* and *Enter the Ninja* (2010). Die Antwoord then formed the label Zef Recordz (2011–) and released its second studio album, *Ten$ion* (2012). Four videos released for the album included the highly controversial "Fatty Boom Boom," an anti-music industry, anti-Lady Gaga, anti-imperialist track whose music video has scenes featuring Yolandi covered in charcoal-black body paint (including blackface—the trio identifies with Black culture over white culture). The hype for their third album, *Donker Mag* (2014), started a year before its release, with the highly controversial single and video "Cookie Thumper." Videos for *Donker Mag*'s tracks "Pitbull Terrier" and "Ugly Boy" were later released, the latter directed by Ninja.

"Ugly Boy" is entirely in F minor. The recorded song's structure is as follows: refrain (repeats); verse 1 (A, trifurcated); prechorus; refrain (repeats); verse 2 (A', quadfurcated); bridge; refrain (repeats); middle-eight (B, bifurcated); prechorus'; refrain (repeats, extended, and used as an outro). The song begins without any intro whatsoever, but rather with the refrain, which features Yolandi's childlike, whispering soubrette (a soprano). She begins her melody on the pitch C (scale step 5 in F minor), doubled by the lead synth only, which creates the song's sparsest instrumental texture. She sings short lines filled with plosives (to mirror the "popping" effect of the synth voice). The lines are sometimes clipped to sound more breathless, and her vocals are multi-tracked and made wet through applied reverb, which plays up their ethereal nature. Slight delay is also used with her voice (appearing first on the left speaker with the delay appearing on the right one).

Yolandi's vocals and the lead synth melody heavily sample the main melody from Aphex Twin's (Richard David James, 1971–) "Ageispolis," which appears on his debut studio album, *Selected Ambient Works '85– '92* (1992). Much discussion on the Internet focuses on Aphex Twin's gear used in this IDM (a.k.a. intelligent dance music) song; however, his lead synthesizer melody, likely played on a Yamaha CS-5 analog monosynth (at the time, already a vintage synthesizer), has not been discussed. (This instrument was also used on Aphex Twin's follow-up 1994 studio album, *Selected Ambient Works Volume II*.) In this song as well as in "Ugly Boy," the lead synth melody has a slightly distorted bubbling sound, with heavy reverb. Its sound is somewhat reminiscent of an ARP 2600 or another kind of ARP synthesizer (the sound may be emulated on a Yamaha DX7 digital synthesizer). The refrain celebrates Yolandi's love for and adoration of ugly boys and their fondness for her studied ugliness (a bowl/mullet haircut, stringy peroxided hair, pale make-up, ratty-looking clothing, and the aforementioned otherworldly nature of her contact lenses). In this refrain, the lead synth melody continues but is now marked by the emergence of beats (furnished by DJ Hi-Tek, who appears in the music video as God) that feature a heavy kick (left) as well an accompanying synth voice, which is also sampled from "Ageispolis" yet is remixed and placed in the background so that it can easily disappear from the mix during certain verses. This new accompanying synth voice is nimbus-like and resembles strings. Technically, this accompanying (and harmonic) function is known as a *synth pad*.

Ninja's low tenor voice enters with his talk-singing against the beat set up in the refrain's repeat. His verse 1 is filled with staccato lines that allow Yolandi opportunities to add vocalizations and tags, which divide the section into three parts. In the first part, Ninja starts with the spoken word "yeah" and moves on to talk-singing until Yolandi adds her "ow" tag. In the second part, he starts to rap, followed by her child-like laugh, which also serves as a punctuating tag. He continues this in the third part, which is marked by the addition of synth bass. Ninja's booming low tenor voice is set against the bubbling lead synth melody and a synth-generated beat that resembles a conga, as well as a secondary woodblock-sounding beat (likely created by an 808). Contrast also exists vocally between his booming voice and Yolandi's gossamer-sounding voice. In the prechorus, Ninja talk-sings lyrics from the refrain of Roy Orbison's "You Got It" (1989) into a call-and-response while the synth bass continues—near its end, the lead synth melody and beat both slow to a caesura, and conclude with Yolandi's answering tag. The refrain then returns with her lead vocals, but this time her accompaniment is fuller and includes the doubling lead synth melody, synth pad, synth bass, and the conga-woodblock beat. After the first utterance of this refrain, Ninja's "uh" furnishes the tag. The same instrumentation is used the second time.

Against the same instrumentation as verse 1, Ninja raps in verse 2, but this time his voice breaks into an approximation of Jamaican-style toasting (he goes so far as to use an affected patois). As this verse continues, the lead synth melody takes on an echo (possibly multi-tracked), which makes it sound slightly faster and more energetic. A synth bass is added. In contrast to verse 1, verse 2 is quadfurcated, and Yolandi does not punctuate as much here. She adds an "uh" tag to the first part, is quiet in the second part, and returns to punctuating briefly in the third and fourth parts. The synth bass drops out in this section but returns by part three and continues through the bridge and refrain. The ensuing bridge brings in a new point of listening interest because it is the only part of the song where both Ninja and Yolandi both talk-sing; her talk-singing employs the same whispery or breathy approach taken with her vocals (which have applied reverb and delay). The elongated sound of their talk-singing is somewhat reminiscent of the second part of verse 1, but instead of a call-and-response, Yolandi repeats Ninja's final word of each line ("magic"). The refrain here repeats and uses the same instrumentation as the previous one.

The middle-eight (B section) contains the most lyrical passages in the song, marked by a distinct sonic shift toward a quieter, more atmospheric sound. Ninja's vocables punctuate lyrics, and he uses vocables as tags. Yolandi starts on the pitch E-flat, though the home key remains in F minor. A new deeper-sounding synth pad is used here as she talk-sings against it and the popping synth beat. The bass, which drops out in the first part of the middle-eight, returns in the second part. Ninja continues the mood and instrumentation of this section in prechorus', which uses Orbison's lyrics again in a call-and-response, but this time vocally delivered in a downtempo R&B style. He comes close to actually singing, and his voice is multi-tracked so that he can sing both in his dry tenor and in a more processed, breathy voice in alternating lines. Yolandi's answering tag returns, cuing the final refrain, which also serves as the song's outro. The final refrain uses the song's full instrumentation again and is extended. Here, Yolandi is multi-tracked so that she can both sing the refrain and offer spoken-word counterlyrics. The song ends on the final note of the refrain and Yolandi's final line, "crazy about me," after which she is heard laughing, making a playful "pew" gun sound vocal effect, and then whispering girlishly.

In addition to its own projects, Die Antwoord has appeared in a few films, including the two South African short films *Straight from the Horse's Piel* (2010) and *Umshini Wam* (2011). Ninja and Yolandi Vi$$er also appeared in the full-length American feature science fiction film *CHAPPiE* (2015).

A$AP ROCKY: "SUNDRESS" AND "KIDS TURNED OUT FINE"
ALBUMS: NON-ALBUM SINGLE (2018) AND *TESTING* (2018)

Harlem's A$AP Rocky (Rakim Athelaston Mayers, 1988–), is a rapper, actor, producer (under the name Lord Flacko), and music video director. He started out as a member of A$AP Mob (2006–), a Harlem-based collective of rappers, producers, music video directors, fashion designers, and bikers. From the crew he adopted his moniker. Like A$AP Mob, which debuted with the mixtape *Lords Never Worry* (2012) as a free download, A$AP Rocky's solo debut was also a mixtape, *Live. Love. A$AP* (2011). It led to a record deal with RCA Records (under its Pluto Grounds imprint) for a debut album, *Long. Live. A$AP* (2013). The album hit No. 1 on the Billboard 200. In 2015, his second studio album, *At. Long. Last. A$AP*, also hit No. 1. His 2018 album *Testing* (RCA) reached No. 4 and was certified gold in Denmark and Canada, producing two minor hits in "A$AP Forever" and "Praise the Lord (da Shine)." The album also included the experimental hip hop song "Kids Turned Out Fine."

Testing was preceded by "Sundress" (2018), a non-album single co-produced by Danger Mouse (Brian Joseph Burton, 1977–), Syk Sense (Joshua Scruggs, n.d.), and Hector Delgado (a.k.a. Héctor el Father, Héctor Luis Delgado Román, 1979–). In its drum beat, the song samples the 2010 Tame Impala song "Why Won't You Make Up Your Mind?" (from *Innerspeaker*, 2010). The result is a mid-tempo sweet soul and pop-rock infused track with elements of psychedelic alternative rock, with both singing and rapping by A$AP Rocky. The song's lyrics tell a story of lost love, anger, and jealousy, as its narrator takes pleasure in knowing that his ex is miserable with a new lover, although the lyrics betray a sense of lingering love on his part.

"Sundress" is entirely based on a three-chord progression in B major: A-sharp minor-B major^7-C-sharp major^7 (or B major: vii-I^7-II^7). The structure of the recorded song is as follows: intro; refrain; verse; refrain; bridge; rap interlude (bifurcated); refrain; bridge; instrumental outro. The song fades in slowly with the Tame Impala beat: a 4/4 kick and snare drum interplay (left speaker), combined with barely discernible vocals (left), some of which foreshadow lines in the refrain, in the background. An electric guitar also appears (right speaker), as do cymbals. By the intro's end, the drums get louder, and an electric piano tag (right speaker) foreshadows the sound of A$AP Rocky's falsetto tenor lead vocals in the following refrain. These falsetto vocals sound soul-inspired, alternating between lines about his ex's being with the wrong guy and repeated vocables ("ooh," "oh," and "ah") that take the place of lyrics. As the refrain continues, clapping (reverbed), synth notes (a 1980s Roland electric piano voice), and guitar fret noises are added to create an atmospheric musical landscape, caused by the fact that everything except the lead vocals is placed in the mix's background, so even the falsetto refrain and unidentifiable vocables (yells, sounding like they are made by children) are treated equally with the beat and instrumentation.

In verse 1, A$AP Rocky's low tenor takes the lead vocals while the falsetto tenor vocals, which become the bridge, serve as a countermelody. The low tenor lead vocals that appear in the verse are sung with little pitch fluctuation, almost in a monotone, which is mirrored during both parts of the rap interlude, where A$AP Rocky's voice is multi-tracked to sound fuller; here his rap flow seems to be an updated version of old-school in that it is smooth, with almost no inflection. During the rap, a jazz organ that resembles a Hammond B3 organ is added, as well as a heavily auto-tuned second voice post-produced to sound extremely deep (a post-production pitch lowering effect usually referred to as "Barry White"). In the first part of the rap, the beats shift to a downtempo sound. High-pitched voices double on A$AP Rocky's last words. The Barry White sounding voice marks the beginning of the second part, which ends with a falsetto tenor tag. In the final refrain, this organ continues, and the earlier beats return. This time, cymbal crashes and the hand claps are louder than before. The organ and beats, as well as electric guitar, are heard in the bridge. All fade into a hiccupped synth noise, which gives way to the instrumental outro, which features a quiet electric piano, followed by the earlier Hammond B3-sounding organ. The song concludes by using this organ, which ends with a lot of vibrato (evoking the use of a half-moon switch found on the actual instrument).

"Kids Turned Out Fine" is a sardonic commentary on the state of the younger generation, with the repeated line (which almost sounds like a prayer) that the kids will "turn out fine," despite problems with drugs, alcohol, and sex. The song's upbeat message and general positivity are undercut in its final line, "I lose my mind." More dream-like than "Sundress," "Kids Turned Out Fine" is stylistically more R&B-focused. The song is in F-sharp minor, and the recorded song structure of "Kids Turned Out Fine" is as follows: intro; verse 1; verse 2; rap interlude (trifurcated); verse 3. Within these verses appear a couple of memorable lines that mention either the title of the song or that "the kids will be alright." These may also be heard as short hooks that behave a bit like refrains; however, A$AP Rocky interprets these lines as part of the verses.

The song samples the instrumental intro of the indie rock band Good Morning's "Don't Come Home Today" (2014), using two electric guitars. The song's intro relies on a two-chord folk music progression, moving back and forth on F-sharp major to G-sharp minor (or F-sharp major: I-ii). Played by two electric guitars, these chords create the song's dream-like and sleepy atmosphere. One electric guitar (appearing in the right speaker) uses a buzzed/distorted sound while the other (left speaker) plays clear, bell-like tones and sounds a bit like an electric piano. These guitars slowly fade into the foreground while introducing vocalizations by actor and rapper Will Smith's son, Jaden Smith (1998–) in the background, which set the stage for the song as he talks about "crazy kids."

As the guitars increase in volume into the foreground, they are set against an 808 drum beat, which marks the beginning of verse 1. Emerging in the foreground in this section is A$AP Rocky's soft low tenor; he sings in a 1960s R&B ballad style, his vocals multi-tracked to achieve a fuller sound. Some crackle can be heard, suggesting that this music comes from an old vinyl album. Shortly after he begins verse 1, the 808 drum beats pull out of sync with the verse's music. In the background, Smith's vocalizations are heard, and trombone slides (downward *glissandi*) add to the verse's slow unraveling. The dreamlike quality is still maintained with the guitars' alternating between F-sharp major and G-sharp minor and the R&B-style voice. When lyrics mention drugs, the entire song gets slowed down and all sounds drop in pitch, in much the same way as a vinyl album can be manipulated. Here, the song nearly comes to a halt, but then returns to the original tempo and the F-sharp major home key just as the lyrics return to the line, "the kids will be alright." Though verse 1 sounds like an album, and the guitars are sampled, the lyrics and R&B song are originally composed elements. Verse 2 is much shorter than verse 1 and is interrupted by A$AP Rocky's rapped interlude.

A$AP raps against the same instrumental accompaniment that precedes the rap interlude section. In the first part of the rap interlude, he uses a staccato vocal delivery with dry vocals that sound natural (no effects added). The second part is marked by heavy, distorted reverb for four lines, which indicate an altered mind state (much like the slowed-down drug-induced effect used previously). This passage stands out as being in a sonic space that is separate from the rest of the song. The accompaniment takes a quick break, but returns in the third section, bringing back the original sonic space as well as the instrumentation, singing style, and vocalizations heard in verses 1 and 2. Verse 3 marks a return to the home key and brings back the trombone slides in the background. As earlier, the trombones slide create another disorienting element in this song. This verse is slowed down the same way as verse 1 (prompted again by the mention of drugs), but this time the slowing-down effect lasts longer. Then instrumentation is suddenly reduced to just the electric guitars, against which sung vocals continue until the song's end—which slows the electric guitars and vocals down, makes their pitches descend further, and then fades out, giving the impression that the descent continues forever.

BABYFACE: "IT'S NO CRIME" AND "THERE SHE GOES"
ALBUMS: *TENDER LOVER* (1989) AND *FACE2FACE* (2001)

Babyface (Kenneth Brian Edmonds, 1959–), an Indianapolis-born R&B and new jack swing songwriter, singer, bassist, producer, and entrepreneur/businessman, is best known for his work with the Atlanta label LaFace Records (1989–2001, 2004-2011), which he co-founded along with L.A. Reid (Antonio Marquis Reid, 1955–). Babyface also co-founded Edmonds Entertainment (a.k.a. Babyface Entertainment, 1997–). As a singer, he began as a member of the groups ManChild (1974–1980) and the Deele (1981–1993, 2007–), but struck out on his own to work with fellow Deele member L.A. Reid, who continued his career managing and producing benchmark hip hop and R&B acts such as Paula Abdul, Boyz II Men, Whitney Houston, and TLC. Babyface has won 11 Grammy Awards and received the BMI Songwriter of the Year Award in 1989, 1990, 1991, and 1995. He has also had two albums certified double platinum: *Tender Lover* (1989) and *For the Cool in You* (1993).

Originally a guitarist and singer, Babyface decided he needed to learn keyboard to be a successful R&B and hip hop musician. Despite his self-definition as more of a writer than a musician or singer, his *Tender Lover* produced the hit "Whip Appeal." In 1993, Babyface's song "End of the Road," performed by Boyz II Men, became one of the best-selling singles of all time and broke long-standing chart records, earning him a Grammy as producer (he won the Grammy for Producer of the Year from 1995 to 1997). Around this time, Babyface began to concentrate on a solo career. In 1995, he won five Grammy Awards, including one for Best Male R&B Vocal Performance.

"It's No Crime" (1989), a star-crossed relationship song written by Babyface and produced by Babyface and L.A. Reid, became his first Billboard Hot 100 hit. It peaked at No. 7, reaching the top spot on the Hot R&B/Hip Hop Songs chart. It was also his only song to enter the Dance Club Songs chart, where it peaked at No. 5. The beginning of "It's No Crime" uses an open D5 chord (consisting of the root and the fifth without the third or filling voice to suggest if the chord is major or minor). On bass, the Deele's Kayo (Kevin Roberson, n.d.) plays the pitch of D, which is the song's pitch center. The recorded song's structure is as follows: intro (bifurcated); verse 1 (A); prechorus; refrain; instrumental bridge 1; verse 2 (A'); prechorus; refrain; middle-eight (B); instrumental bridge 1'; interlude 1; prechorus; interlude 2; instrumental bridge 2; vocal bridge; refrain (outro).

The song begins with a synth sweep, an industrial-sounding air loop that fades in. A timbale (right speaker), a snare drum, and a synth-based beat quickly join in this first part of the intro. These continue as a spoken-word media sample (left speaker) repeats "calling all cars" in the background. Synth strings also enter in this part, emphasizing the minor third and establishing D minor as the home key for a moment. But verse 1 quickly shifts to D major as Babyface begins to sing. His voice and delivery are comparable to those of Michael Jackson: his vocal range is between first and second tenor, and his boyish-sounding voice gives a sense of innocence. Babyface sings the verse against synth bass, timbale, and a new synth voice (1980s keyboard) that accentuates the first word in his phrases. The prechorus starts on G minor (iv or the subdominant of D minor) and builds up to the refrain, which introduces two new synth voices: horns and electronic piano. Kayo plays both bass guitar and synth bass and is heard especially in the refrain, as well as later on in instrumental bridge 2. Both instruments are used to give the impression of a slap bass, slightly predating the same approach used by composer Jonathan Wolff (n.d.) on his Korg M1 synthesizer-produced funk slap bass for the contemporary television comedy *Seinfeld* (1989–1998). During the refrain, Kayo's melodic bass line outlines D minor.

Instrumental bridge 1 (as well as 1', modified only by Babyface's sustained falsetto vocalizations) is related to the intro and returns to emphasizing the song's industrial sound. Verse 2 (A) returns to D major and sounds similar to verse 1, though Babyface's voice is now echoed a bit more. This is followed by a repetition of the prechorus and refrain. This time, the synth horns complete Babyface's refrain and become prominent in the middle-eight, which begins on a B-flat major chord (VI of D minor). Harmonically, this section is the song's bright passage. Here, the horns are more prominent, emphasized against the timbales. In the second half of this section, starting on G minor, the song ascends back to D5 then D major (D minor-G minor-A minor-B-flat major-C major-C5-D5-D major or D minor: i-iv-v-VI-VII-I). The intro-related instrumental bridge 1' and interlude follow; the latter recycles the "calling all cars" sample. The final repetition of the prechorus leads to a second interlude instead of immediately to the refrain. This interlude contains a new synth voice (bells), which is played against the timbale and synth bass beat. Instrumental bridge 2 places Kayo's melodic bass in the foreground, which continues as accompaniment in Babyface's vocal bridge. Both bridges are refrain-related and are followed by the final refrain, which serves as the song's outro. Here, concluding in D minor, Babyface sings in his deepest register, leading up to a partial instance of the refrain, which echoes out abruptly on the words "baby" and "why."

"There She Goes" (2001), a song about being in love from afar and being unable to act on the feeling, was co-written by Babyface and The Neptunes (Charles "Chad" Hugo, 1974– and Pharrell Williams, 1973–) for Babyface's sixth studio album, *Face2Face*. Produced by The Neptunes, it peaked at No. 31 on the Billboard Hot 100 (Babyface's final Top 40 entry as of 2021). "There She Goes" uses E minor as its home key except during its refrains, which are all in F major. This ascending move to F major underscores the elation of the male singers while describing the woman of their dreams. The recorded song's structure is as follows: intro (bifurcated); verse 1; prechorus; refrain; verse 2; prechorus; refrain; bridge; refrain; outro.

The song's intro is a combination of a heavy synth melody with a hiccup effect, intermittent electric bass mirrored by heavy kick drum, male vocalizations (in the form of breathing and the "ahhh" sound), and dry hand claps. The first part of the intro is an instrumental vamp, followed by a brief electric guitar tag; Babyface's spoken-word vocals mark the second part of the intro, which is also punctuated by an electric guitar tag. Here, he employs staccato lines in his deepest register (low tenor), using a smooth and cool delivery with little inflection. The same music continues into verse 1, in which Babyface's low tenor lead vocals are also featured. In this section, Babyface sings in a laid-back R&B style. The electric bass now holds off until ends of phrases; however, the kick drum becomes more prominent and frequent, especially at beginnings of phrases. Into and throughout the prechorus and refrain, the instrumentation remains the same as in the song's verses, but vocally the song's mood shifts into sounding urgent and becomes heavily multi-tracked with Williams's falsetto, funk-based tenor voice taking over the lead vocals in the prechorus. These not only contrast with the deeper register of Babyface's earlier vocals, they also contrast with Babyface's high-pitched and low-pitched commentaries in the background of the prechorus.

The refrain returns Babyface's low tenor vocals to the foreground, accompanied by Williams's harmonies. At the end of each phrase in the refrain, Williams's falsetto tags enter the foreground (mostly left speaker). The refrain ends on B major (the dominant or V of E minor), which harmonically leads to verse 2, back in the home key of E minor. Musically, verse 2 sounds similar to verse 1, but this time there is more emphasis on the vocalizations (male breathing and the aforementioned "ahh"), which slowly become emphasized as a kind of beatboxed part of the groove that is slightly reminiscent of The Zombies' "Time of the Season" (1968). Toward the end of the song, the bridge, in E minor, combines the instrumental vamp in part one of the intro with fragments of the prechorus, which are sung by Williams in his funk falsetto; Babyface talk-sings in his deepest range again, with emphasis on the word "dance." This section, with its repeated couplet rather than verse, functions more like a bridge than a middle-eight section. The final refrain has a small extension with tag, performed *a cappella* (unaccompanied), and a beatboxed gesture. The outro, in E minor, starts like the bridge and contains the same prechorus fragments, alternating between E minor and A minor as it slowly fades out (E minor: i-iv).

In 1997, Babyface Entertainment, a film production company, produced *Soul Food* (1997), which spawned a double-platinum soundtrack. In 2000, Babyface co-founded Babyface Sports Group, which provided agent representation for professional athletes. He has released more solo albums: *Face 2 Face* (2001), *Grown and Sexy* (2005), *Playlist* (2007), and *Return of the Tender Lover* (2015). In 2014, he released a Grammy Award-winning duet album with Toni Braxton titled *Love, Marriage and Divorce*. The L.A. Reid/Babyface team is considered one of the most prolific producer and songwriter teams in the history of popular music. At one point, the production duo had six singles in the R&B Top Ten at one time.

BEYONCÉ: "RUN THE WORLD (GIRLS)" (SINGLE VERSION) ALBUM: *4* (2011)

Beyoncé (Beyoncé Giselle Knowles, 1981–), who as of 2021 has won 28 Grammy Awards and had six solo studio albums certified platinum, is more of an R&B and pop singer, but she has also recorded hit hip hop songs. If her R&B trio Destiny Child's (1990–2006) and her own hits are taken together, Beyoncé is one of the best-selling and most acclaimed music artists in Billboard history. As the standout soprano in Destiny's Child, Houston-born Beyoncé also pursued solo projects. Her solo studio albums featuring hip hop elements include *B-Day* (2005), *I Am . . . Sasha Fierce* (2008), *4* (2011), *Beyoncé* (2013), and *Lemonade* (2016). In addition, she has collaborated with a long list of hip hop artists and producers. Her Billboard Hot 100 No. 1 and No. 2 hit singles that contained hip hop elements were "Check on It" (2005), "Single Ladies (Put a Ring on It)" (2008), and "Drunk in Love" (2013). Her participation in hip hop songs usually entails her singing contrasting lyrical passages to

Must-Hear Music 47

Beyoncé started the Dallas, Texas stop of her 2007 Beyoncé Experience Tour with this choreographed pose, which took place shortly before the release of her 2008 hip hot hit, "Single Ladies (Put a Ring on It)." (Michael Bush/Dreamstime.com)

the song's rap; however, since the Destiny's Child days, she has taken to performing rap-singing within R&B songs.

Her fourth studio album, *4* (2011), which followed a career hiatus and severing of her music profession from her erstwhile manager Mathew Knowles (her father), did not do as well commercially as did her first three albums, although it was her fourth consecutive album to debut at No. 1 on the Billboard 200 (it also reached No. 1 in Brazil, France, Ireland, South Korea, Spain, Switzerland, and the U.K.). Fans were not prepared for Beyoncé's emphasis on traditional rhythm and blues (R&B), albeit with elements of Afrobeat, funk, hip hop, and soul, or the album's mellow tone and diverse vocal styles, with lyrics that trumpeted female empowerment. The album also spawned five hit singles with "Run the World (Girls)," "Best Thing I Never Had," "Party," "Love on Top," and "Countdown," with "Love on Top" winning the Grammy for Best Traditional R&B Performance. The album's final song, "Run the World (Girls)," was its sole offering for music fans who were used to "the old"

Beyoncé, reminiscent of the energetic music on *I Am . . . Sasha Fierce*. It was released internationally as the lead single from *4* in April 2011, and it reached number No. 29 on the Billboard Hot 100, as well as the Top Ten in Australia, Japan, the Netherlands, New Zealand, Norway, and Scotland. It reached No. 1 on the U.S. Hot Dance Clubs Songs chart and was RIAA-certified gold.

"Run the World (Girls)," co-written by Beyoncé and The-Dream (Terius Youngdell Nash, 1977–), who also contributed to the composition of "Single Ladies," heavily samples Major Lazer's "Pon de Floor" (2009). Produced by Beyoncé, The-Dream, Switch (David James Andrew Taylor, n.d.), and Shea (Robert Taylor, n.d.), its constant military marching drum beat makes it stand out, especially given Beyoncé's cheerleader-styled chanted delivery. "Run the World (Girls)" can best be described as electropop dancehall with an R&B-infusion. Like "Pon de Floor," the single version of "Run the World (Girls)" uses C as its pitch center or home pitch, favoring C minor over C major as its home key. Despite its radio-friendly length, the structure of this song is modeled on classic rock's epic song structure ambition. As a miniature version of the epic song, instead of having many separate sections, its few sections frequently contain divisions. The single's recorded song structure is as follows: intro (bifurcated); refrain (trifurcated); verse 1 (quintfurcated); prechorus; refrain (trifurcated); verse 2 (quintfurcated); prechorus; refrain (trifurcated); outro.

With no more than a quick synth sweep, the first part of the intro begins. This part, starting on A-flat major (VI of C minor) contains Beyoncé's muted soprano voice, accompanied by the "Pon de Floor" Latin percussion beat created by lower-pitched claves (left speaker), castanets (right speaker), and timbale, with a kick drum accompaniment (mostly left speaker). The second part of the intro clarifies C as the pitch center and features the military-style marching beat of a snare drum. The entire song is in quadruple meter (four beats per measure), and this military beat, at times doubled by the kick drum, reinforces its predictable rhythm. Beyoncé's introductory vocals use call-and-response among three distinct vocal tracks: her main chant-like cheerleader-style vocals (slightly auto-tuned and double- or triple-tracked to sound fuller); vocalizations (a clipped "yeah!"); and by the intro's very end, female backing singers that reinforce the pitch center, singing the single word "girls!" Their one-word entrance creates a break between the intro and the refrain. In addition, their "girls" is elongated and made to sound wetter (fuller). It also has a sweep quality, like the song's opening sound.

The song's refrain also uses call-and-response, but with only two voices—Beyoncé's lead chant and the word "girls" (which is an answer to the question raised by Beyoncé about who runs the world). The refrain also introduces the song's various instrumental and vocal textures (to create points of interest) and recycles its earlier sounds. Its first part includes the military-style snare drum, which accompanies Beyoncé's voice; the second part brings back the castanet (on right speaker), claves and kick drums (left speaker), and introduces an oscillating synthesizer (running an octave between lower C^4, also known as middle C, and a higher C^5); and the third part introduces some synth-generated sonic background effects. A synth sweep marks another division between the first and second part of the refrain. More noticeable, however, is how Beyoncé sings from the pitch G to C (scale step 5 to scale step 1) in the first part, followed by folding in more octaves on C in the second part. The third and final part starts like the first part, but Beyoncé's last two double-tracked lines introduce E-flat, which suggests the key of C minor and gives a darker, more ominous sound at the end of the refrain (scale steps ♭3, 2, 1, sung just above middle C and then sung again an octave higher). In just these brief sections, "Run the World (Girls)" recontextualizes two musical aspects that have often been associated or interpreted as masculine musical tropes: the military snare beat (as an important element of her anthem for girls and women) and fifth and octave relations (which in the past have been described as assertive or masculine sounding). At the same time, the song uses the minor third (the E-flat pitch that suggests C minor), enabling a feminine or more sensually associated gesture to firmly establish the song's home key. The refrain folds pitch-altered, and thus impossibly high, hiccupped female vocalizations into the background.

An 808 hiccup leads to the verse, which starts with Beyoncé's more auto-tuned staccato sung lines about how men treat women. Initially, the verse may sound like a lengthy section; however, this section is quintfurcated (contains five parts). The first part of the verse provides the song's most dramatic key change and texture change. It starts in F minor (iv or the subdominant of C minor) and includes just Beyoncé's voice with overdubbed close harmonies, accompanied by the military-style snare drum. This part concludes on C major (or borrowed I, which uses C, E, G instead of C minor's darker sounding C, E-flat, G). Like the first part, the second part of this verse contains four lines. The lyrical content shifts to a warning to the opposite sex. The accompanying oscillating synthesizer and castanets heard in the second part of the refrain, as well as the cartoonish sonic sounds (from "Pon de Floor"), highlight the quirky vocalizations. Here, Beyoncé starts on G, but soon reinforces C as the pitch center, underscoring her mention of Houston, her home city. The accompaniment continues in the third part of the verse, which is also four lines, but this time Beyoncé celebrates the "girls" who party in clubs and find success. The rhythm of the kick drums changes here. Beyoncé starts singing on A-flat, but F minor is the key here (returning to iv), with harmonizing overdubs. The chord progression of this verse is the same as the first verse, ending again on C major (and borrowed I). The fourth part, also four lines, brings back the sonic sounds and returns to reinforcing C as the pitch center through Beyoncé's use of octaves and the oscillating synthesizer. The fifth and final part of the verse, which has just two lines, contains a more lyrical, sinewy melodic line in comparison to the verse's previous parts. Accompanied by the military snare drum, Beyoncé starts on F minor, but returns to C major. The lyrical aspect of this final part foreshadows the prechorus. Sonic effects in the background accompany a swirling sounding synth sweep.

The prechorus starts on A-flat major (VI of C) and then moves to C minor (i). Beyoncé's darker, sequential melody is accompanied mostly by her R&B-style backing vocalizations (elongated "ooohs"). Her voice is at its most songlike in this section, which builds up to the refrain. A synth-generated sonic sweep (panned from left to right speaker) cues in the refrain, which is then followed by verse 2. The accompaniment pattern for each part is recycled, and Beyoncé's staccato vocalizations return in the first part; however, the lyrical content continues (with celebrating female college graduates), and the last two lines of this first part include some triplets, Beyoncé coming close to rap-singing. In the second part, she sings about how she cannot be held back and has worked fully to earn her pay. The third and fourth parts, which celebrate women who work hard, succeed, and still have children, as well as men who respect them, feature Beyoncé's vocal grinding. The final part returns to warning the opposite sex and ends with the same line as the final part of verse 1. The same prechorus and refrain follow.

The song's outro, starting in A-flat major (VI of C minor) and moving to C major (borrowed I), is an R&B chant that is sung, with backing vocalizations, against the military-style snare drums, claves, castanet, and timbale instrumentation. A synth sonic sweep and hiccup effect mark the return of Beyoncé's question. When she repeats her question, the kick drum starts doubling the military-style snare drums. Throughout the outro, Beyoncé's main vocals are harmonized by her overdubbed vocals, her filtered voice echoing some of her lines. The end of each of her lines is in C major (she ends on E, the middle pitch), a brighter conclusion than C minor. The outro, like the prechorus, is also more songlike, though it is more declarative, now appropriating C major instead of C minor.

BLACK EYED PEAS: "BOOM BOOM POW"
ALBUM: *THE E.N.D.* (2009)

The Los Angeles-based Black Eyed Peas (1995–) is a hip hop and electronica rap and dance (the act originally including breakdancing) quartet formed in 1995 by members apl.de.ap (Alan Pineda Lindo, 1974–), Taboo (Jamie Gomez, 1975–), and will.i.am (William James Adams Jr., 1975–), along with guest vocalist Kim Hill (1962–). Before the quartet became successful, Hill left and was replaced by singer Fergie (Stacey Ferguson, 1975–) in 2001, completing the four-person lineup that would make up the group until 2016. Originally an alternative hip hop group that gained popularity by playing college campuses, Black Eyed Peas evolved to become a hip hop, R&B, soul, funk, dance, and techno fusion group. It set itself apart from other rap groups by emphasizing not the gangster life—violence and materialism—but social causes, romance/sex, and community. It was the band's first album to feature Fergie and its third overall, *Elephunk* (2003), on A&M Records (1962–), that made the group a success, peaking at No. 14 on the Billboard 200, selling more than 8.5 million copies worldwide, and spawning the group's first three Billboard Hot 100 hits: "Where Is the Love?," "Hey Mama," and "Let's Get It Started." Pop legend Justin Timberlake produced the "Where Is the Love?," and the group joined him on his tour with Christina Aguilera. Its 2005 album, *Monkey Business*, performed better, reaching No. 2 on the Billboard 200 and selling more than 10 million copies worldwide. It also gave the band its first Billboard top-10 hits, "Don't Phunk with My Heart" and "My Humps."

The next album, *The E.N.D.* (i.e., *Energy Never Dies*, 2009), followed a hiatus wherein Fergie, Taboo, and will.i.am pursued solo careers, and apl.de.ap worked on an English and Tagalog music project and video (apl.de.ap is Filipino and was adopted by Americans). On *The E.N.D.*, the band debuted what was a harder, more energetic electronic sound influenced by will.i.am's trip to Australia. Reaching No. 1 on the Billboard 200, it sold 11 million copies worldwide and spawned three Billboard No. 1 songs, "Boom Boom Pow," "I Gotta Feeling," and "Imma Be." The skills braggadocio "Boom Boom Pow" (2009), the lead single from *The E.N.D.*, became the group's first No. 1 on the Billboard Hot 100. It also topped the Australian, Canadian, and U.K. singles charts, and reached the Top Ten in more than twenty countries. It sold more than seven million copies and was nominated for a Best Dance Recording Grammy Award.

Like the official music video, the album version of "Boom Boom Pow" is in A major. It employs a modified AABA structure commonly used in pop. The recorded song's structure is as follows: intro (quadfurcated); refrain; verse 1 (A); verse 2 (A′); refrain; verse 3 (A″); rap and vocal interlude 1; middle-eight (B); bridge 1; rap interlude 2; vocal bridge 1; bridge 2; vocal bridge 2; instrumental bridge; verse 2 (A′); refrain; outro (trifurcated). The intro's first part begins with a slow synthesizer overtone series that is panned from left, then center, to right speaker. This synth voice evokes science fiction versions of space and is accompanied by a synth sub-bass drone. The first part, especially the sub-bass drone, emphasizes C-sharp as the intro's initial pitch center. The second part includes a deep, robotic spoken-word voice (which references MTV's Max Headroom through its hiccup effects and delays). The voice here prepares listeners for the changes they are about to hear in the group's music, pointing out that fluidity is the nature of reality. As the speaker continues, a distorted, energetic egg-shaker sound (this gives the impression of a beat) is introduced, and it evolves into a second oscillating synth voice that sounds like a cross between helicopter blades and many science fiction film lasers. As the voice concludes, the third part is marked by the introduction of a new synth voice (reminiscent of bees); it is used like a sympathetic string, a consistent, continuous sound against which most of the song will be constructed. Here, a sustained synth emphasizes a pitch between G-sharp and A as the new pitch center. The fourth part of the intro features the first human voice heard in the song—will.i.am's low tenor vocal hook—also hiccupped, followed by snares. Both cue the refrain in A major with its pitch center now on A.

The refrain contains the new "boom boom boom" hook, sung by Fergie and Taboo, both of whom are highly auto-tuned (to sound robotic). The interval they sing is an octave, which emphasizes A as the new pitch center. Fergie and Taboo's hook is punctuated by will.i.am's earlier hook. All are sung against a kick drum and hand clap beat. The descending chord progression of the refrain is A major-F major-D minor (A major: I-VI-iv). This descent is enhanced by the pitched kick drum. Will.i.am takes the lead vocals on verse 1, alternating between rapping and singing. Verse 1 is also in A major and consists of will.i.am's singing an octave that emphasizes A as the pitch center. In verse 2, Fergie's mezzo-soprano lead vocals also alternate between rapping and singing against the same instrumentation, with the addition of an intermittent 808 drum as contrast to the kick drum. With little instrumental change, the refrain follows. Verse 3 consists of Taboo's muted low tenor vocals. Here, he mostly raps, chanting a couple of lines, which are highly auto-tuned. Sonic effects are added as well.

A rap and vocal interlude features apl.de.ap's muted low tenor vocals, which alternate between rap, funk-infused rap singing, and singing. His vocals are the most auto-tuned section of the song. The middle-eight, which occurs only once, features Fergie's singing with little auto-tuning, belting her lines and using vocal grind (or rasp) in a way that resembles house music. This contrasting section with its new vocal texture and a new oscillating synth voice starts in D minor (the subdominant or iv of A major). Fergie invites listeners to dance, then prompts will.i.am to "drop the beat." Will.i.am raps a quick tag that leads to bridge 1, which features his vocals. It also uses synthesizer keyboards in much the same way as energetic rhythm guitars.

Bridge 1 marks where "Boom Boom Pow" evolves fully into house music. It is followed by a rap interlude, which features will.i.am, then a vocal bridge. This brief bridge features will.i.am's singing against the same synthesizers used throughout the first bridge and second rap interlude. These synthesizers become the foreground of the next bridge and accompaniment of the low voice heard in the intro in the next vocal bridge. Before the instrumental bridge, the second bridge has a tag, which recycles will.i.am's comment about the rocking beat. The instrumental bridge features sustained synth voices that lead to a repeat of Fergie's verse 3, followed by the refrain. This time, Fergie's voice fades in like the synth sweep at the beginning of the verse. The first part of the outro is marked by a new ascending synth voice, followed by the low spoken-word voice alternating with will.i.am's higher-pitched repetition of his line. The outro's second part features a wobbling high-pitched synth voice that sounds a bit raga- or Middle Eastern-influenced. The third part features just the sustained synth string voice, a sound that was introduced in the intro's third part. The song then fades out.

In 2004, will.i.am, who had produced most of the Black Eyed Peas songs, launched his record label, the will.i.am Music Group. In 2009, the Black Eyed Peas set the Billboard Hot 100 record for longest No. 1 chart run for a group when "I Gotta Feeling" (14 weeks at No. 1) assumed the Billboard No. 1 singles spot held by "Boom Boom Pow" (12 weeks at No. 1), making the group the top slot holder for a record 26 consecutive weeks (as of 2021). It also won various Grammy Awards, such as the

2004 award for Best Rap Performance by a Duo or Group; the 2005 awards for Favorite Pop/Rock Band and Favorite Rap/Hip Hop Band, Duo or Group, 2005; and the 2006 award for Best Pop Performance by a Duo or Group with Vocal. Overall, the band has won seven Grammy Awards, eight American Music Awards, and three World Music Awards.

BOYZ II MEN (FEATURING MICHAEL BIVINS): "MOTOWNPHILLY"
ALBUM: *COOLEYHIGHHARMONY* (1991)

Philadelphia R&B sensation Boyz II Men (1988–) was best known for its ballads and *a cappella* (unaccompanied) harmonies; however, the quartet's first big breakthrough hit on Motown Records, "Motownphilly" (1991), included elements of danceable hip hop and new jack swing. Currently the trio is comprised of baritone Nathan Morris (1971–), tenor Wanyá Morris (1973–), and tenor/second tenor Shawn Stockman (1972–); the group originally also included bass Michael McCary (1971–), who retired in 2003 due to health issues. In 1991, Boyz II Men debuted with *Cooleyhighharmony* and two Top Ten Billboard Hot 100 singles: "Motownphilly" reached No. 3 and "It's So Hard to Say Goodbye to Yesterday" (dedicated to tour manager Khalil Roundtree, who was murdered in Chicago) peaked at No. 2. The following year, the group had the first of five No. 1 singles (four as artist, one as guest artist) with the non-album single "End of the Road," co-written by Babyface, which stayed in the top spot for 13 weeks. The group had two more long-standing No. 1 hits with "I'll Make Love to You" (1994, 14 weeks) and as featured artists on Mariah Carey's "One Fine Day" (1995, 16 weeks). Boyz II Men can be counted among the music industry's elite, with 50 cumulative weeks at No. 1, ranking fifth behind Carey, Elvis Presley, Rihanna, and The Beatles.

Cooleyhighharmony, produced by Bel Biv Devoe's Michael Bivins (1968–), is an album that introduced drum-heavy new jack swing with soul-styled vocals in place of rapping and hip hop singing. The album sold more than nine million copies and won the Grammy Award for Best R&B Performance by a Duo or Group with Vocals. Its biggest single, the Dallas Austin (1970–) produced "Motownphilly," featured a rap cameo by Bivins, who co-wrote the song, which can best be summed up as the narrative of the quartet's beginnings, complete with the story of how Boyz II Men approached Bivins backstage at a concert and auditioned on the spot. Two other Bivins-associated acts, Bell Biv DeVoe and Another Bad Creation, both new jack swing groups, are mentioned as part of what was nicknamed the East Coast Family in the first verse. The song also references two of the group's main musical influences, Motown (1960s) and Philly soul (1970s), describing the band's brand of music (which also included elements of hip hop and R&B) as "East coast swing / . . . / not too hard, not too soft."

Entirely in D minor, the song's structure is as follows: intro (trifurcated); refrain; verse 1; verse 2; prechorus (bifurcated); refrain; bridge; rap interlude; verse 3 (interrupted with a vocal break); verse 4; prechorus (bifurcated); refrain; bridge; prechorus (part 2 only); bridge; rap interlude; vocal interlude; refrain; bridge; outro. It's no exaggeration that the first part of the song's intro jumps out at listeners, with an immediate combination of synth chord stabs (high-pitched brass), kick drum, hiccupped 808 drum, snare drum, and voices. At times, vibraslap also appears (usually faintly and on the left speaker). Bivins's speaking voice asks the quartet's members if they are ready, with the response being energetic, incoherent mumbling. Voices state "and it's about time," which cues in the intro's second part. Sustained low synth horns, followed by sustained high trumpets, enter. A stuttered and harmonized repetition of the name Boyz II Men takes place here as well. All are set against deep electric bass guitar (mainly on the E string), kick drum, timbale, snare drum, 808, and vibraslap. The synth chord stabs begin the intro's third part. Like the second part, the third part includes hiccupped snare drum rolls. As the band begins singing the refrain, vocalizations—energetic, quick-chanted repetition of the word "go"—appear in the background. Snare drum, timbale, and horns appear (right speaker) here along with synth bass and kick drum (left speaker) and remain as accompaniment into verses 1 and 2. In these verses, Nathan Morris sings lead low tenor vocals and uses a funk-style delivery with elongated syllables. McCary sings the bass commentary on specific lines here.

Punchier synth horns are reintroduced in the beginning of the prechorus, which features Wanyá Morris's R&B-style bright tenor vocals, featuring lots of vibrato (his voice is comparable to Stevie Wonder's) and Stockman's soft falsetto. These turn-taking vocals create a pleasant-sounding balance between the verses and prechorus, from low to high. A bifurcated prechorus is unusual partly because the role of the prechorus is to build up to the refrain and dividing it could lessen this effort. Here, it works, with just Wanyá Morris's voice in the first part and the group's four-part harmony in the second part. The prechorus begins in D minor and ends on A major, the dominant (V) of D minor, which strongly leads back to the home key used in the refrain. In the

56 Listen to Hip Hop!

second part, Wanyá Morris hits the prechorus's highest notes to create a dramatic build-up.

The refrain follows: a tightly harmonized vocal section that features similar instrumentation to the first refrain, with added cymbal crashes. This time, the "go" vocalizations are dropped. The first bridge features vocal and instrumental hiccups, with the quartet half-stuttering the repetition of "boys" while the 808 hiccups—both evoking scratching. The ensuing rap interlude features Bivins using more spoken word than rap, with Boyz II Men's harmonies as counterpoint in the background. Here, synth chord stabs are reintroduced against the heavy bass beat.

Verse 3 uses the same instrumentation as verse 1, but after two lines, a vocal break is inserted with all four members singing. Nathan Morris starts as lead vocalist, but in the tightly harmonized vocal break, McCary stands out for his walking bass vocals (mostly right speaker). Verse 4 starts with Stockman taking lead, followed by Nathan Morris again. The return of the prechorus, with the same instrumentation, features Wanyá Morris's lead vocals along with Stockman's commentary falsetto again, followed by the entire quartet in the second part. The refrain returns with the "go" chants in the background appearing later.

After this refrain, a second bridge follows, containing new higher-pitched vocalizations while at the same time the same sustained horns (heard for the first time in the second part of the intro) and the stuttered repetition of the group's name return. The second part of the prechorus, which features the quartet, is inserted in between this bridge and the third bridge, which features a couple of 808 hiccups and cues another rap interlude, which features Bivins's old-school rap against the rhythm section, plus the 808 and actual turntables. The following vocal interlude features the quartet, accompanied by timbale (right speaker). Here, the quartet harmonizes, singing bell-like pitches (ostensibly, this is how they auditioned for Bivins). By the end of this section, McCary's bass vocals appear prominently (right speaker). The refrain returns with the "go" chants heard throughout, followed by a repetition of the third bridge, which brings these chants into the foreground. The short outro is marked by sustained low synth horns and the stuttered repetition of the band's name from the second part of the intro, joined by the harmonized repetition of the name Boyz II Men (sung). The song ends with a harmonized shout out to the other groups—ABC and BBD—of their East Coast Family.

Boyz II Men's third album, *II*, mostly written and produced by Tim Kelley, Bob Robinson, Babyface, Jimmy Jam, and Terry Lewis, sold more than twelve million copies and spawned the singles "On Bended Knee,"

"I'll Make Love to You," and "Water Runs Dry." Boyz II Men's next studio album, *Evolution* (1997) sold more than three million copies, but McCary's health issues made its tour difficult. Its next two albums did not do well commercially. *Full Circle* (2002) would become the group's final album as a quartet. It would release more albums, but none would have the commercial success of its first three efforts. Boyz II Men received a star on the Hollywood Walk of Fame in 2012. In June 2017, Philadelphia renamed the street that runs near the High School for the Creative and Performing Arts, where the group was originated (as Unique Attraction by friends Nathan Morris and Marc Nelson in 1985), as Boyz II Men Boulevard. As of 2021, Boyz II Men continue to perform worldwide, as a trio, having released their thirteenth album, *Under the Streetlight*, in 2017.

BRETT DOMINO (THE BRETT DOMINO TRIO): "PINOCCHIO" NON-ALBUM SINGLE, 2014

Brett Domino (a.k.a. C-Bomb, Rob J. Madin, 1986–), a musical comedian from Chesterfield, North Derbyshire, England, had a minor U.K. hit with "Gillian McKeith" in 2010, but he is best known as a YouTube sensation for his "how to create hit songs" videos. In his 2014 *How to Make a Hit Pop Song* (Parts I and II) video, he creates the hip hop songs "You Look Sexy When You Do That" and "Pinocchio," both of which were released as non-album singles. The videos demonstrate humorously that hip hop hits can sometimes be boiled down to auto-tuning, 808 drums, one or two quirky ostinatos and sound effects, and a rhyming dictionary, as well as conventions like referencing other hip hop artists and name dropping. His band, The Brett Domino Trio, currently consists of only two members, himself and fellow deadpan comedian Steven Peavis (Ste Anderson, n.d.), both graduates of Leeds College of Music in West Yorkshire, England. In 2009, original third member Mitch Hutchinson (Michael Denny, n.d.) left the band.

The videos for *How to Make a Hit Pop Song* (Parts I and II) offer a textbook description of hip hop songs: a catchy instrumental ostinato on an oddball instrument to create a hook; a funky drum beat; a brief but sexy, melodic, and simple vocal hook that doubles as the song's title (Brett Domino explains that "the most important thing is not to overthink it. Sing the first thing that comes into your head"); auto-tuning; vocal effects (such as hiccups and pitch-altered vocals); 808 drums; euphoric build-up (he uses the sound of his washing machine on spin cycle); name dropping (contemporary only); and a "sprinkle" of bass, percussion, keyboards, backing vocals, and rap. His discussion of lyrics is memorable comedy, as he comes to the conclusion that most people don't listen to them anyway, so it doesn't pay to put too much effort into them (in the videos, he googles "sexy phrases," "sexy women," and "capital cities" to get ideas for lyrics, followed by using a rhyming dictionary). As long as what you do/rap/sing is sexy, he adds, "it doesn't need to make a lot of sense."

Brett Domino's Part II song, "Pinocchio," is an unrequited-love snap song where he is attempting to win over a woman who doesn't quite trust his motives (hence, the theme of lies versus truth, as represented by Pinocchio). Entirely in quadruple meter (four beats per measure) and G minor, the song's structure in the video is as follows: intro; refrain; verse 1; verse 2; verse 3; refrain (extended); verse 4; verse 5; interlude; refrain (extended); interlude; refrain; outro. "Pinocchio" begins with a synth-generated bass ostinato in the foreground that resembles a Blue Man Group keyboard (a 37-key toy synth made to look like the band's PVC instruments). This ostinato (G-F-D-B-flat-C-G) basically outlines the G minor chord (G-B-flat-D) and emphasizes the home key. It is backed by a higher-pitched synth countermelody, snaps, and synth-generated beats. Brett Domino's slightly auto-tuned talk-singing soon shares the foreground with the bass ostinato, declaring that he would never lie to the woman in question. Just after a simple 808 hiccup, a euphoric build-up sound (sounding like a radio tuner) takes place and works here like a sweep into the first refrain. Several aspects of the earlier part of the video for *How to Make a Hit Pop Song: Advanced Techniques* (Part II) are informative in determining the actual sound sources. According to Brett Domino in the part of the video that precedes the song, he demonstrates that the euphoric sweep sound was originally a recording of his washing machine "towards the peak of its spin cycle." This part of the video also shows how he generates 808s by pressing a key on his keyboard-based beat controller: the same one used in his "Sexy When You Do That" video as well as in this video and the one for the extended version of "Pinocchio." In these videos, Steven Peavis is shown playing more than just one key on this keyboard; he is later shown during the ostinato as he hovers his hands over a toy synth, pretending to play the part.

In the first refrain, simple 808 beats continue in the background, punctuated by high-pitched dings—the same ones used to introduce captions in the instructional part of the video. Brett Domino's low tenor vocals are multi-tracked and highly auto-tuned here, accompanied initially by only the two synth voices and snaps. In contrast to the intro and verses,

Brett Domino sings the refrain. His auto-tuned harmonies are added here as backing vocals. In contrast to the intro, more auto-tuning is used here, making his voice sound slightly robotic. The same euphoric sound effect used at the end of the intro appears here, but the build-up is not as lengthy as it was the first time.

Verse 1 begins with a post-production vocal effect, a hiccup on the long "o" of "Pinocchio" along with the 808s. Verses 1, 2, and 3 are talk-sung against the simple synth beat, snaps, the 808, and intermittent occasions of the build-up sound. Some sounds are introduced, however, to offer listeners brief points of interest: in verse 1, Brett Domino breaks up his flow on his fourth phrase by emphasizing the word "round," as a cosmic-sounding synth-produced effect completes this section. Verse 2 is introduced with another vocal hiccup, then accompanied by "whoop-whoop" synth sound effects on the beat, followed by a complete dropping-out of all the previous accompaniment, as Brett Domino talk-sings alone, with only snaps for accompaniment. Verse 3 is marked by a return of the accompaniment, including hiccupped 808s and the bass ostinato, followed by another dropping-out of the accompaniment and Brett Domino's voice being doubled by his voice processed to sound in the bass range.

A whirring build-up sound introduces the second instance of the refrain, which sounds just like the first refrain but is extended. In this extended part, marked by the 808 drum rolls, new lyrics are introduced. Here, Brett Domino's multi-tracked vocals are accompanied again by synth-produced "whoops." Verse 4 is a return to Brett Domino's talk-singing, this time with a chime-like and more prominent—perhaps science-fiction sounding—synth accompaniment. The other accompanying instrumentation is the same as that used in verse 1. Here, Brett Domino interrupts his flow with pauses. The same whirring effect is used as a sweep, marking the end of verse 4 and the beginning of verse 5. In this verse, a continuous bell dings at rhythmic intervals as the chime-like synth continues. At this point, vocal effects are ramped up, with more hiccups, build-ups, and multi-tracking.

The first interlude brings back the sounds of the intro section, including Brett Domino's talk-singing about never lying to the woman in question as well as the bass ostinato and their accompaniment. A build-up with 808s and the cosmic-sounding/science fiction-inspired effects leads to the third iteration of the refrain, which is again extended. This time, the refrain begins with a highly auto-tuned Brett Domino singing (his voice multiplied a great many times with a lot of applied reverb) with only snaps as accompaniment; the bass and the 808s completely drop out. After two phrases, a synth-generated strings voice emerges, creating a *crescendo* (gradually getting louder). The climax of the song employs a lengthy build-up of these strings against the euphoric whirring sound effect. The extension takes place while this build-up is still happening. Here, Brett Domino's highly processed vocals (the word "though" distorted heavily) sound cavernous (echoing on the word "no") and the built-up intensity marks the song's false ending. After a brief caesura, the second interlude brings another return of the bass ostinato in the foreground, accompanied by 808s; in other words, the opening sounds of the intro. Brett Domino signs off by talk-singing his name, then giving the title of the song, followed by the year of composition (2014)—a way of giving the song his signature and a common practice used in not only hip hop but songs composed as long ago as the troubadours and trouvères, if not earlier. His voice hiccups and echoes on his name and a moment later his processed bass-sounding voice repeats it. The 808, played against vocals processed to sound like gibberish, marks the song's second fake ending. Though the second interlude may initially sound like the song's outro, it is followed instead by the fourth instance of the refrain. This time, the synth-generated "whoops" are used to accompany Brett Domino's final singing of the refrain. A brief outro brings the bass ostinato back to the foreground. Here, the song's title is sung or talk-sung in various ways, including his processed synth-sounding high-pitched "Pinocchio," until Brett Domino announces "that's it."

The music video that features the extended version of "Pinocchio" is simply a lengthier version of the original; however, the recording mix sounds clearer and some more sounds have been added. The F pitch in the bass ostinato—the flattened seventh scale step of G minor that gives the chord a bluesy sound—sounds crisper and more boldly attacked. Brett Domino's vocals in the intro are also clearer in the foreground and sound re-recorded; not only are more snaps included, but they also sound crisper and drier than the original. Structurally, very little has been done to differentiate it from the original. The major change is a bridge inserted between the second refrain's extension and verse 4. The bridge includes Brett Domino's repeating the song title and places the bass ostinato in the foreground, accompanied by the 808s and synth's cosmic sound effects. Another major structural change is that the last refrain gets extended and followed by a lengthier outro. Overall, the extended version is roughly thirty seconds longer than the original.

As of 2021, Brett Domino's *How to Make a Hit Pop Song: Advanced Techniques* YouTube video alone has received nearly two million views. Besides his comic original songs, Brett Domino is also known for his hip hop covers and medleys (both viewable on YouTube), which usually feature unusual or dated instruments such as the *keytar* (an analog then digital synth that requires a guitar strap that is made portable for performance onstage, which became especially popular in the 1980s) and *stylophone* (an analog stylus-operated miniature synth keyboard, which gained popularity after its invention in 1968 through use by recording artists such as David Bowie and Rolf Harris). The Brett Domino Trio has competed on *Britain's Got Talent*. It has also created songs for the series *Young Apprentice* and *8 out of 10 Cats*. In between 2012 and 2014, Brett Domino also produced regular musical segments for the U.K. children's show *Blue Peter*.

BTS: "IDOL"
ALBUM: *LOVE YOURSELF: ANSWER* (2018)

Seven-member South Korean boy band BTS (a.k.a. Beyond the Scene, Bangtan Boys, or Bangtan Sonyeondan, 2013–) was formed by Big Hit Entertainment CEO Bang Si-hyuk (a.k.a. Hitman Bang, 1972–). The group, consisting of high tenors Jin (Kim Seok-jin, 1992–), Suga (Min Yoon-gi, 1993–), J-Hope (Jung Ho-seok, 1994–), RM (Kim Nam-joon, 1994–), Jimin (Park Ji-min, 1995–), V (Kim Tae-hyung, 1995–), and Jungkook (Jeon Jung-kook, 1997–), won fans over with its single "No More Dream," which sold more than fifty thousand copies and led to the hit albums *Dark & Wild* (2014) and *Wings* (2016), the latter selling more than one million copies in Korea. As of 2021, BTS has had two songs reach the top spot on the Billboard Hot 100, "Life Goes On" and "Dynamite." Their last three albums, *Love Yourself: Tear* (2018), *Map of the Soul: 7*, and *Be* have all reached No. 1 on the Billboard 200.

By the time of their 2018 album *Face Yourself*, the group had achieved platinum status in Japan and was beginning to make inroads in the United States, eventually appearing on *Saturday Night Live* in 2019. BTS had already debuted on the Billboard Hot 100 in 2017, with "DNA" (No. 67) and "Mic Drop" (No. 28). "Mic Drop" made BTS the first Korean group to get a platinum certification. In 2018, the group had its first of five (as of 2021) Top Ten hits on the Hot 100 with "Fake Love" (No. 10). That same year, "Idol," the lead single from *Love Yourself: Answer* (2018), reached No. 11. *Love Yourself: Answer*, on the Bit Hit label, became the first Korean album to be RIAA-certified gold.

"Idol" also reached No. 5 in Canada and was RIAA-certified gold. It inspired The Idol Challenge, a dance challenge to the choreography of the refrain in the song's music video. A songwriting team comprised of Si-hyuk, Roman Campolo, Pdogg (Kang Hyo Won, the track's producer), RM (of BTS), Supreme Boi (Shin Donghyuk, a founding member of BTS who departed from the group before their debut single), and Ali Tamposi composed "Idol." Supreme Boi nevertheless continues to produce and compose for Big Hit, including BTS's subsequent recordings. Frequently, BTS's songwriting team includes American songwriters—here, represented by Campolo and Tamposi; the latter is best known for co-composing Kelly Clarkson's most successful hit, "Stronger (What Doesn't Kill You)" (2011) and Camila Cabello's (formerly of Fifth Harmony) "Havana" (2017).

"Idol" is K-pop (Korean pop), but it is also a fusion of an impressive number of elements from hip hop, electronic dance music (EDM), house music (especially *gqom*, which originally emerged in Durban, South Africa), samba, and West African-inspired drumming and polyrhythm (multiple interlocking rhythmic patterns that take place at the same time). The song is a self-reflective statement of BTS's role inside K-pop's "idol" culture, and its video consists of intense audiovisual content (combining brightly colored clothes, computer-generated graphics, and intricate chorus dance choreography). The group's vocal and dance training comes across as an intense version of Motown artist grooming, which was often started at a young age. BTS's songwriting uses Korean and English phrases, and both are present in "Idol," a song about self-love and pride in the face of criticism. Musically, "Idol" exhibits mostly the EDM side of K-pop, but also, like many K-pop songs, it folds in traditional Korean musical instruments as well as influences from traditional Korean music. For example, the drum and bass sound of the song is enhanced by the *janggu* (a.k.a. *seyogo*), an hourglass- or waisted-shaped wood drum with two heads made of animal skins (each representing a man and a woman). Used in traditional court music and shamanistic music as well as other kinds of vocal and dance music, the janggu are played with sticks (*chae*, named *gungchae* and *yeolchae*). The *haegeum*, a very popular kind of bowed fiddle used in many kinds of Korean traditional music (played by a Korean farmer's ensemble, which typically consists of amateur musicians), can also be found in the song, especially in the prechoruses. Yet both traditional instruments are used to enhance or accompany Western sounds and only briefly stand out aurally on their own. Most of the time, the *haegeum* doubles with Western-sounding synth-produced strings. Other traditional Korean music is used more as a visual inspiration than an aural one. In the music video, some of the elaborate costumes featured come from *P'ansori*, a staged traditional epic narrative work; however, none of the singing style or use of the *puk* (the most important drum used in P'ansori) is aurally detectable.

The band is known for its intricate dance choreography, especially for how it positions singers to trade off lines (moves include two singers ending up back-to-back, so that as both turn the new singer appears; having the next singer make his way to the side of the others so that he can move toward the camera, seemingly coming out of nowhere; and having the next singer end up in back, so as the others part he can move up through dance moves). This choreography lends itself to songs that involve a lot of trade-off among the group's members, with each one singing a few lines until the next breaks in. "Idol" is an excellent example of this technique, with constant switches between singers, including a clever metatextual lyrical call at one point to "trade off."

Entirely in C-sharp minor with a fast quadruple meter (four beats per measure), the song's structure is as follows: instrumental intro; verse 1 (A, bifurcated); prechorus; refrain (bifurcated); verse 2 (A′, bifurcated); prechorus; refrain (bifurcated); middle-eight (B); refrain (bifurcated); instrumental outro. "Idol" kicks off with a brief bass-drum flourish (likely janggu-reinforced and reminiscent of a powerful and resonant Japanese *taiko* drum). The intro quickly follows with a vamp played by an alto saxophone that sounds synth-produced with applied reverb. This vamp, with its melody outlining the home key chord pitches (C-sharp, E, and G-sharp), later turns into the song's most important melodic hook and ostinato. The alto saxophone sound is close to the same range and timbre as the haegeum. The introductory vamp sounds offbeat against uneven 808-sounding beats that employ dry snare and kick drum with applied reverb. Also accompanying, though placed far into the background to add sonic depth, are sustained synth-produced strings (reinforced by haegeum) and a synth-produced sub-bass with applied reverb. Altogether, these instruments sound reminiscent of gqom's drum and bass and synths (rooted in South African *kwaito techno* with its use of a catchy ostinato against heavy bass beats).

After an 808-sounding flourish, the first part of verse 1 begins. Here, the saxophone drops out and is replaced by synth-produced chords and constant Brazilian samba-style whistles. The sub-bass continues as part of the accompaniment. Verse 1 initially features RM and J-Hope rapping and aggressively talk-singing. RM almost shouts his lyrics, as a synth string voice builds up in intensity and a military-style snare beat emerges. In the second part, the synth strings and military-style beat are placed more into the foreground when RM and Suga aggressively talk-sing while other band members provide vocalizations such as grunts and howls—the whistles are placed in the background, and new beats are introduced. The prechorus starts with the group's auto-tuned and sung descending scales, which contrast strongly with the previous vocals. V,

RM, and Jimin continue with spoken-word vocalizations with a slower flow than heard in verse 1, all set against aggressive 808-sounding beats. The prechorus concludes with the song's main vocal hook, which is in English ("You can't stop me lovin' myself"), sung by Jimin.

In the song's highly energetic refrain, the whistle (right speaker) becomes loud and the beat (center) and bass (left speaker), along with the saxophone vamp from the intro, are now played by synthesizer. The first part of the refrain is sung, whooped, and howled melodramatically by RM, Jungkook, and Jimin. This instrumentation continues into the hook, also sung by Jimin, which prompts the second part of the refrain, where members use what has come to be called the Millennial Yodel (a.k.a. Millennial Whoop), the belted vocalization of "oh," followed by "whoa-oh" and/or "whoa-oh-whoa-oh-oh." The yodel takes up the saxophone and synth-produced ostinato, contributing to a new dense texture.

The first part of verse 2 is a sudden return to a sparser texture, with the same whistle from before in the background. The dry synth-based snare drum is played against a kick drum with applied reverb, and thus the beat is now lighter sounding than before. Here, a new synthesizer voice takes on the ostinato, and it resembles the *daegeum*, a bamboo Korean traverse flute traditionally used in both folk and court music. J-Hope and Suga give listeners a new dose of the aggressive talk-singing used throughout, followed by Jungkook and V in the second part, in which the military-style drumming of the second part of verse 1 is reintroduced. V is slightly auto-tuned so that his voice reverberates, which works well with the verse's working toward a dramatic, angry, echoing finale. The following prechorus and refrain feature leads by Jin, Suga, Junkook, Jimin, RM, V, and J-Hope, and harmonies and vocalizations by all. The refrain also repeats its second part, the Millennial Yodel.

The middle-eight provides a lyrical contrast with its downtempo beats and a highly auto-tuned Jimin and Jin singing R&B style against a slower beat and a modified (more clipped) version of the saxophone ostinato (in the Nicki Minaj version, her rap follows this section). The instrumentation is much sparser than in the previous refrain. Tenor falsetto vocalizations transition into the refrain, and a reiteration of the vocal hook brings the faster beat back. This time, the Millennial Yodel ends abruptly, leaving just the alto saxophone from the intro to play the ostinato one more time. Heard mostly on the right speaker, some delay is applied to the solo saxophone, which concludes the song on a single sustained pitch of E, the third scale step of C-sharp minor as well as the third of the home chord (the very pitch that gives C-sharp minor its more ominous sound in comparison to C-sharp major), followed by a descending synth-produced sound effect.

The video for "Idol" got more than 56 million views within 24 hours of its release, breaking previous records. An alternative version, featuring Nicki Minaj, was released digitally, and its music video received more than 45 million views in its first 24 hours on YouTube. Known for its songs' references to literature, paintings, psychological concepts (mental health, youth, loss, self-love, and individualism), and alternative universe storyline (the BTS Universe), BTS were the most retweeted celebrities in the world for 2017 and 2018. In 2018, the group reached No. 1 on the Forbes Korea Power Celebrity list, which ranks South Korea's most powerful and influential celebrities. The group is also known for its philanthropy.

CEE-LO GREEN (FEATURING TIMBALAND): "I'LL BE AROUND"
ALBUM: *CEE-LO GREEN . . . IS THE SOUL MACHINE* (2004)

Cee-Lo Green (a.k.a. Cee-Lo, Thomas DeCarlo Callaway, 1975–) is an Atlanta-born keyboardist, singer-songwriter, rapper, and record producer known for his smooth and lyrical high tenor voice and his mastery of R&B, hip hop, neo-soul, and gospel singing. He is known for his collaborations more than for his own solo output, having been a member of the psychedelic neo-soul duo Gnarls Barkley (2003–2010) and the hip hop and R&B duo Goodie Mob (2003–), both with producer DJ Danger Mouse (Brian Joseph Burton, 1977–). His solo output includes his first two studio albums, *Cee-Lo Green and His Perfect Imperfections* (2002) and *Cee-Lo Green . . . Is the Soul Machine* (2004), both of which almost broke into the Billboard 200's Top Ten. His third, *The Lady Killer* (2010), was No. 9, and became RIAA-certified double platinum in the United States. His major hits have also become iconic; they include "Crazy" (with Gnarls Barkley, 2006) and the solo "F*** You" (2010), both of which reached No. 2 on the Billboard Hot 100 and were certified, respectively, four-times platinum and seven-times platinum.

"I'll Be Around," appears on *Cee-Lo Green . . . Is the Soul Machine* on the Arista Records label. It was recorded at Criteria Studios in Miami, Florida—the same recording studio that produced many classic rock smash hit albums, such as parts of the Eagles' *Hotel California* (1976), Fleetwood Mac's *Rumours* (1977), and R.E.M.'s *Automatic for the People* (1992) and *Monster* (1994), as well as a few hip hop hit albums, such as Lil Wayne's *Tha Carter III* (2008) and Nicki Minaj's *Queen* (2018).

"I'll Be Around" was recorded after The Hit Factory purchased Criteria (becoming Criteria-The Hit Factory) in 1999; since 2017, the studio has reverted to its original name. Like "SexyBack," which is discussed in one of our Must-Hear Music entries, Timbaland partnered with his engineer, Jimmy Douglass, on mixing the album.

"I'll Be Around" features Cee-Lo with producer, turntablist, rapper, and singer-songwriter Timbaland (see the Must-Hear Music entry on Timbaland for biographical details), who is a baritone. A rapping skills braggadocio song, "I'll Be Around" also boasts about sexual prowess. The entire song is in B-flat minor and quadruple meter (four beats per measure). Its structure is as follows: intro (bifurcated); verse 1 (bifurcated); refrain (twice); verse 2 (bifurcated); refrain' (twice); verse 3 (bifurcated); refrain" (four times); vocal outro (four times); instrumental outro (twice). Here, Cee-Lo's vocals are unique in that he moves back and forth between singing, talk-singing, rapping, and spoken word so effortlessly that his style could at times be described as rap-singing.

The intro's first part features horns against the song's beats, which consists of kick drum, toms, snare drum rim shots, drumstick hits, and congas. The album credits Timbaland as the performer and programmer of all instruments; however, musicians Jimmy Brown and Russell Gunn on horns and Charles Pettaway on electric guitar are given credit for many of the album's other tracks. An unidentified impersonation of Louis Armstrong's singing "mm, mm, better," scatting, and growling emerges as the accompanying instrumentation functions like a vamp, cuing Cee-Lo to start performing. Armstrong performed and recorded Alec Wilder's popular standard "I'll Be Around" (1942) on trumpet; however, the songs have only their title in common. Armstrong does sing "mm, mm, better" as part of a line in "Would You Like to Take a Walk?" (1930, Harry Warren, Mort Dixon, and Billy Rose) on *Ella Fitzgerald and Louis Armstrong: For Lovers* (1951). These vocalizations continue into the background in the second part, as Timbaland adds some spoken-word hype vocals that call out Cee-Lo Green and also cue him to start. Both vocals echo throughout the intro. The two then banter, layered over the scatting and hype to create multiple voices—as well as a New Orleans frontline parade party atmosphere. The first part concludes with a trumpet-dominated horn trill, whereas the second part concludes with four quick triplet flourishes from high to low, creating a drum-kit version of an 808 hiccup.

The horns and beats continue into the first part of verse 1, which features Cee-Lo's dry vocals as he talk-sings his initial lines (with a couple of pauses), creating a descending melody. Timbaland punctuates the passage with "uh-huhs," as backing voices (from the intro) remain in the background. The same trumpet-led horn trills that conclude the intro's first part conclude this passage's first part. Cee-Lo continues talk-singing for the first two measures of the second part and then changes his flow in the second two measures. Here, he continues to talk-sing, but his lines become elongated and he comes close to rapping. In the first part, he boasts about being from the South, which he suggests is the reason his flow is so good and his words sound so beautiful. In the second part, where his flow changes, he decides to give people "somethin' to talk about." Throughout this verse, Cee-Lo uses old-school rhyming. The same tom flourish concludes this passage.

The refrain is a call-and-response passage that features Timbaland's lead vocals as Cee-Lo answers and comments, using spoken-word, chant-rap, and singing. This most melodic passage in the song emphasizes their contrasting vocals: Timbaland sings in his low register, and his vocals are multi-tracked (using octave doubling) and highly auto-tuned, whereas Cee-Lo responds in his middle and high register, sounding more natural, with just a little applied reverb. The horns and beats continue from the previous verse, but male backing vocals now use sustained "ahs," and a new electric guitar countermelody emerges. The tom drums from the intro and verse 1 conclude the second iteration of this passage.

Verse 2 features Timbaland on lead vocals, using the same multi-track effect, against the same instrumentation from the intro and verse 1, but with added tambourine. In the first part, Timbaland talk-sings like Cee-Lo, but although he maintains the same descending melodic line heard in Cee-Lo's verse 1, he is less melodic and more monotone. In verse 1, Cee-Lo was autobiographical, so this time it is Timbaland's turn. Here, he explains how he's from the South, suggesting that he is from the country and not the city, and he mentions his family and what he likes. Cee-Lo adds soul- and R&B-style backing vocals and vocables, including a growl when Timbaland mentions having a big dog. The refrain' differs from the first by its inclusion of the tambourine only.

In verse 3, the tambourine drops out in the first part as the horns and beats continue. This verse showcases Cee-Lo's impressive flow and speed as he moves between short, *staccato* (short and detached) lines and lengthy prosaic lines. His fastest lines approach the chopper style of rap. Cee-Lo starts the verse using spoken word but flows into rap. The tambourine from the refrain' drops out as softer horns continue with the beats in the first part of this verse. The backing vocals in the refrain' also drop out, and verse 3 stands out as the only verse without a prominent secondary lead vocalist. This sparser texture puts more focus on

Cee-Lo's vocals. The tambourine reappears four measures later, marking the beginning of the second part. The refrain" is sung four times, with the same instrumentation and backing vocals as earlier. Listeners may expect that the song will fade out on the refrain, but instead it concludes on a vocal outro that features both lead vocalists one more time, followed by an instrumental outro, which concludes the song.

Together, the vocal and instrumental outros are a minute in length. The outro consists of refrain-related material that is bifurcated. The refrains' electric guitar countermelody returns and plays against Timbaland's new R&B-style melody, which is sung four times. Timbaland uses his high register, and his multi-tracked vocals provide harmonies. The horn and beats groove continues, but without tambourine, as Cee-Lo comments in the background. The same tom flourish heard earlier concludes this passage. The electric guitar drops out in the instrumental outro, which frames the song with its returning horn and beats groove from the first part of the intro. All singing ceases, and vocals trickle down to Timbaland's spoken-word hype in the background. The instruments play the first four measures, concluding with the same horns' trill, then play four more measures as they fade out.

"I'll Be Around" has been sampled on a couple of lesser-known recordings. In 2003, Chris Read sampled Timbaland's spoken-word cue to start from the intro's second part in "Diary Rap Megamix" on his album *The Diary (World's Greatest Rap Megamix)* (later released in 2007). In 2006, Charles Hamilton sampled "I'll Be Around"'s horns and beats groove for "Boredom," on his mixtape *The Binge Vol. 1: Staring at the Lavalamp.* Cee-Lo has released three more solo albums, *Cee-Lo's Magic Moment* (2012), *Heart Blanche* (2015), and *Cee-Lo Green Is Thomas Callaway* (2020). He was also a judge and coach on *The Voice* (2010–) for four seasons. As of 2021, he has won five Grammy Awards and a Billboard Award.

CHILDISH GAMBINO: "THIS IS AMERICA"
ALBUM: NON-ALBUM SINGLE, DIGITAL MEDIA (2018)

Actor, writer, producer, and director Donald Glover (1983–) is known on many fronts: his writing on the absurdist parody of TV studios in the series *30 Rock*; his acting in a co-starring role (as Troy) in the comedy series *Community*; his creation of, writing for, and starring in the dark rapper/manager comedy *Atlanta*; and his eight-year stint as a musician and singer under the stage name Childish Gambino (which he retired for the second time in 2019). For *Atlanta*, Glover won the Primetime

Donald Glover, whose stage name is Childish Gambino, performs on stage in September 2014 at the iHeartRadio Music Festival Village in Las Vegas. (Kobby Dagan/Dreamstime.com)

Emmy for Outstanding Lead Actor in a Comedy Series and for Outstanding Directing for a Comedy Series, a Golden Globe for Best Television Series–Musical or Comedy and for Best Actor–Television Series Musical or Comedy. As Childish Gambino, he realized similar success, releasing three studio albums: *Camp* (2011), *Because the Internet* (2013), and *Awaken, My Love!* (2016). His Grammy Award-winning single "Redbone," from *Awaken, My Love!*, charted at No. 12 on the Billboard Hot 100, but it was his non-album single "This Is America" that literally took the country by storm, debuting in the top spot on the Hot 100 and burning its icon-filled music video into the minds of Americans. It debuted with 78,000 downloads sold and 65.3 million U.S. streams in the first week; its video accounted for 68 percent of the total.

"This Is America," written by Glover and Ludwig Göransson, also topped the charts in Australia, Canada, and New Zealand. The song won four Grammy Awards: Record of the Year, Song of the Year, Best Rap/Sung Performance, and Best Music Video. It features Glover both singing and talk-singing against various hip hop beats, including gospel-influenced ones, as well as featured vocals by Young Thug (Jeffrey Lamar Williams, 1991–), who is in some sources given writing credit, as well as background vocals by Slim Jxmmi, BlocBoy JB, Quavo, and 21 Savage. The song's groundbreaking and exceptionally brilliant video, directed by frequent Glover collaborator Hiro Murai (1983–), achieved iconic status with unexpected moments of extreme gun violence, suicide, and references to school shootings and brutality against Black people. In its scenes where innocent people are shot and murdered, a teen appears carrying a red cloth onto which the gun used is gently placed, while bodies are left where they lie.

Though the song's structure is straightforward, it contains musical details that underscore the complexity of its video. The song's structure of the official video is as follows: intro (trifurcated); refrain; verse 1 (bifurcated); interlude (trifurcated); refrain (truncated); verse 2 (bifurcated); interlude (trifurcated); instrumental bridge; outro. The first part of the intro includes a nearly *a cappella* gospel choir (accompanied by shakers) singing a harmonized chant (with harmonized backing vocals). After four iterations, the second part begins with an acoustic guitar played by Calvin the Second (Calvin C. Winbush II, n.d.), set against an intermittent kick drum, as two voices (Childish Gambino and Young Thug) are heard (both left and right speakers). The home key established here is F major. The acoustic guitar adds an element that is reminiscent of highlife, a popular music genre from Ghana that combines traditional Akan music with elements of Afro-Caribbean popular music such as the popular 3-2 *son clave* rhythm (Afro-Cuban music). Highlife is also played with Western musical instruments. The acoustic guitar introduces sixteenth notes that are juxtaposed against the choir's triplets, creating *polyrhythm* (two rhythmic patterns that take place at the same time and interlock). As the chant continues in the background, it appears that they lightheartedly sing of partying, dancing, and women. But these vocals are slightly off-pitch and they become distorted, gain an echo, and develop into a more ethereal sound (giving the impression of a dreamlike state). An 808 and hand claps (with a lot of reverb) are introduced, hinting at an upcoming and ominous sonic shift. The third part includes the gunshot sound effect, which brings this section to an abrupt (but crossfaded to sound seamless) end.

The refrain starts with a trap music beat. Here, the song title is used as a hook (and creates more triplets) and is repeated four times. Childish Gambino uses his low tenor vocals to talk-sing and chant staccato lines that are filled with street slang, warning Black Americans not to be caught "slippin'" (to be off-guard or lazy), perhaps an allusion to the intro's laid-back and comparatively naïve music. Just about every line in the refrain features a vocalization, ranging from grunts and hollers (evoking Black slave work songs) to expected and unexpected words, as tags. Virtually every line is punctuated by additional vocalizations that give the refrain a sense of dramatic build-up. A synth sub-bass and chords, soon joined by 808s, congas, and metal clanking effects (the last evoking chains) accompany Childish Gambino. The instrumentation of the intro and refrains clearly represents two worlds of Black Americans: the first a peaceful beginning that reflects cultural diversity in a positive light, though this diversity is nevertheless imposed by colonialism and white brutality; the second is a horrific displacement into a violent society. The intro's use of traditional African instruments such as shakers and African American as well as Afro-Caribbean musical cross-pollination (e.g., gospel choir and highlife) is lighthearted, whereas the refrain's use of modern synth-based instrumentation and beats is threatening and dark.

The refrain's lyrics describe the full spectrum of African American culture, from style and fashion, to drugs, illegal money, and gun violence. Its most telling lines are "guns in my area / I got the strap," which make the point that violence breeds more violence, in an endless downward spiral, a stark contrast to the intro's celebration. The sudden shift to the refrain's pitch center, E-flat, jolts listeners into the harsh reality. The refrain's home key reveals a subtle complexity. Its use of a sub-bass clouds a clear sense of the key, which shifts at times from E-flat minor to E-flat major, uses an E-flat power chord ($E^{\flat}5$, a chord built on a root and a fifth and missing its third, the fill-in or middle voice that suggests major or minor), and occasionally moves down to D major or D minor (VII or vii of E-flat major or minor). D major/minor is used here as a neighboring harmony to E-flat major/minor, giving a sense of movement while at the same time reinforcing the home key or pitch. Generally, the refrains as well as the verses mostly use E-flat minor. The refrain pauses when guns are mentioned.

Childish Gambino reintroduces the triplets in his vocals in the first part of verse 1, which are still accompanied by the sub-bass, hollers, and beats. A high-pitched synth voice is introduced to the mix, soon joined by the sustained notes of male backing vocals. In the second part of this verse, Childish Gambino changes the rhythmic flow of his chant. Like the refrain, this part of verse 1 contains a short pause. An 808 hiccup cues the first interlude, which is based on the intro's music. This time, the gospel choir sings of reparations and/or illegal activity (the meaning is unclear), both methods of attaining money. Though the instrumentation is similar to that of the intro, the vocals are placed more in the foreground and heavier beats are added. Like the intro, the interlude ends with gunshots. Before this effect is heard, the words "Black man" signify the return to the refrain.

This time, the refrain is truncated; the hook is used only twice. This refrain also contains a pause, though this one introduces more echoes in the vocals, with the synth keyboard voice being introduced eight lines later in verse 2 (in an interesting twist, whereas the mention of guns invoked the keyboard earlier, here it is the mention of a cell phone—perhaps alluding to the fact that the phone has become the new weapon of choice against police brutality and discrimination). Verse 2 consists of harmonic stasis similar to verse 1. Though some listeners may identify verse 1 as section A and verse 2 as section B, they are too closely related to be distinguished this way (a better interpretation would be to think of verse 1 as section A and verse 2 with its new words and varied rhythmic vocal flow as A'). The first part of verse 2 focuses on appearance and fashion, whereas the second part alludes to drug dealing and illegal money. As vocals disintegrate into vocalizations, Childish Gambino singsong chants and brings back triplet note values during this second part. The video differs from the recording here: In the video, the song comes to a false ending in which the music stops (after Childish Gambino pantomimes aiming a gun, at which point the children all run and scream). Urban sounds, in addition to running and screaming, are faintly heard in the background, while Childish Gambino, now alone, lights a joint.

The second reference to gun violence cues the second interlude, also featuring the gospel choir and based on the intro's music in the first part. Like the intro and first interlude, the second interlude is in F major. Childish Gambino uses spoken word in the second part to address America directly. In the third and lengthiest part, the acoustic guitar and the same lyrics addressing a Black man return. Beats are folded in, as is an oscillating bass drone. On the phrase "get down" (a reference to both dancing and ducking), the sounds from the intro and verses are finally united, with an electric bass (almost in the sub-bass range) taking the place of the earlier keyboard voice. The instrumental bridge, consisting of 808 kick drum hiccups that sound like heartbeats, leads into the outro, also in F major. The synthesizer's keyboard voice, the 808, and the hand claps with heavy reverb return, against which Young Thug's R&B-style, low yet bright tenor vocals are juxtaposed against more grunt-like vocalizations. Young Thug's voice is highly auto-tuned to sound robotic, yet it is filled with sadness and despair: his voice breaks on some words. As this outro fades out, it functions as commentary on the previous music: it offers little hope to the Black man in America, who despite being a "big dog" is "kenneled."

Glover, winner of the Writers Guild of America Award for Best Comedy Series in 2009 for his work on *30 Rock* and ex-member of the sketch comedy group Derrick Comedy, holds the distinction of having appeared in two guises at the 2011 Bonnaroo Music Festival: in 2011, he took the stage both as Childish Gambino and as himself doing a comic duo stand-up. In 2018, Glover released the EP *Summer Pack*, which contained the songs "Summertime Magic" and "Feels Like Summer," but neither had the same chart success as "This Is America." His film *Guava Island* was released in 2019 through Amazon Prime Video.

CHINESE MAN: "I'VE GOT THAT TUNE" (YOUTUBE SINGLE VERSION) ALBUM: *THE GROOVE SESSIONS: VOL. 1* (2007); NON-ALBUM SINGLE REISSUE, 2014

Aix-en-Provence, France, trip hop collective Chinese Man (2004–) is composed of three musicians who prefer to remain anonymous: Zé Mateo (a.k.a. Marseille Zé Mateo, n.d.), High Ku (n.d.), and SLY (n.d.). The trio produces original music and remixes that show the influence of funk, dub (dubstep), and jazz. Chinese Man periodically uses the services of two other anonymous song composers and beat makers, Leo le Bug (n.d.) and Le Yan (n.d.), as well as two live collaborators, Taiwan MC (n.d.) and MC Youthstar (n.d.). As of 2021, the collective group had released 10 albums: *The Bootleg Sessions* (2005), *The Groove Sessions: Volumes 1, 2, 3, and 5* (2007, 2009, 2014, 2020), *Racing With the Sun* (2011), *Remix With the Sun* (2012), *Live à la Cigale* (2012), *Sho-Bro* (2015), *The Journey* (2015), and *Shikantaza* (2017).

Chinese Man's first big break came with "I've Got That Tune" (2007, re-released 2012 and 2014), an updating of the 1932 Washboard Rhythm Kings' "Hummin' to Myself (I've Got That Tune)" on the Victor label, which features lead vocals by member and banjo player Steve Washington (ca. 1900–1936). A small jazz ensemble, the Washboard Rhythm Kings (a.k.a. the Alabama Washboard Stompers, 1930–1935) featured washboards in their rhythm section and resembled a Dixieland ensemble with its frontline (consisting of clarinet, trumpet, and trombone). Its main swing-band-era feature was its use of saxophones. The band's 1932 recording of "Hummin' to Myself" is in G minor. In 2004, Linda Ronstadt covered the song (in D minor) on her album, *Hummin' to*

Myself. Chinese's Man's version, "I've Got That Tune," was first released on the band's album *The Groove Sessions, Vol. 1* (and a live version on *Live à la Cigale*) and later released as a seven-inch single, along with a remix by the Vietnamese and French duo Tha Trickaz, who added more bass; a harder, more prominent synth-produced beat; a couple of break beats; and hiccups in the lead vocals. The Chinese Man version, however, was chosen by Mercedes-Benz for a promotional campaign and became a YouTube favorite. Because of its music video's ingenious animation, which uses characters from the 1930s *Betty Boop* cartoon series dancing on a turntable record (non-animated), with real-life DJ hands seen scratching in the background, it has garnered 37.9 million views as of 2021.

In the song, Chinese Man samples the 1932 recording significantly, speeding up its foxtrot pace and raising the pitch so much that the home key of the song is moved up to B minor. This manipulation of the recording also raises the pitch of Washington's low tenor voice in his refrains and scatting vocal interlude, which gives the impression that Chinese Man's recording features a lead female singer with a boyish soprano voice. In addition to these lead vocals, Chinese Man's recording features a soft and at times menacing-sounding male baritone voice as well as some female-sounding vocalizations (both likely processed versions of Washington's voice, as no vocalists are credited). The latter is likely the result of some painstaking editing to create Betty Boop's "oh" vocable and the pitch-altered (to approximate a female voice) phrase "four-four, four-four." The lengthiest passages of the Washboard Rhythm Kings' recording that are not used in "I Got That Tune" are the trumpet and alto saxophone solos.

"Hummin' to Myself" is a song about unrequited or lost love, where the singer expresses that he has many beautiful words and knows his music well, but has no one to sing them to. This thematic concern is made slightly comic by the sped-up, pitch-altered Betty Boop voice, even though she sings of the same loneliness. The recorded song structure of Chinese Man's "I've Got That Tune" is as follows: intro (trifurcated); refrain 1 (repeats); instrumental interlude 1; refrain 2 (repeats); vocal bridge; instrumental interlude 2; instrumental interlude 3; instrumental interlude 1'; refrain 2; vocal interlude; outro. The song's intro is a faithful sampling of the Washboard Rhythm Kings' recording, which features clarinetist Ben Smith (Benjamin J. Smith, 1905–n.d.), accompanied by a rhythm section that contains washboards, piano, guitar, and banjo. A notable aspect of the clarinet's melody, in B minor, is its use of chromaticism—descending here by half steps on the pitches F-sharp, F,

E, and then a whole step (two half steps) to D—as well as the accompanying sped-up harmonic progression now on each beat (which may be heard as B minor-B diminished-F-sharp dominant$^{6/5}$-B minor$^{6/4}$ or B minor: i-i°-V$^{6/5}$-i$^{6/4}$). The first part is filtered so as to sound like it is coming from a Victrola (an early phonograph that was also known as a gramophone). It features the acoustic rhythm section in the background, chugging along via washboard scratches, as well as piano, guitar, and banjo chords (a skiffle sound that became highly popular during a revival of interest in 1950s England). The second part is marked by a clearer sound than the first, as well as by the entrance of a walking bass (mostly left speaker). The third part is the clearest and is marked by placing a downtempo drum beat (a snare beat that mirrors the notes of the bass walk and creates flourishes until the cadence) into the foreground. In addition, a synth bass now reinforces the song's acoustic rhythm section. Male vocalizations such as subtle evil laughter and banter appear in this lengthiest part of the intro. Male laughter, which is sonically matched by a vibraslap, is heard as a tag just before refrain 1.

The same instrumentation in the third part of the intro accompanies the Betty Boop vocals. She sings the refrain, which is followed by instrumental interlude 1. This section begins with the material from the intro's second part, followed by the third part. Instrumental interlude 1 introduces turntable scratching and clever metatextual and slightly filtered rhythmic male voices chattering in the background. One of these voices repeats the phrase "on the beat," followed by the aforementioned "four-four, four-four" (talk-sung lines which cleverly explain that the song is in 4/4): each beat of a measure is in quadruple meter (four-to-the-floor). Some hiccups are also present in these voices.

The ensuing refrain 2 resembles refrain 1 because it uses the same music, including instrumentation; however, some subtle changes take place here. This time, the female lead vocalist's voice echoes toward the beginning and end (the echo is heard from left to right speaker). She starts on a higher pitch than in verse 1 (B^4 or scale step 1 here instead of F-sharp^4 or scale step 5 of B minor) and applies more vocal grind; both make her sound more assertive this time. One of the main reasons that this passage sounds like a sped-up Washboard Rhythm Kings' recording is because of the vocal grind, especially on the word "humming," which is identical to that in Washington's 1932 vocals in that song's refrain 2. Vocal bridge 1 features the beats, percussion, and male vocals in the foreground, as Washington's voice introduces instrumental interlude 2 (this two-line bridge is included in the band's live performance of the song).

Instrumental interlude 2, a 40-second jam session in B minor, features a walking upright bass solo, accompanied by turntables, beats, and snare drum. As the beat changes to a shuffle, instrumental interlude 3 starts, marked by saxophones and horns. More male banter takes place here in the background. The horns' sustained notes temporarily emphasize F as the pitch center of this section; however, after a brief male vocal tag, instrumental interlude 1 returns (slightly modified with more turntables), bringing back a strong sense of the B minor home key as well as introductory material. The music here is nonfiltered, like the third part of the intro. The male banter continues in the background. The pseudo-female singing voice repeats refrain 2 a final time and then scats, accompanied by plucked bass strings in B minor and then F-sharp minor (the dominant of B minor), thus strongly gravitating back to the home key, which is used in the outro. The song concludes by bringing back the introductory material one last time; this time, the material is modified by pauses that allow for brief turntable solos. About thirty seconds in duration, the outro reverses the overall timbre of each part of the intro, moving from the clarity of the third part and ending with the filtered first part. Male and female banter are recycled. More plucked strings and turntable scratches are prominently added. At the very end of the song, just the instrumental material of the intro's first part is left, which is concluded by the male vocalist's evil-sounding laughter.

In 2004, the collective formed its own label, Chinese Man Records, in Marseille, France. Its members wanted the independence of owning its own label. Artists who have been associated with Chinese Man Records include Scratch Bandits Crew, Taiwan MC, Baja Frequencia, and LeYan. Its members consider themselves part of a hip hop family.

GEORGE CLINTON: "ATOMIC DOG" (ATOMIC MIX LONG VERSION) ALBUM: *COMPUTER GAMES,* 1982

Singer, songwriter, and record producer George Clinton (1941–) created the Plainfield, New Jersey-based iconic electro-funk collective Parliament–Funkadelic, which released songs under both the names Parliament and Funkadelic, as well as the P-Funk All Stars. To say that these bands were influential to funk music would be a gross understatement; they literally changed expectations for 1970s funk, introducing into its musical conventions elements such as electronica, rock, and electro-psychedelia, and into its larger aesthetics ideas such as

Afro-futurism, outlandish fashion, psychedelic culture, and absurdity. Clinton himself launched a solo career with *Computer Games* (1982), which spawned the iconic song "Atomic Dog," one of the most sampled songs in rap music.

During the 1970s, Clinton and Parliament–Funkadelic had more than 40 hit singles on the Hot R&B/Hip-Hop Songs chart, including four No. 1 songs: Parliament's two 1978 hits "Flash Light" and "Aqua Boogie (A Psychoalphadiscobetabioaquadoloop)," and Funkadelic's "One Nation under a Groove" (1978) and "(Not Just) Knee Deep" (1979). Clinton's bands also had three platinum albums: Parliament's *Mothership Connection* (1975), an album whose tour performances ended with a giant spaceship transporting "Dr. Funkenstein" as it descended to the stage; *Funkentelechy vs. the Placebo Syndrome* (1977); and Funkadelic's *One Nation Under a Groove* (1978). In 1982, Clinton signed to Capitol Records both as a solo artist and as a member of the P-Funk All-Stars, releasing *Computer Games*, which reached No. 40 on the Hot 200. Its first single, "Loopzilla," reached No. 19 on the Hot R&B/Hip-Hop Songs chart. The follow up single, "Atomic Dog," topped that chart.

Clinton, along with David Spradley (1954–), and music director, lead guitarist, lead vocalist, and songwriter Garry Shider (1953–2010), composed The Atomic Extended Mix of "Atomic Dog." This recording is pure danceable and enjoyable funk energy, purportedly completed as an improvised jam session over Spradley's previously recorded keyboard and temp vocal tracks (proto-tracks used by recording musicians to help guide them through various aspects of a piece). The four-and-a-half-minute radio single was the P-Funk collective's last to reach No.1 on the Hot R&B/Hip Hop Songs chart, although it did not chart on the Billboard Hot 100 (it got close, hitting No. 1 on the Bubbling Under Hot 100 Singles chart). Most of the lyrics, which are basically about the nature of male-female relationships and about men being slaves to their libidos, were extemporized during recording. Helping the song's sales were its music video, featuring both animation and live dancers performing in a surreal cityscape while in cat and dog suits; the video was nominated for two Billboard Video Music Awards (Best Special Effects and Best Art Direction).

"Atomic Dog" is in D major, but at times briefly makes connections with its home key's relative minor (B minor). The 12-inch album version of the recorded song contains many bridges or transitional sections that create points of interest for listeners. It is also constructed of several refrains. Further details on the recorded song's structure will be discussed here, but the iconic part of the song is refrain 2, which contains the "bow wow wow, yippie yo yippie yay" hook by P-Funk's original bass-baritone singer, Sting Ray Davis (Raymond Davis, 1940–2005). Here, his vocals are highly processed to sound robotic and thus serve as one of the song's elements of Afro-futurism. Davis's other iconic vocals can be heard in the intro of Parliament's "Give Up the Funk (Tear the Roof Off the Sucka)" (1976), and his now-iconic passages from those two songs have become widely sampled in hip hop. For the purpose of listening to this lengthy recording, which has a duration of ten minutes, we will refer to refrain 2 as the centerpiece of the recording's structural orientation. As expected, the song builds up to refrain 2 and its repetitions.

The song structure of the 12-inch album version, which is extremely complicated, is as follows: intro (quadfurcated); spoken-word intro section; bridge 1 (repeats); refrain 1; refrain 2 (hook, repeats); refrain 1′; bridge 2; refrain 1″; bridge 3; refrain 3 (repeats); refrain 4 (repeats); refrain 3′ (repeats); bridge 4; refrain 2′ (extended); bridge 5; bridge 6; instrumental interlude 1; instrumental interlude 2; instrumental bridge; refrain 2 (repeats); instrumental bridge′; instrumental interlude 3; refrain 1‴; instrumental bridge; refrain 4′ (repeats); refrain 3″; bridge 7; refrain 3‴ (repeats); refrain 4″ (repeats); refrain 3⁗; instrumental bridge′; bridge 1′; bridge 8; refrain 2 (repeats); bridge 9; refrain 3⁗; instrumental bridge; outro. Here, prime markings, such as refrain 2′, indicate slight changes to the original passage. The passages marked as prime may also indicate the use of different singers (from the original section) or other instrumentation and slight lyrical modifications. As previously mentioned, the song is extremely complex in that it offers constant changes.

The first intro of "Atomic Dog" is mostly an instrumental one. Its first part fades in a gospel-influenced mixed chorus, which is concluded by Davis's processed bass voice singing the word "dog," and the choir's contrasting "ooh." Light turntable scratches, a Minimoog bass line, and a lead synthesizer melody on a Prophet-5 follow. Bernie Worrell (George Bernard Worrell Jr., 1944–2016) plays both keyboards, which were well-known 1980s instruments used in a variety of music (including funk, R&B, and pop-rock). The lead synth melody foreshadows refrain 3's melody. Hand claps (with reverb applied) and a funky bass, tom, and snare drum kit beat mark the intro's third part. The turntables and bass from the second part continue as accompaniment as well, but in the third part, additional turntables (left) appear in the foreground. Two new Prophet-5 synth voices emerge: a lower-pitched one (right speaker), followed by a higher-pitched one (left speaker). The latter has a timbre resembling that of the turntables, and it approximates the sound through hiccupping and sliding (*portamento*) effects. Both then become involved in a call-and-response exchange of the melody, with the low synth voice taking the role of the leader and the high synth voice acting as the follower. The fourth and final part of this intro introduces two new lead synth melodic voices from the Minimoog. The higher voice (right speaker) also foreshadows refrain 3's melody, which gets answered by a funkier lower voice (left speaker), which foreshadows that refrain.

The spoken-word intro follows, featuring Clinton's breathy, soft-spoken, low tenor vocals (over mixed-chorus vocalizations in the form of rhythmic panting placed in the background). Here, he uses a folk music technique, explaining to listeners what the song (the "story") will be about. As Clinton continues to speak, the Minimoog bass and Prophet-5 voices are reintroduced and used as effects. Here, the Minimoog foreshadows Davis's hook. Following the bass voice's "dog" tag, bridge 1 features a mixed chorus (with men and women) that announces the song's title. After bridge 1's repetition, refrain 1 introduces mostly low tenor lead vocals (and a female contralto sometimes added) with Clinton's singing commentary over them, much of it in a way that resembles a gospel choir with a lead singer. This section leads to refrain 2 with the song's iconic hook by Davis, using a highly processed (to sound robotic) voice. After the hook repeats, refrain 1 reappears with new lyrics (becoming 1'), though with the same music and instrumentation. Hand claps, drums, and turntable effects continue throughout this section, which is followed by bridge 2, a gospel-inspired mixed chorus with more female vocalists than earlier singing "ooh" against Clinton's rhetorical question (foreshadowing refrain 3). Here, his delivery is dramatic and impassioned, with lines reaching his highest register and resembling James Brown's melodic funk outbursts. Refrain 1″ then follows, containing male voices, with "woof" sounds in the background that punctuate the end. These "woofs" continue into the foreground of bridge 3, which also features the aforementioned synthesizers as accompaniment. Toward the end, the Prophet-5 synthesizer foreshadows refrain 3's melody.

Refrain 3 enters and is repeated a total of four times, with some changes to the vocal texture. The first time begins with a combination of Clinton, Shider, and Spradley's low tenor and falsetto vocals. The second features Sting Ray's bass-range voice doubling against a tenor singer, followed by a falsetto tag. The third and fourth focus on unison male vocals. Refrain 4 sounds like a call to perform what is called the "dog catcher" (likely a dance for women). Like refrain 3, this refrain includes a hook that is less memorable than that of refrain 2. The soprano-range female (and possibly falsetto male) backing vocals that sing at the end of refrain 4 continue into refrain 3′, with this time female vocalists asking the rhetorical question about why men are ruled by their libidos (and preoccupy themselves with chasing cats, a metaphor for females). Bridge 4 recycles the earlier panting material that was in the background in the spoken-word intro, but here the panting is placed in the foreground. Refrain 2′ includes an extension of the material and differs from the earlier appearances of this refrain by being slightly longer and featuring a mixed chorus instead of just Davis. A chime-like voice on the Prophet-5 appears briefly (right speaker). Bridges 5 and 6 recycle the Prophet-5 and Minimoog synth sounds. Mixed chorus is featured in bridge 5, whereas Clinton's spoken-word voice is briefly featured, pointing again to the futuristic orientation of the song, in bridge 6.

Instrumental interlude 1 begins with a lengthy extension of the bass solo (left speaker) and beats found in the second part of the intro. The entrance of the Prophet-5's new main melody (left speaker) over the continuing beats marks the beginning of instrumental interlude 2, but this section most notably introduces a new Prophet-5 sliding (*portamento*) effect that has a bouncing sound. This effect seems awkward because of its timbre and its being slightly out of sync with the continuing groove. It occurs between beats two and three in a syncopated quadruple meter (four beats per measure), which places the heaviest emphasis on beats two and four. It does, however, offer a new point of interest for listeners. The instrumental bridge uses the Minimoog bass synthesizer and beats from the intro's second part as a vamp that builds up to refrain 2, which repeats and this time returns with Davis's singing the hook. After a return of the instrumental bridge, instrumental interlude 3 takes place and sounds reminiscent of the first part of the intro.

Next, more female singers appear, singing in unison, in refrain 1‴. The instrumental bridge briefly returns to cue in refrain 4, which repeats. The "dogcatcher" part of this refrain, juxtaposing a woman's voice and likely Davis's, using more vocal flourishes than earlier. Refrain 3″ reappears, but this time the soprano's lead vocals asks the rhetorical question, followed by the male vocalists' "woof" tag. Bridge 7, sung by Clinton, leads back into the third refrain (refrain 3‴). These call-and-response vocals feature male singers, followed by Clinton's answer (repeated six times). Refrain 4″ returns and repeats, but this time Clinton's spoken commentary and the *portamento* synthesizer effects from instrumental interlude 2's return. These continue as accompaniment in the next version of the third refrain (refrain 3″″), which now features a mixed chorus, followed by a modified instrumental bridge that works as a vamp, then bridge 1, which announces the song's title again with mixed chorus. A spoken-word bridge 8, which is related to the "woofs" of bridge 3, builds up to the final return of refrain 2. Bridge 9 is also a spoken-word bridge. It leads to refrain 3′′′′, which modifies the original third refrain melody and features a high tenor vocalist accompanied by alternating synthesizers on both speakers. The last appearance of the instrumental bridge leads to the outro. Against the same instrumentation, the outro features more applied reverb, with Clinton's vocal improvisations, including a stream-of-consciousness spoken-word absurd list of types of dogs in the foreground, which continues as the music fades. The last sounds are the echoing hand claps, the Prophet-5 synthesizer-produced sound effect of a spaceship landing, and the word "dog" echoed (using a ping-pong vocal effect).

"Atomic Dog" highly influenced Public Announcements' "D.O.G. in Me" (*All Work, No Play*, 1998)—so much so, in fact, that Clinton, Spradley, and Shider won a lawsuit against that band. It has been included in TV commercials and series (most notably, *The Fresh Prince of Bel-Air*), as well as many films, including *102 Dalmatians*, *Toy Story 2*, *Legally Blonde 2: Red, White & Blonde*, and *Menace II Society*. As a musician, George Clinton is regarded as one of the foremost innovators of funk. He also produced albums, including one for Bootsy Collins (*Ultra Wave*, 1980) and one for the Red Hot Chili Peppers (*Freaky Styley*, 1985). He and 15 other members of Parliament-Funkadelic were inducted into the Rock and Roll Hall of Fame in 1997. In 2019, Clinton and Parliament-Funkadelic were given a Grammy Lifetime Achievement Award.

DJ APS: "TABBA"
ALBUMS: *BOBBY FRICTION & NIHAL PRESENT . . .* (2004), *VIBES 2* (2005), AND *ROCKIN' BEATS* (2011)

DJ APS (Ajay Paul Singh, n.d.) is a ground-breaking Canadian turntablist and sampler who began creating remixes that combined R&B, hip hop, Bollywood, and Punjabi music for dance clubs in 1994. His song "Tabba" is a mix of hip hop and *bhangra-beat* music, the latter a hybrid itself of hip hop, rap, and the folk dance and music of Punjabi farmers. "Tabba" incorporates traditional Punjabi instrumentation such a *tumbi* (a plucked single-string chordophone). The *tumbi* has since emerged as a distinctive bhangra beat sound alongside the *dhol*, a large shoulder-strap drum or membranophone with two heads usually made of goat skin and played as two different but simultaneous patterns, with two separate sticks. In bhangra-beat music, the dhol provides the distinct beat and is essential. The tumbi has also been featured in international hits such as Panjabi MC's bhangra-beat song "Mundian to Bach Ke" ("Avoiding the Boys," a.k.a. "Beware of the Boys," 1997), which was remixed and featured American rapper Jay-Z (2003); as well as Missy Elliott's "Get Ur Freak On" (2001, produced by Timbaland).

"Tabba," which first appeared on *Bobby Friction & Nihal Present...* (2004), was later reissued on *Vibes 2* (2005) and *Rockin' Beats* (2011). The song, known for its frenetic melodic line (the tumbi) and high energy (various synth stingers and raucous vocalizations), is in F-sharp minor. Musically it is divided between instrumental sections and vocal sections accompanied by instruments. The main melody has two parts, with the lower first part played much more often than the higher, answering second part. The first part of the tumbi-heavy melody appears in the foreground and serves the purpose of an *ostinato*, a persistent and repeating melodic and rhythmic pattern in a song. The song's structure is as follows: intro (bifurcated); bridge 1; instrumental verse 1; bridge 1'; instrumental verse 2 (bifurcated); vocal verse 1 (bifurcated); vocal verse 2 (bifurcated); bridge 2; bridge 3; vocal verse 1'; vocal verse 2'; bridge 1; outro. Every section in which the verse is bifurcated (having two distinct parts) also indicates the appearance of the second part of the melody.

The first part of "Tabba"'s intro begins with a somewhat gruff low tenor male voice that encourages listeners to "yo, turn this up." Reverb is applied to the vocals, as well as echoing and some slight panning between left and right speakers at the end. The second part of the intro is marked by the tumbi, whose melody is actually a sample from the intro of songwriter Babu Singh Maan's (a.k.a. Maan Maraarhan Wala, 1942–) Punjabi song "Mitran da Tabba" (a.k.a. "Mitran da Dhaba" or "Mitran Ne Dhabha Kholiya," loosely "Friends of the Tabla"), found on the album *Siddique Da Pehla Akhada* (2000). In his creation of "Tabba," basically a dance and party song, DJ APS manipulates the "Mitran da Tabba" sample (the first part of the main melody) to give it a hiccupping sound and uses post-production effects such as filtering to make it sound as if it is coming from an old radio or television set. This first appearance of the catchy, energetic tumbi melody starts out unaccompanied. As the tumbi sample continues, more hype man calls to "turn this up" are interspersed into the mix. This second part of the intro gives way to an alternation of the male vocalization "yo" and the tumbi. By the end of the intro, the song shifts from its sparse texture to a fuller one, with James Brown funk-inspired Hammond organ and horn section voices. Together, these added voices build up to a climax by outlining the F-sharp minor (F-sharp-A-C-sharp) and then adding the pitch E that leads to a large cadence on F-sharp major (the parallel major of the home key, F-sharp minor). Looking at the song's structure in the previous paragraph, one may wonder why the first entrance of the main melody isn't labeled as instrumental verse 1, because this part of the melody is certainly there. The reason is that the role of that main melody, very much introductory material, differs from the next section of the song, when it becomes instrumental verse music.

A brief bridge 1 just features the tumbi's few plucked pitches just on F-sharp minor. These strums return the song immediately to its home key; against these strums, a bass-heavy drum beat (either a dhol or a synth dhol voice) is introduced and continues into instrumental verse 1. Here, the tumbi's first part of the main melody is played again, but this time without the post-production effects applied in the intro. It is now the main melody in the foreground, punctuated by a hype man ("yeahhhh!"). Turntables enter the background as flourishes begin to enhance the song's beat, reminding listeners that this is a hip hop song. At the end of the section, an effect that sounds like tape quickly winding quickly emerges.

Bridge 1 occurs again and is followed by instrumental verse 2. The same tumbi plays the first part of the main melody as the beats continue, and a chorus of male shouts rhythmically punctuates it in the background (the sound is similar to that of rowers rhythmically chanting "stroke"). The second part of the verse consists of the continuation or second part of the main melody, suddenly played an octave higher on the tumbi. This time, the tumbi is played with *tremolo*, which gives the second part of the melody a tremoring and more urgent sound in contrast to the lower-pitched tumbi in the main melody's first part. Distorted gong-like synthesizer sounds emerge (mostly right speaker) in the background. A slight slowing-down (*ritardando*) concludes this section.

Instead of a return of bridge 1, the song moves immediately into its vocal verses, which are faithful excerpts of section A and A′, verses 1 and 2, of the vocals and accompanying tumbi in "Mitran da Tabba" (the remaining part of the original isn't used). A popular Punjabi duet song that celebrates friendship, food, and good cheer ("Mitran da Dhaba" is a frequent name of restaurants), the song features film playback singers Mohammed "Mohd" Siddiq (a.k.a. Mohammed Siddique, 1942–) and Ranjit Kaur (1950–). Though Siddiq is also an actor and politician, he is best known as the male low tenor counterpart to the duo Siddiz and Kaur, who sang most of Babu Singh Maan's songs. These two, who recorded and gave live performances together for decades, were one of the most famous singing couples of Punjab in the 1970s and 1980s. The pair trade verse sections in DJ APS's "Tabba," effectively making it into a duet. Vocal verse 1 is also the first verse found in the original song's recording and features Siddiq, who takes over the first and then the second part of the main melody. For "Tabba"'s vocals, DJ APS adds very few post-production effects, which leaves the vocalists to demonstrate many of the conventions of Punjabi singing: high-pitched, nasal timbres; lots of end rhyme and end-of-line repetitions (the same words ending more than one line); and predictable, repetitive vocal rhythms. In vocal verse 1, Siddiq is accompanied by the higher pitched tumbi's repetition of the pitch F-sharp (as the home pitch, it is being used here as a pitch center) on the beat, which also appears on the original recording. DJ APS adds a sample of the large cadence from the intro and female laughter to mark the end of the first part of Siddiq's main melody. Siddiq's voice continues into the second part of the main melody, now accompanied by DJ APS's addition of more dhol-heavy beats, hand claps, and sampling of the intro's "turn it up" vocals.

Vocal verse 2 of "Tabba" is also vocal verse 2 in the original recording. Kaur, a female high soprano, takes over the first part of the main melody and, and mirroring Siddiq's flow and delivery, she continues singing the second part of the main melody as well. Her section, however, differs from Siddiq's verse 1 because APS reintroduces the organ and horn voices heard in the second intro. Here, the organ and horns take on the role of the high tumbi found in Siddiq's earlier verse, playing the pitch F-sharp on the beat. The second part of the main melody and the second part of vocal verse 2 use the same accompaniment as Siddiq's verse, but end with a boyish female spoken-word tag ("yo baby"). This is followed by bridge 2, a return of the lower-pitched tumbi heard in bridge 1, punctuated by the sampled boyish female voice, dhol beats, and turntable scratches. In bridge 2, the tumbi plays the first part of the main melody in the foreground, followed by a male vocalization ("yeahhhh!"). Bridge 3 reintroduces the "yo, turn this up" spoken-word samples. The lower-pitched tumbi plays the first part of the main melody again in the foreground. A quick synth keyboard sweep ends the bridge as it heads into vocal verse 1', sung by Siddiq.

In DJ APS's "Tabba," vocal verse 1' simply copies and pastes Siddiq's vocals and the tumbi from vocal verse 1, along with some of the accompaniment. This time, however, male vocalizations ("hey!") boost and rhythmically punctuate the main melody and the tumbi's repeated F-sharp notes. At the end of Siddiq's second part of the melody, his voice is distorted and hiccupped through post-production effects, and more synth keyboard effects are added than the first time. Kaur's vocal verse 2' also simply copies and pastes Kaur's verse 1 vocals, but more modifications are present than in Siddiq's preceding verse. The organ and horn section that played on the beat in vocal verse 2 have been replaced by the high-pitched tumbi, which also emphasizes the F-sharp home pitch as the pitch center.

Bridge 1 returns again with the lower-pitched tumbi pitches, leading into the outro. Here, the lower-pitched tumbi plays the first part of the main melody again as a siren effect builds. Based on the context of the song, listeners may interpret the siren as being the arrival of the police to break up the party. As the song draws to an end, the tumbi and dhol beats drop off suddenly and clumsily (on purpose), leaving the sampled voice only. It is about to say "hey, yo, turn this up," but gets cut off after "yo." The siren closes the song as it fades out.

DJ APS continues to record and release his mixes. His 2019 release about the dangers to musicians of free downloads, "You Want the Record," features rapping against a funk and hip hop beat. His fan base remains loyal because of his ability to create complex, detailed, and ingenious mixes.

DONATAN/CLEO: "MY SŁOWIANIE" (POLISH VERSION) ALBUM: *HIPER / CHIMERA* (2014)

Kraków, Poland's Donatan (Witold Czamara, 1984–), a DJ and producer, redefines hip hop by using traditional Slavic instruments (especially the accordion) to create songs about Polish pride that counter the stereotypical view of Poles as being rural and simple. Through his beats and collaborations with rappers and singers, he introduces a Poland that is full of fast cars, alcohol, and beautiful (not to mention well-endowed) Slavic women. He co-founded RafPak with R&B- and Dirty South-influenced DJ and producer Teka (Tomasz Kucharski, 1982–) and became a much sought-after producer himself. After returning to Poland from Russia, he released his first solo album, *Równonoc: Słowiańska Dusza* (roughly translated, *Equinox: Slavic Soul*), in 2012. The album and its lead single, "Słowiańska Krew" (a.k.a. "Słowiańska Dusza," in English "Slavic Blood" or "Slavic Soul"), both hit No. 1 on the OLiS (Oficjalna Lista Sprzedaży), Poland's official music sales chart. The album's third single, "Nie Lubimy Robić" (literally, "We Don't Like Doing") has had almost 41.2 million YouTube views as of 2021.

In 2013, Donatan, along with his sometime musical partner, Polish singer Cleo (Joanna Klepko, 1983–), was nominated for Best Polish Act at the MTV Europe Music Awards, and both were chosen to represent Poland at the 2014 Eurovision Song Contest, with their duet "My

Słowianie" (literally "We Are Slavic" or "Us Slavs"), which reached No. 2 on the OLiS in 2013. The duo finished in fourteenth place overall because the live performance was deemed too sexual by some judges, who docked points for the performance's not being family-friendly. The song, a parody of Polish stereotypes, had a popular video that hit fifteen million views on YouTube in less than three weeks (almost 79.2 million total views as of 2021). The two collaborated to produce an album, *Hiper / Chimera* (2014), which the Polish Society of the Phonographic Industry certified as double platinum. One of its singles, "Slavica" ("Slavik"), used elements of Western hip hop (particularly g-funk), and its video, which garnered nearly sixteen million views in just weeks, features twerking Slavic women wearing skin-tight leather shorts, juxtaposed against images of farm roosters, honey harvesting, and powdered amber (believed to have medicinal properties in Polish folk medicine). The song is notable for its use of a distorted synth-distorted voice, which can best be described as a human approximation of a hen cackle.

The Polish version of "My Słowianie" was released as a digital download; it was mixed and mastered by Jarosław Baran (n.d.). An English version, "Slavic Girls," was released in Austria, Germany, Hungary, and the U.K. The song is braggadocio in nature, but it does not brag about music skills; rather, it pays homage to Polish culture by pointing out how beautiful its women are and how sexual they can be. The Polish version of "My Słowianie" is entirely in quadruple meter. The song's structure is as follows: intro (bifurcated); refrain (repeats); verse 1 (trifurcated); refrain; bridge; instrumental interlude; verse 2 (trifurcated); refrain (repeats); outro (bifurcated).

The first part of the intro opens with a synth-produced horn voice that resembles a *shofar* (a kind of bugle made from a ram's horn, associated especially with Jewish synagogue services such as Rosh Hashanah and the end of Yom Kippur). This horn plays C^4 (panning quickly from the left to the right speaker) but does not establish the song's home pitch. In the music video, a shofar is used in a secular way: to wake up all the people sleeping at a Polish farm. Animal sounds heard earlier in the video, such as a rooster, depict that everyone has overslept. A high-pitched, processed vocalization ("eeeeeeeeeya!") at the end of the intro's first part creates a sonic match to the horn's C and slightly resembles the kind of factory whistle that signals everyone to start working. The key A minor, with its home pitch on A, is suddenly established by accordion at the beginning of the second part of the intro. Here, "My Słowianie" becomes an energetic and rhythmic song whose beat in quadruple meter (four beats per measure) is established early by consistent, multi-tracked clapping with a lot of applied reverb that is at times doubled with rhythm sticks and clappers (both often used in Polish or other kinds of Slavic music). A rumbling sound resembling a soft roll on a cymbal or a storm drum effect builds up here (creating a *crescendo* by growing increasingly louder) and sound effects such as an acoustic piano's highest pitches (made to sound like wind chimes) and vocal hollers are added. Cleo's shout out to her musical partner Donatan kicks off the refrain.

The rumbling sound and effects disappear by the beginning of the refrain, which features a multi-tracked Cleo singing lead vocals (to sound like backing singers performing her melody with her in unison). The accordion and hand claps (the latter doubled by rhythm sticks and clappers) remain in the refrain, while kick drum beats are added. Underneath all of this instrumentation is a synth-produced horn voice that is sustained like a drone. Cleo, often compared to Fergie of Black Eyed Peas both for her appearance and her powerful mezzo-soprano voice, belts the refrain, which contains lines that start out as staccato syllables, but end with elongated ones. As she repeats the refrain, the high-pitched screams return, as do the rumbling sound and effects, which build up again; all contribute to the song's first climax.

This energy briefly drops off a bit as Cleo brings her loud voice down to a softer level (closer to *mezzo forte* or medium loud) in verse 1. The first part of the verse (four measures) uses sparse instrumentation. The clapping (still with a lot of applied reverb and doubled by rhythm sticks and clappers) continues accompanying her, but the drone drops out. The accordion also accompanies her by playing at the end of each of her lines. Kick drum beats and the "eeeeeeeeeya!" scream lead into the second part (two measures), which include other female vocalizations (e.g., "mmm"). The third part (also two measures) is marked by a brief shift in vocal texture from just Cleo's lead vocals to more lyrical and harmonized female vocals.

The refrain returns as before, this time using the "eeeeeeeeeya!" scream as a tag just before it repeats again. The rumbling sound returns and builds up again during this repeat. In the following bridge, Cleo uses the same approach to her vocals as she does in verse 1. Initially, the bridge sounds reminiscent of verse 1's first part; Cleo's four lines are almost the same and her melody repeats. Here, she chants, "*To co nasze jest, najlepsze jest, bo nasze jest (to)*" ("what is ours is the best because it is ours") as her first and third lines. For her second and fourth lines, she alternates "*jest*" ("ours") at the end with "*wiesz*" (changing the meaning to "what is ours is the best, we know it"). This display of braggadocio builds up with each vocal line, against a combination of the accordion, clapping, and the synthesizer's pulsating use of its horn voice (the last is the same voice as the drone).

The instrumental interlude stands out for its use of accordion as the main instrument and its use of folk music. Also in A minor and quadruple meter, the folk-style melody plays twice over this chord progression: A-minor-C-major-D-minor-A-minor (in A minor: i-III-iv-i). The brief move from A minor to its relative major, C major, creates a bright moment in the music. A solo accordion begins with the main melody, followed quickly by another accordion (left speaker) in the background that uses *tremolo* (a quivering sound that resembles a *balalaika*, a Russian instrument that is played like a guitar). One of these accordions pushes chord buttons, furnishing the bass. During the second iteration of the folk-style section or interlude, a violin enters and doubles the accordion's melody, adding ornaments. Here, rhythm sticks accompany the song, instead of the usual hand claps and kick drum beats. In the music video, women are shown during the instrumental interlude via overhead and over-the-shoulder shots, wearing traditional Polish dresses with multi-layered skirts and performing a spinning dance in a circle surrounding Cleo. The dance most closely resembles an *Oberek*, a Polish national dance (*oberek* means "to spin"). These dresses are the most traditional-looking costumes in the video; however, Cleo's dress, as well as those of the women featured in most of the video, are altered to show cleavage. The music video employs many images of Polish folk objects, from the traditional skirts and dresses, to farm equipment and animals and accordions—conveying not only Polish identity but also its connections to neighboring Slavic and German cultures. The accordion, featured not only visually but also in the music itself, carries a broader meaning of community—a meaning that is not only Polish but is also understood by other cultures that use this instrument in their music.

The same instrumentation as in verse 1 is used in verse 2, followed by the final iterations of the refrain. The rumbling sound that builds up returns, as do its accompanying effects and drone, now hinting that the song is coming to an end. In the outro, all instruments save the clapping disappear, and an accordion voice takes over. Here, Cleo talk-sings the final few lines, then all voices disappear except the accordion, which plays one last descending flourish. As soon as the accordion hits its final note, one final echoing clap ends the song.

In 2015, Cleo signed a solo record deal with Universal Music Poland and released her first single, "*Zabiorę Nas*" ("I Will Take Us") in December. In 2016, Cleo was nominated for the MTV Europe Music Awards in the Best Polish Artist category. Her second album, *Bastet* (2017), spawned the singles "*Pali się*" ("It's on Fire") and "*Serce*" ("Heart").

FIFTH HARMONY (FEATURING KID INK): "WORTH IT" ALBUM: *REFLECTION* (2015)

Miami-based girl pop group Fifth Harmony (a.k.a. 5H, 2012–2018) began as individual contestants on *The X Factor*: Ally Brooke (Allyson Brooke Hernandez, 1993–), Normani Kordei (Normani Kordei Hamilton, 1996–), Dinah Jane (Dinah Jane Milika Ilaisaane Hansen, 1997–), Lauren Jauregui (Lauren Michelle Jauregui Morgado, 1996–), and Camila Cabello (Karla Camila Cabello Estrabao, 1997–, who left the group for a solo career in December 2016). These five were brought back for the group competition, which led to a joint record deal with co-host and "Groups" mentor Simon Cowell's label Syco Records and co-host and "Over-25" mentor L.A. Reid's label Epic Records. Fifth Harmony's debut EP and its three studio albums all charted in the Billboard 200, with *Better Together* (2013) hitting No. 6, and *Reflection* (2015), 7/27

Fifth Harmony models during the February 12, 2015, Go Red for Women fall fashion show in New York City. At the time, the group's members, who also sang, included (pictured from left to right) Normani Hamilton, Camila Cabello, Ally Brooke, Dinah Jane, and Lauren Jauregui. (Fashionstock.com/Dreamstime.com)

(2016), and *Fifth Harmony* (2017) peaking at Nos. 5, 4, and 4, respectively. The quintet's debut single "Miss Movin' On" was RIAA-certified gold in the United States. *Reflection* and *7/27* were both certified platinum. The latter reached the Top Ten in thirteen countries, producing the group's only Billboard Top 10 hit with "Work from Home" (No. 4). *Reflection* produced the group's first two Billboard Top 40 hits, "Sledgehammer" (No. 40) and "Worth It" (No. 12, triple platinum certification). "Worth It" also reached No. 3 on the U.K. Singles and No. 9 on the Australian ARIA charts.

Touting feminism, self-worth, and confidence, "Worth It," written by Priscilla Renea Hamilton (1988–) and the trio Stargate (Mikkel S. Eriksen, 1972–; Tor Erik Hermansen, 1972–; and Hallgeir Rustan, 1966–), the latter serving as the song's producer, was a hip hop dance and R&B song that incorporated Balkan and Middle Eastern instrumentation. Its video, which depicts band members as business executives (although the song is simply a romance/sex song where the woman is as assertive as the man), had received more than 1.9 billion views on YouTube as of 2021. A Spanish version, *"Dame esta noche"* ("Give Me This Night") was released to iTunes, featuring the group singing in Spanish, as well as rapper Kid Ink, for whom the song was originally written (as "Wit It"), rapping in English. The song's instrumentation includes an eight-note Middle Eastern-sounding alto saxophone ostinato (a persistent melodic and rhythmic pattern) that serves as the song's main instrumental hook, in addition to a second shorter alto sax ostinato, Middle Eastern-inspired synth strings, and a snap-inspired Roland 808 drum machine.

"Worth It" features four of Fifth Harmony's singers exchanging lead vocals; Lauren Jauregui sings backing vocals only. An interesting vocal aspect of this girl group is that the four singers' ranges are extremely close together: all can be classified as mezzo-sopranos with minor distinguishing features based on individual timbres. The most distinct voices in the song belong to Dinah Jane, whose voice is the lowest and hits contralto range (as with many contraltos, she has more strength in her low and high registers than her middle one), and Normani Kordei, who is a lyric mezzo-soprano. Kid Ink's high and low register of his low tenor are used in this song, which gives the impression that another male singer (hitting the baritone range) is accompanying him; however, he performs his own vocal overdubs. The song, basically a female-to-male dialogue, is entirely in C minor and quadruple meter. The recorded song's structure is as follows: instrumental intro; refrain (repeats); rapped verse (bifurcated); sung verse 1 (bifurcated); prechorus; refrain' (repeats); sung verse 2 (trifurcated); prechorus; refrain" (repeats); rapped verse (bifurcated); prechorus; refrain''' (repeats). The refrains and verses start in the home key (C minor or i) and end on the dominant key (G major or V of C minor), which strongly leads back to the home key in the sections that follow. The prechorus tonicizes (very briefly changes key) from A-flat major (VI of C minor and a typical substitute for the home key that creates a brief sense of brightness) to E-flat major (V/VI) in its first line and moves from C minor to B-flat major (C minor: i-VII) in the second line; this second chord progression substitutes G major with B-flat major. But the progression repeats again in the third line and is followed by ultimately moving to G major and harmonically building up to the refrain and return of the home key.

The song begins with a brief instrumental intro that features Ori Kaplan (1969–) who plays the alto saxophone ostinato (left speaker) and the song's instrumental hook, accompanied by hand claps (instead of snaps), likely created by an 808, with a lot of applied reverb, and an 808 kick drum. After two iterations of the hook, synth strings enter (left speaker), followed by the shorter and lower-pitched sax ostinato with new synth-produced sonic sound effects in the background (right speaker). Camila Cabello takes lead vocals in the refrain while the saxophone, beats (including claps), synth strings, and sonic effects continue as accompaniment. The kick drum is set to echo more so that it sounds like an electric bass. Her vocals, as with all of Fifth Harmony's members, are slightly auto-tuned. In the first iteration of the refrain, she sings by herself; in the second, Kid Ink's voice enters with punctuating vocables (e.g., "uh" and "ah") and an 808 snare drum flourish is introduced.

Both Kid Ink's vocables and these 808 flourishes build up to his rapped verse. Added to the accompaniment, a new synth marimba voice, doubled by a new synth bass, enters as a prominent instrument as Kid Ink talk-sings. His voice is multi-tracked (with different effects on his higher and lower vocals) so that it not only sounds fuller and wetter, but also has moments of reverb and echo; these studio production multi-tracking techniques also allow for him to sing chant-like vocalizations against his own lines. The saxophone drops out here, but the hand claps remain as accompaniment. In the first part, Kid Ink's talk-singing is in the low tenor range, and the kick drum beats drop off, whereas the second part is marked by his lower vocal punctuations as well as a synth's low sustained pitches, which resemble a baritone saxophone. The same instrumentation, in addition to 808 flourishes, continues as accompaniment into the second part of the sung verse 1, which is sung by Dinah Jane. Toward the end of his section, Kid Ink's voice raises in its inflection, which foreshadow Dinah Jane's idiosyncratic talk-singing in the second section.

The first part of sung verse 1 features Dinah Jane, whose voice begins with talk-singing. She slides up—like up-speak—at the end of each third staccato phrase in the first half of her verse, so that she can hit a reverbed high-pitched "oooo" sound. In the second part of this verse, she sings in a dance music style that sounds sultry. Normani Kordei sings the first prechorus, in which the beat changes to sixteenth-note hand claps that emphasize a four-to-the-floor beat. These are joined by two synthesizer voices (one of which uses a Doppler effect and the other, a nimbus-like synth pad, yields sustained chords and behaves like accompanying strings). The prechorus serves as a lyrical contrast to the earlier material. Even though saxophone does not play here, the instrumentation sounds full; it includes a sustained 808 flourish at the end and builds up to the second refrain'. Though the first part of the second refrain' is basically a repetition of the first one, Camila Cabello's words, "worth it," include backing harmonies. In this second repetition, however, a few background female vocalizations are added. Some of these background vocalizations are processed through a filter. Kid Ink's punctuating vocalizations return and build listeners' expectations that his verse is next; however, it comes later. Instead, Camila Cabello continues, talk-singing in sung verse 2. Though her accompaniment is the same as in her previous verse, and she begins with the same idiosyncratic sliding used earlier by Dinah Jane, her verse is trifurcated. The second part features her voice (highly auto-tuned and multi-tracked), but because of the members' close ranges, it is too difficult to tell if she sang her own backing harmonies or if others performed them. Rather than returning to the sultry dance music–style vocals that were heard previously, her lines here are delivered in a more energetic diva or house music style. Camila Cabello's last couple of lines are taken from Lathun Grady's "Gimmie What I Want," featuring Katrina, which appears on the compilation album *So So Def Bass All-Stars, Vol. 3* (1998).

Ally Brooke sings the following prechorus, which uses the same instrumentation as the earlier prechorus that featured Normani Kordei, with an additional 808 snare shuffle beat. The refrain" is then repeated, with Camila Cabello and Kid Ink's same vocalizations. This third iteration (and its repeat) sound almost identical to the second one. In the repeat here, the background contains spoken-word voices processed through a filter (to sound like either a telephone or a "bad radio" voice). Kid Ink's verse finally returns, followed by Normani Kordei's prechorus (in live performances, both Ally Brooke and Normani Kordei sing this final prechorus). This time, the prechorus includes more sexualized vocalizations. The song concludes with a final iteration of the refrain''', now

Must-Hear Music 93

including the phone-styled spoken word voice. The song ends abruptly, on Camila Cabello's phrase, "Give it to me. I'm worth it," with the final word echoing.

Since Camila Cabello's departure, Fifth Harmony has made it clear that the remaining four have burned bridges with her. At the MTV Video Music Awards, five girls in costume appeared on stage to begin the song "Angel," but one flew/flipped off the stage and disappeared behind it as the song began (perhaps the group was both literally and figuratively flipping Cabello off, as the four felt betrayed by her departure). The now four-person group performed at the 2017 *People's Choice Awards*, singing the hit "Work from Home." In 2017, Fifth Harmony teamed with Gucci Mane to record "Down," which as of 2021 was their last Hot 100 hit, at No. 42. In March 2018 Fifth Harmony went into indefinite hiatus; its members wanted to pursue solo careers and to pursue possibilities in philanthropy. As of 2021, all members have released solo singles and have confirmed debut albums. Normani Kordei and Dinah Jane have released EPs, and Normani Kordei has had three Top Ten Billboard Hot 100 solo hits. Camila Cabello has released two albums. The first, *Camila*, hit No. 1 on the Billboard 200 and produced the No. 1 song "Havana" and the No. 6 song "Never Be the Same." She has also had two additional Top Ten hits as a featured artist with Shawn Mendes.

DOMINIC FIKE: "3 NIGHTS"
ALBUM: *DON'T FORGET ABOUT ME, DEMOS* (2018)

Like Frank Ocean (whose single "Swim Good" [2011] is discussed in another Must-Hear Music entry in this book), Naples, Florida, singer-songwriter and rapper Dominic Fike (1995–) is an anomaly in the hip hop world in that his songs fuse R&B, alternative rock, and hip hop elements. He started learning how to play acoustic guitar when he was 10 years old, and his earliest hip hop work was making beats with producer 54 (Hunter Pfeiffer, n.d.) and posting their songs on the music-sharing and distribution digital platform SoundCloud. In 2017, Fike was sentenced to house arrest for battery of a police officer. At the time, he recorded and released his debut EP *Don't Forget about Me, Demos*, which sparked a bidding war between major label record companies. During this bidding war, Fike took down all of the songs he had self-released on Internet streaming services and then served jail time for violating the terms of his house arrest. In late 2018, he signed a $4 million contract with Columbia Records, which officially released the EP. Its first track, "3 Nights," started getting heavy rotation on BBC Radio 1. It reached No. 2 in Ireland, No. 3 in Australia, and No. 4 in Belgium, and charted in Germany, New Zealand, Scotland, and the U.K., prompting Billboard to name Fike a breakout act. It became No. 1 on Billboard's Alternative Songs chart, reached No. 21 on the Bubbling Under Hot 100 Singles chart, and was eventually RIAA-certified platinum in the United States.

Fike and his producer Capi (Kevin Carbo, 1994 or 1995–) co-wrote "3 Nights." Wanting to compose an upbeat song, Capi initiated it by selecting an ascending and walking four-note electric bass guitar loop as the song's *ostinato* (a persistent melodic and/or rhythmic pattern that plays throughout a musical piece). While Capi used Ableton Live (a brand of digital audio workstation) to repeat the loop and to add a basic drum beat, Fike wrote the words, and the two later worked together on the melody and harmonies. The thematic concerns of "3 Nights" are similar to those of "Swim Good," which focuses on relationship problems and the resulting sadness and a sense of loneliness and despair caused by being in an emotional rut; however, whereas Frank Ocean's song is dramatic and incredibly sad, Fike's take is one of slight amusement, almost a sense of absurdity (the chorus includes the lines "call me what you want when you want if you want / and you can call me names if you call me up"). Entirely in E-flat major, the song may initially appear to use a simple verse-refrain form with four or four-plus-four measure parts; however, there is more complexity. The song's structure is as follows: intro; refrain (repeated with modifications); verse 1 (hexfurcated with the last two parts also functioning as a prechorus); refrain' (repeated with modifications); verse 2 (hexfurcated); refrain' (repeated with modifications); instrumental outro. The complex features that stand out are that the refrain (a four-plus-four measure passage) already has modifications made to it in its initial repeat, just after the very first time, and the last two parts of verse 1 not only conclude the verse but also create potential energy that builds up to the refrain, hence functioning as a prechorus. In addition to structure, Fike sometimes elides between not only lines but also verse parts (a great example is in between verse 1's second and third parts when he suggests that maybe the person he's addressing would like some company). At times, the predictable four-measure parts break down into two-plus-two measures, as will be described further.

The instrumental intro features the bouncy electric bass ostinato in the foreground, set against percussion (cymbals played with brushes and rim shots or drumsticks played together), hand claps, and an acoustic rhythm guitar. The electric bass guitar's ascending ostinato consists of E-flat, G, B-flat, C, which are the roots of its chord progression (E-flat major-G minor-B-flat major-C minor [I-iii-V-vi in E-flat major]; the last chord, C minor, is the relative minor of E-flat major). A synth-produced bowed cello pitch appears (left speaker) in the background during the fourth measure both times in this four-plus-four-measure intro. The intro concludes by introducing an 808 snare drum tag and Fike's vocals: he does some comic *scatting* (using his voice like a musical instrument by singing vocables or nonsense syllables) in his falsetto range.

The song's refrain starts with the hook (which evokes the song's title). Fike's baritone singing voice is featured in the initial refrain with some applied delay. Throughout the refrain, he is accompanied by the continuing instrumentation heard from the intro. Fike's nasal and laid-back singing style and his vocal delivery, notably slurring lines, suggest that his persona suffers from boredom and sleepiness—a soul-crushing insomnia due to a relationship that has turned sour (the song returns to this refrain three times, a clever reference to each sleepless night). The refrain's repeat, however, starts with a brief break as the bass and beats drop off momentarily and then restart. It features Fike's singing in the same register, backed by his octave-higher doubling vocals.

Fike's bored and sleepy vocals reappear, now echoing more due to applied delay, in the first part of verse 1. All the accompaniment continues but with drier-sounding hand claps. His low vocals continue into the second part, but here they are less breathy, and he is backed by his own falsetto, harmonized vocals that sing "oohs." In between the end of the second and beginning of the third part, where he elides between two lines of text, an 808 snare drum strike followed by a clap—both with applied reverb—sounds as the second part's concluding tag. The claps become more prominent in the third part. Here, Fike's low voice starts the part and is answered by his own multi-tracked backing vocals, set an octave apart. Due to changing musical gestures, the third and remaining parts can be heard as two-plus-two measures each. The fourth part repeats the structure of the third one, with Fike singing the first two measures, followed by his same backing vocals singing the second two measures. The fifth and sixth parts both conclude the verse and also function as a prechorus in the sense that they are more melodic. They build up tension dramatically and musically through Fike's anxiety expressed in his lyrics and vocal delivery as well as through the alternation of various kinds of vocals. The fifth part's first two measures start with Fike's auto-tuned voice, backed by "oohs," with acoustic guitar only—the bass and beats drop out momentarily and then reappear. In its second two measures, Fike yodels between his mid-range and falsetto. The verse's sixth and final part's first two measures feature his harmonized multi-tracked vocals. In its second two measures, the accompaniment drops out. Here, his auto-tuned voice singing *a cappella* (unaccompanied) in his high register just appears in the last two measures, which lyrically dovetail back into the refrain′. Unlike the first refrain, the second iteration reuses Fike's backing vocals, which are an octave higher than his lead vocals, which appeared in the earlier refrain's repeat. Toward the end of this iteration, his multi-tracked singing is backed by his highly auto-tuned vocals that sometimes repeat his words. In the refrain's second iteration, the multi-tracked lead vocals and backing vocals continue, but this time more sustained backing vocals are placed far into the background. At the end of this iteration, Fike's highly auto-tuned backing voice harmonizes with his lead vocals. He includes a falsetto "ooh" as a concluding tag.

Though the instrumentation in verse 2 is just like that of verse 1, Fike's vocal delivery and the song's use of vocals differ greatly. The first four parts feature Fike's voice without any multi-tracking or backing vocals, which underscores his alienation and loneliness. Instead of returning to his low register, in the first part, Fike jumps right into his high register and applies vocal grinding to express the elevation of his persona's emotional state, from boredom to desperation. In the second part, his flow changes as he becomes whiny, and his voice breaks (while still maintaining control of his pitches). Gone is the elision between lines that existed in verse 1's second and third parts; instead, Fike continues to use his high register and the vocal delivery, just changing his flow in the third and fourth parts. Instead of having the last two parts both conclude the verse and act as a prechorus and become more melodic than the previous parts, the desperation of Fike's persona becomes so palpable that the last two parts of verse 2 are rapidly talk-sung. Emotionally spinning out of control from being trapped inside his own head, Fike becomes self-referential about being by himself with his music as a way to handle his desperation. In the fifth part, his lead vocals are backed by his sustained harmonized "oohs," which serve as a countermelody. The bass and beats drop out initially but return immediately. His flow speeds up into the sixth part, as his backing vocals and accompaniment also continue. At the end of this concluding part, he comes to a dramatic pause after he mentions that he is thinking about his partner (addressed as "you"). But his singing and the accompaniment pick up again, dovetailing back into the refrain′, which is the same as the previous one and represents the third night of insomnia. The monotony of being in the same place but at a different time, continually stuck in one's mind, seems to have won. His concluding falsetto "ooh" tag, which appeared previously, is more suggestive here of someone who has descended into madness. But the song must still end. The instrumental outro features the electric bass ostinato in the foreground with the same beats, hand claps, acoustic guitar, and occasional synth-produced bowed cello. After playing the ostinato twice, the song suddenly ends like a crash with a final strike on the 808 snare drum followed by a clap.

In January 2019, Fike revealed that he was working on an album. In the same year, he released four singles: "Açaí Bowl," "Rollerblades," "Phone Numbers," and "Hit Me Up" and, in 2020, "Chicken Tenders." The singles were planned to be part of his debut album *What Could Possibly Go Wrong* (2020) and world tour. "Rollerblades" and "Chicken Tenders" made it onto the album, the latter being the album's first single. Fike is also featured in "Dominic's Interlude," which appeared on American singer-songwriter Halsey's (Ashley Nicolette Frangipane, 1994–) album *Manic* (2020).

FUGEES: "NAPPY HEADS" (REMIX)
ALBUM: *BLUNTED ON REALITY* (1993)

Hailing from South Orange, New Jersey, Fugees (1992–1997) challenged hip hop listeners with a new sound that fused the beats they were used to hearing with reggae and neo soul. The band was best known for the album *The Score* (1996), which hit No. 1 on the Billboard 200, was certified sextuple platinum, and won a Grammy for Best Rap Album. *The Score* contained a hip hop rendition of the 1974 Roberta Flack hit "Killing Me Softly (with His Song)" (1971), composed by Charles Fox and Norman Gimbel. Fugees' version won a Grammy for Best R&B Performance by a Duo or Group with Vocals.

The band, which consisted of American singer-songwriter Lauryn Hill (Lauryn Noelle Hill, 1975–), Haitian singer-rapper Wyclef Jean (Nel Ust Wyclef Jean, 1969–), and American rapper-songwriter-producer Pras (Prakazrel Samuel Michél, 1972–), stemmed from an earlier Hill and Pras band, Tranzlator Crew (a.k.a. Rap Translators, 1989–1992), which Jean, Pras's cousin, had joined by 1993. Hill made the group a trio that recorded demos and signed on the Ruffhouse Records label. The trio changed its name to Fugees, inspired by the derogatory name given to Haitian Americans. In addition to its name change, the group shifted musical direction from pop and R&B to hip hop for its debut studio album, *Blunted on Reality*, which reached No. 62 on Billboard's Top R&B/Hip-Hop Albums and did not chart on the Billboard 200, with its top single, the Black Power anthem "Nappy Heads," peaking at No. 49 on the Billboard Hot 100, although it did top the Billboard Dance/Electronic Singles Sales chart.

"Nappy Heads (Remix)," the final track on *Blunted on Reality*, was written by the trio and produced by Pras and Jean. The original "Nappy Heads" is a series of sociopolitically informed harsh, angry rap vocals that threaten revolution and hard rock-based instrumentation (the sound achieved is similar to that of Public Enemy in "Fight the Power"). Conversely, the remix is melodic, funky, and light-hearted, a love song more concerned with personal statements on African American culture and the Black community. The song's video, directed by Max Malkin, is notable for its use of red filters that de-emphasize colors, making everything look reddish brown, almost colorless, playing up the song's sense of history and nostalgia. The song itself samples or interpolates Woody Guthrie's "This Land Is Your Land" (1940), parodies Corey Hart's "Sunglasses at Night" (1984), alludes to the Mighty Tom Cats' "Love Potion—Cheeba-Cheeba" (1973, released as a funk and soul 45 rpm single) and/or the Harlem Underground Band's "Smokin' Cheeba-Cheeba" (1976, released on a 33-1/3 rpm album), and contains an impersonation of Louis Armstrong in "What a Wonderful World" (1967). Jean and Pras use one or two lines of each original song and then change or undercut the meaning by adding new, original lines. Unlike the original "Nappy Heads," the remix goes beyond rapped vocals to include Jamaican toasting, talk-singing, singing, and scatting.

Entirely in C-sharp major, the structure of the song is as follows: intro (trifurcated); verse 1; refrain; verse 2; refrain; verse 3; bridge; refrain' (three times and extended); outro. Both the intro and the outro contain refrain and vamp (or bridge) materials as well as trumpet and synth keyboard *ostinati*. The first part of the trifurcated intro features Jean's singing the unaccompanied refrain, a calypso-inspired melody that asks for a date from a girl named Monalisa in what appears to sound like Caribbean patois. Jean's tenor vocals are dry and raspy yet playful. The second part of the intro features a trumpet ostinato, which is an arpeggiation of a C-sharp major chord, made bluesy by its additional pitch (C-sharp-E-sharp-G-sharp-C-sharp-B; the last pitch is a ♭7 scale step of C-sharp major). This trumpet ostinato is actually sampled from The Caroleer Singers and Orchestra's recording of "Santa's Birthday," which appeared at the end of Side One on their album *"Sleigh Ride"/"Jingle Bells"* (1960). While this ostinato is played (just over three times), a dialogue between Jean and Hill can be heard in the background. He teasingly calls her "nappy head," and she informs him that she has some "cheeba-cheeba," another name for marijuana. A turntable scratch and a descending, whirring hiccup created by overprocessing Jean's last vocalization (the word *word*) are reminiscent of the sound effects used in Buster Williams's "The Hump" (1975), the same song that furnishes the bass in this remix of "Nappy Heads."

In the third and final part of the intro, the whistle-sounding keyboard ostinato is introduced with the bass and drums, as Jean continues to mention "cheeba-cheeba." Together, these form a four-measure vamp that leads into verse 1. Here, the instrumentation continues, all of which creates a downtempo but danceable beat. The whistle-sounding keyboard ostinato plays F-sharp-D-sharp-E-sharp (resolving to E-sharp, the ostinato reinforces C-sharp major). In verse 1, Jean raps. His voice is kept dry (without any reverb applied) and measured, with instances of whimsical delivery, such as scatting (using nonsensical words) and sing-jaying (using a sing-song delivery) in a Jamaican-sounding patois, briefly singing an allusion to the hymn "I'll Fly Away" (1929, composed by Albert E. Brumley). The refrain follows, but unlike the intro, it is now accompanied by "ivory-tickling" on an acoustic piano, followed by the bluesy trumpet ostinato first heard in the intro's second part.

In verse 2, Hill partly raps and partly talk-sings. Her voice is multitracked to sound full and assertive. This verse repeats the instrumentation of the first verse, with the addition of drum flourishes at the end of some lines, especially when Hill inserts an unexpected pause in her flow or a surprising vocal jest by shaking her voice. As her verse concludes, she elongates her lines and then switches to singing. Jean joins her at the end, again playfully alternating between Jamaican-style vocalizations and actual words, and, at times, scatting. The refrain appears again and uses the same instrumentation. Here, Jean becomes sprightly, allowing himself to play around some more with his vocal delivery.

In verse 3, Pras begins by rapping, his voice deeper than Jean's, approximately in the baritone range. Reverb is applied to his voice, which serves as a distinct contrast to Jean's soft, dry tenor vocals. The same instrumentation is used as in the previous verses, though about a third of the way through, Hill joins in for a quick call-and-response line, then Jean takes over the verse. Here, Jean quotes "This Land Is Your Land," using a more sing-song, almost puckish approach, and then does a Louis Armstrong impersonation by singing part of the refrain from "What a Wonderful World," allowing his voice to break for comic effect and playing with inserting deliberate pauses. Despite his playful delivery, however, this verse is the most political one in the song, with references to slavery and questions about how it could be part of a wonderful world. He returns to rapping, which is punctuated by the same descending whirring effect used in the intro's second part.

The bridge consists of the same vamp that was used in the intro's third part (here used as a bridge). It also consists of Jean's chanting about cheeba-cheeba and is therefore related to the intro's third part. The refrain' follows and repeats. Here, Jean's Monalisa tune in the first part of the intro recurs, still accompanied by trumpet ostinato and punctuated by the descending whirring effect but now with acoustic piano, bass, and Pras's accompanying vocals. The whistle-sounding keyboard ostinato returns, and turntablism is introduced at this point. After the repeat of the refrain', it is then extended by an inserted passage (Jean's singing an off-key allusion to Corey Hart's 1984 new wave rock and synth pop song "Sunglasses at Night"). The refrain' is then repeated a third time, as both *ostinati* continue.

The outro follows, extending Jean's cheeba-cheeba chant material found in the earlier bridge as its main melody. As in the bridge, Jean is accompanied by the trumpet ostinato and punctuated by a bass, which now starts, stops, and starts again. The sudden introduction of saxophones, electric guitar, and slightly discordant synth keyboard voices gives the song a sense that it is breaking down instrumentally. Just like a fantasia, the only way it can all end is with a fadeout (underscoring that they're really "not goin' home," but continuing on).

Despite *Blunted on Reality's* lack of success, Ruffhouse Records gave Fugees an advance that would enable it to record a second album in a relaxed atmosphere. Fugees' second and final album, *The Score*, featured the group at its best, fusing hip hop, dubstep, and reggae. In addition to "Killing Me Softly," the album featured a rendition of Bob Marley and the Wailers' reggae classic "No Woman No Cry" (1974). Another rendition, the Delfonics' R&B and soul song "Ready or Not Here I Come (Can't Hide from Love)" (1968), appeared on the album with a sample from Irish new-age composer Enya's "Boadicea" (1987).

Despite success, the group disbanded in 1997. Hill began to pursue her successful solo career, and her solo album *The Miseducation of Lauryn Hill* (1998) made her the first female artist to win five Grammys in one night. Jean and Pras also continued with solo endeavors. The former's *The Carnival* (1997) and *Ecleftic: 2 Sides II a Book* (2000) were both certified platinum. Jean became politically active, filing for candidacy in 2010 in the Haitian presidential election and getting involved in philanthropic efforts for Haiti. Pras's first solo studio album, *Ghetto Supastar* (1998), peaked at No. 55 on the Billboard 200 and charted internationally. The title track peaked at No. 15 on the Billboard Hot 100. Since 1999, Pras has pursued acting and film production.

GORILLAZ: "CLINT EASTWOOD"
ALBUM: *GORILLAZ* (2001)

Although it is technically a virtual band, Gorillaz, the brainchild of ex-Blur lead singer Damon Albarn (1968–) and comic and cover designer and *Tank Girl* creator Jamie Hewlett (1968–), has had two albums certified multi-platinum (its 2001 debut *Gorillaz* and 2005's *Demon Days*, which hit No. 14 and No. 6 on the Billboard 200, respectively). A Grammy Award-winning virtual band, Gorillaz was formed in 1998. The musicians behind the virtual band, which was made up of four animated members (2-D on lead vocals, keyboards, and melodica; Murdoc Niccals on bass guitar; Noodle on guitars, occasional keyboards, and vocals; and Russel Hobbs on drums and percussion) included Albarn, Del tha Funky Homosapien (Teren Delvon Jones, 1972–), Dan the Automator (Daniel M. Nakamura, 1966–), and Kid Koala (Eric San, 1974–). Albarn, however, is the only consistent behind-the-scenes member, as his goal is to collaborate with diverse musicians, allowing him to eschew Blur's Britpop sound in favor of hip hop (rap and non-rap), electronica, and world music.

Dan the Automator produced "Clint Eastwood" (2001), Gorillaz's debut single from their eponymous album. *Gorillaz* spawned three other singles: "19-2000," "Rock the House," and "Tomorrow Comes Today." "Clint Eastwood" hit the Billboard Hot 100 at No. 57, reaching No. 4 on the U.K. Singles chart and topping the Italian chart as well. "19-2000" hit No. 6 on that chart and hit No. 1 in New Zealand.

"Clint Eastwood" is so named due to its use of melodica as its main instrument, which was thought by band members to resemble Tommy Morgan's (Thomas Morgan Edwards, 1932–) harmonica playing heard in Hugh Montenegro's 1968 hit rendition of Ennio Morricone's main theme from *The Good, The Bad and the Ugly* (1966). The song's lyrics reference a few lines from the film, which is about the pursuit of money (in the form of gold). Although "Clint Eastwood" has been interpreted in various ways, the references to money and to a corrupt system indicate that it, like many hip hop songs, is a song about the music industry, in particular about beating the system and making money. (Here, *The Good, The Bad and the Ugly* is used in much the same way that Brian De Palma's 1983 crime drama *Scarface* gets used in mobb rap culture.) The lyrics also have moments of braggadocio, especially in the song's rapped verses. Instrumentally, the song is a downtempo mix of electronic music, dubstep, reggae, hip hop, and rock. The strings featured in the song are produced from a string machine synthesizer called a Solina String Ensemble; the drums are a combination of Albarn's standalone sampler (MIDI Production Center), which was used to create the song's prototracks, drum track demos, and main drum loop, and the drum kit played by punk rock drummer Cass Browne (Cassian Ingmar Browne, 1971–) of The Senseless Things. Other instruments include Albarn's Suzuki Omnichord, an electronic musical instrument once intended by Suzuki as an updated replacement for the autoharp but often used as a keytar, and the electric bass guitar played by reggae musician Junior Dan (n.d.).

Entirely in E-flat minor, the structure of "Clint Eastwood" is as follows: instrumental intro (bifurcated); refrain (repeated); verse 1; refrain (repeated); verse 2 (bifurcated); refrain (repeated and extended); instrumental outro. A drum flourish with crashing cymbals kicks off the song's bifurcated instrumental intro, followed immediately by a vamp, which drops the bass, accompanied by cymbals, tom, snare, and other percussion sounds such as jingle bells. This vamp establishes a reggae-inspired groove in quadruple meter (four beats per measure). The bass plays an ostinato that rocks between the pitches E-flat and B-flat. To add variety, the ostinato occasionally finishes off a phrase by going from E-flat to B-flat, then overreaching quickly to B-natural, followed again by B-flat and returning to E-flat (the home pitch and chord). Albarn sings the refrain's first entrance by himself, not quite using falsetto but with a boyish quality and tenor range that fit his virtual character, 2-D. On the second iteration of the refrain's vocals, Albarn is multi-tracked to harmonize with himself (right speaker). On his words, "the future is coming on—it's coming on," his vocals are panned from left to right, adding a psychedelic touch.

Verse 1 features rapping by Del tha Funky Homosapien. As he begins, a sustained vocalization (possibly "aighhhhhht") is heard, followed by cymbal crash. His voice is processed to have more reverb and echo than Albarn's, which works well against the continuing bass vamp (left speaker). Discordant acoustic piano notes are introduced into the instrumental mix here; they double the bass. As Del raps in a relaxed manner, a secondary, deeper voice in the background adds tags to the ends of lines and commentary within them (usually one or two words). As the verse continues, the Solina String Ensemble plays *glissandi* (here, moving up and down pitches) to create a whirling psychedelic studio effect. Another sound effect, the sound of inhaling (implying marijuana being smoked), appears in the background. The verse ends with the same cymbal crashes heard in the intro, which lead into the next refrain. Like the earlier one,

Albarn's voice is initially heard alone, and then his harmonies appear in its repetition. This time, though, his voice is accompanied by melodica (with applied reverb) which plays a brief ostinato. The cymbal crashes end the refrain.

Verse 2 is also rapped, but this time it contains a distorted version of the previous refrain's melodica, rather than the discordant piano chords introduced in verse 1. The whirling string *glissandi* of verse 1 reappear in verse 2. The structure is played with here: the cymbal crashes used to end sections are used in verse 2 to bifurcate it. In contrast to the first part, the second part is rapped against just the intro's sparser instrumentation. The refrain is then reintroduced, with the singing voices used the same way. This time, however, there is the addition of slightly oscillating synth-based string voices (left speaker) that play an ascending scale, set against turntables processed to sound like frog croaks (center), processed and hiccupped vocalizations, and whirring synth-produced *glissandi* (right speaker). All create a sense of a grand finale. The words "it's coming on" are alternated with cymbal crashes and extend the refrain. Delay is used here as another psychedelic effect. This instrumentation plays through to an outro that lasts for more than a minute and thirty seconds wherein the melodica is reintroduced. Just before the music fades out, the melodica is at first on right speaker, then pans, then alternates quickly between the left and right speakers.

Gorillaz's No. 1 album (on the U.K. chart) *Demon Days* produced three U.K. Top 10 hits: "Feel Good Inc." (No. 2), "Dare" (featuring Shaun Ryder, No. 1), and "Dirty Harry" (featuring Bootie Brown and the San Fernando Valley Youth Chorus, No. 6). The rock-based "Feel Good Inc." hit No. 14 on the Billboard Hot 100 and topped the Hot Modern Rock Tracks chart in the United States for eight consecutive weeks. It peaked in the Top 10 in 17 countries, reaching No. 1 in Spain and Greece and also won the Grammy for Best Pop Collaboration. Gorillaz have gone on to produce other albums: *Plastic Beach* (2010), *The Fall* (2010), *Humanz* (2017), *The Now Now* (2018), and *Song Machine, Season One: Strange Timez* (2020). The band has been nominated for ten Brit Awards, and it won Best British Group in 2018. *Plastic Beach*, *Humanz*, and *The Now Now* all hit the Top 10 in both the U.K. and the United States. In 2007, a compilation album titled *D-Sides*, containing previously unreleased tracks, B-sides, and remixes of singles and songs from *Demon Days*, was released. In 2012, the band released "DoYaThing" to promote the Gorillaz-branded Converse shoes, with collaborators James Murphy of LCD Soundsystem and André 3000 of Outkast.

GREAT BIG SEA: "BEGGAR DUDE"
ALBUM: *PLAY* (1997)

Known for their award-winning live performances, the four members of Canadian (Newfoundland and Labrador) band Great Big Sea (GBS, 1993–2013)—Alan Doyle (1969–; vocals, guitar, bouzouki, mandolin), Séan McCann (1967–; vocals, bodhrán, guitar, tin whistle), Darrell Power (1968–; vocals, bass, guitar, bones), and Robert "Bob" Hallett (1967–; vocals, fiddle, accordion, mandolin, concertina, bouzouki, whistles, bagpipes)—bring to their music a sense of humor and playfulness. GBS usually alternates between two sounds: traditional Irish, Scottish, and Cornish tunes and highly energetic rock songs and rock-influenced covers of traditional folk songs, including sea shanties. Power, McCann, and Hallett had already been playing together as early as 1989. Their band, NRA (Newfoundland Republican Army), won the Memorial University Winter Carnival Talent Show, and its members started honing their live performances early, touring nearly constantly, sometimes traveling as many as 300 days a year; Doyle had already joined the band by its debut album. GBS's second album, *Up* (1995), was awarded four-times platinum status and charted on the Canadian Album's Chart at No. 45. The band's next seven albums all went to the Top 10 on that chart, three of them achieving Canadian platinum status, with *Sea of No Cares* (2002) topping the chart.

The band's one foray into the realm of hip hop is a memorable, raucous version of an Irish traditional song, "The Beggarman," which focuses on a wanderer who brags about the lifestyle of the beggar, including living on the run, sleeping wherever he can find a place, and meeting young, beautiful women. The Great Big Sea version was an untitled bonus track on its third album, *Play* (1997). The song is usually known by the name "Beggar Dude," but has also been referred to as "Beggarman," "Little Beggarman," "Ragadoon," and "Jolly Beggar Dude." For the song, the quartet took what is normally an uptempo, innocuous ditty and turned it into an energetic, danceable song with raw, aggressive lead vocals, highly aggressive (bordering on shouts) backing vocals, and a bodhrán beat (sometimes doubled by toms and other drums) that approximates the 808 drum hiccup normally associated with hip hop music. In addition, McCann, who sings lead, changes the order of the verses in the traditional song to create lyrics that tell a new narrative, one that hints at the conventional "farmer's daughter" and "farmer's wife" sexual jokes. In addition, McCann adds a line to suggest that a musician (singer) is the perfect beggar/wanderer to engage in such nefarious activity. These lyric changes create a sexually suggestive song, but more to the point, an unapologetic one with an attitude.

The structure of "Beggar Dude" is as follows: intro (trifurcated); verse 1; refrain; instrumental interlude 1; verse 2; refrain; instrumental interlude 2; verse 3; refrain; instrumental bridge 1; instrumental bridge 2; verse 4; refrain (extended); instrumental bridge 3; outro. The verses may also be heard as bifurcated; this sectioning is created by shifting from a heavy emphasis on the song's home key, C major (I), very briefly to B-flat major ($^{\flat}$VII) and back again. This kind of $^{\flat}$VII-to-I sound is often heard in traditional as well as popular Celtic music.

The first part of the intro begins with an energetic bodhrán beat (sixteenth notes with a pause at the end of phrases, which gives the drum a sense of an 808 hiccup) that is panned from the right speaker to the left speaker and then from left to right. This beat continues in the second part and accompanies a repeated spoken-word sample (i.e., "aye, aye," with a long pause between the two so as not to sound like a pirate). This sample is filtered to sound as if it is being heard through an old radio. The "ayes," which also hiccup, are panned from right to left as electric bass enters (left speaker). What next sounds like aggressive gibberish is actually McCann's first parody of folk music vocalizations. Later these vocalizations (e.g., "high diddly, diddly") become part of the refrain. McCann's gibberish (his creation of a hiccupping vocalization, through fast, aggressive, throaty random stuttering of the sounds "did," "lee," "dee," and "die") marks the beginning of the third part of the intro, in which a horn drone (right) appears with a small *crescendo* (gradually getting louder) and builds up with the addition of accordion.

In verse 1, McCann's lead vocals enter, still aggressively spouting a run-together parody of the vocalizations "diddle," "diddly," "hi," and "do." His low tenor vocals are quick and breathless (a sung version of chopper-style rap). In fact, he does not pause to take a breath at the end of his lines. The bodhrán, bass, and drum kit continue to accompany him as he is joined in the refrain by a chorus of backing singers and sustained horns. This is the most instrumentally sparse refrain, as more instruments are folded in gradually. Here, McCann and the chorus together aggressively sing traditional vocalizations, and these always end on a raspy "do da da." Instrumental interlude 1 follows, introducing a memorable melody on the tin whistle (also known as a pennywhistle and here made to sound wetter through applied reverb), accompanied by funky electric guitar (using distortion and wah pedals), synthesizer, bass, and drums, punctuated by the hiccupped "aye, aye" sample (left speaker). In live performances, Doyle often plays the tin whistle melody on guitar, distorted and with wah effects.

Verse 2 sounds similar to verse 1 but includes sustained accordion and strings that continue into the second refrain, which has higher harmonizing vocals. Instrumental interlude 2, which is related to instrumental interlude 1, also includes the tin whistle melody, funky electric guitar accompaniment, synthesizer, bass, and drums, again punctuated by the "aye, aye" media file. Toward the end, the sustained horns and strings emerge and build up again while McCann's gibberish, heard in the third part of the intro, returns in the background. Instrumental interlude 2 closes with a false ending, as a gruff-sounding sampled "hey, hey, and away we go," also filtered to sound like an old radio, leads to a caesura (in live performances, either Doyle or Hallett, who both have gruff voices, performs this line).

Verse 3 also sounds similar to the previous verses but includes the funky electric guitar and more snare drum. After the third refrain, which resembles the second one, two instrumental bridges appear. Instrumental bridge 1 features ascending fiddles and sustained horns and continues into instrumental bridge 2, which features the tin whistle melody fading into the foreground. Verse 4, the final verse, is a metatextual one which announces that the song is coming to an end, as it is time for the beggar man to call it a night after a day full of sexual exploits. The fourth and final refrain consists of the fullest vocal harmonies and is extended, introducing an acoustic guitar, which continues to the end of the song. The extended refrain ends on McCann's voice only, as he literally shouts "do da, da, da, da, da, da!" Instrumental bridge 3 follows, featuring a strummed acoustic guitar solo that leads directly into the outro. This final section reintroduces the tin whistle, which plays against the acoustic guitar, bass, drum kit, bodhrán, and McCann's gibberish vocalizations (the last very much set into the background), until fadeout.

Consecutively between 1996 and 2000, Great Big Sea won the Entertainer of the Year award at the East Coast Music Awards. They have also been nominated for several Juno Awards, including Group of the Year in 1998, 2005, 2009, and 2011. Although the band has retired, Doyle and McCann have gone on to successful solo careers, typically including music from GBS in their set lists.

HAMILTON (CAST): "TEN DUEL COMMANDMENTS"
ALBUM: *HAMILTON: AN AMERICAN MUSICAL* (ORIGINAL BROADWAY CAST RECORDING, 2015)

Lin-Manuel Miranda's (1980–) *Hamilton: An American Musical* is concerned with the life of Alexander Hamilton, inspired by the 2004 biography by historian Ron Chernow. Achieving both critical acclaim and box-office success, *Hamilton* debuted on Broadway in August 2015 at the Richard

Rodgers Theatre. In 2016, it received a record-setting 16 Tony nominations, winning 11, including Best Musical. It also won the 2016 Pulitzer Prize for Drama for its representation of Hamilton's life as well as his interactions with contemporaries, including Aaron Burr, Elizabeth Schuyler Hamilton, Angelica Schuyler, and King George III, as well as George Washington, James Madison, and Thomas Jefferson. The soundtrack was the recipient of the 2016 Grammy for Best Musical Theater Album. Its songs incorporated elements of not only R&B, soul, pop, and Broadway musical show tunes, but also elements of hip hop, both non-rap and rap.

One of its songs, "Ten Duel Commandments," is particularly interesting for its inclusion of hip hop elements, but with singing and talk-singing as well as rapping. The song occurs in Act I, when the Washington-appointed General Charles Lee proves to be incompetent and is fired and then challenges South Carolina Lieutenant Colonel John Laurens to a duel, with Hamilton and Burr as their seconds. Laurens injures Lee, who yields. Washington later temporarily suspended Hamilton over the duel, until the Siege of Yorktown.

"Ten Duel Commandments" explains ten rules for dueling, which were influenced by both the biblical Ten Commandments and The Notorious B.I.G.'s "Ten Crack Commandments," from his posthumous album *Life After Death* (1997). There are two reprises of elements from the song, during "Blow Us All Away" (when Philip Hamilton and George Eacker are about to duel) and during "The World Was Wide Enough" (which leads up to the Burr and Hamilton duel). Entirely in F minor and quadruple meter (four beats per measure), the song consists of a quadfurcated intro, followed by four verses that contain couplets that enumerate and describe each of the "ten duel commandments." Cadences offer internal points of conclusion, so the song may be heard as having four verses that group couplets for commandments one through three (verse 1), then four through five (verse 2), and six through eight (verse 3), ending on a bridging dialogue to nine and ten (verse 4). Unlike hip hop singles or album tracks, "Ten Duel Commandments" contains no refrains or vocal hooks. Though it may be used as a place to begin listening to the musical, the song is not a standalone, as it relies on listeners' previous knowledge of its subject matter.

The first part of the song's bifurcated intro features synth-produced turntables that resemble sweeps or air loops that pan slowly from the right to the left speaker. The second part features an *a cappella* (unaccompanied) male chorus (using close harmonies) that counts from one to nine while a ticking sound is heard in the background, giving the impression that time is inevitably moving forward toward the duel. Vocals also give this impression as they get gradually louder (*crescendo*). Once the count reaches nine and the song title is sung by Burr (Leslie Odom, Jr., 1981–), Hamilton (Miranda), Laurens (Anthony Ramos, born Anthony Ramos Martinez, 1991–), and Lee (Jonathan Rua, 1993–), the ticking ends. The third part of the intro brings back the panning turntables and announces the title of the song. Here, the ticking clock is no longer present. In the fourth and final part, all voices repeat the song's title. The song's beat then emerges full force. It is comprised of a heavy kick drum and tom combination, set against what seems like horror-influenced, siren-like ascending *glissando* sound effects (sliding up pitches) that are reminiscent of Falco's "Rock Me Amadeus" (1985) or Cypress Hill's "Insane in the Brain" (1993). These sound effects appear both on the right and left speakers, accompanied by turntables (right speaker) and the kick drum (left speaker).

The couplets are all either talk-sung or rapped in an old-school style (focusing on end rhymes) by two main vocalists, Ramos (Laurens) and Miranda (Hamilton). Although both sing in the tenor range, their voices contrast with each other: Ramos has a smooth, boyish high tenor voice, whereas Miranda's voice is a raspy and throaty lower tenor. In addition, Miranda employs a more aggressive delivery than Ramos. The rapping or talk-singing takes place against a simple old-school drum kit beat, with a peppering of various instruments that create points of interest (e.g., glass and metal bells, sub-bass, piano, the high-pitched siren voice, a distorted synth-produced drum voice that sounds similar to scratching, and dramatic oscillating string voices). Each commandment is introduced by the male chorus's singing its corresponding commandment number, and lists vary between one and two couplets, with single couplets at the beginning and end of the list, bookending doubled couplets, which occur in the third, fourth, and fifth list items.

By Commandment Three, rapping is done by all four major characters in the scene: lower tenors Rua (Lee) and Odom (Burr), Ramos and Miranda, as well as the male chorus (occasionally, for variety). At the end of the third commandment, the kick drum halts for a brief moment. The chorus then concludes the verse, accompanied by the sound effects. A cadence takes place (also reminiscent of "Rock Me Amadeus"), and it kicks off Commandment Four. Like the mention of Commandment One, the bass doubles the chorus. A similar combination of instruments is employed for Commandments Two and Three, and Commandment Four ends with Odom's rapping against a drum break (and a sudden sparse musical texture as the other instruments drop out). This marks a moment in which Burr answers Hamilton with "You have to turn him around so he can have deniability": ironic given that Burr ultimately kills Hamilton in a later duel. For the first time, the chorus introduces a commandment by only its number, "five." Commandment Five employs a synth stinger before the chorus concludes the couplet and verse, followed by a metal bell ding. The next verse, starting with Commandment Six, begins much like Commandments One and Four. It is followed by Commandment Seven, which is introduced by only its number, as "seven." During Commandment Eight, Rua, Odom, Ramos, and Miranda rap together (following the chorus, which introduces it). The aforementioned sound effect concludes this commandment, followed by a brief pause; most notably, the bass and tom beat ceases.

At this point, the song evolves toward Hamilton's and Burr's dialogue on the uselessness of dueling. Here, the previous accompaniment is replaced by a synth-produced popping sound, which resembles the ticking clock. This new accompaniment stops and is followed by drums as all decide to continue. Commandment Nine prefigures the duel. Here, the bass returns, and accompanying strings swell, ascend, and become louder and more dramatic. The male chorus then counts from one to nine against the ticking clock, indicated the duelers' ten paces. The ticking abruptly ends, and the male chorus shouts "Number Ten. Places. Fire!" The song ends on the last word.

"Ten Duel Commandments" was released as part of the 2015 cast album on the Atlantic label. The album featured Miranda, Odom, Rua, and Ramos, as well as Phillipa Soo, Renée Elise Goldsberry, Christopher Jackson, Daveed Diggs, Okieriete Onaodowan, Jasmine Cephas Jones, Jonathan Groff, Thayne Jasperson, Sydney James Harcourt, Ariana DeBose, and Sasha Hutchings. Its musicians included Alex Lacamoire, Kurt Crowley, Andres Forero, Robin Macatangay, Richard Hammond, Benny Reiner, Jonathan Dinklage, Erin Benim Mayland, Anja Wood, Mario Gotoh, and Laura Sherman. The album reached No. 1 on three Billboard charts: Broadway Cast Albums, Top Rap Albums, and Top Internet Albums.

HERBIE HANCOCK (FEATURING DXT): "ROCKIT" (LONG ALBUM VERSION) ALBUM: *FUTURE SHOCK* (1983)

Chicago-born jazz composer, keyboardist, bandleader, and actor Herbie Hancock (Herbert Jeffrey Hancock, 1940–) produced quite a few iconic hits, with his most famous foray into hip hop being "Rockit" (1983, a fusion of hip hop and jazz), the first turntable-heavy mainstream hit.

Herbie Hancock plays his keytar at the Cemil Topuzlu Open Air Theater on July 2008 in Istanbul, Turkey. (Petitfrere/Dreamstime.com)

The song was the opening track on his 1983 platinum album *Future Shock* (his only other RIAA-certified platinum album was 1973's *Head Hunters*, which was also his highest charter on the Billboard 200, at No. 13). "Rockit" was recorded, edited, and engineered at several sound-recording studios, with bass guitarist Bill Laswell (1955–), drum machine and synthesizer programmer Michael Beinhorn (n.d.), and turntablist GrandMixer DXT (as Grand Mixer D.ST, Derek Showard, 1960–). Hancock had previous connections to hip hop, as his songs had served as source music for samples, and he would develop further connections, as he worked later in his career with hip hop artists such as Kanye West, The X-Ecutioners, and Rob Swift and was a go-between who introduced fellow musicians who would then work together on hip hop projects.

Hancock studied classical piano, but his interest was in jazz's complex harmonies. In 1962, he recorded his first album, *Takin' Off*, which so greatly impressed eminent jazz composer-trumpeter Miles Davis that he invited Hancock to join his quintet. Hancock's work in Davis's Second Quintet resulted in a more prominent rhythm section that became the one he used increasingly in post-bop as well as in jazz-rock fusion. Hancock shifted between piano, electric piano, and synthesizer, exploring jazz-funk fusion, which incorporates Afro-Caribbean and Latin percussion instruments and rhythms.

In 1983, "Rockit" attained mainstream popularity and encouraged interest in hip hop turntablism and breakdancing; in addition, it reached No. 1 on Billboard's Hot Dance Club Play, No. 6 on Hot Black Singles, and No. 64 on the U.S. Cashbox charts. It reached only No. 71 on the Billboard Hot 100 despite *Future Shock's* platinum status; however, its music video became famous in its own right. Godley and Creme (1977–1988), a London-based rock duo who became a successful and influential music video team, directed "Rockit," which featured action shots and jump cuts of English installation artist and inventor Jim Whiting's movable and danceable sculptures—hybrids of broken mannequins and robots. They were filmed to appear as though they are dancing within a house in London. Hancock appears, playing keyboards, on a television that is smashed by the end of the video.

"Rockit" was composed by Hancock, Laswell, and Beinhorn. In the song, Beinhorn used a new Oberheim DMX drum machine to lay down a basic beat, and Laswell brought in percussionist Daniel Ponce to augment the track with Afro-Cuban batá drums by multi-tracking himself to sound like three drummers (in other words, Ponce recorded the small, medium, and large batá drums separately). Grand Mixer D.ST and two DJ friends from his group Infinity Rappers scratched for the track, using a Celluloid Records single, "Change the Beat" (1982), by Fab 5 Freddy. Laswell added an electric guitar sound inspired by Led Zeppelin's (1968–1980) cover recording of Willie Dixon's (1915–1992) "I Can't Quit You Baby," from the band's debut album (1969). Originally intending to use a drum sample, Laswell finally decided to play the chord as a double-stab on his own electric guitar, using his Lexicon Prime Time digital delay set on repeat hold. Toward the end of the recording, Hancock, Laswell, and Beinhorn composed the song's melodic line on the spot by humming out loud to each other. Laswell and Beinhorn then added a vocal sample from "Planet Rock" (1982), by Afrika Bambaataa & the Soul Sonic Force (1980–). D.ST and his colleague Grandmaster Caz (Curtis Brown, 1960–) then finalized the scratching. In addition, Laswell's bass guitar melody, which appears as a countermelody to the main theme, uses as its basis the end of saxophonist Pharoah Sanders' (Farrell Sanders, 1940–) "Upper Egypt and Lower Egypt," from his 1966 spiritual-jazz album *Tauhid*.

The song begins with a bifurcated intro. Typically, bridges come in between sections of songs; however, the first part of this intro gets re-used often—as a bridge—and therefore may be thought of as bridge 1.

It contains ascending turntables and heavy kick drums and toms (right speaker). A lighter variation of bridge 1 with less emphasis on kicks and toms (though still using turntables) is also heard. Here, the turntables are followed by two snare drum strikes, to create bridge 2. This lengthy and elaborate intro includes a bifurcated bridge 1 (electric guitar double-stab), followed by a bifurcated bridge 2 (electric guitar double-stab and snare strikes). It then returns to bridge 1 (snare strikes). The bridges serve as short rhythmic breaks that would be typical of early hip hop dance music. The intro features the Oberheim DMX drum machine employing sixteenth-note beats (in the range of the toms), with turntables scratching as accompaniment. After bridge 1 and the electric guitar double-stab, there is a switch to a funkier beat, produced by bass guitar with drum machine-produced kick and snare drums (right speaker) and a light jangling sound (left speaker), along with more prominent and playful scratching (left speaker). Turntables continue in the second part of bridge 2, but this time with batá drums (right speaker) also in the foreground. In the background, the bass guitar plays a melody, and this part of the intro is punctuated by synth sweeps (panned from left to right). Bridge 1 returns with a drum machine hiccup (that sounds like a Roland TR-808 or 808 percussion sound) and snare strikes, leading into "Rockit's" iconic synth melody.

The rest of "Rockit" employs bridges 1 and 2, the iconic melody, and several instrumental interludes. Its structure is as follows: intro (discussed in the preceding paragraph); main theme; bridge 2; instrumental interlude 1; main theme'; bridge 1; instrumental interlude 2; main theme''; bridge 1; main theme'''; bridge 1; instrumental interlude 3; bridge 2; instrumental interlude 4; bridge 3; instrumental interlude 5; bridge 2' (as a brief outro). Hancock composed the song's iconic melody (labeled here as the main theme) and recorded it by using his Fairlight CMI synthesizer, accompanied by batá drums (right speaker), as well as drum machine-produced snares and toms with a bass guitar countermelody (left speaker). The main theme establishes the home key of the song as A minor, and its melody is based on a seven-note (*heptatonic*) A minor blues scale (using A, B, C, D, D-sharp, E, and G or scale steps 1, 2, ♭3, 4, ♭5, 5, and ♭7; the "♭" or flat sign indicates that the notes are lowered by a half-step). The A-minor sound of the main theme sounds so satisfying here because the lengthy intro may be interpreted as being in V or the dominant of A minor: the prolonged wait and emphasis on the pitch E makes the listener want to hear A, which takes place as the main theme appears. This first entrance of the main theme concludes with an autotuned robotic voice (via vocoder) that says "don't stop it."

Bridge 2, with its machine-produced hiccup (snare and cymbal ranges), reintroduces the electric guitar double-stab. Instrumental interlude 1 features the batá drums (right speaker) and staccato-sounding turntables, accompanied at first by bass-range robotic vocables. Here in bridge 2, the bass is replaced by a synth bass, which plays intermittent notes rather than the funky countermelody heard earlier. Synth sweeps, panned from left to right, return. The main theme repeats with some variation; this time, the melody slows down slightly and sounds more detached because of its use of pauses. The batá drums continue (right speaker), along with accompanying synth sweeps, including a swelling one that pans several times between left and right speakers at the end of this repetition of the main theme. Bridge 1 returns, leading into instrumental interlude 2, which features more prominent turntables and rests. The main theme returns again, and this time it is similar to the first version. Vocoder-produced robotic vocals return to punctuate this section, as batá drums (right speaker) remain part of the accompaniment.

Instrumental interlude 3 takes place after the return of bridge 1 and introduces a new turntable's rhythmic pattern, accompanied by bass. This lengthiest interlude eventually features a ticking turntable rhythm (left speaker), accompanied by synth sweeps. Batá drums return midway (right speaker). At the end of this section, the turntables introduce a triplet rhythmic pattern, followed by more synth sweeps (panned left to right). Bridge 2 leads to instrumental interlude 4, which reintroduces turntables with electric guitar (left speaker) in an exchange with new robotic vocalizations (right speaker). Bridge 3 combines the kick drums and tom sound of bridge 1, with synthesizer as a new sound in a transitional passage (a percussive hiccup). Interlude 5 uses the electric guitar double-stabs with a keytar solo (left speaker) and features turntables and bass guitar, punctuated by drum machine-produced snare drums. It is during this interlude that Hancock finally jams, adding a more funk-based melody. Bridge 2 is modified to serve not as a bridge but as a very brief outro, which is notable for its percussive hiccup and abrupt sudden snare-strike conclusion.

In 2001, Hancock, Laswell, and Swift collaborated again on a remix of "Rockit" for Hancock's album *Future 2 Future*. This time, Swift and A Guy Called Gerald (Gerald Simpson, 1968–) programmed beats. The remix expands on the original hit's use of electronica. Hancock later went on tour with Swift and the X-Ecutioners, who performed a new concert version of "Rockit." The original version has been sampled by Knights of the Turntables, the B-Boys, De La Soul, Charizma and Peanut Butter Wolf, Janet Jackson, and the duo of Neeraj Shridhar and

Suzanne D'Mello. Hancock's further hip hop activities can be found on his albums *Sound-System* (1984), *Perfect Machine* (1988), and *Dis Is da Drum* (1994).

JANET JACKSON: "RHYTHM NATION"
ALBUM: *RHYTHM NATION 1814* (1989)

Singer, dancer, and actress Janet Jackson (1966–) was the youngest child of the famed Jackson family, which also launched the highly successful careers of The Jackson 5 and Michael Jackson. Janet Jackson began her own music career at the age of 10 with *The Jacksons*, a short-lived 30-minute television variety show. Initially, though, she became well known not for music but for acting, appearing on television as a main cast member of the final two seasons of *Good Times* (1974–1979) and the fourth season of *Fame* (1982–1987, on which she sang), as well as becoming a recurring cast member for three seasons of *Diff'rent Strokes* (1978–1985). In 1991, she appeared in her first starring role in the John Singleton film *Poetic Justice*, which also starred Tupac Shakur. She also starred in *Nutty Professor II: The Klumps* (2000), opposite Eddie Murphy.

Janet Jackson's vocal range is high soprano with the same smooth, youthful, and muted timbre found in her brothers Michael and Jermaine and her sister LaToya's voices. In 1982, Janet Jackson began turning her attention to music, signing with A&M Records. Her early solo studio albums included *Janet Jackson* (1982), *Dream Street* (1984), *Control* (1986), and *Janet Jackson's Rhythm Nation 1814* (1989). The latter was titled after the year Francis Scott Key wrote the poem "The Defense of Ft. McHenry," which was then set to the tune of John Stafford Smith's British drinking song "To Anacreon in Heaven" (a.k.a. "The Anacreontic Song," named after a London gentlemen's club of amateur musicians), and was then retitled as "The Star-Spangled Banner." On *Control* and *Rhythm Nation 1814*, Jackson collaborated with the iconic production team of Jimmy Jam (James Samuel Harris III, 1959–) and Terry Lewis (1956–). *Control* started a string of multi-platinum albums that included itself, *Rhythm Nation 1814*, *janet.* (1993), *The Velvet Rope* (1997), and *All for You* (2001). The album *janet.* marked her move to Virgin Records, though she continued to work with Jimmy Jam and Lewis. These were followed by the platinum *Damita Jo* (2004), named after Janet Jackson's middle name, and *20 Y.O.* (2006). Overall, Janet Jackson has sold more than 180 million records.

"Rhythm Nation 1814" is the second track on her album of the same title. Jackson composed and produced the song, working with Jimmy Jam and Lewis. Her aim was to create a sociopolitically conscious song with upbeat dance music. It fuses elements of hip hop, R&B, funk, and soul with some industrial effects, and thus is an example of new jack swing. It reached No. 2 on the Billboard Hot 100 and topped Billboard's Hot R&B/Hip-Hop Songs and Dance Club Songs charts. It was also RIAA-certified gold in the United States. Internationally, it reached No. 2 in Canada, Japan, and South Africa, and hit the Top 10 in France and the Netherlands. Dominic Sena (1949–) directed the song's black-and-white music video, set in what looks like a postapocalyptic warehouse and featuring Jackson and her dancers in unisex military attire. The video won two MTV Video Music Awards (Best Choreography and Best Dance Video).

In comparison to the album version, the music video includes Jackson's lengthy spoken-word first track, "Interlude: Pledge," which serves as a prelude to the song. This preliminary track features Jackson's voice, doubled by a male-sounding voice that is distorted to sound deep and robotic. They point out their solidarity and that they are part of a nation (a multitude of people) who have no boundaries and no divisions or limitations based on color. The background consists of bells and electronically produced industrial sound, along with ominous sustained notes on the Oberheim OB-8, a keyboard-controlled subtractive polyphonic analog synthesizer that was a bit dated at the time, as most were manufactured between 1983 and 1985. This synthesizer's powerful sound, however, remains a producer favorite, and it is used on nearly all of the tracks on the album. Recording for the album began in January 1989 at Flyte Time studio in Minneapolis, Minnesota. "Rhythm Nation 1814" was one of the first songs recorded. The album was released on September 19, 1989, and the single was released on October 24, 1989.

The song structure of "Rhythm Nation 1814" is as follows: intro (hexfurcated); verse 1 (A, bifurcated); refrain (bifurcated); verse 2 (A′, bifurcated); refrain′ (bifurcated, played twice); bridge 1; instrumental interlude 1; middle-eight (B, bifurcated); instrumental bridge 1; instrumental bridge 2; instrumental interlude 2; bridge 1′; instrumental bridge 3 (vamp); bridge 1″; instrumental bridge 3 (vamp); bridge 1‴; refrain″ (bifurcated, also twice); B′ (used as the outro and played three-and-a-half times). The intro may be heard as either hexfurcated (four small one- or two-measure parts plus two larger eight-measure parts) or trifurcated (adding the earliest four parts together as one part, followed by the fifth and then the sixth part). The first part establishes the song's quadruple-meter time signature (four beats per measure) and moderately fast tempo through its beats, performed on the E-mu SP-1200 drum machine, a state-of-the-art sampler and sequencer that was released the same year as the song was recorded, and the Sequential Circuits Drumtraks drum machine and sampler (which also contributed to some of the song's industrial sound effects). The E-mu SP-1200 had a greater variety of sampled drum sounds than its predecessor, the LinnDrum (the earlier LM-1, manufactured between 1980 and 1983), and used samples of real drum components, such as the kick drum, toms, snare, snare rim shots, hi-hat, ride cymbal, crash cymbal, congas, cabasa, and tambourine, as well as hand claps.

"Rhythm Nation 1814" starts with a heavy beat on kick drum in the first part of its intro. Its beats also include dry triangle strikes (which resemble a low timbale cowbell), tambourine, and snare drum. Jackson punctuates these beats by whispering "yeah," which is hiccupped, and briefly establishes A as the home pitch. A sampled turntable scratch and drop (resembling a "whoo" scream) is also folded into the beats (predating Rob Base and DJ E-Z Rock's use of the same in "It Takes Two" by less than a year). Jackson and her backing male vocalists repeat the word "dance" four times, accompanied by the kick drum on each word, in the second part. This is followed by 808 snare drums, an alarm-like bell (or quick triangle flourish), and tambourine shakes, followed by a synth strings stinger, with Jackson whispering the word "nasty" and then calmly saying "three" (her voice is distorted to sound like a male's), and turntables, respectively, in the third and fourth parts. The intro's fifth part establishes the song's home pitch, E, and features electric guitars and bass guitar playing a distinctive funk groove. Here, Jimmy Jam sampled and looped from the bridge (after the refrain) of Sly and the Family Stone's 1969 funk rock hit, "Thank You (Falettinme Be Mice Elf Agin)," using an AMS DMX 15–80 S computer-controlled digital delay. The electric guitars also serve as a lengthy vamp (cuing the singer to begin). These guitars establish E minor as the home key; however, placed far into the background is a very soft synth strings melody that foreshadows the middle-eight's melody, which outlines E major. What is being underscored with the minor/major combination is the lyrics: "major" and "minor" are the color or quality of chords, and the song is about blurring the lines of color. Though the combination does blur the lines, listeners have a tendency to hear one key over another when *bitonality* (two or more tonalities) is present. Here, the electric guitars and bass dominate and will do so during verse 1 as well, so E minor (the darker sounding key) weighs more heavily than E major. These electric guitars are joined by new beats that include snare drum and the same triangle, tambourine, and turntables used earlier. Synth horns create a concluding tag for the fifth part. A new synth pan flute melody emerges in the sixth part, sharing the foreground with the continuing instrumentation. Meanwhile, male vocables (clipped and slightly distorted whoops and grunts) are placed far in the background. A major aspect of the song's production approach is its economy: the intro's small parts get reused again in the song's later sections and passages.

Verse 1 features Jackson's ethereal and filtered R&B style vocals against the continuing beats. Here, the electric guitars are placed in the background, and the synths drop out. The division of first and second parts is heard through the lyrical content. The refrain is in E major, the parallel major to E minor. Male and female backing vocals join Jackson in singing the refrain, sliding chromatically from D to C-sharp to B (against E dominant^7-A major-E major, respectively, or in E major: V^7/IV-IV-I), as the beats continue and the strings synth melody heard in the fifth part of the intro reappears in the background. Layered over this synth melody is the synth pan flute melody of the intro's sixth part. Jackson's vocals are doubled again by the male-sounding robotic voice. Together, everyone sings the song's hook, "we are a part of the rhythm nation," which most strongly affirms the E-major home key. Through use of multi-tracking, Jackson is able to punctuate these vocals and create tags at the end of lines.

Verse 2 is similar to verse 1, but with more electric guitar effects, as well as some additional reverb on Jackson's last two lines (and two measures) in the second part. The electric guitars continue to play in E minor, but the weight of this key comes across as not being as heavy after listeners have just heard the refrain's E-major hooks. The beats continue throughout the first part, but in the second part, they drop out against Jackson's harmonized multi-tracked vocals. The refrain' is repeated twice. Bridge 1 is a hiccupped alternation of Jackson's saying the word "bass" against the beats and soft synth strings melody. Its material is related to the second part of the intro, bringing back a rapid, psychedelic alternation between the right and left speakers. This eight-measure bridge sounds like a breakbeat passage for dancers and leads to instrumental interlude 1 for another eight measures. Here, the synth pan flute melody, initially heard in the foreground of sixth part of the intro and the refrains' backgrounds, is the main instrument. It is accompanied by new jazzy synth flutes and punctuated by electric guitars and bass, all against the continuing beats. These remain in the next section as accompaniment in the background.

118 Listen to Hip Hop!

The middle-eight features the chorus of backing singers' soaring melody, singing the song's title, punctuated by Jackson's more gospel-inspired vocals (e.g., "Sing it, people"). All are juxtaposed against robotic, drawn-out male vocals that almost sound like a vocal drone: here, Jackson hits her highest and most dramatic notes of the song. The vocalists' melody here is doubled by the synth strings, and both outline E major while the electric guitars and bass play in E minor.

The second part varies the first part's melody just slightly, but the jazzy synth flutes drop out. The second part concludes with a *ritardando* (slowing of the tempo), which gives way to instrumental bridge 1. The alarm clock-sounding bell and tambourine shakes sound against the song's sparsest texture—some percussive effects and the synth pan flute melody—for two measures. Instrumental bridge 2, the very electric guitar and bass vamp material heard in the intro's fifth part, reappears with the returning beats for another two measures. Interlude 2 is also breakbeat-focused and showcases funk drumming (especially on the kick and tom drums), accompanied by funk bass and occasionally punctuated by loops of Jackson's whispered "nasty" (heard in the intro's third part) and hiccupped "bass" (heard in bridge 1 and related to the intro's second part); the latter alternates from the right to the left speaker. Gear-shifting sound effects are introduced here. Interlude 2 is surprisingly cut off (lasting six instead of eight measures) by the return of bridge 1′ and its quick alternation to instrumental bridge 3 (the electric guitar vamp, jazzy synth flutes, pan flute melody, and intro's beats), bridge 1″, instrumental bridge 3′, and bridge 1‴. Jackson adds a tag inviting everyone to start singing the following refrain″, which is played twice. The instrumentation is the same as before, but more synth horns are added. The middle-eight (B′) reappears with the same instrumentation, this time with continuing synth horns, and is played three-and-a-half times. Used as the outro, it is a final showcase of Jackson's vocals, which punctuate her chorus of backing singers. The third time they sing, instruments drop out to create a sparse texture of voices against industrial metal-against-metal effects and beats. They fade out as waves of white noise emerge. This white noise foreshadows the album's third track, "Interlude: TV."

As of 2021, Jackson holds the record for women, with the most consecutive Top 10 songs on the Billboard Hot 100 at 18, from "Miss You Much" (1989) to "I Get Lonely" (1998). In 2019, she was inducted into the Rock and Roll Hall of Fame. In addition, the music videos for singles from the album *Control* introduced Paula Abdul's choreography and led to Abdul's own recording contract. Janet Jackson's *Rhythm Nation World Tour 1990* became the most successful debut tour at the time, and she established the Rhythm Nation Scholarship fund. She also received a star on the Hollywood Walk of Fame. In 2004, she made Super Bowl history as Justin Timberlake tore open the top of her costume, exposing her right breast to 140 million viewers (both musicians claimed that it was a wardrobe malfunction). The incident, nicknamed "nipplegate," was one of the most controversial events in television history. As a curious result, CBS and Viacom (as well as subsidiaries MTV, VH-1, Clear Channel Communications, and Infinity Broadcasting) blacklisted Janet Jackson—but not Timberlake.

JESSIE J (FEATURING ARIANA GRANDE AND NICKI MINAJ): "BANG BANG"
ALBUM: *SWEET TALKER* (2014)

Singer-songwriter Jessie J (Jessica Ellen Cornish, 1988–) began her music career early in London. At 11 years old, she got a part in Andrew Lloyd Webber's West End production of *Whistle Down the Wind*. At 16, she began studying at the BRIT School for Performing Arts and Technology (which boasts other famous alumni singers such as Adele and Amy Winehouse), before joining the group Soul Deep. A powerful dramatic soprano who specializes in soulful belting, Jessie J didn't really find her audience until she signed with Lava Records and Universal Republic and released her debut single "Do It Like a Dude" (2010). International success came with her next single, "Price Tag" (2011), which featured B.o.B. (Bobby Ray Simmons, Jr.). The song became an iconographic megahit, topping charts in the U.K., Ireland, and New Zealand and reaching No. 23 on the Billboard Hot 100.

Her debut album, *Who You Are* (2011), produced four more Top 10 U.K. singles: "Nobody's Perfect," "Who You Are," "Domino," and "Laserlight" (featuring David Guetta) as well as "Who's Laughing Now," which reached No. 16. Across the Atlantic, "Domino" reached No. 6 on the Hot 100, making it her second U.S. hit. Her second album, *Alive* (2013), included the U.K. Top 10 hit songs "Wild" and "It's My Party." Her third album, *Sweet Talker* (2014), peaked at No. 5 in the U.K. At No. 10 on the Billboard 200, it became Jessie J's highest charting album in the United States as of 2021. Its lead single, "Bang Bang," features Boca Raton, Florida, singer-songwriter and former childhood actress Ariana Grande (Ariana Grande-Butera, 1993–) and Port of Spain, Trinidad-born and Queens-based Nicki Minaj (Onika Tanya Maraj, 1982–). Grande's vocal range is soprano; her vocals, comparatively thinner and more willowy than Jessie J's, are mostly suited for pop songs. In contrast, Nicki Minaj is better known for rapping and talk-singing; however, she is also an accomplished singer who is moving from soprano to the slightly lower mezzo-soprano range. She mostly raps, though she sings a bit on "Bang Bang."

In addition to appearing on Jessie J's *Sweet Talker*, "Bang Bang" also appeared on Ariana Grande's album *My Everything* (2014), which was No. 1 on the Billboard 200. Because of the trio's popularity, "Bang Bang" debuted at No. 1 in the U.K. and went platinum. It also reached the Top 10 in Belgium, Bulgaria, Canada, Denmark, Finland, Ireland, Israel, the Netherlands, New Zealand, Scotland, and South Korea. By November 2017, the song was RIAA-certified six-times platinum in the United States. "Bang Bang" was team-written by Max Martin, Savan Kotecha, Rickard Göransson, and Nicki Minaj. Martin, Göransson, Ilya Salmanzadeh, and Kuk Harrell produced the song.

A high-energy R&B and soul-infused dance song in quadruple meter (four beats per measure), "Bang Bang" incorporates hip hop elements such as synth-produced beats, hand claps, and rapping. The song's structure is as follows: instrumental intro; verse 1 (trifurcated); refrain (bifurcated, repeated); verse 2 (trifurcated); refrain' (bifurcated, repeated); rap interlude (trifurcated); singing interlude; refrain" (repeated four times and used as the outro). The very brief intro in C minor consists of a bass guitar riff, which is quickly followed by a jam block or tom beats and a trumpet; the last functions like an exclamation point for the riff.

Jessie J is featured belting in verse 1. Her vocal melody consists of pitches from the C-minor blues scale (C, D, E-flat, F, G-flat, G-natural, B-flat, C) along with blue notes (bent pitches). In the first part, the same electric guitar riff with toms and trumpet exclamation point that cued her in for the intro now answers her. Jessie J's raspy and booming voice is then accompanied by more tom beats (mostly left speaker) and combinations of four-to-the-floor (on the beat) and eighth-beat hand claps (in between and on the beat). In the second part, the riff initially drops out. Here, Ariana Grande's lower breathy, more sexualized and elongated vocals join in; together, their vocal delivery is slow and syllabic (one syllable per note). More resonant sounding toms dominate the accompanying beats, along with claps. The riff returns as a concluding tag to this part. Jessie J and Ariana Grande continue singing in the third part, this time returning to the bluesy vocal melody of the first part. Both voices are divided by an octave, blending well together, with Jessie J's voice (with a delayed effect) singing the high part and Ariana Grande singing the lower part. Snare drums replace the toms but then drop out by the end of the verse. Another structural detail is now revealed in the song: each verse contains a smaller aba' form, meaning that the melody labeled as a (mentioned earlier here as the first part) repeats as a' (third part) with new lyrics, and it sandwiches a different sounding b melody (second part). A drum roll concludes the verse.

The refrain's first chord is C major, the parallel major of C minor; its raised third scale step (E-natural instead of E-flat) is mainly responsible for the comparatively brighter sound. In the first part, Jessie J sings the refrain, joined in unison by backing female vocals in the foreground. Their melody outlines the C-major chord in the first part. Throughout the refrain, these vocals are boosted by more female backing vocalizations (singing, for example, "ahhhhh" and "hey!"), which serve as tags for the end of some of Jessie J's lines. The second part features Jessie J as she returns to the C-minor blues scale. Also in the first part, horns are added, accompanied now by snare, tom, and kick drum beats, as well as hand claps and bass. In between the first and second parts, a new cosmic-sounding siren effect emerges in the background. The claps, which begin on the beat (four-to-the-floor) shift to eighth-note claps (separated on left and right speakers).

Verse 2 initially features Ariana Grande, who is quickly joined by harmonizing female backing vocals, including Jessie J's. The same mini-form and instrumentation used in Jessie J's verse 1 reappear. Ariana Grande mimics Jessie J's soulful style, and is joined on some lines by Jessie J, who uses vocalizations, including hiccupped syllables, to give the verse more energy than the first one. Like the first verse, the second and third parts feature Jessie J and Ariana Grande in a duo; however, this time the second part ends on two breathy lines, creating a "shhhhh" sound. Like verse 1, this verse ends with Jessie J and Ariana Grande singing together an octave apart, but this time, Jessie J adds high-pitched "hey!" vocalizations. The same refrain returns.

The rap interlude features Nicki Minaj, who raps a chopper-style braggadocio half-verse against eighth-note claps in the first part. Jessie J's vocables and the bass guitar riff and horn exclamation point are used together as stingers at the end of some of Nicki Minaj's lines. Her lengthier flow and shift to old-school lines mark the beginning of the second part, and the eighth-note claps shift back to four-to-the-floor. Here, the toms also return, and the stingers are replaced by backing female vocalizations ("ahhhhh!"). In the third part, Nicki Minaj's rap ends with her chanting, spelling out "Bang Bang" old-school style ("B, to the A, to the N to the G . . .") and harmonized with Jessie J's hiccupped spelling in the background. Snare drum strikes replace the previous beats.

The instrumentation comes to a halt for the song's only singing interlude, Jessie J's brief four-measure *a cappella* (unaccompanied) solo. The same drum roll that kicks off the other refrains reappears. The final refrain is a higher-energy, extended iteration. Repeating four times, it is used as the song's outro. The same instrumentation as earlier is used, but this time Jessie J's vocalizations enhance every line, making it clear that the song is a vehicle for her to showcase her vocal abilities. As before, the four-to-the-floor claps shift to eighth-beat claps in the second iteration. Ariana Grande joins in, followed by Nicki Minaj's spoken-word tags. Laughter is heard and then all the instrumentation stops during the Jessie J-led second part of the final iteration. In the middle of her last line, a final "ahhhhh!" and horn exclamation point suddenly conclude the song.

After her third studio album and "Bang Bang," Jessie J released a fourth one, *R.O.S.E.* (*Realisations, Obsessions, Sex, and Empowerment*, 2018), which was a further stylistic move to R&B, as well as her first Christmas album, *This Christmas Day* (also 2018). As of 2021, she has sold more than 20 million singles and 3 million albums worldwide. In 2016, Ariana Grande appeared as host and musical guest on *Saturday Night Live* to market her R&B-infused third studio album, *Dangerous Woman* (2016)—her first album to top the U.K. chart. Her next two albums, *Sweetener* (2018) and *Thank U, Next* (2019), exhibit a more experimental style. *Sweetener* won a Grammy for Best Pop Vocal Album, and she became the first solo artist to hold the top three spots on the Billboard Hot 100 simultaneously, with "Thank U, Next" (2018), "7 Rings" (2019), and "Break Up with Your Girlfriend, I'm Bored" (2019); the first two hit No. 1, and the latter peaked at No. 2 on the Billboard Hot 100. In 2017, Nicki Minaj surpassed Aretha Franklin for having more songs chart on the Billboard Hot 100 than any other female artist. She has also turned her attention to philanthropy.

MATEO KINGMAN: "SENDERO DEL MONTE"
ALBUM: *RESPIRA* (2016)

Ecuador is one of the most ecologically friendly nations in the world, as exemplified by its most popular current hip hop singer, spoken-word artist, and rapper, Mateo Kingman (1991–), member of the rap crew EVHA (a.k.a. El Viejo Hombre de los Andes, or the Old Man of the Andes, 2014–). Kingman's solo debut was in 2016, with the album *Respira*, on the pioneering Latin American label ZZK Records. His lyrics, usually in Spanish, examine life and spirituality in the rain forest, and his music fuses traditional Latin American sounds with hip hop, rock, pop, cumbia, bolero, and street party music, all created with both modern and Andean instruments. His songs are informed by chanting as much as rapping. His instrumentation uses a combination of African drums and traditional instruments from the Ecuadorian Pacific, sometimes run through a synthesizer. In other words, he is a study in contrasts, with music that fuses hip hop with Andean rhythms and electronica, and lyrics that connect urban concerns (his grandfather migrated to Ecuador from Philadelphia) with the natural world and nature-based mythological belief systems.

Respira's first track, "Sendero Del Monte" ("Mountain Trail") is a song about finding oneness with nature. Here, Kingman narrates a realization he had while hiking in the mountains. In his vision, he becomes more animal, yet more aware of his humanity. His mind becomes like water, and he becomes part of the air. The song's lyrics, written by Kingman himself, represents the Earth as almost a lover, and the mountain as the place where a singer can find his voice. He also invites his listeners to join him by taking their own natural journeys. Kingman and Ivis Flies (Ivis Cuesta, ca. 1975–), a Quito-born, award-winning producer known for his work in rock, folklore, jazz, and funk, produced "Sendero Del Monte." Flies's other projects include folklore-based recordings that promote the culture and sounds of Ecuador.

"Sendero Del Monte" is entirely in G minor and quadruple meter (four beats per measure). The song alternates between two chords: E-flat minor (vi, or E-flat-G-flat-B-flat) and G minor (i, or G-B-flat-D). The structure of the recorded song is as follows: intro; verse 1 (trifurcated); verse 2 (trifurcated); bridge 1; refrain (twice); verse 3 (trifurcated); verse 4; bridge 2; refrain' (three times); outro (bifurcated). Although it has a clear, observable structure, there are short melodic passages that appear as the third parts of verses 1, 2, and 3. These are free-form sounding, for they do not resemble one another. In contrast to Kingman's rapping in the first two parts of each verse, he sings these third parts. The lyrical content of each third part is thematically connected to the previous parts of their respective verses—so, rather than standing alone as separate parts, these sound more like ways to conclude each verse. (Another way of hearing this structure is with the verses as bifurcated, followed by melodic extensions.)

With this structure clearly in mind, Kingman generally uses variations in live performances of the song. On stage, his instrumentation relies heavily on his use of keyboard synthesizers, drum controllers, and a soundboard, though he is often accompanied by a live drummer who places (and plays) indigenous drums within the instruments in his drum set.

The song's intro begins with a male low tenor singing "oooooh" in his falsetto range, sounding as if he is in an echoing cavern or canyon. A second track with the same voice emerges a moment later, harmonizing *a cappella* (unaccompanied) with the first track. To create this cavernous-sounding atmosphere in the studio, a lot of reverb is applied to the vocals; to achieve the same sound during live performances, Kingman uses pre-recorded vocals. Before the intro concludes, a keyboard-generated kick drum enters to set the beat.

The first and second parts of verse 1 feature Kingman's talk-singing, using an almost monotone delivery, which makes his voice evocative of religious or sacred chant. Digital keyboard synth-generated and acoustic instruments join in to give the rhythm section an indigenous Ecuadorian, and thus traditional Andean, flavor. The beats, which emerge and mark the beginning of the first part of verse 1, sound like a combination of kick drum and *bombo* (an indigenous South American bass drum), with rim strikes on a *tinya* or *caja*, both snare-range drums. Rattles (shakers) soon join in, initially sounding like an effect, though they become incorporated in the beats. Altogether, these instruments create a low-fi sound that straddles the sound between indigenous beats and industrial ones—this aspect underscores the song's message about escaping the city into nature. The rattles most closely resemble the *chajchas*, which are made from hollowed-out goats' hooves, yet they also possess a chiming sound. Rattles or shakers (both idiophones) are used not only in traditional Andean music, but also within shamanistic Andean cultures: a shaman (a medicine man who is also considered sacred for his ability to heal) will use chajchas and other kinds of rattles, such as ones made of seeds, in rituals and ceremonies. Other instruments that accompany Kingman's (as shaman) talk-singing include finger-picked acoustic guitar and electric bass (in live performances, these are synth-produced). In verse 1, two parts that contain four lines each (which vary in length so the phrases are asymmetrical) are heard first, with the second part marked by Kingman's new flow, punctuated by his own backing vocalizations. After Kingman sings his couplet in the third part, the chajchas enter the foreground, accompanied briefly by the indigenous-sounding beats, which conclude the verse. The third part's melody and lyrics appear only once.

Verse 2, like verse 1, is trifurcated, with Kingman talk-singing in the first and second parts and singing more melodically in the third. This time, however, the first part has more reverb, using the same cavernous backing vocals heard in the intro. Like the first part of verse 1, there are only four lines. The second part of verse 2 differs from that of verse 1 by having breathier vocals and being two lines long. Kingman sings a new melody with new words in the third part. The melody, unrelated to the third part of verse 1, contains three lines and is slightly longer. Bridge 1 follows, resembling the end of verse 1 by its placing the chajchas in the foreground, accompanied by the beats. The acoustic and bass guitars drop out and do not appear in the bridge, which creates the bridge's sparser texture. The cavernous male vocals, this time chanting, reappear toward the end of the bridge.

The refrain returns to the verses' fuller texture (and a return of the guitars). A snare drum with a lot of applied reverb establishes the refrain's four-to-the-floor beat, which sounds more industrial or urban-inspired than the indigenous bombo with tom beats that alternate with it. Kingman's brief Millennial Yodel (see the entry on BTS, although here the yodel takes the form of "oh-oh-oh-ohhh") kicks off the most melodic and memorable passage of the song. His voice is multi-tracked as he sings to the mountain trail about looking for his love, his "*canario*" (canary) or his "*pajáro*" (bird), two words that connote song. Again, the chajchas and indigenous-sounding beats that briefly conclude the verses also conclude the refrain.

The first and second parts of verse 3 use the same vocal delivery and trifurcated structure as verses 1 and 2; however, the chajchas compete with Kingman's talk-singing, as they play against the tom and bombo beat with synth bass. The first part contains six lines, ending with a new, slowly oscillating cosmic-sounding synth voice that resembles a sine wave. It is quickly followed by a loud, crashing percussion strike, which takes the place of strings typically used in a stinger. This new synth and dramatic effect underscores Kingman's sixth line, an invitation for listeners to cross into the forest. The second part also contains six lines, but the length of the lines remains uneven. The synth and tom beat drops out by the third part, leaving just the chajchas and bombo that softly accompany Kingman's three sung lines. A lot of reverb and delay are applied to Kingman's singing here. His voice echoes, sounding as cavernous as the male backing vocals heard in the intro and bridge 1. At the end of this verse, sustained synth-produced string voices (mostly left speaker) emerge and continue into the final verse.

In contrast to the previous verses, verse 4 just has one part, and it therefore sounds truncated. This verse resembles the first part of the previous verses. As the sustained synth strings and indigenous-sounding beats continue, Kingman talk-sings the first three lines, then raises his pitch and sings the last line, which creates a segue into bridge 2. The acoustic guitar reappears prominently (right speaker), backed by electric and bass guitars (left speaker), as the beats continue against Kingman's echoing vocables. Both guitars continue into the final iteration of the refrain, which repeats three times. Just before the final repetition, a track of Kingman's previous vocals that sing the Millennial Yodel accompanies his lead ones. These vocals continue into the first part of the outro, now in the foreground, accompanied by the acoustic guitar, synth strings, electric bass guitar, and bombo, tinya, and chajchas beats. The vocals fade and then stop. The synth electric bass guitar and tinya suddenly drop out, marking the beginning of the outro's second part. The song concludes with Kingman's vocables, accompanied by a four-to-the-floor bombo beat with chajchas and sustained synth strings. The second part brings a sonic shift, because it is filtered and sounds as if the music is moving away as it continues to fade out.

In 2019, Kingman released his second album, *Astro* (*Star*), another collaboration between Kingman and Ivis Flies that fuses hip hop with electronica—but incorporates more trap. As in *Respira*, Kingman approaches his songs as a source of healing and spiritual exploration. The songs of *Astro* draw connections between earthly beings and the cosmos, and narrate tales of the fine line between the sacred and spiritual (with a small "s").

K'NAAN: "TAKE A MINUTE" (ALBUM VERSION)
ALBUM: *TROUBADOUR* (2009)

Somalia-born Canadian singer and rapper K'Naan (Keinan Abdi Warsame or Keynaan Cabdi Warsame, 1978–) is a socially conscious rapper-lyricist. His "Wavin' Flag" (2009) was originally written for the Somalian people to inspire their fight for freedom, and it reached No. 2 on the Canadian Hot 100. "Wavin' Flag" was re-released twice in 2010: once by Young Artists for Haiti and as a remix recorded for use as Coca-Cola's promotional anthem for the 2010 FIFA World Cup, hosted by South Africa.

K'Naan came from a musical family. His aunt, Magool (Halima Khaliif Omar, 1948–2004), was a traditional Somali singer known for patriotic songs during the Ethio-Somali War (a.k.a. the Ogaden War, 1977–1978), and she sang to him, becoming his earliest exposure to poetry and lyric writing. However, the Somali civil war (1989–) led to the suppression of music and the exile of musicians. By the time he reached age 13, in 1991, he and members of his immediate family had moved to Toronto, Ontario, Canada. To help himself learn English, K'Naan memorized rap lyrics and studied patterns of internal and end rhymes. He began writing and rapping while growing up in one of Toronto's toughest neighborhoods, focusing not only on his experiences during the Somali civil war, but also his experience as a Somali immigrant often exposed to his new home's street violence.

K'naan, whose texts favor English but who also raps in Somali, has achieved international fame not only as a rapper, but also as a poet, multi-instrumentalist, and philanthropist who fuses hip hop with indie, R&B, neo soul, Ethiopian jazz, traditional Somali music, and afro beats. His warm singing style and use of positive-message rap is comparable to that of Chance the Rapper. His four studio albums are *My Life Is a Movie* (2004), *The Dusty Foot Philosopher* (2005), *Troubadour* (2009), and *Country, God, or the Girl* (2012). *Troubadour* charted internationally, peaking at No. 32 on the Billboard 200 and No. 7 on the Canadian Albums chart. His texts and musical choices were strongly influenced by Nas, who tied autobiographical storytelling about his urban upbringing to positive messages in versatile ways.

From his album *Troubadour*, "Wavin' Flag (Celebration Mix)" and "Is Anybody Out There?" were both Music Canada certified platinum singles and made him the most famous Somali rapper in the world; however, the song that is most representative of his array of talents is "Take a Minute," in which K'Naan uses his voice in a variety of ways that include singing, sing-jaying (more melodious toasting than the usual monotonous sound of toasting), talk-singing, and rapping, in addition to spoken word. The lyrics tie his social consciousness to his personal life—specifically lessons of forgiveness and thoughtful quiet taught him by his mother. "Take a Minute" was released as a promotional single for *Troubadour* (its twelfth track). It features K'Naan's down-to-earth, gentle, yet nasal-sounding low tenor voice.

Entirely in D-flat major and quadruple meter (four beats per measure), the song's structure is as follows: refrain (bifurcated); verse 1 (quadfurcated); refrain (bifurcated); verse 2 (quadfurcated); refrain (bifurcated, extended); instrumental interlude; spoken-word interlude; refrain (bifurcated); outro (bifurcated; an extension of the previous refrain plus a repeat of the refrain's second part). "Take a Minute" begins with a sparsely textured refrain, which features K'Naan's gentle, nasal low tenor singing voice, accompanied by acoustic piano. In the refrain's first part, the latter instrument plays the ostinato, which gets used in both the background and at times in the foreground. The melodic pattern here (B-flat, C, D-flat, then G-flat, A-flat, B-flat) is played against a persistent harmonic pattern. The acoustic piano plays the chords G-flat major-A-flat major-D-flat major, followed by G-flat major-A-flat major-B-flat minor (or D-flat major: IV-V-I; IV-V-vi; here, I or the home chord alternates with vi, which is a typical substitution chord for I). This gospel music-influenced harmonic pattern gives the song its uplifting sound. In the second part of the refrain, the song's other gospel-influenced element, also used in soul music, appears: the organ's sustained notes support and add more intensity to K'Naan's sung melodic hook and message: "I'm just gonna take a minute and let it ride / I'm just gonna take a minute and let it breeze." The refrain's message is a simple one, that with knowledge comes the understanding that we know less than we think, and we don't understand pain at all, which requires that we take a minute to think about acceptance and the point of life.

In verse 1, the organ disappears, but the synth-produced bass that carries on the melodic ostinato (B-flat, C, D-flat, then G-flat, A-flat, B-flat) joins the acoustic piano. The beat consists of snare and tom drum sounds that are muffled with a sub-bass through a filter. Verse 1 features K'Naan combining talk-singing, rapping, and sing-jaying about pain, suffering, and survival. In the first part, he considers the plights of great leaders like Mandela and Gandhi, which leads to the second and third parts in which he mentions his mother and how much she suffered from racism and war, at one point requiring hospitalization. She beat death, forgave her attackers, and returned to raise K'Naan and teach him about giving and forgiveness. At the end of the third part, a descending electric guitar-sounding synth effect is used as a concluding tag. In the fourth part of verse 1, a synth-produced horn voice is added, and a chorus of backing vocals is introduced, singing higher harmonies against the ostinato (D-flat, E-flat, F). For a brief moment, this dense texture drops out, concluding with K'naan's voice against acoustic piano and then a drum set is introduced, which enhances the synth-produced beats throughout most of the rest of the song.

In the return of the refrain, more instruments are added, such as a cymbal ticking along with the beat, sustained synth-produced strings, and yet another gospel and soul music element, tambourine. The other accompanying instruments from verse 1 also continue, creating a much denser texture than heard in the opening refrain. The backing chorus (which may be thought of as another gospel element) returns in the second part of the refrain, singing D-flat, E-flat, F. The lower instruments answer the chorus with G-flat, A-flat, B-flat (with chords played by an acoustic piano's left hand and broken chords in the right hand). The chorus and lower instruments therefore create a call-and-response pattern out of the ostinato. The chorus then answers its D-flat, E-flat, F with D-flat, E-flat, D-flat, reinforcing D-flat as the home pitch and key. By the end of this second iteration of the refrain, a delay is applied to K'Naan's singing voice, which may be detected on the right speaker.

Verse 2 parallels the first verse instrumentally, as well as with its quadfurcated text. K'Naan also returns to combining talk-singing, sing-jaying, and rap. This time, however, a new arpeggiated and distorted ARP-like synth voice replaces the acoustic piano chords. With a new synth-created air loop or muffled sweeps (resembling turntable scratches), this new voice plays a call-and-response accompaniment against the ostinato. The addition of these new voices with the ostinato gives the first and second parts of the verse a bouncier feel than earlier (in the video single, these synth voices are placed in the background). K'Naan starts by talk-singing and rapping about Somalia. In the third part of verse 2, after recognizing Senegalese-American rapper-songwriter Akon for collecting awards for recording covers, K'Naan identifies himself and that he represents his home city and country, Mogadishu, Somalia. The electric guitar-sounding synth tag from verse 1 returns as a tag in this section and continues by doubling with the bass ostinato. K'Naan then combines sing-jaying with more melodious talk-singing on the word "homie," which repeats. He separates himself from Akon and others by pointing out that he draws from his horrible experiences in Africa. By the fourth part, the two synth voices disappear; the texture tapers off and becomes briefly sparse again, concluding with just K'Naan, acoustic piano, the synth-produced bass doubled with the electric guitar synth voice, and beats. Here, K'Naan takes a moment to thank Africa for making him who he is. The subsequent refrain is similar to the second iteration, most strikingly bringing back the sustained synth-produced strings. It ends with a short extension with K'Naan's multi-tracked voice singing a descending *melisma* (adding several notes to one syllable) on "breeze" and thus elongating the word (also giving a quick instance of word painting or musically depicting the meaning of "breeze").

An instrumental interlude follows and creates a quieter, more sparsely textured passage. It features an electro-acoustic guitar's broken chords, still reinforcing the ostinato and accompanied by synth-produced bass and beats. This use of a brief, comparatively gentler acoustic guitar passage in a hip hop song pre-dates Childish Gambino's song "This Is America" (2018), which is discussed in a previous Must-Hear Music entry in this book. Toward the end of the instrumental interlude, the synth string returns and concludes the melodic phrases. This instrumental interlude segues into K'Naan's spoken-word interlude. The acoustic guitar remains, but is now part of the background with its broken chords (in the song's music video, this instrumental space is filled with K'Naan's making a metatextual statement that he decided to replace a third verse with a spoken word message).

K'Naan comes to the realization that he needs to be a messenger, in his case making sense out of and finding beauty in heinous situations. In this spoken-word interlude, he continues this lesson on acceptance, embracing that the world is imperfect, living in the moment, and being in the wonderful position now of getting to give back. As the instruments pause, the last word of his spoken-word message is echoed and panned from left to right, then back to the left speaker. The refrain returns again, using the cymbal ticks and crashes as well as tambourine to enhance the beats. This time, the choir emphasizes the home pitch by singing D-flat, E-flat, F, then D-flat, E-flat, D-flat during the second part. In this second part, the electric guitar-sounding synth voice returns, doubling with the bass and sub-bass.

The outro starts out as an extension of the refrain, with the choir initially in the foreground singing the pitches of the ostinato as "yeahs," this time ascending with the pitches D-flat, E-flat, F and now answering themselves by descending with G-flat, F, D-flat, also reinforcing D-flat as the home pitch by returning to it repeatedly. The bass remains, but the sub-bass and electric guitar-sounding synth voice briefly drop out. K'Naan speaks over the choir one last time, followed by singing the second part of the refrain, as the choir continues singing its part. Some backing vocalists add vocalizations in the background while K'Naan sings for the last time. The song concludes with a cymbal crash from the drum set, followed by a tambourine shake.

K'naan has won many awards, including Juno Awards for Rap Recording of the Year for *The Dusty Foot Philosopher*, Artist of the Year (2010), and Single of the Year for "Wavin' Flag" (2011). In 2011, he visited Somalia and wrote an opinion piece in the *New York Times Sunday Review*. Since the 2012 release of *Country, God, or the Girl*, K'naan has not recorded an album. In 2016, HBO picked up his pilot for *Mogadishu Minnesota*, directed and written by K'naan. As of 2021, K'naan is still the most famous Somali rapper; his plans are to return to recording.

LITTLE BIG: "SKIBIDI"
ALBUM: *ANTIPOSITIVE, PT. 2* (2018)

Like Black Eyed Peas (discussed earlier in a Must-Hear Music entry in this book), St. Petersburg, Russia's Little Big is a hip hop and electronica rap and dance group. The 2019 lineup of this electro-rave hip hop band and performance artist, founded in 2013 by Ilya Prusikin (1985–) and video director Alina Pasok (ca. 1989–), includes Prusikin, Sergey Makarov (1982–), Sonya Tayurskaya (1991–), and Anton Lissov

(1989–). Two other female vocalists, Olympia Ivleva (1990–) and Anna Kast (1982–), both quit the band. Little Big released the first of its four full-length albums, *With Russia from Love*, in 2014, following the success of its debut single, "Every Day I'm Drinking." With the song "Skibidi" (2018), Little Big became an Internet sensation. Its absurdist video, which ends with a dance-off a la Michael Jackson's "Beat It" video and a dancing Godzilla, had more than 527 million views as of 2021. It not only went viral but also spawned a "Skibidi" dance craze and dance challenge.

"Skibidi," a fairly innocuous sex song written by Prusikin and producer Lubim (Lyubim Khomchuk, 1991–), is the second track on *Antipositive, Pt. 2* (2018). Also released (along with various remixes) as an EP, it debuted at No. 1 on Tophit in the Russian Commonwealth. "Skibidi" uses a four-to-the-floor groove, meaning that each beat in quadruple meter (four beats per measure) is accompanied by a drum beat. The song's structure is as follows: intro (bifurcated); verse; refrain; instrumental bridge; verse; refrain; interlude (bifurcated); second interlude; refrain (repeats and is used as the outro). "Skibidi" is entirely in A minor. Musically, it is extremely well crafted, which balances its ridiculous refrain lyrics, which are a parody of scatting consisting almost entirely of nonsense words and vocables (e.g., "skibidi," "ua-pa-pa," "boom," and "ay") that are combined in various patterns. Each of these words is also assigned a synth voice (e.g., a distorted squeeze toy, a frog croak, a dog bark), and these synth voices appear and disappear throughout the song. In its instrumental section, the synth voices are used instead of vocals for two instances of the refrain (the first time unaccompanied, the second time with a beat). Instead of fading out during the final repetition of the refrain, animal sounds end the song abruptly.

The intro's first part also features an animal sound, a synth-created rooster crow that is clipped abruptly into a sonic match via pitch with the song's central melodic instrument, a synthesizer (using a calliope voice), which plays a repetitive four-phrase passage that contains a caesura between each iteration (which both throws the listener off and creates a point of interest, as well as leaving room for remixers to add sounds). The entrance of this synthesizer voice marks the second half of the intro and establishes the home key. It emphasizes the pitch E (the fifth of an A-minor chord), first moving up a half step to F, then moving down to B, the latter creating an unexpected yet playful dissonance. A descending scale using the pitches A, G, F, and E concludes each second instance of this melody. The accompanying groove is a simple synth bass and snare beat, with a percussion voice in the background that sounds like a cross between snaps and drumsticks played against each other. All instruments except the melodic synth voice continue into the first verse, which is introduced by a caesura (caesurae actually occur at every transitional point in the song). Verses are sung by Tayurskaya, whose tinny and nasal yet breathy mezzo-soprano voice is auto-tuned and pitch-altered to sound girlish, doubled, and robotic, which is highly ironic given the verses are about a "booty call." Her lines are tagged by sounds and vocalizations (e.g., phone clicks and female voices sighing "ah," "unh," and "ooh").

The same instrumentation is carried into the refrain, scatted aggressively by Prusikin's low tenor vocals with little or no auto-tuning. Refrains feature the aforementioned nonsense vocals, with words (the only exception being "ua-pa-pa") doubled (seemingly randomly) by their assigned synth voices. An instrumental bridge that is based on the second part of the intro with its high-pitched synthesizer melody leads into verse 2. Both verse 2 and the second refrain mirror verse 1 and the first refrain musically, followed by the aforementioned two instrumental interludes and the song's outro. The first interlude is related to the intro, using another high-pitched synthesizer voice that replaced the rooster's crow in the first part, then including a pause, and employing more animal sound effects in the second part. The heaviest beat of the groove returns, marking the second interlude, which also consists of the high-pitched synthesizer and animal sounds. This time, the animal sounds continue, accompanying the entire refrain and its final repeat, which serves as a grand finale, featuring virtually all the synth voices that have been used in the song, which combine and exhibit a sense of complexity and fun. The song concludes on a dog bark and frog croak.

Little Big's song "Uno" was chosen to represent Russia at Eurovision 2020 in Rotterdam, but the event was canceled due to COVID-19. Overall, the band considers itself a satirical art collective whose main target is Russian stereotypes. It is often compared to another band which satirizes local stereotypes, Die Antwoord (also discussed in this book's Must-Hear Music section), the band for whom Little Big opened in its first concert appearance. Little Big has its own label, Little Big Family, which produces Little Big, The Hatters, Tatarka, Khleb, and Lizer.

M.I.A.: "PAPER PLANES"
ALBUM: *KALA* (2007)

Sri-Lankan (Tamil) and English rapper, hip hop artist, visual artist, and activist from Hounslow, a borough in West London, M.I.A. (a.k.a. Maya, Mathangi Arulpragasam, 1975–) incorporates elements of hip hop, dance, electronica, and world music into her songs, many of which are concerned with political and cultural activism. As a six-month-old, M.I.A. experienced first-hand the political upheaval in Jaffna, Sri Lanka, where her family lived in poverty. Her father became a Tamil activist, marking him for death, so when she was 10, she and her siblings were moved to London as refugees.

Originally a visual artist, M.I.A. got her start in the music business after designing cover art and producing videos for the London-based band Elastica and Canadian alternative hip hop, electropunk, and dance-punk musician Peaches (Merrill Nisker, 1966–). Peaches encouraged her to start making music with a Roland MC–505, which M.I.A. used to record a demo tape. Before signing a record contract, her 2003 song "Galang" (Jamaican patois for "Go On") earned her a large following online. In 2005, M.I.A. signed to a label and released her first album, *Arular*. Featuring MC-505 beats and sequences, the album is a mix of dance and hip hop, with inspiration taken from Tamil film and Indian music. *Kala* (2007), her second album, was supposed to have been recorded in the United States but ended up being recorded in different locations around the world after she was denied a visa. Its songs are infused with an array of traditional dance and folk elements from Trinidad, India, Liberia, and Jamaica—set against M.I.A.'s politically charged lyrics about immigration and war. "Bird Flu" (2006) was the first single released, followed by "Boyz" (2007), "Jimmy" (2007), and finally "Paper Planes" (2008), the track that was the most commercially successful from the album, hitting No. 4 on the Billboard Hot 100 and being RIAA-certified triple platinum. It also hit the Top 10 on the Canadian Hot 100, peaking at No. 7.

A snap song, "Paper Planes" is a satire that plays on the right-wing stereotypes of migrants. Produced and co-written by Diplo (Thomas Wesley Pentz, Jr., 1978–), the song features a liberal sampling of the intro keyboard voices of "Straight to Hell," The Clash's 1982 song from *Combat Rock*. Written by Joe Strummer, "Straight to Hell" satirizes right-wing views on immigrants through a narrator-singer who comes across as inhumane and cruel (Joe Strummer wrote the song as a response to the right-wing views of his brother David, who was a member of the Neo-Nazi National Front). M.I.A.'s lyrics are peppered with various clues that make it clear she is portraying the more ridiculous claims that right-wing conservatives make about immigrants: they sit around all day making fake visas, get rich once they immigrate, take jobs from citizens, behave violently and lazily (using weapons and taking hits off of bongs), sell drugs, do heroin, make themselves "poison for the system" (a reference to both the aforementioned heroin and the anti-Semitic trope about Jewish blood polluting Christian lineage), and have children who just want to steal.

Like "Straight to Hell," "Paper Planes" is a downtempo song in quadruple meter (four beats per measure). The music video of "Paper Planes" was filmed in Bedford-Stuyvesant, a New York neighborhood infamous for street violence and organized crime yet nevertheless famous for being the home of many hip hop pioneers and innovators; it was censored by MTV for its cannabis reference and the gunshot sounds in its refrain, which features singing by immigrant street children from Brixton, England. The video accentuates the song's satire, as it juxtaposes images of immigrants working hard to sell food, jewelry, videos, magazines, and similar exotic products to appreciative Americans, juxtaposed against lyrics that position immigrants as thieves, drug dealers, and murderers.

Entirely in D major, the song's structure is as follows: instrumental intro (bifurcated); verse 1 (bifurcated); verse 2 (bifurcated); refrain; verse 3 (bifurcated); verse 4 (bifurcated); refrain; bridge; verse 5 (bifurcated and truncated); refrain; instrumental outro. "Paper Planes" is in the same key as "Straight to Hell" and borrows the latter's pulsating synth ostinato and electric bass accompaniment. This ostinato is heard at the very beginning of the intro's first part. Also like "Straight to Hell," an added kick drum beat and the entrance of a synth-produced sub-bass mark the intro's second part.

The synthesizer-produced ostinato (mostly left speaker) in "Paper Planes," however, is fuller and deeper sounding, with a more prominent electric bass guitar (right speaker). But by verse 1, the synth voice disappears and is replaced by synth-produced strings as the bass carries on. This ostinato simply repeats the pitches D, C-sharp, and G (scale steps 1, 7, and 4 in D major). Overreaching, by descending from D to G instead of A (scale step 5), gives a brief sense of dissonance throughout the song, which works well at underscoring M.I.A.'s message of frustration and discontent. This dissonance, however, is carefully placed in the background, layered underneath other sounds yet still detectable (examples of it can be heard at the end of each part of the bifurcated verses, as well as in the refrains).

In addition to M.I.A.'s chant-singing, which is in the foreground, accompanied by the synth-produced strings, the kick drum beat continues, and snaps appear (high-pitched and low-pitched snaps double on both speakers with some applied reverb). This instrumentation is consistent throughout the song's refrains and its verses; however, subtle and less aurally detectable details are added to the song's beats as well as its vocal production (such as an added sixteenth note in the kick drum on the last beat of the third measure of verse 1 and the slight delay applied to M.I.A.'s voice at the beginning of verse 3 to create a sense of off-kilter or disconcerting reverb). M.I.A., a mezzo-soprano, uses sing-song vocals that are nasal and slurred (though not to the degree of mumble rap), while also breathless. Lines begin as soon as previous lines end. Her vocal pattern in verses 1, 2, and 4 has two long lines that descend in pitch, with the next two (both shorter and employing *staccato* notes—detached pitches) ascending, sometimes to the point of making her voice break. This is usually followed by one long line that descends again and concludes a thought. Verses 1, 2, and 4 also share the same bifurcated pattern. M.I.A.'s dispassionate lead vocals and purposefully limited range are part of the song's dark humor.

The refrain features additional percussive sound effects: four gunshots followed by a cash register ring. Children's vocals are also heard, repeating the right-wing stereotype of immigrants four times: "All I wanna do is take your money." Here, the aforementioned sound effects are heard in the foreground, breaking up this line into the following: "All I wanna do is / [4 gunshots and cash register, with the word "and" on the register sound] / and take your money." The satirical imminent threat of immigrant violence is none too subtle.

Verse 3, which follows the first refrain, is characterized by M.I.A.'s lengthier lyrical flow. Here, her words are elongated, even though the instrumentation, including the doubled snaps, is the same as in verses 1 and 2. In verse 3, M.I.A. uses a rising inflection on odd-numbered lines and a downward tick in vocals on even-numbered ones. Verse 4 follows and is related to verses 1 and 2 through its instrumental accompaniment and M.I.A.'s vocal delivery. It is followed by a second iteration of the refrain.

The bridge starts out as an instrumental one, featuring the intro's pulsating synth voice and electric bass guitar. M.I.A.'s spoken-word vocals begin, now accompanied by kick drum. Here, M.I.A. talks partly as braggadocio and partly as a political statement, as she readies her listeners for verse 5. As in verse 3, M.I.A. uses elongated words and a lengthier lyrical flow than in verses 1, 2, and 4. This playful sing-song verse, however, is truncated: instead of being comprised of several lines with a bifurcation created by repeating the first line, it is created by M.I.A.'s simply singing and repeating a couplet. Here, interpretation of lyrics becomes essential, and sources disagree on what exactly M.I.A. sings in verse 5. The beginning of the couplet sounds like the lines "some-some-some-I some-I murder," with her voice descending on this line but ascending on the beginning of the next one, giving a sense of playful upspeak as she

136 Listen to Hip Hop!

hints at what seems to be gangsta activity. Here, her voice is doubled on both speakers with a slight delay, making her voice on the right speaker more prominent than that on the left one.

The third and final iteration of the refrain follows, transitioning into the instrumental outro. This section concludes with the synth-produced ostinato and previously heard snaps (the latter now has applied delay). Toward the very end, the synth oscillates more, creating a sense of warbling, though not quite *tremolo* (a quick alternation between two pitches), which is reminiscent of the sound of the ostinato used in "Straight to Hell," though introduced originally here. This ostinato is set solely against the song's snap beat, giving the ending a sense of sadness—a pleasing juxtaposition with the song's tongue-in-cheek tone.

M.I.A. has since released three more studio albums: *Maya* (2010), *Matangi* (2013), and *Aim* (2016). An iconoclast, M.I.A. has never shied away from shocking people into sensibility. The video for the single "Born Free" (off of *Maya*), for example, was considered a too explicitly violent and controversial video about genocide, but M.I.A. and its director Romain Gavras again collaborated on the video for the *Matangi* single "Bad Girls." Filmed in Morocco, the video for "Bad Girls" featured women in traditional Middle Eastern clothing performing car driving tricks, such as spinning and skidding across the desert. In 2015, M.I.A. released the song "Borders," which is about the struggles and stereotypes faced by migrants and refugees.

M.I.A.: "P.O.W.A."
NON-ALBUM SINGLE, 2017

Although M.I.A.'s "Paper Planes," discussed previously, was more successful and popular, "P.O.W.A." better represents her typical musical style, which is EDM (electronic dance music), with elements of electronica, reggae, R&B, alternative rock, and hip hop (both grime and rap). Other examples of her more typical style are her song "Galang" (*Arular*, 2005; originally released as a single in 2003), which uses synth drums and an ARP synth-based voice, as well as distorted hand claps, giving it a midtempo dance EDM feel; and "Bird Flu" (*Kala*, 2007), which employs world music percussion instruments such as Tamil (specifically, Gaana) *urumee* drums (double-headed drums made from goat hide), and a shawm. "Bird Flu" has elements of industrial and noise music and has an aggressive EDM feel.

M.I.A., a mezzo-soprano, has influences that range from Missy Elliott and Timbaland to the Pixies, from the Beastie Boys and Public Enemy to A. R. Rahman and Björk. She uses various styles of vocal delivery that range from aggressive rapping and chant-rapping to spoken word, talk-singing, and singing. An additional influence comes from punk rock; thus she favors using very little studio post-production manipulation of her vocals, opting for a natural sound. This approach allows for vocals that have a nasal twinge, vocal breaks and grinding, vocal fry (forcing the voice downward and into a creaky sound, often at the end of spoken or sung phrases), and singing that is slightly off-pitch or pitchy. Using music as social activism, her multilingual lyrics touch on identity politics, poverty (the working class in London), revolution and war, gender and sexuality issues, and a more personal political interest, Tamil independence. Despite the popularity of her stances, her lyrics and political statements led to the United States' refusal to grant her a travel visa. From 2006 until 2016, U.S. Homeland Security had her on its security risk list, mainly due to her politically charged lyrics. "P.O.W.A." contains some lyrics that appear to be a reaction to this designation.

M.I.A.'s 2017 non-album single "P.O.W.A." was produced by New Orleans-based, Miami bass-influenced Kid Kamillion (Bryan Normand, ca. 1985–). Here, he uses a distorted and rearranged sample of the scatting intro to the hit doo-wop version of Rodgers and Hart's "Blue Moon" (1961) by The Marcels (1959–1962). The letters P.O.W.A. reference the late 1970s People Opposing Women Abuse (POWA) movement in Africa, while also serving as a stand-in for the word "power." Basically a feminist braggadocio/defiance song, its central image is that of giving those in authority the middle finger. Its lyrics, full of astutely rhymed pop culture references that mention Barack Obama, Osama bin Laden, Monsanto, Rihanna, Madonna, Mariah Carey, and Ariana Grande, call out critics/haters, and establish M.I.A.'s musical dominance.

"P.O.W.A." uses the pitch E as its pitch center, emphasizing it mostly through a sample of the intro of "Blue Moon," sung by The Marcels' bass singer Fred Johnson (1942–). "P.O.W.A." speeds up The Marcel's sample, transposing it from E-flat major up a semitone to emphasize E, which makes Johnson's deep bass voice sound more like a low tenor (as well as thinner). The looped sample's use of E as a pitch center sounds like a drone, while simultaneously feeling unstable, as if it is going to be resolved, which it never is—this sound is jarring for listeners familiar with The Marcels' recording, where the introductory melody descends from E-flat to A-flat, the song's home pitch. The emphasized E in P.O.W.A. does not sound like a home pitch, but rather the fifth scale step above the goal pitch (A in "P.O.W.A." and A-flat in "Blue Moon").

After listening to the loop continuously, it becomes easier to discern another frequent pitch, B; the loop therefore presents constant fluctuation but never any tonal arrival. M.I.A.'s vocal melody, however, gives the sense that E is the home pitch. There is no sense of the song being in a major or minor key.

The song structure of "P.O.W.A." is complex and challenging. Typically, refrains differ from verses by being entirely repeated (using the same text and music). In "P.O.W.A.," however, the first verse is used like a refrain. An added complexity is that the intro, as well as many of the verses, including the refrain-like verse (or verse-like refrain), have two or more parts. Our interpretation of the song structure of "P.O.W.A." is as follows: intro (quadfurcated); verse 1 (A, bifurcated); verse 2 (A′, bifurcated); verse 3 (A″, bifurcated); verse 1 (A, truncated); bridge 1; verse 4 (A‴, bifurcated); verse 5 (A⁗); bridge 1′ (truncated); bridge 2 (bifurcated); middle-eight (B, bifurcated); bridge 3; bridge 4 (bifurcated); bridge 1″; verse 6 (A⁗′); verse 1 (A); outro. This interpretation takes into account that verse 1 (A), which repeats like a refrain, functions more strongly as a verse, especially given that verses 2 and 3 (A′ and A″) sound so much like this verse, share the four-plus-two phrase structure that makes these verses sound bifurcated, and have lyrical content that is thematically connected. Typically, refrains tend to be the most memorable part of a song, not only because of their repetition but also because they have the catchiest melodies. Here, verse 1 does repeat like a refrain; however, it does not stand out because the same vocal melody is used elsewhere, and its verse-like attributes keep it from sounding as catchy as a refrain.

Bridge 1 is a short passage used repeatedly in an expected way: going somewhere, including to another bridge such as bridge 2, which includes phrases and sounds different from the other verses. Unexpectedly, bridges 3 and 4 also contain text but are more concerned with sound than with meaning (M.I.A. uses vocables, for example, in bridge 3 and nonsense words in bridge 4). Bridges 3 and 4, which are verse-like due to their sound if not their phrase structures, could be viewed as verses of an entirely new song section, or together they may be taken as an interlude, since here M.I.A. scats, thus using her voice more like a musical instrument.

Exploring the song's sounds, the first part of the intro of "P.O.W.A." starts *in medias res*—it immediately starts in the middle of the "Blue Moon" intro sample. A hiccupping beat is created by this sample's being sped up (pitch altered), distorted (clipped and rearranged), and repeated (looped). In The Marcels' recording, the scat intro starts with the vocable "bom," followed by some labial plosives and nonsense words that start with the letter "b," and these soon shift to the vocable "dang" and some dental plosives and nonsense words that start with "d." But in "P.O.W.A.," the dang/d vocables, repeated and clipped (i.e., "d-d-dang, d-d-dang, d-d-dang, d-d-dang dang"), are first heard in the intro, followed later by the bom/b vocables, also repeated and clipped (i.e., "b-b-bom, b-b-bom, b-b-bom, b-b-bom bom"). Furthermore, the hiccupping dang/d vocables are heard in the first four phrases and the bom/b ones are heard in the second two phrases of the bifurcated verses. This pattern of alternation continues as a loop throughout the song. Not all verses are bifurcated or the same length, so the four dang/d plus two bom/b phrase accompaniment pattern is at times broken off, creating an off-kilter sound. For example, the first return of verse 1, which is truncated and only contains the first four phrases, uses only the bom/b accompaniment, whereas bridge 1, which follows, uses only the dang/d.

In all parts of the intro, beats accompany these vocables. In the first part, synth-generated drum kit sounds (on the tom and snare end) and hand claps, as well as a beat that resembles a tambourine or *chimta* (a South Indian percussion instrument, an idiophone shaped like tongs that have metal jingles) are the consistent rhythmic accompaniment. Adding to the beat are male vocalizations in the low tenor range (the *bhangra*-beat "hey!" call). After a brief break in the loop, a separate baritone voice, singing "dup dup, doh" (with the long "o" sound elongated), slides upward, for the second part of the intro. Grunts and growls (some human-sounding, some animal-sounding) are used here to punctuate the beat. The second part closes the same way as the first. The intro's third part uses more reverb and a more prominent sub-bass drone, made to sound expansive and resembling a thunder drum. The looped sample emerges, followed by M.I.A.'s whispering about making a million dollars and an electronic chiming effect that resembles a cell-phone notification. All accompaniment pauses as a distorted, slightly robotic male voice says "power." The fourth part restarts the sample on bom/b initially, with a lot of reverb applied, as well as a sub-bass drone. M.I.A.'s whisper and the cell-phone notification repeat, now more prominently placed in the foreground.

Set against the intro's accompanying instrumentation (with one exception: the bom/b vocable combination becomes more prominent than the dang/d one), M.I.A. half-chants, half-sings her verses, starting with the first part of verse 1. Her nasal delivery is unprocessed (other than minimal multi-tracking to make it sound fuller), her voice allowed to crack and wander off pitch (again, much like in punk music). From this point on, the instrumentation stays mostly consistent, with little change between verses, bridges, and the outro beyond the alternation between the dang/d and bom/b parts of the looped sample. To offset the monotony, sections have uneven phrases and, more notably, M.I.A. changes her vocal delivery often, during and in between verses and refrains, including their parts. For example, she cuts her vocals off short in the second use of the A part of verse 1, creating a brief instrumental interlude where growls and distorted words (e.g., "power") are heard. M.I.A. hints at some autobiographical details on how others see her as causing drama in the first three verses, where she also takes a jab at the Monsanto Corporation and anyone who would farm for it. In verses 4 and 5, she directly counters these negative perceptions of her by mentioning how she is actually thoughtful and benevolent. She also directly mentions the FBI's watching her and brushes off the problem of not being allowed to tour and make money in the United States by claiming that she doesn't need it.

In contrast to bridge 1, which uses materials found in the first part of the intro and places the looped sample in the foreground, bridge 2 includes M.I.A.'s voice, changing her chant-rapping flow to statements with rests interspersed between her phrases as her instrumental accompaniment continues in the first part. The accompaniment pauses, and in the second part of bridge 2 she scats to answer herself. In the first part of the B verse (which can be heard as a middle-eight), M.I.A. uses the same-sounding chant-rap heard in bridge 2. In the second part, she shifts to scatting, which continues in bridge 3 and into bridge 4. In the first part of bridge 4, M.I.A. chants a politicized wordplay on "supercalifragilisticexpialidocious" (the word "racist" can be clearly understood) from the American film musical *Mary Poppins* (1964), and in the second part, she speaks. Bridge 1″ leads to a return of the music of verse 1. In verse 6, M.I.A. suggests that she is more powerful than Rihanna, Madonna, Mariah Carey, and Ariana Grande. The first part of verse 1 returns, and the outro follows. Here, the same instrumentation as the intro is used but with more alternation in the looped sample's vocables. As the song moves toward its end, a lot more reverb is applied to the sample. Once again, M.I.A.'s whisper and the cell-phone notification appear. The song ends on the booming sub-drone, a thunder drum-type effect that is heard in the third part of the intro.

M.I.A. directed the highly acclaimed music video for "P.O.W.A." in India. The video focuses mostly on her, initially riding on a flower-filled pickup truck bed, dressed in a floral jumpsuit and wearing a veil, then appearing in a sari with a sleeve marked M.I.A., standing or walking on an unpaved gravel road, and sitting on cliff rocks. It also features a chorus of male dancers in the same uniform and hats, standing together and passing various versions of a "wave" back and forth. M.I.A. also directed the video for "Borders" (released on *AIM*, 2016), a song about the plight of refugees escaping persecution in their home countries and being turned back. The video contains haunting imagery of refugees (instead of actors, she used people she met on the streets) climbing a border fence to spell out "LIFE" with their bodies, wearing drab clothing and positioned (standing and crouching on an arid, sand-filled landscape) to form a human sand sculpture of a ship, with M.I.A. as its jibboom and/or figurehead, and refugees lying shoulder to shoulder on a boat, filling every inch of space, with M.I.A. also sitting among them. Many of the vocal techniques mentioned earlier, such as vocal fry, are also heard in this song.

In 2007, *USA Today* named M.I.A. one of the 100 Most Interesting People of the year, and *Esquire* listed her as one of the 75 Most Influential People of the 21st century. In 2009, she was cited in *Time* magazine as one of the world's most influential people. In 2010, *USA Today* listed M.I.A. in its 100 People of 2010 list. *Rolling Stone* had also named her one of the artists who defined the 2000s in popular music.

MIX MASTER MIKE (FEATURING DJ QBERT): "COSMIC ASSASSINS"
ALBUM: *SPIN PSYCLE* (2001)

Turntablist Mix Master Mike's (Michael Schwartz, 1970–) signature sound includes a heavy dose of bass and intricate, extremely quick, and precise two-turntable scratch routines, including what became known as the *tweak scratch*, which involves suddenly stopping the turntable's platter motor to change pitch while scratching. In his live performances, his speed and precision separate him from other turntablists, as does his showmanship: for example, he will throw a behind-the-back scratch into the middle of a routine, or pick up and bend his vinyl record while scratching, or use a wah pedal (intended for electric guitar). His solo albums include *Needle Thrasher III* (1997), *Anti-Theft Device* (1998), and *Bangzilla* (2004), and one of his EPs, *Eye of the Cyklops* (2000), is considered a classic of turntablism.

Mix Master Mike and DJ Qbert (Richard Quitevis, 1969–), both San Francisco-born turntablists and producers, met during a DJ battle held in a high school cafeteria. The two have been good friends and frequent collaborators ever since, beginning with their 1990 formation of the group FM20, with DJ Apollo, an anonymous turntablist who would later co-found Buckshot LeFonque and Triple Threat. Legendary hip hop dancer Crazy Legs (Richard Colón, 1966–) invited FM20 to join the b-boy Rock Steady Crew, and they adopted the name Rock Steady DJs. In 1989, DJ Qbert, Mix Master Mike, and DJ Apollo co-founded the Filipino-American hip hop DJ collective Shadow of the Profit, which soon became the award-winning Invisibl Skratch Piklz. In 1992, Mix Master Mike became the first West Coast DJ to win the DMC World DJ Championships and, in 1993 and 1994, he and DJ Qbert won the DMC championships as a duo. By 1995, the two had become judges at the event, which is still considered the highest honor among turntablists.

Mix Master Mike's "Cosmic Assassins" features DJ Q-Bert, who originally released the song on *Wave Twisters, Episode 7 Million: Sonic Wars within the Protons* (1998), an album that inspired the first turntablist-based musical film, an animated feature of the same title. DJ Qbert's "Cosmic Assassins" is a collage of samples that includes Herbie Hancock's "Suite Revenge" (1974), Beatmaster's "Lipservice" (1984), Dynamix II's "Feel the Bass" (1988), Bobbi Humphrey's "Please Set Me at Ease" (1975), "Destruction of Death Star I" from *Star Wars Episode IV: A New Hope* (1977), KRS-One's "I Got Next/Neva Hadda Gun" (1997), Fab 5 Freddy and Beside's "Change the Beat (Female Version)" (1982), Big Audio Dynamite's "BAD" (1985), Venom's "Live Part One" (1991, an unofficial release that was recorded in 1986 at City Gardens in Trenton, New Jersey), "Blastin' on Fools!" from *Murder Was the Case: The Movie* (1995), and Wade Denning and the Port Washington's "It's about Time" (1966). The most notable nerdcore element found in the song is the use of samples from *Star Wars Episode IV*.

Mix Master Mike's version of "Cosmic Assassins" appears on his DJ mix album *Spin Psycle*. Though the intros of the two versions start off differently, Mix Master Mike uses the same samples as DJ Q-Bert throughout his version and adds some more to the composition. Both recordings share the same structure. "Cosmic Assassins" does not have a key, but Mix Master Mike's version immediately uses the pitch A^1 in the bass and sub-bass, which serves as a home pitch or tonal center. Sometimes the basses will move up a half step to the neighboring B-flat, but they always return to the home pitch. Although the song consists of samples and turntablism, a structure can nevertheless be heard as follows: intro (bifurcated); bridge 1; section 1 (trifurcated); interlude 1 (trifurcated); bridge 2; section 2 (trifurcated); interlude 2; interlude 3 (bifurcated); section 3 (trifurcated); bridge 3; outro (trifurcated, with the first part of section 1, bridge 1, and a modification to section 1's conclusion). The logic behind thinking of the structure this way is that the main sections place the samples in the foreground, whereas the interludes feel more instrumental, with turntablism becoming a focus (these serve as turntablist jams). The bridges are so designated here because they are brief passages that clearly take the listener to a section.

In the bifurcated intro's first part, Mix Master Mike adds another sample to those used by DJ Q-Bert: a sped-up excerpt of the horn-section fanfare of Blood Sweat and Tears' (1967–) hit "Spinning Wheel" from their eponymous album (1968). The horns' chords lead into a sampled file of a male hype man and a heavy bass, doubled with booming sub-bass hiccups that assert A as the home pitch. The second part features combinations of turntablist scratches such as *baby scratches* (the foundational forward then backward scratch) and *tears* (two pushes forward and a pull back), followed by some *chirps* (a crossfader-applied high-pitch scratch). The words "get set up," sampled from "Death Star I" are cut and hiccuped repeatedly as a second spoken-word line from "Death Star I" appears in the background. The context of this sample suggests that one should get ready for a battle; however, "get set up" is also being used like a metatextual vamp, which typically cues in the main performer. Meanwhile, the second part establishes an eight-beat loop that gives the section its sense of beats. The intro reaches a break as the "get set up" line is dropped long enough to reveal the complete sentence, "get set up for your attack run." The intro's basses and turntable scratches drop out in bridge 1, which, as in DJ Qbert's original, consists of hi-hat cymbal strikes (left speaker) from "Suite Revenge," followed by brief tom strikes, Humphrey's "Ooh," and warped-sounding jazzy acoustic piano chords from "Suite Revenge."

Section 1 reintroduces the basses and the eight-beat rhythmic loop, which now accompany a media file of actor Ricky Harris's spoken-word line as an eyewitness, "Blastin' on fools!" During the first part, the line is hiccuped. A new sample from "Change the Beat (Female Version)" enters the foreground in the second part, which features a robotic voice and some sonic firing from "Death Star I." Here, turntable chirps double the robotic voice and take over the foreground, accompanied by continuing eight-beat loops. An unintelligible sample of a woman's voice concludes this section.

Interlude 1 showcases elaborate combinations of turntable scratching and more *beat juggling* (alternating and maintaining turntable loops or scratching patterns between two or more turntables at the same time). Some of the turntable sounds that appear in the foreground include forward and backward baby scratches, tears, and *flares* (both can be performed backward and forward to create triplet sounds with the use of a crossfader), as well as *transformers* (hiccupped-sounding turntables that sound like scratching with skips). The entire duration of interlude 1 is accompanied by the same eight-beat loops that appeared in section 1. These also continue into bridge 2, which features faster turntable scratches that accompany a new sample, the line "go ahead" from "BAD" (originally sampled from the 1966 Great Britain television marionette-science fiction adventure show *Thunderbirds*).

The bass and turntable loops continue in the background in section 2, which features the line "sit yo a** in the back" from "I Got Next/Neva Hadda Gun" in its first part. Turntable scratching re-emerges in the foreground in the second and third parts, initially with *stabs* (short, detached, high-pitched scratches that are quickly executed by using a crossfader or fader) and then folding in lengthy scratches that sound punctuated by horns. A brief psychedelic production detail is heard here as the scratches are panned from left to right speaker. Section 2 ends with a kick drum break by having the basses drop out completely, applying reverb to the turntables, and using a media file of a man saying "got it."

Interlude 2 is another lengthy turntable solo. It stands out for its lack of bass. It contains a new loop consisting of synth-produced snare hits and toms. The bass's absence gives the sense that this is the most distorted turntablist solo; the entire solo seems to be at a higher pitch than the rest of the song. It ends abruptly and is followed by a more elaborate turntablist solo in interlude 3. Here, the earlier basses and beat loops reappear. Lengthy scratches, approximating a thin brass section, alternate between high and low pitches in the first part. The rhythm of the scratching changes in the second part, which features a hiccupped sample of "Change the Beat's" computer and robotic sounds as well as some left-right-left panning of the turntable scratches. Interlude 3 ends with turntablist chirps that sonically match the sample, the same technique used in the second part of section 1.

Section 3 places a sample of Venom's lead singer and bassist Cronos Lant saying, "you're wild, man" in its first part. This is accompanied by the basses and looped beats, which continue into the outro. The second part features a sample of a commercial from "It's about Time." The third section quickly alternates two samples from "Beatmaster" and "Feel the Bass." Bridge 3 briefly places turntable scratching in the foreground and leads to the outro.

Initially, listeners may think that the outro is just a reiteration of section 1; however, the outro suddenly concludes by copy-pasting bridge 1's hi-hat and discordant piano chords as its second part, followed by a

Must-Hear Music   145

sample of a woman's indistinguishable voice that was also heard at the end of section 1. This time, so much reverb and distortion are applied to the sample that her words become even more unintelligible. The song ends abruptly here.

In the early 2000s, DJ Qbert worked with The Vestax Corporation to develop the QFO, an all-in-one scratching instrument that combines a turntable with a mixer's crossfader. In 2006, he introduced the Qbert turntable cartridge, which stresses the mid-range frequencies of active sound to help cover up wear-and-tear sounds that are caused by scratching. At the 2016 DMC World DJ Championships, he was awarded a DMC Legend jacket. In 2013, Mix Master Mike had the honor of being the first turntablist to perform at the John F. Kennedy Center for the Performing Arts for the Kennedy Center Honors. At the awards, he was involved in a performance of "Rockit" (1983) to honor Herbie Hancock. Mix Master Mike has also appeared in various television venues, ranging from the sublime (performing for the Vancouver Winter Olympics in 2010) to the ridiculous (remixing the theme song "Puffy AmiYumi" for *Teen Titans Go* and performing in 2010 on the children's show *Yo Gabba Gabba*, for its "Cool Tricks" segment). Mix Master Mike was also known for his tenure with Beastie Boys (1978–2012), working on their later albums such as *Hello Nasty* (1998), *To the 5 Boroughs* (2004), and *Hot Sauce Committee Part Two* (2011). In 2012, along with Beastie Boys, Mix Master Mike was inducted into the Rock and Roll Hall of Fame.

NICKI MINAJ: "ROMAN HOLIDAY"
ALBUM: *PINK FRIDAY: ROMAN RELOADED*

At age 5, Onika Tanya Maraj (1982–) came to Queens, New York, with her mother. Artistically gifted, she successfully auditioned for the prestigious Fiorello H. LaGuardia High School of Music and Art and the Performing Arts as an acting major. Incorporating her drama and music background with her love of wearing provocative fashion and penning equally compelling lyrical content, she quickly became one of rap's most successful and critically acclaimed female acts. Releasing sexually graphic mixtapes, she launched her career as video vixen and rapper Nicki Minaj. Her rapid-fire flow—filled with wordplay and clever, humorous, sometimes hyper-sexualized imagery (used for songs about sex, for bragging rights, and for diss tracks)—combined with her electrifying videos full of colorful costumes (including multicolored dyed hair and wigs), have earned her a large fan base and popularity both as

Nicki Minaj combines rapping, spoken-word, talk-singing, and singing, using a variety of personae. Her Pink Friday Tour in 2012 showcases these talents as well as her flair for drama and fashion. (Michael Bush/Dreamstime.com)

a soloist and as a featured rapper. Her solo album *Pink Friday* (2010) became RIAA-certified three-times platinum; *Pink Friday: Roman Reloaded* (2012) and its follow-up, *The Pinkprint* (2014), were both certified double platinum. Two songs from *The Pinkprint*, "Anaconda" and "Only," reached No. 1 on both the Hot Rap Songs and the Hot R&B/Hip-Hop Songs charts.

Generally, Nicki Minaj's rap flow varies between chanting, carefully pronounced mid-tempo rapping, and speed rapping, at times approaching chopper style. Her lyrical concerns include braggadocio (skills bragging and diss tracks about other rappers), sex/romance, and ethnic minority and feminist issues. Stylistically, her raps are based on sharp-witted wordplay and the occasional use of internal rhymes and near-rhymes, although she relies heavily on old-school style rapping in her mid-tempo raps (sing-song lines, lots of end rhyme, lots of repetition on the ends of lines). Regardless, she is consistently an aggressive, in-your-face rapper who pulls no punches.

Her album *Pink Friday: Roman Reloaded* can best be described as electronic post punk rap. One of its best songs, "Roman Holiday," is expertly produced by BlackOut (Winston Thomas, n.d.), credited as BlackOut Movement. The song is a combination of self-study, diss rap, and dramatic personae depiction with a couple of modern and postmodern compositional techniques. For example, she uses *bitonality* (two keys at the same time) and the mashup or post punk aesthetics. In short, "Roman Holiday" is a high-energy, creative, and complex mix of instrumentation and production, against which Nicki Minaj, a flexible mezzo-soprano, sings with a pronounced lilt; its rapped verses showcase her various styles and voices (as personae).

"Roman Holiday" starts out in E-flat major, but its key is primarily in the relative minor, C minor. Most of this song centers on the relationship between these two chords. Although it is entirely in quadruple meter (four beats per measure), at times the predictability of the beat and *tempo* (the speed of the song) rely more on Nicki Minaj's interpretation and expression than on consistency. The song's structure is as follows: refrain (trifurcated); verse 1 (A, quadfurcated); refrain' (trifurcated); verse 2 (A', quadfurcated); refrain' (trifurcated); middle-eight (B, trifurcated); verse 3 (A", trifurcated and truncated); refrain" (extended). Nicki Minaj sings this song in her Martha Zolanski persona, who addresses her son, Roman Zolanski, one of Nicki Minaj's most used personae.

"Roman Holiday" begins with its trifurcated refrain. In the first part, it uses sparse instrumentation of just a synth-produced organ voice that doubles Nicki Minaj's punk-style singing. Her delivery is aggressive, consciously lilting, and slightly off-key, with playful elongated syllables at the end of lines. Her voice is somewhat raspy, including when she initially sings as Martha Zolanski in her high register; however, by the second part, she sings in a husky low register to produce the male-voice responses of her Roman Zolanski character, who represents her anger. The sense of beat is most erratic here, giving preference to Nicki Minaj's dramatic expression rather than strictly following an expected, consistent rhythm. Synth-produced cosmic effects also emerge in the second part; these sound like laser guns and punctuate the rest of the refrain. The third part features her returning to her Martha Zolanski voice, accompanied by 808 snare drum beats, setting the stage for the harsher-sounding beats that are to come in verse 1. Nicki Minaj uses her hardest, almost comic lilt and elongation on the final syllable of the word "holiday," which brings the first refrain to C minor, the key of verse 1.

In contrast to the sung refrain, verse 1 features Nicki Minaj speed-rapping in her low register as Roman Zolanski. During the first part, she is accompanied by frenetic congas with a lot of applied reverb, 808s, and synth bass stingers, all of which are punctuated by cosmic sound effects such as laser gun shots. In the second part, her speed-rapping continues into its most braggadocio lyrical content. The accompanying instrumentation, however, changes. Though the beats and tempo are the same, the conga beats are replaced with drum machine-produced typing beats (approximating drumstick hits). These are soon joined by machine-produced drumstick hits that appear on the right speaker and are slightly delayed. In the third part, the conga beats and synth bass stingers return and are then quickly switched out with the second part's accompaniment. The cosmic sound effects return in the fourth part, which ends comically with Nicki Minaj's vocalized sonic laser gun effect as a tag. The refrain', now modified, returns. This time, it includes a new loud and melodramatic synth-based string voice that suggests the continuation of C minor. Nicki Minaj's phrases, however, still end on E-flat major (III of C minor), and the third part repeats the harmonic movement from E-flat major to C minor as her elongated notes descend (sliding down from the pitch E-flat to C). Her vocals are accompanied by synth bass and a heavy hiccupped 808 snare drum beat.

The quadfurcated verse 2, in C minor, uses the same accompaniment pattern as verse 1, though the text and Nicki Minaj's vocal delivery, flow, and use of vocals are different. As Roman Zolanski again, she is now backed by a humming female chorus. The reverb applied to their hums resonates against the synth bass stingers and conga beats of the first part. Minaj uses spoken-word vocals (she insults haters with the repeated word "b****") and then quickly switches to a speed-rapped line in the second part that threatens her critics with war, which leads into the rapped part of this verse. As the conga beats and synth bass stingers return in the third part, she switches to using huffy, stuttering chant-rapping, which is multi-tracked with applied reverb. The second refrain' reappears.

The middle-eight features Nicki Minaj singing in her Roman Zolanski voice, which is multi-tracked with a lot of applied reverb in the first and second parts. Here, she sings a parody or mashup of the traditional Christmas song "O Come All Ye Faithful"; however, despite using the "O Come All Ye Faithful" text, her melody begins with the first vocal line of another song played often at Christmas, Franz Schubert's "Ave Maria" ("Hail Mary"), D. 839 (a.k.a. Op. 52, No. 6 or "Ellens dritter Gesang" ["Ellen's Third Song"], 1825) before she actually sings the "O Come All Ye Faithful" melody. Originally composed in B-flat major, the melody is transposed to C major in "Roman Holiday" and set against the C-minor-sounding synth bass stingers, accompanied by conga beats, that initially play in the middle-eight's first part. The congas are now more separated with delay applied; these give way to the typewriter-sounding beats with drumsticks and conclude with an ascending cosmic sound effect. The second part repeats but now consists of conga beats and synth bass stingers accompaniment as well as the typewriter and drumsticks beats. More synth-produced cosmic sound effects appear, and by the end of this part, her voice becomes shaky. In the third part, she repeats the same melody but this time it is sung in her own singing voice rather than in character. Here, the typewriter beats are folded in as the conga beats and synth bass stingers and cosmic effects continue. In all three parts, her lyrical content suggests that her skills deserve worship.

Verse 3, also in C minor, is trifurcated and truncated. Here, Nicki Minaj returns to her husky-voiced chant-rap as Roman Zolanski. The three parts use the same instrumentation as verses 1 and 2, but the fourth part is missing. Instead, the refrain″ returns and gets used as the outro. The instrumentation is the same as the repeat of the refrain′ but slightly extended. The 808 beats are louder, and Nicki Minaj is accompanied by the synth strings as well in all three parts. After the third part and her final sliding descent from the pitch E-flat to C, the song ends abruptly on the echoing sound of a synth-produced slamming effect.

Nicki Minaj continues to release albums and singles that perform well on the Billboard charts. After *The Pinkprint*, she released *Culture II* (2017) and *Queen* (2018). From *Queen*, "Fefe"—her collaboration with 6ix9ine (Daniel Hernandez) and Murda Beatz (Shane Lee Lindstrom)—reached No. 3 on the Billboard Hot 100. In 2020, the song "TROLLZ," her collaboration with American rapper 6ix9ine, debuted and hit No. 1 on the Billboard Hot 100. Less than a month after its release, "TROLLZ" became RIAA-certified gold. She also continues acting, appearing in *Barbershop: The Next Cut* (2016) and as the voice of Pinky in the animated *The Angry Birds Movie 2* (2019).

NKOTBSB: "DON'T TURN OUT THE LIGHTS (D.T.O.T.L.)"
ALBUMS: *DON'T TURN OUT THE LIGHTS (D.T.O.T.L.)* (EP, 2011) AND *NKOTBSB* (2011)

NKOTBSB was a project-band supergroup that combined members of New Kids on the Block and Backstreet Boys. It featured A.J. McLean (Alexander James McClean, 1978–), Brian Littrell (1975–), Danny Wood (1969–), Donnie Wahlberg (1969–), Howie Dorough (1973–), Joey McIntyre (1972–), Jonathan Knight (1968–), Jordan Knight (1970–),

150 Listen to Hip Hop!

and Nick Carter (1980–). The NKOTBSB Tour was short-lived, starting in May 2011 and ending in June 2012. Of the supergroup's three songs, the single "Don't Turn Out the Lights (D.T.O.T.L.)" became its biggest hit. Featuring singing by nearly all members, it debuted at No. 14 on the U.S. Billboard Bubbling Under Hot 100 Singles. The only member not involved was Backstreet Boys' Kevin Richardson (1971–), who was concurrently pursuing his own solo career and working on his own album, *Cover Story*, which was supposed to be released in 2012 but has, as of 2021, yet to appear.

"Don't Turn Out the Lights" is a breakup song (of the "give it one more chance" variety) composed by Jess Cates, Claude Kelly, and the song's producer Eman Kiriakou. It combines elements of pop (such as lyrical content and form, catchy and simple refrains, and an energetic prechorus) and hip hop dance music (retro-sounding 808 beats, a four-to-the-floor dance sound added at times for dramatic effect, and synth-produced sweeps that vaguely resemble turntable sounds). NKOTB singers, with Backstreet Boys' Carter and Dorough, are most prominently featured, and overall the song is notable for its sparse use of auto-tuning (used only briefly during the prechoruses and refrains). Mostly in E major and in quadruple meter (four beats per measure), the song's structure is as follows: intro (bifurcated); verse 1 (A); prechorus; refrain (bifurcated); verse 2 (A′); prechorus; refrain (bifurcated); middle-eight (B); bridge; refrain (repeats with bifurcation); instrumental outro. It uses a modified pop-oriented AABA form with added prechoruses and refrains. A recording that modifies this structure in a similar way to this one is BTS's "Idol," which is discussed as another entry in this book's Must-Hear Music section.

The first part of the bifurcated intro features a synth keyboard voice in the foreground, with a repeated melody heard in other sections of the song (pitches E, D-sharp, F-sharp, and E over above E major-B dominant$^{6/5\text{-}7}$-E major or I-V$^{6/5\text{-}7}$-I). This progression reinforces both the home pitch and chord by using leading or lower neighboring tones and an upper neighboring tone, and it is the song's most prominent ostinato. In the intro, this ostinato acts as an introductory vamp. The synthesizer continues into the second part of the intro, which now includes Jordan Knight's auto-tuned low tenor background vocals as he sings the song's title. A synth-produced drum beat (creating a heavy use of a snare drum beat with applied reverb to sound like hand claps) kicks in as Wahlberg's low tenor voice speaks the band's name in the baritone range. The intro concludes with an 808-sounding hiccup and a synth-produced sound effect that transitions into verse 1.

In verse 1, low tenors Jordan Knight and McClean take turns singing lines. The synth melody and accompanying chords from the intro continue in the background, along with a new synth-produced bass and a four-to-the-floor kick drum pattern. The prechorus serves as contrast to verse 1 by featuring two softer, muted, and higher tenors, Littrell and McIntyre (starting out with McIntyre's solo voice and then harmonizing together); a new, faster-moving synth accompaniment that oscillates at a higher pitch than the intro; and a beat that uses an occasional 808-sounding quick double-time drum sound when singers trade off. The vocal melody initially begins on B (scale step 5 of E major), but the key remains E major; this home key is reinforced by the ostinato in the accompaniment, which continues from the intro and verse 1. An 808-produced drum flourish kicks in the refrain, harmonized (with some vocal tags as well) by all the group's members against the prechorus instrumentation. The refrain is made to sound fuller with the addition of a melodic synth string voice, cymbal crashes, and lengthier sweeps than used in the prechorus (though employing the same synth voice). After the prechorus's whirring sound effect, which works like a sweep, the refrain begins in B major (V of E major) and offers, albeit briefly, the most significant harmonic shift in the song. Here, the entire group sings, accompanied by the synth and electric guitars. The refrain quickly takes the song back to E major in the first part. The second part features high-pitched descending vocals that take the song back to verse 2, also in E major.

Verse 2 features Knight, Littrell, and low tenor Nick Carter. Carter has the group's most rock-styled voice, employing rasp or vocal grinding. The instrumentation of verse 1 reappears, but with distorted backing vocalizations (words like "yeah" and "ha") added as tags, as Wahlberg's low tenor answers in the background to the lead voices that appear in the foreground. The prechorus returns with the same instrumentation as earlier, though automated clap-sounding beats add some texture and variation to the accompanying beat. The second appearance of the refrain uses the same instrumentation as the first, as well as the high voices found in its second part. This time, in the background, a low tenor emerges, but it becomes interrupted by the middle-eight, in B major.

Dorough, a low and soft-sounding tenor, sings the middle-eight section, which is the strongest sonic contrast, shifting toward quieter, sparser, and less dramatic instrumentation. Cymbal sounds are added to the beat, now with only snare, hand claps, and an occasional 808 sound, and Wahlberg's low tenor voice whispers softly in the background (mostly left speaker). A simple bass ostinato is introduced, which balances a high-pitched but melodic synth string voice. Carter concludes section B with its final rock-sounding line, "till the end, till the end, till the end, yeah, yeah," harmonized with the others from the group. Carter's line concludes this section in E major. Instead of a third A section, a bridge takes place, returning to the synth ostinato and vamp in E major, which were heard in the first part of the intro.

The rest of the song is in the home key, E major. The sparse texture with harmonizing vocals from the middle-eight is prolonged here to help give the last refrain a sense of a big finale. In this bridge, Wahlberg's low voice (right to left speaker) speaks the name of the group, as heard in the second part of the intro. After a caesura and an 808 hiccup, the first part of the refrain returns for a third time and then repeats. The second part concludes with the voice winding down, accompanied by a lengthy synth-produced sweep. The song's instrumental outro is a brief continuation of the synth's ostinato; the outro ends suddenly.

Backstreet Boys had three albums hit No. 1 on the Billboard 200, including *DNA* (2019), as well as three RIAA-certified platinum albums. The group has had six songs reach the Billboard Top 10. New Kids on the Block had four platinum albums, as well as two No. 1 albums. The group had nine Top 10 hits, with three hitting No. 1: "I'll Be Loving You (Forever)" (1989), "Hangin' Tough" (1989), and "Step by Step" (1990). Together as NKOTBSB, the two bands first performed during the 2010 American Music Awards. As a project band, they released one compilation album, *NKOTBSB* (2011), on Sony's Legacy Recordings label. It featured five "greatest hits" tracks from each group and three new recordings by the combined supergroup, including the single "Don't Turn Out the Lights."

FRANK OCEAN: "SWIM GOOD"
ALBUM: *NOSTALGIA, ULTRA* (2011)

Frank Ocean (Christopher Edwin Breaux, 1987–, later legally changing his name to Frank Ocean) is a Long Beach-born, New Orleans-raised singer-songwriter, rapper, record producer, and photographer who began his musical career unlike most hip hop musicians: his mother, a jazz, R&B, and musicals aficionado and album collector, cultivated his love for music. While in high school, he attended concerts and met jazz musicians who encouraged him to start recording. He majored in English at the University of New Orleans; however, he transferred to the University of Louisiana at Lafayette in the aftermath of Hurricane Katrina (2005), which destroyed his family's home and his recording studio. By 2006, he dropped out of college and relocated to Los Angeles, where he flourished as a ghost songwriter for musicians such as Beyoncé, Justin Bieber, and John Legend. He also collaborated with Jay-Z and Kanye West. But he wanted his own recording career and, in 2009, he signed a contract as a songwriter for Def Jam Recordings. But after a lack of support and delays with his progress under the label, he grew frustrated and therefore responded by joining the Los Angeles-based hip hop collective Odd Future. He enjoyed writing songs for the collective and began collaborating often with group member Tyler, the Creator (Tyler Gregory Okonma, 1991–), who was also a singer-songwriter and producer in addition to pianist, music video director, actor-comedian, fashion designer, and visual artist.

In February 2011, Ocean self-released his debut EP, *Nostalgia, ULTRA*, which includes appearances by Tyler, the Creator and another Odd Future member, Hodgy (a.k.a. Hodgy Beats, Gerard Damien Long, 1990–). The album fuses alternative R&B, psychedelic soul, electronica, and hip hop. After he gained traction through a cult following and strong critical acclaim, Def Jam promised to release Frank Ocean's music under its label; however, in July 2011, Def Jam announced that the release would be delayed. In the same month, the label released his first single, "Novacane," which became No. 82 on the Billboard Hot 100 and was eventually RIAA-certified platinum. Def Jam also released his second single, "Swim Good," which was No. 70 on Billboard's Hot R&B/Hip Hop Songs. Despite both songs' success, the label ultimately cancelled the EP. Instead of severing their relationship, Ocean and Def Jam worked to improve it, leading to the album *Channel Orange* (2012); Ocean self-released *Nostalgia, Ultra*.

The structure of "Swim Good" is as follows: instrumental intro (bifurcated); verse 1 (A); prechorus; refrain (bifurcated); bridge; verse 2 (A′); prechorus′; refrain′ (bifurcated); middle-eight (B, bifurcated); refrain″ (bifurcated); bridge′ (repeated and extended); sound effects outro. The structure contains no surprises until its outro, which is unusual for its replacement of music with the natural sounds of seagulls and ocean waves. Frank Ocean, Charles Gambetta (n.d.), and the production duo MIDI Mafia—Bruce Waynne (Waynne Nugent, n.d.) and Dirty Swift (Kevin Risto, n.d.)—co-wrote the song. "Swim Good" showcases Frank Ocean, a low tenor with a wide vocal range, with backing vocals by Tyler, the Creator. Its text is a literal contemplation of suicide as a response to the guilt of breaking a lover's heart (it figuratively or metaphorically expresses a need to escape the relationship). Its lyrics tell the story of a man who has decided he will drive into the ocean, kick off his shoes, and swim away, to escape something "bigger" than himself through drowning. The lyrics express the loneliness and despair caused by being in an emotional rut, and they also hint at the narrator's sense of guilt and remorse for running. Its video by Nabil Elderkin (1982–), which reinterprets the song as a murder-suicide note, was nominated for three MTV Video Music Awards: Best Direction and Best Male Video, with Ocean being nominated for Best New Artist.

"Swim Good" is entirely in A minor and focuses on a four-chord progression that is used as an *ostinato* (a persistent melodic and/or rhythmic pattern that appears throughout a piece): A minor-G major-E minor-F major (or, in the home key of A minor: i-VII-v-VI). The ostinato descends for three chords and then moves up a half step. If the progression sounds familiar, it's because it has been used in numerous popular songs, such as Vanilla Fudge's 1967 hit rendition of The Supremes' Motown classic "You Keep Me Hangin' On" (1966, composed by Brian Holland, Lamont Dozier, and Eddie Holland). Vanilla Fudge gives its song a more desperate feeling by slowing down the tempo and employing the same progression in E minor. Another example is Pat Benatar's new wave rock classic "Love Is a Battlefield" (1983, composed by Holly Knight and Mike Chapman), which uses the progression in D minor. Ocean takes it further in "Swim Good" by turning it into an ostinato; in the contexts of all these song's lyrics, this ostinato may be interpreted as suggesting an ocean—and its repetition and motion (wavelike) keep listeners (as well as the songs' narrators) hanging on. The thematic concerns of love, heartbreak, and suicide are ubiquitous in music. Listeners who have some background in nineteenth-century German art songs will recognize the first image in "Swim Good"—a trunk full of broken hearts—as it recalls the image of Robert Schumann's poet-protagonist's coffin full of sorrows and love. Schumann used lyrics from a poem by Heinrich Heine in the sixteenth and final song, "Die alten, bösen Lieder" ("The Old, Bad Songs") from the song cycle *Dichterliebe* (*Poet's Love*, 1840), Op. 48. Furthermore, the desire to drive into the ocean, suggesting suicide by drowning, is reminiscent of the poet-protagonist's suggested suicide in Wilhelm Müller's text that was used in the twentieth and final song of Franz Schubert's earlier song, "Des Baches Wiegenlied" ("Of the Brook's Lullaby"), from his song cycle *Die schöne Müllerin* (*The Beautiful Miller Girl*, 1823), D. 795.

Ocean's "Swim Good" is entirely in quadruple meter (four beats per measure), and it begins with a bifurcated four-plus-four-measure instrumental intro that features the synth organ playing the ostinato against an intricate combination of drum machine-produced beats: snare drum 808s, hand claps (echoing with some applied delay and added reverb), and a tambourine filtered to sound less jingly and more metallic, resembling the sound of an air loop. The synth bass plays the roots of the ostinato's chords. Together, the beats and ostinato create a funky groove that is also ominous sounding. Toward the end of the intro, the bass quickly drops out as the beats and organ continue, creating a very brief disruption, but all quickly resumes.

The accompaniment, except for the hand claps, continues into verse 1, a bifurcated four-plus-four-measure verse that now features Ocean's R&B-style lyrics, his voice multi-tracked and slightly auto-tuned, with a slight echo effect. Tyler, the Creator is heard at the end of the verse for the first time, singing "yeah" in his gruff baritone voice, which has reverb applied to it. The synth bass drops out, as does the synth organ ostinato in the prechorus, but the beats—except for the claps—continue in this short four-measure passage. The synth organ plays sustained chords to accompany Ocean. Still in A minor, the prechorus builds up anticipation with its sparser texture and melodic stasis. The synth bass and claps return in the refrain (as does the ostinato), but here an acoustic piano replaces the organ. The lower register of the piano (played by the left hand) plays the ostinato (right speaker), doubled by synth bass, while the upper register (played by the right hand) plays chords (left speaker). Ocean's voice here becomes more dramatic, hitting the song's second highest notes as the narrator uses imagery of suicide. The bridge features Ocean's highly auto-tuned and robotic-sounding *scatting* (using his voice like an instrument as he sings vocables or nonsense syllables). Initially, his voice is on the right speaker for two measures, but it then moves to the left for two measures. The acoustic piano (and ostinato), bass, and all elements of the beats but the kick drum and snare strikes drop out. In contrast to his voice, which has a lot of applied reverb, the drums are dry-sounding.

Verse 2 uses the same accompanying instrumentation as verse 1, but there are some differences in the production effects and use of vocals. In the first couple of phrases in the first part, the end of the lines (usually the last one or two words) echo. Ocean's lead vocals are punctuated with his high-register "yeahs" in the first part of verse 2. In the second part, his backing vocals become more complex, with a response sung in a low register contrasted with sung R&B-style "oohs." He uses his falsetto to sing an octave above his lead vocals at the end. The prechorus' returns, this time punctuated by Tyler, the Creator's low "yeah" backing vocals. The refrain' also returns with added backing vocals sung by Ocean. This time, they are multi-tracked, harmonized, sustained vocables that sound like they are played backward (with the decay as a fade-in and ending on an attack), creating a dragging sound.

The middle-eight or bridge, also in A minor, is the song's most dramatic section. In the first part, the groove comes to a complete stop as a synth organ's chord sustains for a moment. The beats continue but without the hand claps and ostinato. The beats, synth bass, and synth organ are placed far into the background. Ocean hits his highest notes in his staccato lines. His R&B and experimental music-style backing vocals—in a lower register, multi-tracked, at times harmonized, and with a lot of reverb—comment on or answer each of his lead vocals' lines. As the first part continues, a hi-hat tick is folded into the beats. By the second part, Ocean's lines are lengthier, and he shares the foreground more with his vocal countermelody, which is sung in his low register with auto-tune applied. In the last measure of this eight-measure section, the instrumentation comes to a pause (right speaker, then moving left) with a sustained chord played by the synth organ. Ocean ends the section by singing *a cappella* (unaccompanied), "waves are washing me," in his high register, with his harmonizing backing vocals. The refrain" also returns with the same instrumentation as earlier but with added vocals. This time, his lead vocals share the foreground more with the same auto-tuned backing countermelody vocals he used in the middle-eight. These vocals harmonize, sing a countermelody, and repeat his words or comment on his lines. The bridge' is twice as long as the earlier one due to repetition. It consists of the same highly auto-tuned scatting, but vocals are now heard on both speakers. The beats continue, along with the hand claps and synth bass, but the acoustic piano drops out and gets replaced by the synth organ. The typical use of a bridge is to lead to another (often more significant) musical passage. Bridges are not expected to fade out—but here it does fade out, giving way to the outro, which contains sound effects only. Seagulls appear, followed quickly by ocean waves, quietly concluding the song.

Frank Ocean's debut studio album *Channel Orange*, which debuted at No. 2 on the Billboard 200, was RIAA-certified platinum, and won the Grammy Award for Best Urban Contemporary Album. Its Grammy-nominated Record of the Year, "Thinking about You" (a.k.a. "Thinkin' 'bout You") was No. 32 and No. 7, respectively, on the Billboard Hot 100 and Billboard's Hot R&B/Hip Hop Singles and has been certified platinum in the United States and gold in the U.K. Another song from the album, "Super Rich Kids," was used in the television show *Gossip Girl* and in the HBO television miniseries *Big Little Lies*. The liner notes for

Channel Orange were going to include Ocean's open letter about being attracted to a man when he was 19 years old, but instead he released the letter on Tumblr blog, thanking that man as well as his mother and others who accepted him. The letter also received a lot of support from the hip hop community. In 2013, Ocean began working on songs for his second studio album. While recording for that album, his rapport with Def Jam crumbled. In 2016, after releasing his visual album *Endless*, Def Jam executives determined that he had fulfilled his obligation to release one more album. During the same year, he released a 360-page magazine, *Boys Don't Cry*, a fashion- and auto-themed publication, and he self- released *Blonde*, which includes further collaboration with Tyler, the Creator and an impressive cadre of hip hop artists and producers that included André 3000, Beyoncé, and Pharrell Williams. *Blonde* was No. 1 on the Billboard 200, as well as in Australia, Denmark, New Zealand, Norway, and the U.K., and was RIAA-certified platinum. In 2017, Ocean published a photo essay titled "New 17" in the British magazine *i-D*. Starting that year and until the end of 2019, he had a Beats 1 radio show, titled *blonded RADIO*, which premiered his new songs, his covers, and other songs performed by musicians. As of 2021, he continues to release charting singles.

PLASTICIAN: "WINDWALKER" AND "TAINTED"
ALBUM: *OVERDUE* (2018)

At the age of 18, a U.K. garage DJ using the stage name Darkstar began to take interest in electronic dance-based hip hop that had an ominous sound. This fascination continued as his act evolved briefly into Plasticman and then into Plastician (Chris Reed, 1982–). Plastician's musical skills developed when he was a member of a community of young producers making dark garage tracks in Croyden, England. Like his colleagues in the Fearless Crew (1999–2002), as well as fellow DJs Skream (Oliver Dene Jones, 1986–) and Benga (Adegbenga Adejumo, 1986–), Plastician used digital music software such as FruityLoops to create hip hop recordings. He sent his tracks to Big Apple Records' South London head buyer and dubstep producer DJ Hatcha (Terry Leonard, 1981–) in hopes that he would play them on his popular pirate radio show Rinse FM (and later his Kiss FM).

By the end of 2001, East London grime pioneer, DJ Slimzee (Dean Fullman, 1978–) discovered Plastician's tracks and signed him (as Plasticman) to the Slimzos imprint. In 2003, DJ Hatcha, impressed by Plastician's grime-infused take on dubstep, signed him, which led to releases on Ammunition Promotions' Soulja and ROAD imprints, as well as a weekly slot on Rinse FM. In 2006, Plastician obtained a slot on BBC Radio 1, which evolved into the show *In New DJ's We Trust*. Two years later, he released *Beg to Differ* (2008), his debut album, on his Terrorhythm Recordings label. It contained some of his most recognizable works, "Japan" and "Intensive Snare." By 2012 and 2013, he was touring the United States and working with EDM icon Skrillex (Sonny John Moore, 1988–), after having worked with rap icons such as Snoop Dogg. During that period, he began to produce dubstep music. His seven-track EP *Overdue* (2018) is an example of this dark dubstep. It includes two standout instrumentals: the panflute-informed "Windwalker" and the g-funk-influenced and steampunk-inspired "Tainted." Both pieces are in quadruple meter (four beats per measure).

Completely in E-flat minor, "Windwalker" uses a structure called *theme and variations* (with the main theme introduced, then followed by variations of it intended to hold listening interest). An intro starts the song, followed by the theme (bifurcated) and its four variations (each extended just slightly in contrast to the original). The variations focus on folding in and layering new sounds, thus creating sonic shifts and diverse textures. The intro begins with thunder, rain, wind, and crickets sound effects, filtered with some added white noise. Soft, high pitches on a synth-produced acoustic piano appear in the background, which builds suspense. A synth-produced Native American flute plays the main theme. This aerophone is called by many names and is played by various Native American people. It is often used in courting rituals. The wind, an overblown sound, is created by a block, usually bird-shaped and tied onto the outside of the flute between the mouth and finger holes. This instrument's most common tuning resembles the Western minor pentatonic scale (a collection of five pitches that use the first, third, fourth, fifth, and seventh steps of the minor scale; here, it would be the black keys on the piano—E-flat, G-flat, A-flat, B-flat, and D-flat). The main tune, however, adds a sixth pitch (F). This synth-produced Native American flute nevertheless sounds like the actual instrument with its overblown timbre and warbles enhanced by reverb.

The theme is initially presented with just the sound effects and synth-piano pitches as accompaniment. Its first part consists of two phrases (two-plus-two measures); its second part answers with two more phrases (one-plus-one measures), followed by a closing phrase that sounds like the end of a sentence (also two measures).

Variation 1 is marked by the replacement of the thunder effect by synth-produced electric bass guitar, which uses the distinctive dubstep wobble sound and 808-sounding snare beats with hiccups that tend to take place at the end of phrases. The wind effect continues, and the synth-produced Native American flute is used again, as it is throughout the rest of the song. In this variation, the phrases are used like melodic modules: rather than directly repeating each phrase using the same sequence as the first time, the first part of variation 1 repeats the first phrase three times, followed by the second phrase just once. The hiccupped beats drop out, and thus fewer beats accompany the second part, which consists of the same phrase sequence as the theme. The dropping-out of these beats gives more focus to the Native American flute's conclusion of this variation.

Variation 2 uses a phrase sequence identical to that of variation 1; however, a new synth string voice emerges to accompany its third iteration of the first phrase. Variation 3 uses the same structure as the two earlier variations, but this time the synth strings disappear along with the hiccupping beats during its second part and use of the main tune's third phrase. Variation 4, the final variation, repeats the theme's phrase structure. Initially, this variation sounds like a repetition with no accompaniment except for the wind and rain sounds; however, echoing hand claps enter during the first part and the final pitch during the second part is hiccupped and echoed. At the very end, the acoustic piano pitches from the intro play softly in the background.

Like "Windwalker," "Tainted" employs the same kind of modular or phrase-focused composition approach. The structure may be thought of as like a theme and variations; however, there is actually no theme. Rather, there are shorter melodies that are prominent here: a synth flute *ostinato* that oscillates and appears in phases and synth strings that sound like the strings used in stingers of horror films, which sustain two or three chords. The song's main compositional focus is on folding in—either subtly or obviously—new sounds as the song progresses. Sounds that suggest the ticking away of time as well as whirring components and other sound effects are layered in as the song continues. "Tainted," in B-flat minor, may be thought of as having an intro and four related sections that break down further into parts. The song's structure is as follows: intro (bifurcated); section 1 (bifurcated); bridge; section 2 (trifurcated); section 3 (quadfurcated; first three parts); bridge; section 3 (last part); section 4 (bifurcated, with the second section serving as the outro).

The first part of the intro consists of eight phases of the oscillating synth flute ostinato with a lot of applied reverb. This ostinato outlines the B-flat minor chord and establishes the home key. As it continues into the second part, a drum kit beat, heavy on the snare and accompanied by an 808 snare drum effect, with hiccups, emerges and becomes the song's g-funk-influenced driving beat.

The first part of section 1 introduces and repeats the synth strings' four-note motive four times. Heavy vibrato is applied to this pitchy melody (starting approximately on E), which marks time like a clock against the continuing ostinato and hiccupped beats. Hand claps with applied reverb are subtly folded into the beats. The second part of section 1 is marked by pitch-bent and sustained chords played by a new bell-sounding synth voice. Also pitchy, the chords sound like B-flat major and create an unsettling dissonance against the ostinato (still emphasizing B-flat minor). The chords are also now backed by a synth-produced bass and sub-bass. The chords repeat three times, enhanced by sustained synth strings and resembling a tone on an alarm clock. The synth flute ostinato returns to the foreground in the bridge as the continuing beat accompanies it. Both continue into the first part of section 2 but now accompany the four-note synth string motive, which slowly pans from the left to the right speaker. The ostinato stops just before the second part, a reappearance of the bell-like chords (repeated twice). Here, new hiccupping mechanical percussive effects are added. Although less vibrato is applied to the chords than during their first appearance, the chord texture is denser, with more pitches added. This time, the chords are played twice and share the foreground with a new oscillating synth voice (repeating E, E-flat, D) that sounds like a combination of flute and recorder. The third part features three repetitions of the sustained chords but slightly softer and at a lower pitch. This time, the synth flute ostinato reappears as accompaniment. The beats shift to an 808-produced downtempo beat, slightly deeper in pitch than earlier, with occasional hollow-sounding 808 bass along with the previous 808 snare effect with hiccups. The synth bass and sub-bass also reappear along with industrial hammering percussive effects.

Section 3 is the song's lengthiest passage. Its first part employs the four-note synth string motive against the synth flute ostinato and the beats heard at the end of section 2, including the hammering effects. All drop out in the second part as the chords repeat twice. Hiccupped beats appear after the second iteration of the chords. The third part serves as the song's climax, as it quickly shifts into double-time, with faster and higher-pitched beats accompanying just one iteration of sustained chords. The same synth flute voice used for the ostinato only has enough time to move up and down in pitch a couple of times. The ostinato then returns, acting as an inserted bridge between section 3's third and fourth parts. By the fourth part, the original tempo returns. Here, the sustained chords play twice, accompanied by the continuing synth flute ostinato, hiccupping beats, and synth bass and sub-bass.

Section 4 places the synth flute ostinato back into the foreground, panned more than earlier, against section 3's continuing beats and basses. All stop, marking the end of the first part. In the second part, the bell-like sustained chords reappear (more left speaker), now accompanied by a peppering of chirping, whirring, and ticking sound effects. The oscillating synth flute-recorder reappears as well and eventually takes over in the foreground, playing by itself with the effects in the background until the song stops suddenly.

Plastician has expanded his musical production and global reach, eschewing the tempo constraints of grime and dubstep while forging strong connections with the Los Angeles weird beat and neo-trap scenes, starting in 2013. He has also begun remixing some of his earlier songs.

PSY: "GANGNAM STYLE" (ALBUM AND MUSIC VIDEO SINGLE)
ALBUMS: *PSY6, SIX RULES, PART 1* AND *GANGNAM STYLE EP* (BOTH 2012)

In 2012, Psy (Park Jae-sang, 1977–) took the music world by storm with his international megahit "Gangnam Style." The song's video was the first ever to reach one billion YouTube views, and its refrain ("oppan Gangnam style") was listed by *The Yale Book of Quotations* for 2012. Born into an affluent family in Seoul's Gangnam District, Psy studied at the Berklee College of Music in Boston, but he dropped out and returned home to become a musician. Despite his eschewal of the popular boy-band K-Pop sound, the part singer-songwriter, part rapper-producer, and part comedian has become one of South Korea's best-known recording artists of the early 21st century. His first album, *PSY from the Psycho World!* (2000), on the Cream Entertainment label, led to his being fined by the South Korean government for inappropriate content. His second and third albums (both 2002), *Cheap* and *3 Mai*, brought the singer notoriety and more censorship, but led to a fourth and fifth album.

Psy's music is hard-edged, techno-based, high-energy dance-infused hip hop. It contains chant-like, catchy refrains, usually in both Korean and English. "Gangnam Style," the lead single from his YG Entertainment-released six-song EP *Psy6, Six Rules, Part 1*, debuted at No. 1 on South

162 Listen to Hip Hop!

Psy and dancers perform his 2012 hip hop mega hit "Gangnam Style" during a concert at the Penang Han Chiang College in Malaysia, in conjunction with the 2013 Chinese New Year Celebration. (Kelvinchuah/Dreamstime.com)

Korea's Gaon Chart. The song's title phrase is a Korean neologism that refers to a lifestyle associated with the ritzy, trendy, and hip Gangnam District—in many ways, an area comparable to Rodeo Drive in Beverly Hills and Century City in California. By the end of 2012, the song had topped the music charts of more than 30 countries, including Australia, Canada, France, Germany, Italy, Russia, Spain, and the United Kingdom.

"Gangnam Style," composed by Psy and producer Yoo Gun-hyung (1979–) of the Korean hip hop duo Untitle, is for all practical purposes a braggadocio song about sex, which in moments fantasizes about an ideal woman. Its lyrics establish that although Psy may look professional and classy, he is quite the lover, as he tries to seduce a likewise classy and quiet woman (the song's "sexy lady"). Before discussing the song's structure, it is important to point out how "Gangnam Style" gives textbook examples of hook versus refrain as well as harmonic function. The hook is Psy's spoken phrase "oppan Gangnam style," a quick and catchy phrase used frequently in the song. The refrain includes the sung "Hey, sexy lady" line and is a lengthier and more melodic passage than the hook. With hook versus refrain clarified here, the song makes a more complex use of both (this point will be returned to shortly).

The song is mostly in B minor (its home key or i) with a prechorus in G major (VI of B minor), a key that is related a bit further away from B minor than B major (its parallel major) or D major (its relative major). But G major moves back very smoothly to B minor via a big F-sharp major (the dominant key of B minor) appearance at the end of the prechorus, and thus leads very satisfactorily to the refrain in the home key. The use of F-sharp major as a large resolution to the home key is not only textbook tonal music theory, it is also the most commonly used device in all classical music to give listeners a sense of a very dramatic return to the home key.

The song's structure is as follows: intro (bifurcated); verse 1; verse 2; prechorus; refrain 1; refrain 2; verse 3; verse 4; prechorus; refrain 1; refrain 2; verse 5; verse 6; refrain 1 (truncated); refrain 2; outro (bifurcated). The song presents a couple of interesting complexities. The hook appears as a hook in the intro, in the last two refrain 2s, and in the outro; however, it also signals the beginning of refrain 1, a lengthy passage that later includes Psy's elongating the phrase as "op, op op, op oppan Gangnam style." Refrain 1 with its hook is the most popular part of the song. Although it uses introductory material much like an interlude, it gives listeners the satisfying resolution expected from a refrain that appears after a prechorus. The other notable structural complexity is found toward the end of the song, when refrain 1 is truncated to immediately kick off refrain 2.

The sounds of the song are also fascinating. The first part of the song's intro starts with a simple combination of a somewhat comical synth ostinato and a synthesizer-produced four-to-the-floor kick drum beat (four beats per measure, also known as quadruple meter or common time). The first vocals heard are Psy's spoken hook, which is followed by a synth-produced whip, used as a sweep. In the intro's second part, the ostinato continues as its higher-pitched frequencies emerge into the foreground and alternate with Psy's voice. A later song, Little Big's "Skibidi" (also included in this book as a Must-Hear Music entry), uses a synth ostinato that resembles the one in "Gangnam Style." Psy's voice resembles that of a young David Bowie in range and timbre—it is mostly in the baritone range, with some flexibility and brightness in the high or low tenor range. In the intro, a lot of reverb is applied to make his voice sound wetter, fuller, and more resonant. A sudden louder occurrence of synth-based distorted strings followed by drums and a cymbal crash are used to create a tag, concluding the intro. The synth ostinato and kick drop off as this stinger-like tag provides a moment of dramatic tension.

Verse 1 is comparatively energetic as the synth ostinato returns, accompanied by a higher-pitched synth-produced kick drum. Psy talk-sings this verse in his high register. A slight multi-tracking effect makes his almost yelling voice sound seem like it is echoing. The tag from the intro reappears at the end of this verse and also at the end of verse 2, which follows immediately after verse 1. Here, Psy talk-sings against the same synth ostinato, doubled now by the same synth voice in a higher pitch. The four-to-the-floor kick drum beat continues here as well.

In contrast to the previous vocal material, the prechorus is completely sung. Suddenly in G major, it also appears as the brightest-sounding section of the song. The ostinato stops and the kick drum is replaced by higher-pitched snare beats that resemble hand claps. The distorted string synth voice used in the previous tags now accompanies Psy's singing, along with new ascending synth voices (as punctuating cosmic-sounding effects) and backing male voices that vocalize dance-call sounds such as "hey!" A whirring synth voice combined with quick 808 hiccups suggest that the prechorus is reaching its end, all building up with the aforementioned large F-sharp major (V or dominant of B minor).

Refrain 1 starts after the caesura and with the song's most memorable attribute: Psy's talk-singing the song's hook *a cappella* (unaccompanied). Afterward, the intro's instrumentation returns with the synth ostinato. The same tag from the intro is also used at the end of this refrain. In contrast, refrain 2 is more lyrical and consists of an alternation of Psy and the male backing chorus's "hey, sexy lady," punctuated or boosted by Psy's talk-singing the hook, with a hiccupped repetition on the vocalization "opp" (which sounds like "whoop"). The same tag line as used in the intro concludes refrain 2.

Verses 3 and 4 sound the same, respectively, as verses 1 and 2—they just use new lyrics. The prechorus, with its energetic build-up and reappearances of refrains 1 and 2, is copy-pasted. This predictable repetition sets up a surprise in verse 5, which presents a different sound mix. More reverb is applied to Psy's talk-singing, which is now accompanied by the synth ostinato and kick drum. All are filtered to sound muffled. Unlike the conclusions of all of the earlier verses, no tag is used between verses 5 and 6; instead, the music simply continues. Verse 6 is unfiltered and uses the higher synth that doubles with the ostinato found in the second part of the intro, as well as in verses 2 and 4. As verse 6 builds up, Psy's nearly shouting talk-singing is multi-tracked. Another caesura takes place, followed by the hook, which begins the third and final iteration of refrain 1 (instead of the expected prechorus).

Here, refrain 1 is truncated and kicks off refrain 2. At first, the outro sounds like it will be short: a caesura takes place, followed by Psy's spoken-word hook and a final-sounding, echoing heavy cymbal crash. This ends the album track, but for the music video single, this marks just the first part of the outro. After the false conclusion, the intro's synth ostinato and accompanying instrumentation return, followed by another echoing cymbal crash doubled with a quick descending synth effect (as if it is being suddenly turned off) and Psy's hook. The second part of this outro finally concludes with Psy's vocable ("uh"), along with one last cymbal crash. This second part of the outro may also be interpreted as a coda—here, a brief additional section that resolves a previous musical idea. The introductory material with its ostinato gets its own big, dramatic conclusion.

In 2012, the South Korean government announced that "Gangnam Style" had brought in $13.4 million to the country's audio sector. Psy earned more than $60,000 from music sales of the song in South Korea alone, and YG Entertainment earned $1 million from advertisements that appeared on the song's YouTube videos. Beyond "Gangnam Style," Psy has also been at the center of controversy for lyrics that criticize the U.S. detention camp at Guantanamo Bay, Cuba, and for the adult-themed lyrics in his songs.

PUNJABI BY NATURE (FEATURING OFFLICENCE AND CHARANJIT CHANI) AND YO YO HONEY SINGH (FEATURING TDO, SINGHSTA, AND NEHA KAKKAR): "JAAN PUNJABI" AND "MAKHNA"
ALBUMS: *JAAN PANJABI: THE ALBUM* (2007; RE-RELEASED ON *HITMAKER: THE STORY SO FAR*, 2013) AND NON-ALBUM SINGLE, 2018

PBN or P.B.N. (Preet Sandhu, n.d.), formerly known as Punjabi by Nature, is a Wolverhampton-born Indian British keyboardist, music producer, and singer-songwriter of *bhangra-beat* (urban desi) music who has been active since 2004. Coincidentally, there was an earlier band that was also called Punjabi by Nature (PBN), which originated from Canada; however, PBN the producer and musician should not be confused with the Canadian band, which was active from 1993 to 1998. Since the early 2000s, PBN has worked with various hip hop singers, mainly with his Limitless Records label and Playback Records. He has become internationally famous, with fans in Australia, Canada, Europe, India, the Middle East, and the United States, earning the nickname "the hit maker." His albums include *Homegrown* (2009), *Crowd Pleaser* (2010), and *Hitmaker: The Story So Far* (2013). Included on *Hitmaker* is "Jaan Panjabi," originally released on *Jaan Panjabi,* his 2007 four-track compilation EP on Limitless Records. The EP featured collaborations with various bhangra-beat artists, including Offlicence (an international hip hop, bhangra, and R&B group from the West Midlands, U.K.) and Punjabi vocalist, high tenor Charanjit Chani (n.d.). On the album, lyrics are credited to Sandhu.

In F-sharp minor and quadruple meter (four beats per measure), the song structure of "Jaan Punjabi" is as follows: intro; refrain; rapped verse 1 (bifurcated); sung verse 1 (bifurcated); refrain; rapped verse 2 (bifurcated, truncated); instrumental interlude (bifurcated); sung verse 2 (bifurcated); refrain; rapped verse 3 (bifurcated); sung verse 3 (bifurcated); refrain; rapped verse 4 (bifurcated); sung verse 4 (bifurcated); refrain' (repeated almost twice). The song has a high-energy beginning, with Charanjit Chani's Punjabi-language singing. Here, he hits high notes (Sunny J of Offlicence is shown in the video singing this part), accompanied by synth strings voices playing a four-chord *ostinato* (a persistent melodic and/or rhythmic pattern that plays throughout a piece). This ostinato consists of the pitches C-sharp, B, A, and B over F-sharp minor-E major-D major-E major or i-VII-VI-VII). The ostinato is accompanied by shakers and a hiccupping 808 snare drum that is punctuated by Lexeye's (also of Offlicence) English-language hype man toasting. Lexeye establishes the song's title and artist (billed as Punjabi by Nature), covertly appealing to listeners' sense of Punjabi pride. Near the end of this intro, *dhols* (double-headed drums that are typically used in bhangra and bhangra-beat music, played with wooden mallets on both ends) enter the mix dramatically, as drummers strike the bass end of the dhols with force, giving the song's refrain a driving beat. Against the synth-based strings and kick drum-sounding alternation of the dhol players, a backing male chorus shouts, using repetitive percussive vocalizations ("hey!" or "hai!") that serve as contrast to the bass sound of the dhols.

Rapped verse 1, a braggadocio and party rap in English by Offlicence, is accompanied by dhols, male vocalizations, and *tumbi* (an Indian chordophone with one string that is played by plucking—specifically by flicking the forefinger backward and forward across the strings). The backing vocals drop out in sung verse 1, in which Chani is featured again. Here, he is accompanied by the same synth ostinato and dhol beats, but with hand claps added and less bass. A dhol roll serves as a concluding tag. The refrain then returns with the same instrumentation and vocals as the verses but with an added *dholki* (a smaller dhol) and *chimta* (an Indian percussion instrument and idiophone that resembles tongs with attached jingling chimes; here, it sounds like sleigh bells).

Rapped verse 2, also performed by Offlicence, uses the same instrumentation and backing vocals as rapped verse 1, but this time the verse's text repeats and the verse itself is truncated. Lexeye completes each sentence with an upward pitch, underscoring the lyrics "what's up?" The first part of the instrumental interlude features a melodica, punctuated by boosting "hey!" backing vocals, the synth ostinato, and dhol beats; during the second part, a sampled media file of a news report shares the foreground with the melodica. Sung verse 2 features Chani, with the same accompanying instrumentation heard in his verse 1. The refrain returns. Rapped verse 3 brings a return of Offlicence, with the tumbi in the accompaniment. Its length returns to the eight-measure original length heard in his verse 1. This is followed by Chani's sung verse 3, a repeat of the refrain, and Offlicence and then Chani's final verses (respectively, rapped and sung verses 4). The refrain repeats twice, with the song fading out on its final iteration.

Singer-songwriter and producer Yo Yo Honey Singh (a.k.a. Honey Singh, Hirdesh Singh, 1983–) is also known for his video directing and film acting, interests that have helped him bridge the gap between bhangra-beat music production and Bollywood film music. Although he was born in the Punjab region of Hoshiarpur, India, he studied music in the U.K. He nevertheless prefers to sing in his native Punjabi and in Hindi rather than in English. His album *International Villager* (2011) featured the hits "Gabru" and "Angreji Beat." His four-year hiatus-breaking hit single "Makhna," co-produced with Bhushan Kumar (n.d.) and Bobby Suri (n.d.), and featuring playback singer Neha Kakkar (1988–), was released in December 2018 via YouTube, where it hit No. 1 on YouTube India views, getting 20 million views in 24 hours (as of 2021, it has more than 312 million views). The song also features playback singer and high tenor, lyricist, and model Singhsta (a.k.a. Singhstation, Manpreet Singh, n.d.), as well as anonymous rapper TDO (a.k.a. Alistair).

Written by Yo Yo Honey Singh, Singhsta, and Hommie Dilliwala (n.d.), "Makhna" is a basic braggadocio, romance/sex, and party song. The title of the song is a Punjabi term of endearment used for a beloved family member; though it is applied mostly to children, it is also often applied to people who are considered a brother or sister. The song fuses hip hop with R&B and reggaetón elements (although the reggaetón elements are heard only in the beats and use of the bass). Entirely in E minor and quadruple meter, the song's structure is as follows: intro (bifurcated); verse (A); prechorus; refrain; middle-eight (B); prechorus'; rap interlude (bifurcated); prechorus; refrain; verse (C, bifurcated); prechorus; outro (the opening of B and a repetition of the prechorus).

The first part of the intro opens with robotic-sounding distorted male vocals. The lowest pitches of this voice foreshadow the bass, which appears in the second part. Here, the intro gives way to a mid-tempo, synth-produced beat that is punctuated by a hiccupped synth-produced drum effect. Against this beat Singhsta adds highly auto-tuned vocables ("do do do"), as TDO serves as the hype man, introducing the song's title and its singers. Accompanying them is a synth-produced electric guitar voice as well as a descending synth-produced cosmic-sounding effect. The same hiccupped drum effect heard earlier serves as the intro's concluding tag.

Singhsta sings the first verse; delay applied to his voice makes it echo. His nasal tenor vocals are auto-tuned and multi-tracked. He sings in Punjabi about the need to win over a woman through romance and commitment. The same hiccupped synth effect used in the intro's tag now punctuates his verse. He is accompanied by the continuing synth electric guitar voice that emerged in the intro's second part. Both Singhsta and Kakkar, the latter a mezzo-soprano, sing the prechorus. Here, the synth bass and beats are added to the accompaniment. A synth-produced shawm motive emerges and punctuates their elongated vocals. On a separate track, Singhsta's "do do do" vocables reappear. Energy picks up in the refrain, which features Kakkar's very robotic-sounding voice more in the foreground, accompanied by chimta and a new synth keyboard voice. The hiccupped drum effect heard in the intro and in Singhsta's previous verse returns as a concluding tag.

The middle-eight starts with the men singing "that girl is trouble" in English. TDO then chant-raps in English, warning men about gold diggers and their method of trapping men with their sexy dance moves. TDO's dry baritone-range vocals are more natural sounding, making a satisfying contrast to all the other auto-tuned voices. Here, the synth shawm continues as triangle and dhol emerge in the accompaniment. At the end of this section, Yo Yo Honey Singh shouts "go!" as a concluding tag. The prechorus' appears again but slightly modified, with more emphasis on Singhsta's "do do do" vocables, and a lot of applied reverb, at the end. The refrain is expected to follow; however, the rap interlude appears instead.

Yo Yo Honey Singh talk-sings and chant-raps in the rap interlude. In contrast to Singhsta's high tenor vocals, Yo Yo Honey Singh's vocal range is low tenor, and he talk-sings here in his low register. His message, in Punjabi, is aimed at men, reminding them about remaining faithful in love. In a sense, his verse complements TDO's earlier chant-rap, as TDO warns about unfaithful women and Yo Yo Honey Singh warns unfaithful men. After a couple of lines of talk-singing, he chant-raps, accompanied by the continuing beats, triangle, dhol, and beats in the interlude's first part. He changes his flow, and deeper drum beats are used to accompany him, in the second part, which concludes with a sound effect that resembles an echoing gunshot. The same hiccupped effect heard in the beginning sections of the song punctuates his vocals in the third part. The original prechorus returns, followed as expected by the refrain.

Singhsta sings a new verse (labeled here as section C), which uses music and text different from the previous verses. He starts the first part by chant-singing in Punjabi in his high register. His voice is also auto-tuned here and set against only synth-produced beats. The music comes to a caesura at the end of his first part, with his voice, just for a moment in English, echoing. In the second part, more dhol and bass emerge, accompanying Singhsta's singing in his low register. The hiccupped tag returns to conclude the verse, which is followed by a reappearance of the prechorus.

Like Psy's 2012 hit "Gangnam Style" (discussed in an earlier Must-Hear Music entry), "Makhna's" outro is a finale that layers previous passages over one another. Here, the prechorus repeats but now appears a bit more in the background as the "trouble" opening of the middle-eight reappears in the foreground. TDO's hype man vocals are also reintroduced in the mix, as he back-sells himself, Yo Yo Honey Singh, and Singhsta. Kakkar sings the song's title one last time in her prechorus. Singhsta's highly auto-tuned "do do do" vocables return and ultimately take over the foreground to conclude the song, which ends with his voice echoing.

Director Daniel Duran's music video for "Makhna" was set in Old Havana, Cuba, and features all the performers in beach, Mardi Gras, and elaborate stage settings. The aesthetic of the film resembles Bollywood movies as well as bling-oriented old-school hip hop music videos. As of 2021, it is one of the most expensive Indian music videos ever made. Since this song's release, Yo Yo Honey Singh has continued collaborating with Kakkar and Singhsta. Both Kakkar and Singhsta have had further success as playback and R&B singers. As of 2021, all three have continued acting in Bollywood films. In 2011, PBN's *Crowd Pleaser* won Best Album at the U.K. Asian Music Awards. As of 2021, he continues producing albums and singles.

MARK RONSON (FEATURING BRUNO MARS): "UPTOWN FUNK!"
ALBUM: NON-ALBUM SINGLE (2014) AND *UPTOWN SPECIAL* (2015)

Academy Award, Golden Globe Award, and seven-time Grammy winning English-American musician, DJ, songwriter, and record producer Mark Ronson (1975–) is known for his collaborations. He has produced music with Amy Winehouse, Lady Gaga, Adele, Lily Allen, Miley Cyrus, Queens of the Stone Age, Duran Duran, and Bruno Mars. Raised in New York City by his stepfather Mick Jones, guitarist for Foreigner, he started out as a hip hop DJ while at New York University. Although his debut album was not a commercial success, he made a name for himself by producing albums for Christina Aguilera and Amy Winehouse. His second and third studio albums, *Version* (2007) and *Record Collection* (2010, as Mark Ronson & the Business Intl) reached No. 2 on the U.K. album chart. "Uptown Funk" (2014), Ronson's collaboration with singer-songwriter, multi-instrumentalist (especially drum and guitar), producer, and dancer Bruno Mars (Peter Gene Hernandez, 1985–), won the Grammy Award for Record of the Year and spent fourteen

DJ, singer-songwriter, musician, and record producer Mark Ronson performs in concert at the September 2016 Dcode Music Festival in Madrid, Spain. (Christian Bertrand/Dreamstime.com)

consecutive weeks at No. 1 on the Billboard Hot 100; it also topped the Canadian chart for fifteen weeks and the U.K. chart for seven.

Ronson and Bruno Mars share a background in funk (both also use elements of R&B, pop, soul, reggae, hip hop, and rock). The latter's debut studio album, *Doo-Wops & Hooligans* (2010), peaked at No. 3 on the Billboard 200 and won a 2010 Grammy Award for Best Male Pop Vocal Performance (as of 2021, Bruno Mars has won a total of eleven Grammys). His second album, *Unorthodox Jukebox* (2012), topped the charts not only in the United States, but also in Australia, Canada, Switzerland, and the U.K. As of 2021, he has sold more than 180 million singles and 26 million albums worldwide, with eight Billboard Hot 100 No. 1 singles.

Ronson (guitars and LinnDrum, an early 1980s drum machine), Bruno Mars (lead vocals and drums), and keyboardist Jeff Bhasker (a.k.a. Billy Kraven and U.G.L.Y., 1974–), produced "Uptown Funk" and wrote it with songwriter Philip Lawrence (1980–). Recognizing its homage to The Gap Band's disco-funk song "I Don't Believe You Want to Get Up and Dance (Oops!)" (1979), additional song credits were given to The Gap Band's Charlie Wilson (a.k.a. Uncle Charlie, 1953–), Robert Wilson (ca. 1957–2010), Ronnie Wilson (n.d.), and co-writers Rudolf Taylor (n.d.) and Lonnie Simmons (1944–2019). Songwriting credits were also given to rapper-songwriter Nicholas Williams (a.k.a. Trinidad Jame$, 1987–) and producer Devon Gallaspy (n.d.). Williams wrote the hip hop song "All Gold and Everything" (2012), which also served as an inspiration. "Uptown Funk" fuses funk, soul, R&B, and disco elements with old-school hip hop.

Because of its retro sound, its elements are considered derivative at best, and as unauthorized copyright infringement at worst. In 2016, the Minneapolis-based funk band Collage had the best-known lawsuit against Ronson for copyright infringement, charging that the electric guitar riffs and other elements were similar to their song "Young Girls" (1983). Both parties agreed to drop the lawsuit in 2018, just as others emerged. The pioneering female hip hop group The Sequence also sued Ronson and Bruno Mars, claiming that "Uptown Funk" sounded similar to "Funk You Up" (1979). Ronson has also been accused of unauthorized sampling. Though the website *WhoSampled* (a resource for finding out where songs are sampled or what samples are used in a song) credited both Trinidad Jame$ and The Gap Band as being sampled in the song, the site's use of the word "sampled" is not strict. "Uptown Funk" samples neither. Rather, it shares lyrics with Trinidad Jame$ ("don't believe me just watch") and employs a chanting flow similar to

The Gap Band's refrain, as well as a strongly similar use of bass vocals and electric guitar. It also is highly influenced by The Gap Band's disco funk groove, which itself is also present in a number of songs, including the horn-driven intro to Kool and the Gang's "Ladies' Night" (1979). Despite the similarities and influences, no actual musical samples are used from these songs. What is for certain is that "Uptown Funk" is an exceptionally well-studied song, with elements that are reminiscent of many other songs.

Ronson, Bruno Mars, and Bhasker recorded in Los Angeles, London, Memphis, New York, Toronto, and Vancouver, with brass being recorded at Daptone Records in Brooklyn by The Dap-Kings (1996–2016), Antibalas (1998–), and the Hooligans (Bruno Mars's band, 2010–). The track required more than 100 takes, being finished at Ronson's studio in London. On the strength of "Uptown Funk," which was RIAA-certified eleven times platinum, Ronson's fourth studio album, *Uptown Special* (2015), hit No. 1 on the U.K. chart and made it into the Top 10 of the Billboard 200 (his only album to do so). Cameron Duddy directed the popular video. Duddy would shortly thereafter direct Fifth Harmony's music video for their hip hop song "Worth It" (also discussed as a Must-Hear Music entry in this book). The official "Uptown Funk" video shows Bruno Mars fronting a chorus of four male backing singers (although only Bruno Mars is credited for vocals on the recording; the male chorus was created as a post-production effect by multi-tracking his voice). The video is also well known for its choreography and sense of humor. At times, Ronson himself appears, having fun with the group and appearing prominently in shots, such as when he rides on top of the front of a stretch limousine, gets his shoes polished, or wears large plastic curlers with Bruno Mars while yakking on a cell phone. As the song continues, more dancers and singers join in on the fun as the scenery changes from being uptown to being onstage with a band, with Ronson shown playing electric guitar.

"Uptown Funk" is entirely in D minor and consists of a compound verse-refrain structure, meaning that each section has more than one verse. The song's structure is as follows: intro (bifurcated); verse 1 (bifurcated); prechorus (bifurcated); refrain; postchorus (bifurcated); verse 2 (bifurcated); prechorus (bifurcated); refrain; postchorus (bifurcated); bridge; interlude 1 (bifurcated); interlude 2; postchorus; outro (twice). The first part of the intro begins with a bass-range vocal riff that emphasizes D minor. The rhythmic male vocables (D, D-G-F, D-G-F, D) are set against hand claps; all have multi-tracking and a lot of reverb. The first part of the intro ends with a vocally produced sweep that sounds reminiscent of the "shhoooot" sound made by John Lennon in the intro to The Beatles' "Come Together" (1969). The second part is marked by the entry of an electric guitar playing a funky counter riff against the continuing bass vocals and claps. Early on, the song emphasizes a bluesy-sounding D-minor-seventh chord (i^7, consisting of the pitches D, F, A, and C), representing the home key, and a bluesy-sounding G-major chord with a minor seventh (IV^7, consisting of G, B, D, and F). The vocal sweeps reappear, and the intro builds up to Bruno Mars's throaty vocable ("ow!") and trumpet with brass notes. This horn accompaniment is reminiscent of James Brown or George Clinton's bands and returns more prominently later in the song.

All the instruments drop out except for the drum kit, heavy on the kick drum in verse 1. Here, Bruno Mars's multi-tracked high tenor vocals are featured, mainly employing smooth-sounding funk-inspired singing, peppered with instances of throaty rock-style vocals. The first part emphasizes i^7 and consists of four lines, whereas the second moves to IV^7 and consists of three lines that possess a lengthier flow. The second part uses a vocalized kiss as its tag. The electric guitar riff and sweeps return and are added to the drum accompaniment in the prechorus, which returns to i^7. A funk bass also appears in the background. This melodic passage consists of some call-and-response from multi-tracked backing vocals (on the words "too hot"). It ends on a metatextual call for a break (ending on IV^7).

This song is a good example of how refrains and hooks distinguish themselves: generally, refrains are lengthier and more melodic than hooks, which are shorter but nevertheless catchy and may appear both in a refrain and in a song's other passages. "Uptown Funk"'s refrain is the most gospel-inspired passage of the song (on i^7), featuring just Bruno Mars and high-pitched responding male voices that are accompanied by kick drums. The first part of each refrain includes a line repeated three times, followed by a different fourth line; the second part is the first hook (containing the song's title). Here, atop hand claps, an ascending synth string *glissando* (sliding upward in pitch) emerges and builds tension as the snare drum enters. Meanwhile, the first hook is followed by a couplet featuring Bruno Mars and the backing singers. Bruno Mars then sings the second hook, "don't believe me, just watch," alone (*a cappella*) and screams "ow!" in a way that is reminiscent of James Brown. This passage's synth strings are not only reminiscent of a sweeping new jack swing keyboard sound; they are also used here as was the glissando in The Beatles' "A Day in the Life" (1967), to build up to a climax. The same trumpet and horns heard in the intro conclude the refrain.

The postchorus follows, initially placing the horns in the foreground and the backing singers' vocalizations (such as "hey" and "ow!") in the background. In the first part of the postchorus, the horns alternate with Bruno Mars, who repeats the second hook. In the second part, he repeats the second hook again but does so three times in quick succession, without the horns filling in. Like the refrain, the three-time repetition pattern is broken up with Bruno Mars's "heys" and another "ow!"

The song's most structurally interesting passage is found where the second part of the postchorus elides into the first part of verse 2. In other words, the music comes to a false conclusion on the word "stop," which concludes the postchorus while at the same time serving as the first word of verse 2. The instrumentation and structure of this verse are identical to those of the first part of verse 1, but with different lyrics, a "come here" whistle vocalized effect, and now shared lead vocals between Bruno Mars and his backing vocals, who alternate lines. This time, the verse appears to be less distinctly bifurcated, due to the alternation between Bruno Mars and the backing vocals as well as the flow of the new lyrics. The second part of verse 2 is also like verse 1 but with different lyrics. The prechorus, second refrain, and postchorus follow, exactly as before. A bridge, which features the same bass-range vocal riff as in the first part of the intro, leads into interlude 1. The first part features Bruno Mars's metatextual spoken word, pointing out the song's three-quarter mark; the second part features his rhythmic chanting against kick drum, snare drum, and (most notably) the funky electric bass. His "uptown, funk you up" chant sounds like an homage to The Gap Band's chanted refrain in "I Don't Believe You Want to Get Up and Dance (Oops)," as it employs the same flow. Interlude 2 continues his chant but adds the funky electric guitar that appeared in the intro's second part. Bruno Mars addresses listeners directly, telling them to dance and flaunt what they have, because they are sexy. He also tells listeners to "come on," which is reminiscent of Brown's and Clinton's energetic calls to action directed at their audiences. Interlude 2 concludes with the couplet and second-hook material from the refrain. The postchorus follows one last time, leading listeners to expect that the song will conclude here; however, "Uptown Funk" introduces another chant using the title in the outro. As the male backing vocals chant, Bruno Mars supplies vocables and funky tag lines (e.g., "say what?"). The horns' descending gesture leads listeners to expect a conclusion a couple of times but the singing continues, fading out just a bit before ending on the same elongated Bruno Mars growl heard in the intro, accompanied by a horns-led instrumental flourish.

Ronson has founded two record labels: Allido Records (2004) and Zelig Records (2018). He also formed the Grammy-winning duo Silk City with Diplo in 2018. His philanthropy includes the Amy Winehouse Foundation, which helps disadvantaged youth; the Hope and Homes for Children charity; and the John F. Kennedy Center's Turnaround Arts program. Bruno Mars's 2017 album *24K Magic* won the Grammy for Album of the Year. He continues to record solo and tour with his soul and funk band The Hooligans, who perform all-band choreographed dancing arrangements influenced by James Brown and the J.B.'s. Bruno Mars and The Hooligans performed "Uptown Funk" at the Super Bowl 50 halftime show.

SHAGGY (FEATURING RIKROK): "IT WASN'T ME"
ALBUM: *HOT SHOT* (2000)

Shaggy (Orville Richard Burrell, 1968–) is a musician from Kingston, Jamaica, who toasts as well as raps. His hit albums and singles fuse dance music, reggae, alternative rock, pop, R&B, dancehall, dubstep, and hip hop. Nicknamed Shaggy because of his wild hair, Burrell began writing songs in high school. When he was 18, his mother moved his

Known for his gravelly voice and toasting skills, Shaggy performs on stage in June 2011 at the Old Fort in Stone Town in Zanzibar, Tanzania. (Robin Batista/Dreamstime.com)

family to the Flatbush area of Brooklyn, New York. Shortly afterward, he took singing lessons and did some busking, singing reggae songs. To escape the tough Brooklyn street life, he enlisted in the United States Marine Corps during the First Gulf War. In the meantime, he developed his melodic and strongly accentuated vocal delivery, as well as his raspy baritone voice. In 1992, he resumed his music career, appearing on Dope's (a.k.a. K-Dope, Kenny Gonzalez, 1970–) hip hop album *The Kenny Dope Unreleased Project* (1992) and released his own debut album, *Pure Pleasure* (1993).

Boombastic (1995), his most critically acclaimed album, stayed at No. 1 on the Reggae Albums chart for 30 consecutive weeks and won a Grammy Award for Best Reggae Album. It peaked at No. 34 on the Billboard 200 and was certified platinum. The album spawned a No. 3 Billboard Hot 100 single with its title track; however, Shaggy's greatest success on the singles chart did not happen until the album *Hot Shot* (2000), also his best commercial success, which was RIAA-certified six-times platinum and topped the Billboard 200. From that album came Shaggy's biggest hit, "It Wasn't Me," which reached No. 1 on the Billboard Hot 100.

The song comes across as a tongue-in-cheek work about infidelity, lying, and gaslighting to cover up those lies. It features guest vocals from Rikrok (Ricardo George Ducent, 1976–), who co-wrote it, along with Shaggy; Sting International (Shaun Pizzonia, ca.1968–), who also produced the song; and Braun Thompson (n.d.). In 2015, Shaggy revealed on *The Tonight Show Starring Jimmy Kimmel* that the original inspiration of "It Wasn't Me" came from an Eddie Murphy comedy routine and that he (Shaggy) believed that infidelity is not really a joke; he also explained that Rikrok composed the song's apologetic verse (discussed later in this entry). Rikrok's vocals, which are some of the most memorable parts of the song, are in the high tenor range, in contrast to Shaggy's gruff baritone. Rikrok's timbre is laid-back, lyrical, and sweet.

"It Wasn't Me," which topped the charts in Australia, Austria, France, Ireland, the Netherlands, the United States, and the U.K., has musical elements that are more complex than its lyrical content. Entirely in the key of C major, the song uses a collection of pitches that are part of the Mixolydian mode. Typically, the C-major scale consists of C, D, E, F, G, A, B, C, whereas the Mixolydian mode starting on C consists of C, D, E, F, G, A, B-flat, C (the difference is found in the seventh scale step, B-flat, which is lowered a half step in the C Mixolydian scale). The use of Mixolydian mode can be found in a good bit of popular music, including folk songs and jazz. Musicians with a jazz background often apply modal theory to jazz, describing entire songs or sections of songs as being in a particular mode; a more thoughtful application of modal theory as a tool for understanding how a song is constructed is to use it when the modal sound is such a distinctive part of the piece. "It Wasn't Me" is a strong example, as it uses the Mixolydian mode throughout. Another jazz element found in Shaggy's hit can be heard in its chords, which are C major^7-B major^9-C major^7-B-flat major^7 (I major^7-VII major^9-I major^7-^{b}VII major^7 or C-E-G-B, then B-flat-D-A-C, followed by C-E-G-B and B-flat-D-F-A). Here, the seventh and ninth added pitches give the chords their jazzy sound and richer texture. The four chords repeat in this sequence throughout the song.

The song structure of "It Wasn't Me" is as follows: intro; refrain (bifurcated); verse 1 (A, bifurcated); prechorus; refrain' (bifurcated); verse 2 (A', bifurcated); prechorus'; refrain" (bifurcated); middle-eight (B); refrain'" (bifurcated); instrumental outro (bifurcated). The intro begins with a light-hearted interplay among downtempo synth string voices, an arpeggiated acoustic guitar, and a cello or double-bass strings stinger (bowed hard to sound piercing), against which Rikrok and Shaggy talk, suggesting what the song will be about: Rikrok has been caught by his girlfriend having sex with his neighbor, and he asks Shaggy for advice. Shaggy tells him to deny everything; in other words, given the song's lyrical details, to gaslight his girlfriend by arguing that who she saw was someone else. The laid-back, arpeggiated acoustic guitar helps set the tone of the music (this same guitar gesture is also heard in Childish Gambino's "This Is America," also discussed in a Must-Hear Music entry of this book); however, the synth strings are distorted by the partial removal of their attack, and they swell as they sustain, which contrasts with the strong attack of the stingers. This effect punctuates Rikrok's singing.

As the intro ends, Rikrok says the word "alright," which cues the electric bass and kick and snare drum beat of the refrain, which now uses the intro's three instruments as accompaniment and adds electric guitar. The passage uses the same pattern with the cello or double-bass strings stinger as the intro.

Shaggy responds to Rikrok in verse 1, in which he toasts, suggesting that Rikrok denies that it was him, despite the physical evidence. Shaggy's baritone vocals are multi-tracked and aggressive. Here, the strings and stingers drop out completely, though the cello or bass strings stinger is used as a tag at the end of his verse. Instead, he is accompanied by electric bass, a kick-snare-hi-hat beat, and a new bubbling-sounding synth voice. The first part of this verse is Shaggy's first four scolding phrases; the second part is Shaggy's suggestion on how to be a player—and there more hi-hat is introduced.

The prechorus, with lead vocals sung by Rikrok, takes the song on a comical turn, as Rikrok describes what he was doing with his neighbor but is denying what has been seen. It uses call-and-response between Rikrok and a chorus of male backing singers. Rikrok sings about the details of his affair, followed by the chorus's denial, which is the song's hook ("it wasn't me"). All take place against the same backing instrumentation heard in Shaggy's previous verse, kicked off very briefly with the new synth, which falls immediately into the background. The first part consists of Rikrok's first four phrases and the second part, continuing the call-and-response, consists of his second four phrases. Drums and the same stinger as earlier create the concluding tag. The refrain' reappears, but the lyrical content has been slightly modified, although the accompaniment remains the same.

In verse 2, Shaggy advises and reassures Rikrok that his girlfriend will forget the past, but warns him to watch out if she turns violent. He also toasts in this bifurcated verse, which consists of the same structure and accompaniment as the first, along with the low strings stinger. This time, more reverb is applied to Shaggy's vocals. Reappearances of the prechorus' and refrain" (modified and without the synth that kicks off the earliest iteration) follow. The acoustic guitar's fret sounds, also called *fret noise*, which appeared in the second refrain', seem more prominent from this point on, especially in the final refrain''' and outro.

Rikrok's apologetic and confrontational verse serves as a displaced middle-eight, appearing almost at the end of the song rather than sandwiched in the middle of the verses. The lyrical content here suggests that Rikrok's song narrative persona has reached an epiphany. Now knowing the difference between right and wrong, he confronts Shaggy's persona about giving bad advice and disses him. Rikrok's new melody seems reminiscent of the laid-back, lyrical melody in refrain 1, but his voice is higher. The electric bass and drum accompany him at first, followed by a marimba. The bubbling keyboard synth voice heard in the background of Shaggy's verses and refrain' (but absent in the second prechorus and third refrain") emerges more prominently in the foreground. There is also a sound effect that resembles glass chimes. A final repeat of the refrain''' leads to the song's bifurcated instrumental outro. This time, the humorous call-and-response prechorus is skipped, underscoring Rikrok's persona's change of heart.

In the first part of the outro, the acoustic guitar from the intro appears in the foreground, accompanied by the string synths and low string stingers and drum beat. The second part is marked by the addition of the electric guitar. The song concludes with a low string stinger, then a timpani rumble (with a lot of applied reverb), followed by the guitars, which sound as if they are beginning a melody—but the chords get cut off. The timpani rumble resembles a tag heard at the end of Shaggy's verses, but it is much louder, creating a sense of finality.

Hot Shot (2000) produced Shaggy's only other No. 1 hit, "Angel." His next album, *Lucky Day* (2002), was RIAA-certified gold. It would take him 18 years to produce another gold album (SNEP certified) in the form of *44/876*—a collaboration between Shaggy and Sting (Gordon Matthew Thomas Sumner, 1951–) of The Police. Although the album got no higher than No. 40 on the Billboard 200, it topped Billboard's Reggae Albums chart, and its lead single, "Don't Make Me Wait" (which did not chart), has had 24.3 million views on YouTube as of 2021. Also known for philanthropy, Shaggy used the proceeds of his song "Rise Again" (2010) to support the victims of the Haiti earthquake.

SUKSHINDER SHINDA (FEATURING CHESHIRE CAT AND TENASHUS): "BALLE"
ALBUM: *BALLE* (2005)

Sukshinder Shinda (Sukhshinder Singh Bhullar, 1972–) is a British *bhangra-beat* producer and singer-songwriter. Since releasing his first professional recording in 1993, he has produced or collaborated on more than 200 albums. His own albums include *Another Level* (1999), *The OG's* (1999), *Moving & Grooving* (2000), *Gal Sun Ja* (2003), *Balle* (2005), *Chakde Boly: The Way It Is* (2005), *Collaborations* (2006), *Collaborations 2* (2009), *Jadoo* (2010), *Rock da Party* (2012), and *Collaborations 3* (2014). From 2006 to 2011, he won six U.K. Asian Music Awards: Best Album and Best Video (2006), Best Act and Best Album (2008), and Best Producer (2010 and 2011).

His party and music skills braggadocio song, "Balle," is the first track on Sukshinder Shinda's 2005 album of the same name. It features Birmingham DJ and Jamaican-style toaster Cheshire Cat (Stephen Cheshire, n.d.), known for his guest vocalist stints with the U.K. electronica duo Leftfield in the 1990s. Cheshire Cat appeared on Leftfield's singles "Release the Pressure" (1992) and "Chant of a Poorman" (1999). "Balle" also features anonymous rapper Tenashus (n.d.).

The song's structure is complex, with sections that resemble previous material but are different enough to be heard as new music. The structure is as follows: intro (bifurcated); verse 1 (A, bifurcated, with the last part sounding like a prechorus); refrain; rapped verse or middle-eight 1 (B); bridge 1; verse 1 (C); refrain; verse 1 (D); bridge 2; verse 2 (C′);

refrain; rapped verse or middle-eight 2 (E); bridge 3; verse 3 (C″); refrain; verse 2 (D); verse 4 (C‴); refrain; bridge 4; verse 1 (A′, again bifurcated, with the last part sounding like a prechorus); refrain; outro. The music used in sections marked C sounds related to section A but is different enough to be labeled as new sections. The intro and song sections B, D, and E, as well as bridge 3 and the outro are in English, though Cheshire Cat employs Jamaican patois in the intro, song section D, and the outro. The rest of the sung sections (by Sukshinder Shinda) are in Punjabi. In contrast to its large-scale structure, the song's harmonic structure is simple. It is entirely in B minor and stresses its home pitch (B or i) as a pitch center, with secondary emphasis on the pitch F-sharp (scale step 5 of B minor) and tertiary emphasis on C-natural (a lowered scale step 2 of B minor).

 The first part of the intro features Cheshire Cat as hype man, shouting out "Sukshinder Shinda," giving the song an immediate signature. This shout-out prompts the song's ostinato, performed with a synthesizer voice that sounds like an *ektara* (a traditional Indian chordophone with one string). This synth ostinato alternates two pitch patterns: G–F-sharp–B–B (in B minor, scale steps 6-5-1-1) and G–F-sharp–C-natural–B (also in B minor, scale steps 6-5-2-1, with a lowered scale step 2). The first two pitches in each pattern ascend, and the second two pitches are either the same or descend. A cymbal tick also accompanies Cheshire Cat, who briefly hypes Sukshinder Shinda's ascension as a music legend. A distorted *dhol* beat, along with 808s, appears at the end of the first part of the intro. The dhol is an essential element of bhangra-beat music—a hybrid of hip hop, rap, and the folk dance and music of Punjabi farmers who live in North India and Pakistan. A double-headed membranophone that is large enough to require a strap, the dhol beats out a quadruple-meter (four beats per measure) beat (bhangra-beat patterns are drummed by hitting two separate sticks against each of the drum's heads, which are usually made of goat skin). These percussive sounds prompt the second part of the intro, which features Cheshire Cat's toasting about music, partying, and women. His vocals are filled with trills and stutters, used for effect. When Cheshire Cat hits his highest note, Sukshinder Shinda chimes in with verse 1 (A), in Punjabi. Cheshire Cat's throaty toasting and singing range between low tenor and baritone, whereas Sukshinder Shinda's singing is a bright, lyrical low tenor that can reach most of the high tenor range. His singing provides the song's lyrical contrasts.

 Verse 1 (A) is bifurcated, with Sukshinder Shinda's voice in the foreground, singing dramatic vocals that hit high and low notes effortlessly in the first part. The *tabla*, a classic Hindustani set of drums, emerges in the background. In the verse's second part, his vocals are punctuated by the male backing chorus's vocalizations (the typical yelled "heys" of bhangra-beat, with applied reverb). Though the second part completes the verse, it also serves as a prechorus, as it takes place before the refrain and builds up energy toward it (with the male chorus vocalizations). Following the conventions of Punjabi and Bollywood singers, Sukshinder Shinda sings in a nasal voice, his pitches sliding constantly. A male backing singer's vocables ("whoa-oa-aah"), which slide up in pitch, give way to the call-and-response exchange between Sukshinder Shinda and the male chorus in the refrain. During this exchange, the dhol beat drops off, and the higher-pitched *dholak* (used similarly to snare drums), along with the tabla (which now sounds like it is being played underwater), sets the beat. Cheshire Cat is briefly heard, rolling his tongue on a vocable ("brrrrrrr") in the background—a sound which is used or sampled later as rhythmic punctuation and for tags. The refrain concludes an elongated note on the word "yeah" (by Sukshinder Shinda).

With the exception of the tabla, the accompanying instrumentation continues into the rapped verse (section B), with the addition of a tabla beat that sounds like the high end of bongos or congas, along with drier-sounding 808 snare drum, and a new oscillating synthesizer voice. This section features Tenashus's rap; although she does not sing a new melody and new music is not introduced here, this rapped verse functions like a middle-eight in respect to providing contrast to the previous material and length (eight measures). She raps in a sultry, low voice that is multi-tracked and post-produced (applied reverb). In contrast to the song's male singing and toasting, Tenashus's section is a chant-rap in English. Her lyrics make clear that if the men (presumably in the song) want her, they need to be able to handle her assertiveness and sexuality. Cheshire Cat's rolled vocable punctuates her rap flow. This verse ends with a tag that consists of sampled and distorted hand claps.

Bridge 1 is primarily instrumental. It places the ostinato into the foreground, punctuated by male chorus vocalizations and accompanied by reintroduced percussion and synth instrumentation. Sukshinder Shinda's singing voice flows in the foreground again in verse 1 (C), which resembles the melodic material in verse 1 (A). The instrumental accompaniment is similar to that of verse 1, but with more distorted hand claps. After the first two lines, the male chorus boosts the rhythmic flow, making the tempo faster. Cheshire Cat's rolled vocable appears for the first time in the foreground here, as a vocal tag.

The second refrain leads to verse 1 (D), which features Cheshire Cat's toasting and rapping. He exalts hip hop music and its ability to make people dance. The instrumentation in this section is similar to that of verse 1, but with more hand claps. The tabla appears in the foreground, as it punctuates Cheshire Cat's toasting and gets used as the verse's tag, this time with applied echo that is especially noticeable on the tabla that concludes the verse. Bridge 2 and verse 2 (C′) follow. Bridge 2, like bridge 1, places the ostinato in the foreground, this time accompanied by tabla. The male chorus's vocalizations appear in the background, right before the call-and-response part of the refrain (built around the word "balle"), which appears further in the background, punctuated by Cheshire Cat's louder rolling vocable. At this point, Sukshinder Shinda and the chorus sound dreamlike and ethereal (via use of vocal filters). The refrain concludes on the synthesizer's completing the ostinato pattern, with applied reverb.

The second rapped verse (E), like the first one (B), has no new melody and no new musical material is introduced here, though it also functions like a second middle-eight for the same reasons as Tenashus's previous rapped verse. This time, Tenashus uses an old-school style to rap in English about what men need to be to attract women. Her voice is multi-tracked, with a lot of applied reverb, to sound more resonant and thus sultry. The instrumentation is stripped to bass-range instruments: mainly the dhol, but five seconds in, as the rap style changes to new school (with more interior rhyme and enjambment), hand claps, the tabla's *daya* and *baya* (high-pitched and low-pitched drums), and dholak (snare) are added, giving the verse more energy. Toward the end of her verse, claps and the *daya* of the tabla disappear, leaving the water-drip sound of the *baya* drum of the tabla, dhol, and dholak, set against the oscillating synthesizer heard earlier. Bridge 3 shifts to a sparse texture. It places the synth ostinato in the foreground, with applied reverb. Tenashus then continues with short, repetitive lines (e.g., "keep it moving" and "don't stop"). Ironically, however, the song reaches a false conclusion, as her voice echoes and creates a caesura.

Verse 3 (C″) reoccurs with different vocables that boost Sukshinder Shinda's singing, this time with the male chorus chanting ("go, go"). Like the verse's two previous occurrences, Cheshire Cat's rolling vocable enters the foreground, as a tag that leads to the refrain. Verse 2 (D) reappears, followed by a new version of verse 3 (C‴) and then the refrain. Bridge 4 is Cheshire Cat's signature shout to Sukshinder Shinda (the same one heard at the beginning of the song). For the first time, all of the musical accompaniment comes to a stop. Verse 1 (A′) appears one last time, with its second part also serving as a prechorus, followed by the last appearance of the refrain. As Sukshinder Shinda's voice trails off with an extended vocal flourish, Cheshire Cat returns in the outro, back-selling the song, accompanied by the dhol and 808 beats only. The song ends with Cheshire Cat's assertive, echoing voice.

As of 2021, Sukshinder Shinda remains active, not only focusing on recordings that feature himself but also producing albums as well. Just recently, he released the single "The World Is Watching." During the past two decades, his production discography include several albums by Jazzy B (Jaswinder Singh Bains, 1975–), Avtar Singh Kang (a.k.a. A. S. Kang, 1949–), and Amrinder Gill (n.d.). Though his focus has been primarily on secular music, Sukshinder Shinda has also released sacred music.

ANA TIJOUX: "1977"
ALBUM: *1977* (2009)

Ana Tijoux (Anamaría Tijoux Merino, 1977–), a Chilean musician born to Chilean parents who lived in political exile in France during the reign of Augusto Pinochet, moved back to Chile after the return of civil power in 1993. Within a couple of years, she formed the group Los Gemelos (The Twins, 1995–1997). In 1997, Tijoux was featured on *Mama Funk*, the debut studio album by Los Tetas (1994–2004, 2011–), a funk band that released five albums and whose *La Medicina* (1997) is considered one of the best Latin American funk albums. That year, she became MC of hip hop group Makiza (1997–2006). By 2001, she and the group's members were pursuing solo careers. Tijoux's big solo break came in 2009 with her second album, *1977*, a collection of Spanish and French autobiographical songs. Its Spanish-sung, half-autobiographical, half-imagistic title track became an underground hit. Both the title of the song and album allude to the year of Tijoux's birth, as well as to being part of a generation born or raised in exile. Songwriter credits on the album are given to Tijoux as well as Nicolás Carrasco, Mauricio Castillo, Eduardo Herrera, and Francisco Martinez; all have also been credited as songwriters on several other songs on the album. Carrasco and rapper Herrera (who raps as Hordatoj) produced the song and the album. On the strength of *1977*, Tijoux began a 2010 North American tour and, in 2011, the popular and award-winning American television show *Breaking Bad* aired a montage using "1977" as the soundtrack, creating new listeners and more fans.

"1977" fuses the *luxe* (luxurious) aesthetic with a classical orchestra and *boom bap* (a mostly East Coast old-school sound that emphasizes kick and snare drums). The song is in D minor and quadruple meter (four beats per measure). It often uses an A dominant seventh (V^7 of D minor) to dramatically build anticipation. The song's structure is as follows: instrumental intro (bifurcated); verse 1 (hexfurcated); prechorus; refrain (bifurcated); instrumental bridge 1; verse 2 (quintfurcated, truncated); prechorus'; refrain' (bifurcated); instrumental bridge 2; instrumental outro (refrain instrumentation used). The song opens with a sample from the beginning of an instrumental version of composer Lionel Bart's theme for the film *From Russia with Love*, which appears on Side Two, track three, of the album *007: The James Bond Thrillers: The Roland Shaw Orchestra* (1964). During live performances, two copies of the mono version are set up and tape-cued on two turntables to turn the sample into a loop or continual groove. The sound of the orchestra comes through lengthy turntablist drops. Here, the horns have the main melody and are followed by descending orchestral strings that sustain an A dominant seventh chord, dramatically building anticipation for whatever may come next. The first part of the intro uses a hiccupped or quickly shuffling sound effect that sounds like when a player has reached the end of a record as the needle passes to the label, also adding to the sonic cliffhanger impression. The second part of the intro both establishes D minor as the home key and sets up a four-measure pattern for each important musical gesture. It features a male speaker who is filtered to sound as if he is speaking on the radio. This media file is sampled from the Spanish dubbed-over version, entitled "Serpiente supreme" ("Supreme Serpent" or "Great Snake") of the television documentary *National Geographic Special: Ultimate Snake: The Death Squeeze* (2003). This file is set against the looped beats or groove of the song: military-style snare drums, acoustic rhythm guitar, and heavy electric bass, punctuated with zills, on the *From Russia with Love* sample, played on turntables, and enhanced by turntablist *baby scratches* (moving the album forward and backward), as well as more brushed strokes on snare drum played on an actual drum set. The radio sample is distorted and sometimes hiccupped, and appears on just the left or right speaker—a psychedelic production effect. The male speaking voice tells viewers to notice the differences between poisonous and nonpoisonous snakes by their marks. At the end of the intro, the sample fades and echoes.

Both verses, also in D minor, constitute a lengthy verse that can be heard as having six parts. Generally, Tijoux alternates between chromatic and monotone talk-singing and breathless talk-sung old-school style rapping, with an added twist of including lines of variant lengths, a practice which gives her carefully articulated words a sense of build-up despite the monotone nature of her flow. The instrumentation from the second part of the refrain continues. In the first part, Tijoux's lilting lines seem to descend chromatically. Here, she mentions how she is also born (as Anamaría) during the year of the snake and takes a breath before continuing. Her flow changes and more pauses are used in the second part, which ends on a tag of hiccupped, sustained *From Russia with Love* strings. The third part begins with all accompaniment briefly dropping out and quickly returning. Tijoux shifts from monotone talk-singing to ending this part with lilting, chromatic-sounding rapping. This part ends with the same hiccupped tag as the previous part. The second, third, and fourth parts tell of her birth and allude to a history that she could not escape from studying and then knowing all too well. Pauses are also used in the fourth part, this time ending with a brushed cymbal strike with applied reverb. The last two parts are marked by having a louder, brushed military snare drum beat. Tijoux's talk-singing starts on a higher pitch as she explains learning while young that people intend to harm others (by alluding to her stuffed animal). The sixth and last part of the verse is punctuated by descending arpeggiating strings, followed by an instance of a four-to-the-floor (striking on all four beats of a measure) kick drum before the hiccupped sustained string tag concludes the part. Here, Tijoux describes the first time she felt helpless. The prechorus features Tijoux's lilting and chromatic-sounding talk-singing (the hook) as she repeats (in Spanish) "one-thousand-nine-hundred-seventy-seven" three times, ending each line with a "shh" vocable, then concludes with an instrumental break, followed by turntable scratching.

In the refrain, she begins by chanting the hook one more time before continuing with talk-singing. She uses the "shh" vocable to create a brief resting place in the prechorus. The accompanying instrumentation, including turntable scratches, continues in the refrain; however, its first part is marked by the entrance of a new trumpet melody, played by Castillo, with a small studio ensemble of horns. During live performances, a media file is used of this melody, prompted by the turntablist. The same melody is repeated in the refrain's second part, which concludes with a four-to-the-floor kick drum followed by Tijoux's "shh." Instrumental bridge 1 hiccups the sustained strings of *From Russia with Love*, again creating an A dominant seventh chord—but this time, instead of a cliffhanger, an acoustic piano arpeggiates and is followed by a brushed cymbal (left speaker) with applied reverb. The song comes to a brief pause.

Verse 2, also in D minor, uses the same instrumentation as verse 1, but it has one less part and some different tags than the previous verse.

Tijoux also employs some different vocal delivery. Instead of the lilting and chromatic-sounding talk-singing of verse 1's first part, the analogous part starts right away with rapid but highly articulated rapping. Her flow becomes lengthy in the second part (without pauses). Here, she alludes to her adolescence and likens her body to drums and head to a guitar. Her laugh serves as this part's concluding tag. She returns to chromatic-sounding talk-singing in the third part, concluding *a cappella* (unaccompanied). Into the conclusion of this verse with the third, fourth, and fifth parts, she refers to herself as both pupil to a poet and a poet herself, and the lines become more imagistic, mentioning the mountain range that witnessed the exit (of those who fled from Chile). The descending arpeggiating strings, followed by the four-to-the-floor kick drum and a concluding hiccupped sustained string tag heard in the sixth part of verse 1, return in the fifth part of verse 2. Here, she explains how her search (for truth or for herself) was never for the purpose of her act but rather something "necessary that already marked my failure" ("*Fue algo necesario que marcaba ya mi fallo*"). She then explains that after talking to the listener (addressed as "you"), she has come to understand that everyone wants to be a privateer (in other words, with the permission and payment of a government, everyone has a price for which they would be willing to attack enemies).

The prechorus' and refrain' repeat one last time, with some modifications: her vocals are more multi-tracked in the prechorus' than earlier; a turntable, vocal, and percussion hiccup concludes the refrain'. She uses her "shh" vocables to punctuate the prechorus' and refrain' and continues with them during instrumental bridge 2, a four-measure vamp for the outro, which prominently features the *From Russia with Love* sample's strings, accompanied by continuing brushed military snare drum beats, zills, and heavy electric bass. Tijoux's vocalizations are reduced to her "shh" vocables, which appear in the foreground after the strings' phrases. The outro is also instrumental and places the refrain's trumpet melody with horns into the foreground as Tijoux, the sample, military snare, and electric bass continue. Turntable scratching becomes more audible in the background; however, the outro abruptly ends after her final "shhh."

In 2014, her collaboration with Uruguayan singer-songwriter musician Jorge Drexler (Jorge Abner Drexler Prada, 1964–), "*Universos Paralelos*" ("Parallel Universes"), won the Latin Grammy Award for Record of the Year. As of 2021, Tijoux has released five solo studio albums, *Kaos* (2007), *1977*, *La bala* (*The Bullet*, 2011), *Vengo* (*I Am Coming*, 2014), and *Antifa Dance* (2020).

TIMBALAND (FEATURING NELLY FURTADO AND JUSTIN TIMBERLAKE): "GIVE IT TO ME" AND "CARRY OUT"
ALBUMS: *SHOCK VALUE* (2007) AND *SHOCK VALUE II* (2009)

Timbaland (Timothy Zachery Mosley, 1972–) is an American record producer, turntablist, rapper, and singer-songwriter who is known primarily for his work with Portsmouth, Virginia, rapper and producer Missy Elliott (1971–); Victoria, British Columbia, R&B and pop singer-songwriter Nelly Furtado (1978–); and Memphis hip hop singer-songwriter Justin Timberlake (1981–). Timbaland's production output began in 1990 under the name DJ Timmy Tim. He became famous after joining forces with Elliott to become part of DeVante Swing's Swing Mob record label (1991–1995), a member of a group of musicians known as Da Bassment Cru. In 1997, Timbaland had his first hit as a featured artist on the song "What About Us," on Missy Elliott's *Soul Food* album. The song was No. 16 and No. 4, respectively, on the Billboard Hot 100 and Billboard's Hot R&B Songs charts and was RIAA-certified gold. In 1998, he had his first hit as a lead artist on "Here We Come," featuring Magoo, Elliott, and Darryl Pearson and appearing on his own debut album *Tim's Bio: Life from da Bassment*. Eventually, he got his own imprint label, Mosley Music Group (2005–), associated from 2005 to 2014 with parent label Interscope Records (1989–) and from 2014 on with Epic (1953–), the latter because of Timbaland's success as executive producer of Michael Jackson's posthumous *Xscape* (2014). As a songwriter he has written or co-written more than 100 hit songs.

Timbaland's second solo studio album, *Shock Value* (2007, the first release on Mosley Music Group), was certified multi-platinum and reached No. 5 on the Billboard 200; it also reached No. 1 in Australia, Austria, and Ireland. An instrumental version was released in July 2007. The album featured guest artists such as Elliott, Timberlake, Furtado, Fall Out Boy, 50 Cent, Dr. Dre, OneRepublic, and Elton John. "Give It to Me," its first single, topped the Billboard Hot 100, becoming Timbaland's first and, as of 2021, only No. 1 hit as a lead artist. Other Billboard Hot 100 hits off the album included "The Way I Are" at No. 3 and "Apologize" at No. 2.

Featuring vocals from Furtado and Timberlake, as well as Timbaland himself, "Give It to Me" was co-written by Timbaland (who also played drums), Furtado, Timberlake, American rapper Attitude (Timothy Allan Clayton, n.d.), and American producer Danja (Floyd Nathaniel Hills, 1982–), who played keyboards and guitar and co-produced the song. Furtado's vocal range is mezzo-soprano, whereas Timbaland's is baritone, and Timberlake's is low tenor. The hip hop dance song uses retro elements found in *electro*, a style of popular music that combines electronic elements (especially 808s, keyboard synths that were used in 1970s and 1980s funk and hip hop, and synth-produced futuristic or sci-fi-inspired sound effects). Also inspired by the electronic dance music (EDM) club music scene, the song criticizes haters and critics, including record producer Scott Storch (Storch's 2007 response diss track was "Built Like That"). The refrains stand out for being more pop sounding. Instrumentally, the song exemplifies Timbaland's eclecticism, using retro or old-school hip hop instruments as well as a heavy tribal-sounding beat that is reminiscent of The Dixie Cups' hit recording "Iko Iko" (1965). The song's structure is as follows: intro (bifurcated); verse 1 (trifurcated); refrain (bifurcated); verse 2 (bifurcated); refrain (bifurcated); verse 3 (bifurcated); refrain (bifurcated); bridge 1; bridge 2; refrain′ used as outro. Furtado is featured the most, singing verse 1 and the refrains; she is also prominently featured in the bridges. The song is in G-sharp minor.

"Give It to Me" opens with *a cappella* (unaccompanied), purposefully off-key singing by Timbaland (and likely either Attitude or Danja). This intro's first part leads directly into its second part, an instrumental vamp created by a tom drum being struck hard in common time (quadruple meter or four beats per measure) and snare drum rim shots, coupled with a sixteenth-note timbale beat, both joined midway by shakers and a fading-in keyboard synth-produced *ostinato* (a persistent melodic and/ or rhythmic pattern that exists throughout a piece). Timbaland's elongated and ascending "oh," followed by the spoken-word phrase "yeah boy, come on," concludes the intro.

Verse 1 is the song's most complex verse. Here, Furtado sings with multi-tracked vocals (for harmony and to sound fuller) against the intro's continuing instrumentation. A synth bass and sub-bass emerge midway in the first part. This instrumentation continues into the second part, which is notable for its use of *stop time* (inserting pauses in the accompanying music), which allows Furtado to sing a phrase *a cappella*. In the third part, vocal effects such as lots of reverb and delayed multi-tracked vocals, as well as hiccupping, are applied.

In contrast to the rhythmic focus of the verse, the refrain has a much more lyrical melody and fuller texture. Here, the accompaniment includes keyboard synth chords, synth bass, a distorted new-age-inspired synth-produced whale-call effect, and synth strings, as well as a snare drum, which replaces the tom. The refrain repeats a harmonic pattern in G-sharp minor four times: G-sharp minor-D-sharp minor-E major-C-sharp minor (or i-v-VI-iv). The first part of this pop passage consists of the song's most memorable melody; the second, a call-and-response, keeps Furtado's multi-tracked vocals in the foreground while using her own multi-tracked vocals to supply the responses or answers, which contain the song's title.

Verse 2 features Timbaland's highly auto-tuned and also multi-tracked vocals, which sound monotone and would come close to Jamaican toasting if they did not sound so robotic. Because he identifies himself as the producer, this is a signature verse. With exception of the sub-bass, which is now present throughout both parts, the instrumentation is the same as for verse 1. The refrain then repeats.

Verse 3 features Timberlake, whose highly auto-tuned and multi-tracked vocals mirror Timbaland's. The bifurcated structure of his verse and instrumentation are also the same as Timbaland's. In contrast to Timbaland's booming baritone vocals, however, Timberlake sings mostly in his light and muted high register. In comparison to the first part of both verses, the second part uses more hiccupped vocals. The refrain is repeated and is followed by two bridges that feature Furtado's vocables sung against the intro's beat and keyboard synth ostinato, punctuated by Timberlake's "uh-huhs" in the background. Bridge 1 slows down briefly to a pause while the synth enters the foreground, whereas bridge 2 immediately returns to the original *tempo* (speed of the song) and concludes with synth-produced turntable scratch effects and a futuristic synth-produced shooting effect. The outro consists of the refrain. This time, however, the refrain repeats with the beats and bass dropping out. Here, Furtado sings against the keyboard synth ostinato only, as the song ends abruptly on Furtado's final line, "give it to me."

"Carry Out," the third single off of *Shock Value II* (2009), features Timberlake, who co-wrote the song with Timbaland, Attitude, and J-Roc (Jerome Harmon, 1968–), who also served as co-producer. The song reached No. 11 on the Billboard Hot 100, but reached the Top 10 in Ireland and the U.K. "Carry Out" is a sex-themed song from the perspective of two men focused on appealing to an amazing looking female who is objectified, addressed as "girl" and "baby." The female object never responds; her persona is unvoiced. The song's absurd lyrical content—that the female object's body is like a carryout—is used to humorously offset its otherwise misogynist catcalling. In D-sharp minor, the song's structure is as follows: intro (bifurcated); verse 1 (A, quadfurcated); refrain (twice); verse 2 (A, quadfurcated); refrain (twice); middle-eight (B, bifurcated); refrain′ (four times, extended); instrumental outro.

The intro's first part consists of a cosmic-sounding and descending synth voice that resembles a bomb being dropped, but at a higher pitch to appear less aggressive, followed by a synth-produced saxophone or xaphoon. Both are quickly joined by a synth-produced voice that approximates the *dagga* (the bass side of a *dhol*, a drum used in *bhangra-beat* music) and timbale cowbell beats, which are punctuated by Timbaland's low "eh-eh" vocables, which are slightly auto-tuned in the background. Both vocalists, sounding vocoder distorted, appear in the foreground during the second part while the beats continue as accompaniment. Here, a call-and-response takes place with Timbaland's low voice starting the lines and Timberlake's falsetto voice answering him, repeating the song's title, both occasionally accompanied by male vocables ("whoo"). The intro ends with Timbaland's spoken-word tag to "check it."

Timbaland continues singing verse 1, this time with highly auto-tuned and multi-tracked vocals. In the first part, the beats and cosmic-sounding synths continue and accompany him, whereas the second part folds in a synth-produced bass. The rhythmic flow of Timbaland's words become more elongated in the third part, which also contains pauses. Here, Timberlake's voice is heard in the background with some applied delay, and the bass drops out; both are still accompanied by the beats and the cosmic-sounding synth. By the end of this part, synth-produced horns play a stinger. The bass returns in the fourth part, accompanying Timbaland as his rhythmic flow resembles the verse's first and second parts. Timberlake remains in the background, and the verse ends again with Timbaland's spoken-word tag to "check it."

Like "Give It to Me," the refrain is the song's most lyrical and pop-sounding passage. The refrain's style also incorporates a new wave synth-pop style with its addition of keyboard synths to the beats and cosmic-sounding synth and its later addition of synth strings and a synth-produced horn; the latter doubles Timberlake's melody. In this passage, electric guitar is also used in the background. Timberlake sings the refrain twice in his low register. Also like "Give It to Me," the refrain is based on a repeated chord progression. This time it is D-sharp minor-B major-C-sharp major-D-sharp minor (or i-VI-VII-i). Timberlake's vocals are multi-tracked so that he can harmonize with himself and supply tags in a higher range.

Timberlake continues singing in his low register into verse 2. His auto-tuned vocals are multi-tracked so that he can supply the same backing vocals as he did in verse 1. The verse's quadfurcated structure and instrumentation are identical to Timbaland's previous one, but this time Timberlake's tag is different ("say"). The second refrain, which is just like the first, leads to the middle-eight; however, unlike a textbook eight-measure middle section with a contrasting melody, this B section is bifurcated, with each part having a four-plus-four measure structure. In the first part, Timberlake sings a series of short questions to the female object, doubled softly an octave lower by Timbaland (the same notes are sung but in a lower register). All are sung against the same beats and cosmic synth as earlier, punctuated by electric guitar chord strums, which continue into the second part. In contrast to the first part's questions, Timberlake now commands the female object to "come closer." The final refrain is sung four times instead of twice. A sustained synth strings chord concludes the final refrain. The song concludes not with voices but with an instrumental outro, which initially consists of just the cosmic synth and the beats. The bass quickly returns as more reverb is applied, making the timbales ring more. The song ends abruptly.

As of 2021, Timbaland has won four Grammy Awards and has had a total of five songs reach the Billboard Hot 100 Top 10, with two, both featuring Furtado, reaching No. 1: "Promiscuous" (2006), on which Furtado is the featured performer, and the aforementioned "Give It to Me." By inserting passages or elements from different musical styles (creating unusual juxtapositions or humorous twists), as demonstrated in "Give It to Me" and "Carry Out," Timbaland's productions often challenge hip hop expectations.

JUSTIN TIMBERLAKE (FEATURING TIMBALAND) AND LA MATERIALISTA: "SEXYBACK" AND "LOS PANTALONCITOS"
ALBUMS: *FUTURESEX/LOVESOUNDS* (2006) AND *TRAYECTORIA* (2015)

American singer-songwriter, actor, comedian, and record producer Justin Timberlake (a.k.a. JT, 1981–) is one of hip hop music's most multi-talented performers. As a child, he appeared on *Star Search* (1983–1995) and *The All-New Mickey Mouse Club* (1993–1996). His fame, however, catapulted in the late 1990s, when he was one of the two lead vocalists of NSYNC (a.k.a. *NSYNC or 'N Sync, 1995–2002). As of 2021, Timberlake has won ten Billboard Music Awards, four Emmys, ten Grammy Awards, and a Songwriters Hall of Fame Contemporary Icon Award. He has had four RIAA-certified platinum albums, five No. 1 hits on the Billboard Hot 100, and 16 Top 10 hits on the same chart. His first studio album, *Justified*, reached No. 2 on the Billboard 200 and was followed by a string of studio albums that debuted at No. 1 on the same chart: *FutureSex/Love Sounds* (2006); *The 20/20 Experience* and *The 20/20 Experience—2 of 2* (both 2013); and *Man of the Woods* (2016). All have topped charts internationally as well and all were produced in teams with American record producer, turntablist, rapper, and singer-songwriter Timbaland (for biographical information on Timbaland, see our Must-Hear Music entry on him). Timberlake, as well as Portsmouth, Virginia, rapper-songwriter and producer Missy Elliott, are among Timbaland's most famous consistent collaborators. The team of Timbaland, Timberlake, Danja (see the entry on Timbaland), JAWBreakers (the production duo of Timberlake and will.i.am), and Def-Jam co-founder Rick Rubin (Frederick J. Rubin, 1963–) produced Timberlake's *FutureSex/LoveSounds* on the Jive and Zomba labels (under Sony Music Entertainment), which includes the single "SexyBack" as its second track.

Composed and produced by Danja (as Nate Hills), Timbaland (as Tim Mosley), and Timberlake, "SexyBack" was Timberlake's first song to reach No. 1. It was also RIAA-certified triple platinum in the United States. The song was recorded in December 2005 at Timbaland's studio, the Thomas Crown Headquarters in Virginia Beach, Virginia, and then released in July 2006 on the Jive label. Timbaland later partnered with his engineer Jimmy Douglass to mix the album. According to Paul Tingen's 2007 interview, "Secrets of the Mix Engineers: Jimmy Douglass," an interview with Douglass in the online magazine *Sound on Sound*, "SexyBack" was recorded in just one day and used a minimal composition and production approach. The synthesizers were all virtual and created on a Mac computer, using ProTools as the digital audio workstation, and the groove was created on an Akai MPC3000 touch-pad-controlled digital synthesizer, sequencer, and sampler and Ensoniq ASR10 keyboard-operated digital synthesizer and sampler.

"SexyBack" is a male braggadocio snap song that is not just about sexual prowess; it is also about sexiness. Timberlake sings in a rock style rather than his usual R&B style. His low tenor vocals are highly distorted (and slowed down slightly) via post-production techniques. Timbaland, a baritone, prominently appears, chant-rapping in the refrains but also as a backing vocalist throughout the song. Missy Elliott also appears briefly. Entirely in quadruple meter (four beats per measure), the song's accompaniment, a synth organ voice, constantly rocks between its home key and pitch, A, and B-flat (suggesting A major-B-flat minor, or I-ii). The song's structure is as follows: instrumental intro; verse 1 (A); middle-eight (B); refrain (bifurcated); verse 2 (A′); middle-eight (B); refrain (bifurcated); bridge 1; verse 3 (A″); refrain (bifurcated); bridge 2; outro (bifurcated). The intro establishes the song's groove with instrumentation that is heard almost throughout: a synth organ is used as the bass voice riff (rocking between A and B-flat) and plays against beats created by synth-produced kick drums, snare, hi-hats, congas, and percussion that resembles a finger snap combined with a claves strike (with some applied reverb). The congas sound has oscillating pitches from low to high that are reminiscent of a keyboard-generated tempo or click track (previous examples abound, but just two are Blondie's 1979 new wave song "Heart of Glass" and Obie Trice's 2004 hip hop song "The Setup"). The organ synth plays *staccato* (detached notes) that resemble stabs. In the meantime, Timberlake pants in the background. The intro is concluded by Timbaland's first vocalization, "uh."

The first part of verse 1 features Timberlake, who sings in his low register. Here, his voice is breathy and distorted through an Izotope trash filter plug-in and further post-production studio techniques, according to Tingen's interview with Douglass (Tingen 2007). A separate track of "yeah" backing vocals punctuates the verse, which concludes with Timbaland's hysterically voiced metatextual spoken-word cue to take the song to the bridge (here, his excited speaking voice has an intentional tremble). In the middle-eight, Timberlake's vocals become higher and more forceful and melodic (he starts on the fifth scale step in A major and his descending melody outlines pitches in part of the D minor scale: D, C, B-flat, A). Each of Timberlake's lines is accentuated with Timbaland's "uh-huh," which creates a pseudo call-and-response passage. This section concludes with another metatextual cue uttered by Timbaland in his Wild West vocals, this time to take the song to the chorus (refrain). The first part of the refrain begins with Timbaland's chant-rapped lines, answered by Timberlake's sung lines, thus creating an actual call-and-response. This vocal pattern continues in the second part, which adds harmonized and multi-tracked female backing vocals. Three new instruments are folded into the background: electric guitar (played by Bill Pettaway) and electric bass guitar (played by Darryl Pearson), which emerge in the first part and continue into the second part. A synth-produced harpsichord (left speaker), which plays quickly arpeggiated chords, punctuates the second part. Far in the background, a new sinewy finger-picked electric guitar melody emerges briefly. Slightly reminiscent of Dick Dale's melody in his 1962 surf rock hit of the Middle Eastern folk song "Misirlou," this electric guitar melody can also be heard as a direct reference to Missy Elliott's 2001 hip hop and mainstream hit (composed and produced with Timbaland) "Get Your Freak On," which is finger-picked on a *tumbi* (a Punjabi single-string chordophone used often in traditional and *bhangra-beat* music). Toward the end of the refrain,

Timbaland also sings but then, as all the accompaniment drops off, he chant-raps his last line *a cappella* (unaccompanied). This last line serves as a break for a refrain with repetitive material.

Verse 2 uses the same structure and most of the same instrumentation as verse 1. This time, more synth effects appear in the background and more studio effects are applied to Timberlake's vocals, such as those that muffle his use of the "f" word. The same middle-eight and refrain then return, but this time the finger-picked electric guitar melody turns into a prominent melody in the foreground of bridge 1, which also features Missy Elliott saying "you ready?" In contrast to other sections, which are eight measures or eight-plus-eight measures in length, bridge 1 is only four measures. For the first time, the synth organ drops out. Here, just the kick drum, snare, closing hi-hat, congas, and snap beat serve as accompaniment. Bridge 1 also serves as a breakbeat passage for dancers.

The synth organ as bass riff returns in verse 3, which uses the same instrumentation and structure as the earlier verses. This verse is followed by the same refrain and then bridge 2, which, like bridge 1, is just a brief four measures in length. Bridge 2 recycles the harmonized multi-tracked female backing vocals heard in the second part of the refrains, the intro's synth organ and beats, and Missy Elliott's asking if Timberlake is ready. He breathily says, "yes," and the music pauses as if it were being played on a record player when the power was suddenly turned off (the pitch quickly descends and the song slows down). All restarts immediately, which leads to the outro. This final, mostly instrumental part of the song, is a continuation of the previous instrumentation except that the synth organ plays a rhythmically more elaborate variation of its riff against the track that consists of its bass riff in the first part. The electric guitar finger-picked melody dominates the foreground in the second part as the backing vocals from the second part of the refrain play into the fadeout.

Like "SexyBack," La Materialista's "Los Pantaloncitos" ("The Shorts") from her 2015 album *Trayectoria* (*Trajectory*, which she produced herself, working with mixer and songwriter Alex Ridha), is a sexual braggadocio song that uses a minimal composition and production approach. La Materialista (Yameiry Infante Honoret, 1985–) is a Dominican reggaetón, hip hop, bachata, and pop music singer, as well as occasional rapper, who is also known for her stints in modeling, film, and television (usually as a TV personality). To Dominicans, she is known as La Reina Urbana Callejera (the Urban Street Queen), their leading female advocate of hip hop. Although she was accused of plagiarizing from the K-pop girl band 2NE1's song, "I Am the Best" (2011) with her song "Chipi Cha Cha" (2013, released as a cover in 2015), La

Materialista has had continual success since 2015 and 2016, when she released three albums on digital media: *Clásicos*, *Trayectoria*, and *A otro nivel* (*At Another Level*).

In "Los Pantaloncitos," La Materialista, a mezzo-soprano, breathlessly chant-raps, talk-sings, sings, and raps (old-school and new school style) about her ability to make a pair of shorts—in the official video, a pair of ripped Daisy Dukes that bare much of her bottom—into a weapon, allowing her to capture any man who is "chulo" (roughly, "cool" or "attractive") and is willing to buy her material things and pay her bills. This fast, energetic song focuses on La Materialista's vocals against percussive beats, a synth-generated sub-bass, and a variety of sampled sound effects. Entirely in quadruple meter, the song structure of "Los Pantaloncitos" is as follows: intro (bifurcated); refrain (twice); verse 1 (A, bifurcated); bridge 1; verse 2 (A', bifurcated); verse 3 (A''); bridge 2; middle-eight (B, bifurcated), refrain (twice); verse 2' (A', bifurcated); bridge 1'; verse 4 (A'', bifurcated); middle-eight (B, bifurcated); refrain' (bifurcated); outro, consisting of verse 5 (A''', bifurcated), instrumental bridge; and last line of verse 5. Most of the passages are four or, when bifurcated, four-plus-four measures; however, the lyrics' lines often have an asymmetrical division (for example, the first part of verse 1 is a couplet whereas the second part is comprised of four lines). Adding to the song's complexity, "Los Pantaloncitos" uses a home key in its middle-eight sections only. Most of the time, the song instead uses home pitches or tonal centers, including F (intro), A (refrains and verses 1, 4, and 5), and D (bridge 1, verses 2 and 3, middle-eight sections, and the outro instrumental bridge to the end).

The first part of the intro begins with La Materialista's brief *a cappella* (unaccompanied) chant-rap line, followed by an ascending then descending bass and her laughter (most of her music videos show that she is extremely playful with her sexuality, comparable to Spanish-American entertainer Charo). The second part establishes the song's main instrumentation, which serves as the beats: a synth sub-bass countered by a warbled siren effect, both set against a frenetic timbale and bass drum—at times, the latter sounds as if it is underwater. A vocal trill and pause signal the end of the intro. The refrain is a continuation of the same instrumentation, but without the sub-bass and siren. La Materialista breaks into a breathy half-chant, half-rap delivery in both parts. In the first part, male screams appear in the background. In the second part, clipped female vocables in the background emerge, sounding childlike, and punctuate La Materialista's lines. A finger-plucked bass guitar also emerges in the accompaniment and plays into verse 1.

In the first part of verse 1, these vocables evolve into "wahs" in double-time, building up energy. They disappear toward the end of the second part. The siren returns to the continuing beats in bridge 1, which features La Materialista repeatedly chanting vocables, punctuated by her use of the vocable "shoo." Kick drum and tom toms are emphasized in this brief four-measure passage, but all drop out at its conclusion, which consists of a synth-produced bomb sound effect, followed by her playful "hey!"

Verse 2, also bifurcated, uses the same structure and vocalizations as verse 1 but with new lyrics. Here, La Materialista uses a *staccato* articulation for her vocal delivery, with her pitched words sounding crisp and detached. The "wah" backing vocals are replaced with boosting "heys." Though the earlier beats continue, the warbled siren drops out in verses 2 and 3. Unlike verse 1 with its uneven division of lines, verse 2 has a couplet assigned to each part. The second part of verse 2 ends with her vocal grinding, accompanied by a quick synth-produced sweep that makes the music sound as if it may come to a crashing halt.

In verse 3, La Materialista's flow becomes smoother and more talk-sung than earlier. The kick drum and sub-bass are emphasized again. Starting from the second part of the intro, a brief timbale jam block flourish had appeared far in the background to accentuate the end of La Materialista's lines; in this verse, because of her elongated talk-singing, the jam block seems more prominent. Gearshift sound effects are now folded in, and all accompaniment drops out at its conclusion: a synth-produced gun shot. Bridge 2 follows and features her bemused laughter against the beats, which all stop to the sound effect of dropping coins.

The first part of the middle-eight shifts to La Materialista's singing, backed by multi-tracked female vocals that sometimes repeat her lines against the beats. This part concludes with an exaggerated sampled turntable backspin effect that sounds as though it is combined with splashing water. The warbled siren effect returns in the second part as La Materialista sings the song's lengthiest passage on the nonsense vocable "chuvidubidu." The refrain and verse 2', with small additions to the lyrics of the original verse, follow, as does bridge 1'. Like verse 2', only slight variation is found in this bridge. This time, it comes to a halt on La Materialista's playfully spoken and elongated "hello."

Verse 4 features La Materialista's chant-rapping again, as well as a reappearance of the gearshift sound effects from the first part. This verse contains four lines and concludes with all dropping out for the cash-register ding. The second part concludes the verse with a couplet and some more recycled sound effects, such as the sweep from the second part of verse 2. All the instrumentation drops out again for another concluding sound effect—this time, the bomb sound effect from bridge 1 gets recycled. The middle-eight returns, followed by the refrain', now with some additional words.

The outro is treated not as a small concluding passage but rather as a large concluding gesture that contains verse 5, La Materialista's signature verse in which she hypes herself for making records on Rompiendo Records, a Barcelona, Spain-based label, against the beats and finger-plucked bass guitar. Another synth-produced, slowed-down turntable backspin sounds after her hype. Her chant-rapping flow also slows down, and she pauses more. The siren reappears, and soon thereafter she is interrupted by a low-pitched robotic male voice, accompanied by a descending synth-produced pitch and bomb sound effect. An instrumental bridge with a new bubbling keyboard synth, which replaces the siren, feels inserted but quickly leads to her last line, a final "hey" boost in the backing vocals, a turntable backspin, and a conclusion on the same exaggerated sampled turntable backspin combined with a splashing water sound effect (used in the first part of the middle-eight sections).

Though as of 2021 information on La Materialista's record sales remains unavailable, her most popular videos, for the songs "Los Pantaloncitos" (2015), "Yo No Quiero Boda" ("I Didn't Want a Wedding," 2015), "Corazón al Revés" ("Upside-Down Heart," 2015), "Buenísima" ("Great," 2016), "Wow ¡Que Rico!" ("Wow! How Rich," 2016), "Niveles" ("Levels," 2018), and "TomaB" (2020), have garnered over 49.6 million views combined. Her most popular video, "La Chapa Que Vibran" ("The A** That Shakes," 2014) by itself has had 193.5 million views.

TIME ZONE (FEATURING JOHN LYDON): "WORLD DESTRUCTION" NON-ALBUM SINGLE (1984)

When compared to "Planet Rock" (discussed in one of this book's previous Must-Hear Music entries), much less is known about the recording of Afrika Bambaataa (for biographical information, see the entry on "Planet Rock") and his electro-funk band Time Zone's (1983–) "World Destruction" (1984), which features ex-Sex Pistols and Public Image Ltd. (PiL) singer-songwriter John Lydon (1956–). As Johnny Rotten, Lydon became best known as the lead singer of the London punk band Sex Pistols (1975–1978). Despite having little musical talent, the band catapulted punk's significance and notoriety internationally through arousing songs such as "Anarchy in the U.K." (1976), "God Save the

Queen (1977)," and "Pretty Vacant" (1977), which charted, respectively, at No. 38, No. 2, and No. 6 on the U.K. Singles Chart.

By the early 1980s, punk and hip hop had both emerged as DIY (do-it-yourself) cultures in New York City, where the art world began appreciating both, and crossover collaborations started taking place. By 1981, Blondie's "Rapture" became an international mainstream hit, charting at No. 1 and No. 33, respectively, on the Billboard Hot 100 and Billboard's Hot R&B/Hip Hop Songs in the United States. "Rapture" fused NYC hip hop and new wave rock, as well as funk and disco (new wave rock was directly related to punk but less confrontational and rough—thus the music industry embraced it over punk). Afrika Bambaataa & the Soulsonic Force's "Planet Rock" was released in 1982 and eventually became the first 12-inch hip hop album to be RIAA-certified gold. Like "Rapture," its musical elements—most notably rap and funk, as well as Kraftwerk-inspired electronica—were meant to appeal to diverse listeners. After "Planet Rock," Afrika Bambaataa continued his hip hop and electro-funk style with "Looking for the Perfect Beat" (1983). During this time, he formed his electro-funk project band, Time Zone. From the start, Time Zone's membership varied, and its participants were solely based on Afrika Bambaataa's performance needs. Time Zone's debut single was "The Wildstyle" (1983), but "World Destruction" was the band's biggest commercial success, peaking at No. 44 on the U.K. Singles Chart. Though it was not the first successful collaboration between hip hop and new wave (or punk), "World Destruction" stands out for its edgy sound and extensive use of punk rock elements. The song also just missed becoming the first rap-rock recording, as the release of Run-DMC's "Rock Box" was eight months prior.

"World Destruction," which brought together Afrika Bambaataa and John Lydon—two polar-opposite musicians—was also a collaboration with producer and bassist Bill Laswell (1955–) and Parliament-Funkadelic's keyboardist-songwriter and Talking Heads' guest and touring keyboardist Bernie Worrell (George Bernard Worrell, 1944–2016). Laswell, who began his musical career as a bassist for R&B and funk bands, was the house producer at French-American owned Celluloid Records in New York City. Both Laswell and his label were interested in producing "collision music." This term was used by *Black Music & Jazz Review* editor Chris May, who later managed Celluloid Records' London office, to describe avant-garde musical fusions, particularly with new popular music. Laswell straddled New York City's hip hop, punk, and avant-garde jazz communities, while producing and playing bass. Laswell and jazz pianist-songwriter Herbie Hancock attended performances by Afrika Bambaataa and his Universal Zulu Nation groups, which helped inspire them to co-write and produce "Rockit" (1983), another song included in this book's Must-Hear Music list. In the same year, Laswell's ambient punk and jazz rock band and production duo Material, Afrika Bambaataa, and Time Zone (together as Shango) released vocal and instrumental versions of "Zulu Groove" and "Shango Message" on the Celluloid Records label. At this time, Afrika Bambaataa still worked under the Tommy Boy label, which gave him permission to work on these Celluloid recordings.

In the autumn of 1984, Laswell and Afrika Bambaataa began working on a new song that would fuse hip hop, electro-funk, and punk. Laswell, who also knew Lydon, brought him onto the project after learning that Afrika Bambaataa wanted an over-the-top main vocalist and that Bambaataa and Lydon mutually appreciated each other's work. Lydon was living in Pasadena, California and, with permission from his label, Elektra/Asylum Records, flew to New York City in October to work on the single. In addition to vocals, Lydon contributed to the song's beats. Laswell oversaw the arrangement of the entire song, which was mostly co-written by him and Afrika Bambaataa. Time Zone's rapper-singer-songwriters Amad Henderson (William Henderson, n.d.) and the anonymous B-Side (a.k.a. Fab 5 Betty, Ann Boyle, n.d.) contributed supporting spoken-word and backing vocals, though both were just credited as Time Zone on the album. Whereas "Planet Rock" relies on electronic instruments to accompany the vocalists, "World Destruction" employs musicians who play rock instruments, such as Laswell on electric bass and his frequent in-house collaborators, Nicky Skopelitis on electric guitar and Aïyb Dieng on percussion. In addition, the song uses electronic instruments: Laswell programmed the LinnDrum and Oberheim DMX drum machines, and Worrell his Minimoog. Worrell was such an auteur on synthesizer that his contribution to the sound of "World Destruction" should not be overlooked, even though he is uncredited for the song's composition; it is impossible to imagine "World Destruction" without Worrell's instrumental refrain and the effects he applies to its melody. The single was recorded in less than four hours in November 1984 at Evergreen Studio in New York City and was released a month later.

Lyrically, "World Destruction" warns of and laments the condition of the world, highlighting political leaders intent on nuclear war (the official video, not the recording, opens with an excerpt from Ronald Reagan's 1984 televised debate with Walter Mondale in Kansas City). It is also a high-energy dance song (and a club favorite in the mid-1980s) that cynically and sardonically (through gallows humor) celebrates the end of the world. The song's structure is as follows: intro (bifurcated); refrain; verse 1 (bifurcated); prechorus 1; instrumental refrain (played one-and-a-half times); refrain'; verse 2 (truncated); prechorus 2; instrumental refrain' (repeated); refrain"; verse 3 (bifurcated); prechorus 3; instrumental refrain"; instrumental bridge; instrumental refrain''' (repeated); vocal bridge; outro (trifurcated, contains instrumental refrain'''', which repeats three times). With one exception in the first part of the introduction, the entire song is in A major. An interesting aspect of this song's structure is that has different texts for its three prechoruses; their purpose is to build up energy to the instrumental refrains rather than to the refrains that feature vocals.

The first part of the intro starts with an unusual fade-in with loud, energetic, and dive-bombing electric heavy-metal-style guitars and fret noise, which give way quickly to the song's cowbell-driven beats. The electric guitars use classic rock pick-ups (such as P-90s) that create a crunchy sound; its power chords ring out. In addition to cowbell, the song's beat is comprised of snare and kick drums played on a drum set: all establish a quadruple-meter (four beats per measure) time signature. The guitars establish C as a very temporary pitch center. As the guitars and percussion continue playing in the intro's second part, the bass electric guitar joins them. All soon become accompaniment to Afrika Bambaataa's booming baritone-range chant-rap, backed by Time Zone's male vocalists. The home key of A major is firmly established as the guitars rock between sustained A major and its relative minor, F-sharp minor (in A major: I-vi). The electric guitars initially drop off at the beginning of the refrain but quickly return with power-chord strums to punctuate Afrika Bambaataa and John Lydon's chant-rap along with the continuing percussion. Lydon's creaky high tenor-range vocals contrast to Afrika Bambaataa's booming ones and they sometimes sound as if they are harmonizing. They chant-rap together but they also take turns echoing a word. As expected, this refrain mentions the title of the song.

Verse 1 features just Afrika Bambaataa against the continuing drum beat. Before the first part ends, 808-generated snare beats are added through a filter to sound like an air loop. Both the first and second parts are eight measures in length, with the first part in A major and the second part again rocking between A major and F-sharp minor chords. Afrika Bambaataa continues into the second part, this time accompanied by sustained guitar chords and Lydon's higher-pitched and whiny "wha-wha" boosting vocables. The brief four-measure prechorus features both chant-rapping together again, at times with Time Zone's backing vocals.

As in the refrain, the guitars drop out initially and then quickly return to punctuate the vocals as the beats continue into the instrumental refrain.

Like "Planet Rock," the song's most memorable melody is its short instrumental refrain; however, this time it was originally composed. The instrumental refrain is comprised of the pitches G-sharp-A-E, G-sharp-A-F-sharp, G-sharp-A-E-C-sharp-F-sharp (the G-sharp is an *appoggiatura*, an accented, crunchy dissonance that quickly resolves up a half-step to A). Worrell plays the instrumental refrain with a voice he created on his Minimoog, used here as the lead synth. This melody sounds reminiscent of a Hammond B-3 organ, while at the same time introducing an eerie atmosphere by Worrell's adjusting the synth voice to sound smooth and cosmic through voltage-controlled filter and pitch-bending controls. Though Worrell plays just the melody, the harmonic motion rocks between A major and F-sharp minor a couple of times, just as it did earlier in the intro's and verse 1's second parts. The electric bass guitar reinforces this harmonic motion by sustaining the roots of the two chords, the pitches A and F-sharp. Worrell is accompanied by mostly Lydon's screams in the background, sonically matched by electric guitar effects. The return of the refrain' interrupts the instrumental refrain. This time, it features Lydon's idiosyncratic vocals only: here, he chant-raps, using his high register and lots of upward inflection, both of which are well suited for punk rock. He is accompanied by the same instrumentation as the earlier refrain.

Verse 2 features Afrika Bambaataa's chant-rapping with the same beats and electric guitar chords. It is just eight measures, unlike verse 1, which has two parts that are eight measures each (for a total length of 16 measures). This time, the electric guitars briefly alternate between left and right speakers, and Worrell plays a synth stinger in the background. The following prechorus 2 is a signature passage for Time Zone, chant-rapped by all the vocalists. This four-measure passage uses different lyrics from prechorus 1, and it ends with the vocalists shouting "kaboom!" a few times. The last "kaboom!" is stretched out over the beginning of the instrumental refrain', which is played twice. The first time, the Minimoog melody sounds like it did earlier, but with more electric-guitar fret noises and thrashing, as well as siren effects (on the right speaker). In the background, B-Side and Henderson's conversation can be heard (she tells him that she is going insane). The refrain" returns with both Lydon and Afrika Bambaataa's chant-rapping in the foreground and accompaniment similar to that in the previous refrains, but with a concluding electric guitar *glissandi* (sliding up and down pitches) here.

Verse 3 resembles verse 1 in structure and instrumentation. It again features Afrika Bambaataa's chant-rapping. In the second part, however, the electric guitars thrash and play more flourishes and dive-bombs, and apply more buzzed effects. Prechorus 3, featuring mostly Afrika Bambaataa, leads to the instrumental refrain″, which plays just once and is punctuated by Afrika Bambaataa and the male Time Zone vocalists. This time, the Minimoog melody is more pitch-bent and distorted as Lydon sings the line "I'm in a time zone." Bridge 1 is a short four-measure passage that emphasizes the cowbell against the percussion beats. It leads to Afrika Bambaataa's and Lydon's squeals and another instrumental refrain‴, which plays twice. Toward the end of the first iteration, the electric guitars simulate computer sounds (right speaker). In the second part, as the Minimoog melody plays, a phaser is applied, along with more pitch-bending using a tone wheel. These effects make the instrumental melody tremble and sound unsettling.

Lydon continues in bridge 2, initially in his angst-ridden, creaky high register, punctuated by Afrika Bambaataa, and ultimately descending to his lowest register by sliding down in pitch. Lydon's last "I'm in a time zone" utterance is in his low range and uses vocal fry.

Lydon's following scream, backed by filtered and distorted electric guitars, initiates the outro. The first part suggests that he has gone mad as electric guitars rock between A major and F-sharp minor chords. The second part features Lydon's "I'm in a time zone" vocalizations heard in bridge 2, as well as Afrika Bambaataa's scream. Lydon slides down with a lengthy descent, accompanied by thrashing electric guitars, this time creating a false conclusion. The third and final part of the song is comprised of the instrumental refrain⁗, which plays three times against the continuing electric guitars and percussion. The Minimoog melody includes pitch-bending and phaser effects again. Starting the second time, a lower Minimoog keyboard voice doubles it, as congas are subtly folded into the percussion. The congas continue into the third time, as all fade out.

After "World Destruction," Laswell collaborated again with Lydon, Worrell, Skopelitis, and Dieng on PiL's alternative hard rock recording *Album*, inviting legendary drummer Ginger Baker and guitarist Steve Vai. *Album* was No. 14 and No. 115, respectively, on the U.K. Albums chart and the Billboard 200. PiL's concerts have since included new versions of "World Destruction" in its sets, using Lydon as the sole lead vocalist and replacing Worrell's synthesizer with several electric guitars during the instrumental refrain. Afrika Bambaataa put the Time Zone project band on lengthy hiatus, reviving it in 1992 with "Zulu

War Chant." Time Zone released a handful of singles in 1990 and 1992, which were compiled in the 1992 album *Thy Will B Funk*. In 1995, the band released another album titled *Warlocks and Witches, Computer Chips, Microchips, and You*. Unfortunately, these albums did not sell well. Nearly ten years later, the band resumed recording and released the album *Everyday People: The Breakbeat Party Album* (2004) and the single "Push Pt. 2" (2005, with "Shake Ya Bodys" on the B-Side), both released on Afrika Bambaataa's (and Universal Zulu Nation's) Bronx-based Planet Rock Music label.

TRICKY: "GHETTO STARS"
ALBUM: *MIXED RACE* (2010)

British record producer, rapper, and actor Tricky (Adrian Nicholas Matthews Thaws, 1968–), who is part Jamaican and part Anglo-Guyanese, is arguably the father of trip hop. He began as a member of trip hop pioneer band Massive Attack (1987–) before going solo in 1995. His debut solo album, *Maxinquaye*, began a partnership with vocalist Martina Topley-Bird (Martina Gillian Topley, 1975–) and a continuation of his gothic musical style that fuses hip hop, alternative rock, electronica, and a reggae-related electronica style called *ragga*. Like reggae, *ragga* emerged in Jamaica, but was much easier to produce because reggae relies on live instrumentation whereas *ragga* employs electroacoustic instruments. Tricky's ninth album, *Mixed Race* (2010), is uncharacteristically uptempo. It spawned the single "Murder Weapon," which charted in France.

Tricky composed and produced *Mixed Race's* "Ghetto Stars," a downtempo (chill-out) cautionary song about the gangsta lifestyle. Although the song is not horrorcore, it nevertheless embraces Tricky's love of horror film soundtrack elements. In addition to his typical whispered vocals (a cross between rap and spoken word), the song also features London-born Irish soprano Francesca Belmonte (a.k.a. Franky Riley, n.d.). She sings verses by herself and with Tricky, a high tenor, who joins in to sing the refrains with her. Tricky also talk-sings and raps, using a whispering voice to contribute to the gothic, atmospheric tone of the song. Both vocalists use personae, with Francesca Belmonte performing as Tricky's gangster moll.

With the exception of the intro, which has no chords and suggests G-sharp as its pitch center, the key of "Ghetto Stars" is entirely D-sharp minor. Also entirely in quadruple meter (four beats per measure), it alternates between two chords every four beats: D-sharp minor (the home key/chord, i, or D-sharp-F-sharp-A-sharp) down to B major (VI or B-D-sharp-F-sharp). Both chords have D-sharp and F-sharp in common, which makes the chord changes a bit static sounding. The song's structure is as follows: intro; verse 1 (bifurcated); verse 2 (bifurcated); refrain; verse 3 (quintfurcated); refrain'; verse 4; verse 2 (bifurcated); bridge; refrain" (twice); bridge'; outro (bifurcated).

"Ghetto Stars" begins with very soft white noise, followed by a synth-generated acoustic piano voice and heavy, hiccupped tom and kick drum. All of these sounds are trash-distorted; in other words, filtered to sound damaged or mangled. Here, the acoustic piano synth voice plays G-sharp, A, F-sharp, and G-sharp and then G-sharp, A, and A before the beats finish the intro and kick off the next song section; however, the way the melody ends on two A pitches makes it sound as if it is cut off. The gothic atmosphere is created by the combination of white noise, trash distortion, an incomplete, almost directionless initial melody that sounds reminiscent of horror film soundtracks (created by neighboring tones to the temporary pitch center, G-sharp), and some added reverb.

Francesca Belmonte's verse 1 is marked by a shift in instrumentation to 1980s-style arpeggiated synth string voices, which become the main accompaniment, as they play against the drum beat and electric bass, with added crash and hi-hat cymbal effects. There is also a peppering of a synth voice that is used to interject science-fiction sounding effects (a clicking sound that coincidentally also sounds like a gun's clip being reloaded). Francesca Belmonte's voice is whispery and ethereal, almost mumbling, and it is multi-tracked and processed to sound as though it is filtered through white noise (sounding like an air loop). Verse 2 uses the same instrumentation. She continues singing the refrain. Here, Tricky is heard for the first time singing an octave lower than Belmonte in a baritone range. The refrain sounds musically related to verse 1, continuing its instrumentation. Most notably, the arpeggiated synth strings sound louder, reinforced by additional electric and bass guitar accompaniment. As the refrain progresses, his part becomes the aforementioned whispered spoken word, adding an eerie effect that is heightened by a return of the distortion and white-noise production techniques that were previously used in the intro and verse 1.

Verse 3, rapped by Tricky, is a five-part verse that consists of some autobiographical details, suggesting that his persona is not just an act. Throughout the verse, he raps and uses some whispered talk-singing, at times almost breaking into regular speech. Matching the downtempo style of the music, he slowly articulates some of his words, which sometimes get hiccupped. His voice is multi-tracked and processed with a delay effect, so that the two iterations of his voice are slightly off, which further adds to the song's atmosphere. A lot of reverb is also applied to the entire mix. The first and second parts of Tricky's verse are marked by the dropping-out of the higher synth strings, as well as the guitars; the only synth strings that remain present are the low ones that double the sustained synth-generated bass. The rest of the instrumentation, including the clicking noises, continues. The higher-pitched arpeggiated synth strings return in the remaining parts of this section. All of these parts are also distinguishable as Tricky starts a new thought (new lyrically thematic material) or changes his rapping flow.

The second iteration of the refrain sounds exactly like the first one but ends with a clicking effect in the foreground. Verse 4, sung by Francesca Belmonte, has the sparsest texture in the song, suggesting a point of arrival. Even though her vocals sound most similar to verse 1, she replaces second person with third person, and mentions that she is now singing to Tricky's character through prison bars. This time, her vocals are accompanied by toms and a snare rim shot beat, the clicking effect, a very soft synth bass, and a new, distorted, ethereal synth flute voice. This short verse ends on a brief pause or caesura, which is followed by her taking a deep breath and singing the second iteration of verse 2.

An instrumental bridge, which continues the previous section's instrumentation but places the arpeggiating synth strings more in the foreground, punctuated by clicking and gunshot effects, builds up to a climax—the final iterations of the refrain. At its loudest, the song repeats the refrain. The same instrumental bridge returns, this time with additional gunshot effects. The instrumentation continues in the outro, which starts with Tricky's whispering one fading, final line (which includes the title of the song). The white noise heard in the intro re-emerges as the song fades out.

"Ghetto Stars" did not chart; however, it is has become a cult favorite, creating new listeners of Tricky's music. In February 2013, Tricky broke a three-year hiatus and announced the release of a new album, *False Idols*. Over the course of his career, he has released thirteen albums and has collaborated with a wide range of artists, including Terry Hall, Björk (whom he briefly dated), Gravediggaz, Grace Jones, and PJ Harvey. He has had one British Phonographic Industry certified gold album (*Maxinquaye*), and two albums reached the Top 10 on the U.K. Albums chart. Six of his albums have charted on the Billboard 200, with his highest ranking being No. 84, with *Angels with Dirty Faces* (1998). He continues to record, and in early 2020 he released the EP *20, 20* and the album

Fall to Pieces. Tricky has also acted in films, with his most important role being in the 1997 Luc Besson film *The Fifth Element*.

TUMI AND CHINESE MAN (FEATURING TAIWAN MC): "BETTER THAT WAY"
ALBUM: *THE JOURNEY* (2015)

Tanzanian-born South African rapper, singer, songwriter, poet, and record label owner Tumi Molekane (a.k.a. Tumi, Boitumelo Molekane, 1981–), is best known as lead singer of Tumi and the Volume (2002–2012), an experimental band that fused hip hop with African and Latin jazz, afropop, reggae, and rock. In 2006, he released his debut album, *Music from My Good Eye*, on his label, Motif Records. By the 2000s, he had a headliner's career, including reinventing himself as the debonair Stogie T and, in 2012, forming the short-lived duo T-Z Deluxe, with Zubz (Ndabaningi Mabuye, 1976–), a Zambian-born, Zimbabwean-raised, South African rapper. As Stogie T, he released two singles in 2016, "Diamond Walk" and "By Any Means" (both from the album *Stogie T*). He also worked with Chinese Man, a French DJ and remix crew discussed in one of this book's Must-Hear Music entries. Tumi and Chinese Man's "Once Upon a Time," from the album *The Groove Sessions, Vol. 3* (2014), featured not only Chinese Man but also usual Chinese Man anonymous collaborator Taiwan MC (n.d.).

In 2015, Tumi and Chinese Man teamed up to release *The Journey*, a self-described "musical trip hosted by Tumi and shaped by Chinese Man." Its songs are rap-based hip hop, with the exception of the album's standout, its third track, "Better That Way," a quirky tune that rivals The Squirrel Nut Zippers for its fusion of gypsy jazz, 1930s swing, hip hop, and klezmer but with reggae thrown in for good measure. For his part, Tumi raps a couple of verses, but he also talk-sings, chants, toasts, and sings (reggae style, along with Taiwan MC). The song's lyrics are an indictment of both the music industry and consumer tastes, pointing out the tendency toward "big songs" (hits by big-name hip hop stars) that result in lots of air play and profit, especially for the big record labels (the song references major label CEOs' willingness to offer payola to get more air time). Against these forces, Tumi and Chinese Man state emphatically that they both do not like the system and that they refuse to be a part of it, opting instead to be "dangerously independent" and produce music the band members can be proud of—and that its more sophisticated fan base wants to hear.

"Better That Way" uses G minor as its home key. The song's structure is as follows: instrumental intro; verse 1 (A); hook; verse 2 (A'); hook;

rap interlude 1 (trifurcated); hook'; rap interlude 1 (concluded); hook"; verse 1 (B); verse 2 (B); verse 3 (B); refrain; rap interlude 2; hook; bridge 1; bridge 2; hook; refrain; verse 1 (A); hook; verse 2 (A'); outro (bifurcated). An alternative way of hearing the structure is as a large AA'BA" form with an intro, inserted hooks, rap interludes, a refrain and outro: consolidating verses 1 (A) and 2 (A') with an inserted hook between them; rap interlude (rap interludes 1 and 2 consolidated and with the hook"); an extended middle-eight (B, verses 1, 2, and 3); refrain; rap interlude (truncated with hook); bridges 1 and 2; hook; refrain; consolidating verses 1 and 2 (together labeled as A"); outro. This entry analyzes the piece the former way because doing so better deconstructs the song.

The intro begins with a sustained and growled trumpet blast (on the pitch D^4) that is sampled from producer, pianist, and songwriter Joe "Fingers" Carr (Louis Ferdinand Busch, 1910–1979) and His Ragtime Band's 1953 recording of "Istanbul (Not Constantinople)" (1953, Nat Simon and Jimmy Kennedy), titled as "Istanbul." This swing rendition was remixed in 1996 and appears as Part I of "Istanbul (Not Constantinople): Parts I and II." It is combined with the 1961 space lounge instrumental recording by 80 Drums around the World, which originally appeared on the album *Staged for Stereo—Highlights*. The 1996 remixed version, credited to Joe "Fingers" Carr/80 Drums around the World, was released on the CD compilation *Ultra Lounge, Vol. 3: Space Capades* on the Capitol label. The 1996 song also keeps the blaring trumpet on the same pitch.

In "Better That Way," the instrumental intro's initial trumpet blast (left speaker) ushers in percussion (shakers and tambourine) and a lightly played snare drum. A male voice is heard chuckling or snickering (as is often heard in klezmer music), followed by a groove created by a synth bass meant to sound like an acoustic upright bass (emphasizing quadruple meter), kick drum, and other percussion (held over from the intro, with the tambourine more prominent, also on the left speaker). Verse 1 (A) features Tumi talk-singing in monochromatic, staccato lines against this accompaniment, punctuated by other percussion instruments such as conga drums and claves. His high tenor vocals are contrasted with the hook, which contains a bass voice that sings "people just like it better that way." This hook samples the bass from Joe "Fingers" Carr and His Ragtime Band's 1953 recording (it appears isolated and therefore easy to cut from the original recording). In 1990, another cover of "Istanbul (Not Constantinople)," this time by They Might Be Giants (a.k.a. TMBG, 1982–) on their album *Flood*, made famous (one could argue iconic) a vocal bass version of the phrase "better that way," where the word "way" is elongated. The idea of that phrase is used by

Tumi and Chinese Man in the song; however, whereas TMBG's John Flansburgh (1960–) ascends on the phrase, the uncredited bass singer's melodic contour on the 1953 recording (sampled here by Chinese Man) descends. This bass phrase sounds comparatively comical when placed against Tumi's vocals, which seems appropriate to the song's meaning: the ridiculousness of consumer taste in hip hop, an epidemic of bad taste that is being led by the music industry itself. In short, Tumi laments the industry standards, while the absurd bass voice concludes that maybe buyers of music just like formulaic, predictable music (created by big names on big labels).

Verse 2 (A′) uses the same instrumentation and is followed by a repeat of the hook. Rap interlude 1 consists of a much heavier bass, reminiscent of a tuba *oompah* heard in some klezmer dance music, and percussion accompaniment (all centered, albeit slightly left speaker). As the beat increases in volume and more reverb gets applied, a kissing sound effect, multi-tracked hand claps, snare flourishes, and occasional cymbals are added—all in this interlude's three parts. Tumi raps the first verse, his lines still staccato and short but his flow smooth. His voice raises, giving the impression of being strained in frustration and anger, as male vocalizations (mainly grunts) in the background add energy during his lines. Just before the trumpet blast appears as a tag and cues in the second part of the interlude, an acoustic piano enters and punctuates this section, playing the pitches F^7 to D^7. Some reverb is applied to the piano, which continues accompanying the return of the hook, which interrupts the interlude. The piano continues into the third and final part of this interlude as well, which underscores Tumi's frustration. Tumi continues to comment on musical taste, adding more to the sense of frustration. The following hook includes a vocal tag of vocables (e.g., "yo").

Section B's verses feature Taiwan MC's low tenor toasting vocals, accompanied by a heavy beat. The use of toasting is purposeful here, for Taiwan MC mentions Jamaican *riddim* later in this section. In verse 1, the acoustic piano drops out, but the kissing sound effect and the trumpet blasts can be heard in the background. Against continued male vocalizations (grunts, the sound "ahwoo," and similar sounds), Taiwan MC talk-sings his words with force, establishing the musician's refusal to become more commercial, even though it may mean living a life as a B-list artist. In verse 2, the acoustic piano reappears, and a middle-range synth voice that combines violin with a sine wave emerges. Here, Taiwan MC's flow hastens. Verse 3 is marked by Taiwan MC's use of triplets. The piano continues and so does the blaring trumpet, both punctuating the end of this section. A synth keyboard voice foreshadows the melody of the upcoming refrain.

Placing a refrain this late in a song is unusual not only for hip hop but for popular songs in general. The refrain is sung by Tumi and Taiwan MC in parallel perfect fourths (Tumi's high vocals sing G, F, E-flat, then D over Taiwan MC's lower D, C, B-flat, and G pitches, respectively). The use of the parallel perfect fourths, like consecutive or parallel fifths, resembles a musical trope used often between the 19th and 20th centuries in Europe and the United States to evoke traditional Chinese music. Chinese Man, comprised of mostly white Europeans, re-appropriates this trope in this refrain as a musical declaration about their commitment to its music, which the song describes as dynamic. Tumi and Taiwan MC sing the refrain using a heavy Jamaican patois, accompanied by the kissing sound, heavy bass-driven beats, and an acoustic piano's high-pitched F^7 to D^7. Their refrain repeats, this time with talking and Tumi's rapping appearing as well (the last especially foreshadowing rap interlude 2). The piano concludes the refrain by adding a tag.

Rap interlude 2 features Tumi again, this time rapping about innovators versus imitators. It includes the acoustic piano and a kissing sound effect in the background, in addition to the heavy bass-driven beats heard in the section A verses. The hook repeats, but this time Taiwan MC adds a tag with his lower pitch. This punctuating vocalization is featured in the next two bridges, which are almost entirely instrumental. Bridge 1 is a continuation of the beats from the refrain as well as some of the vocal commentary in the background. It features an ascending synth-based sound with some echo applied, and it ends with the trumpet blast tag. Bridge 2 features a synth-based keyboard melody that is based on the refrain (with *portamento* slightly applied, which makes the pitches slide) against the ongoing beats and background vocalizations. During the hook that follows, an ascending synth sound related to the one playing the main melody in bridge 2 emerges. This hook cues the second iteration of the refrain, which now includes Tumi's speaking quick, spoken-word comments and some toasting between the sung lines: both express his disgust with the commercialization of music.

He then transitions to talk-singing as the song repeats verses 1 and 2 (A and A'). The trumpet blasts, this time louder and with more reverb applied, return to punctuate his main melodic line, as does the acoustic piano. This time, lower baritone and bass backing singers accompany Tumi. After the final return of the hook, Tumi completes verse 2 with "so pardon me if I just switch it off," followed by clipped mixed-chorus vocals (possibly a quick sampling of those used in the 1961 recording by

80 Drums around the World or the 1996 *Ultra Lounge* remix) and an 808 hiccup, which sounds like a space-inspired sonic effect. The song's outro consists of a female voice's reading lines from Homer's *Odyssey*. These lines, about Odysseus's wandering the world and marveling at its sights, with a prayer to bring him safely home, are set against instrumentation from the song's intro, percussions (tambourine and shaker), and a whirring synth voice (panned from the left speaker, to the center, then right speaker). As she finishes, and the whirring level decreases, the song abruptly ends with her voice echoing into the ether.

In 2018, Tumi (as Stogie T) appeared on Zé Mateo's (of Chinese Man) solo album *Scaglia*. Tumi's style, like most South African hip hop, is inspired by both reggae and some South African Mbube singing techniques.

PHARRELL WILLIAMS: "FREEDOM"
ALBUM: *DESPICABLE ME 3: ORIGINAL MOTION PICTURE SOUNDTRACK* (2015)

Pharrell Williams (a.k.a. Pharrell, 1973–) is a Virginia-born tenor-range singer-songwriter, drummer, keyboardist, and rapper who has also been successful as a music producer and record label executive. Though he

Pharrell Williams smiles while receiving star number 2,537 on the Hollywood Walk of Fame on December 4, 2014. (Turkbug/Dreamstime.com)

often uses hip hop elements, his music is usually a fusion of R&B, funk, neo soul, dance, and electronic music. As a singer, Williams is a high tenor who is best known for his falsetto range. His two solo albums have reached the Top 10 on the Billboard 200, and he was featured on the 2003 chart topper *The Neptunes Present . . . Clones*. He has also had two Top 10 hit songs on the Billboard Hot 100, including a No. 1 song with "Happy" (2013), which was an international hit, topping the charts in Australia, Canada, France, Germany, Ireland, The Netherlands, New Zealand, Switzerland, and the U.K. "Come Get It Bae" (2014), a funk-infused sex song with heavy electric bass and hand claps written and produced by Williams (and with uncredited vocals by Miley Cyrus and Tori Kelly), reached No. 23 and achieved gold status. It reached the Top 10 in Belgium (No. 10) and Poland (No. 4), and peaked at No. 5 on the U.S. charts.

Originally released as a non-album single, "Freedom" did not chart, but its video was nominated for a Grammy, and the song was included on the soundtrack album of the film *Despicable Me 3*. The song has been used for various commercial purposes by many American companies, including Nissan, Aetna, Bank of America, and Walmart. It had international appeal, hitting No. 2 in Belgium and No. 3 in Greece and Israel. "Freedom" explores what it means to be free literally, figuratively, and spiritually. Connections with freedom are drawn from the birth of a child to one's very last breath. The song also explores how the natural world works and the "God-given" potential of everything.

"Freedom" uses elements of hip hop as well as R&B and, most of all, gospel and soul. Entirely in G-sharp minor, the song consists of just two chords that alternate every two beats: E major (VI or E-G-sharp-B) down to G-sharp major (i, also the home key, or G-B-flat-D). The song is in duple meter (two beats per measure). The song's structure is as follows: intro (bifurcated); verse 1 (bifurcated); prechorus; refrain (bifurcated); instrumental bridge; verse 2 (bifurcated); prechorus'; refrain' (bifurcated); instrumental bridge; verse 3; prechorus"; refrain" (used as the outro).

The first part of the intro begins with the song's main *ostinato*, a melodic and/or rhythmic pattern that repeats throughout a piece of music. Here, a breathy chorus sings vocables *a cappella* (unaccompanied), mainly "la," repeated by a female chorus. The sequence of pitches is E-D-sharp-C-sharp-D-sharp-G-sharp-G-sharp-C-sharp-D-sharp. The low and high voices are spaced an *octave* apart (their pitches are the same but separated by twelve half-steps on a piano). A choir synth voice emerges and briefly swells (getting louder, or using a brief *crescendo*), straddling in between the first and second parts of the intro. An acoustic piano takes over the ostinato, which marks the beginning of the intro's second part. While the right hand plays the ostinato, the left hand alternates the chords. The left hand's pitches, E and G-sharp, are the roots of the chords and the bass. To get from E down to G-sharp (a minor sixth interval with eight half steps or piano keys in between the notes), the bass passes through two passing tones (called a *double passing tone*, which is comprised of in-between or on-the-way pitches that are not part of the chord)—in this case, D-sharp and C-sharp. Williams punctuates the piano with accompanying grunts and vocables (e.g., "uh"). Later versions of this vocable are sampled, and their decays are clipped, transforming human punctuation (in a sense, beatboxing) into mechanical loops and manipulated beats (in a sense, *musique concrète* or a distortion of natural sounds). Williams then clears his throat in preparation to sing. Aside from his vocalizations, the second part of the intro may also be perceived as a bridge, with the piano serving as a *vamp*. The piano's repeating ostinato and Williams's throat-clearing suggest that the vamp is preparing him to sing or waiting for him to get ready to do so, which is the very function of a vamp.

But into the first part of verse 1, the ostinato remains and turns into part of the accompaniment, along with the previous vocables and the addition of snaps and drumstick ticks on a ride cymbal. The grunts soften and at times sound like gasps, placed so that each line begins with one. Close to the beginning, Williams sings some sustained notes on the home pitch, G-sharp. Here, he keeps his singing voice low, approaching mumbling. In the second part of the verse, the snaps are replaced by hand claps (mostly right speaker, with some applied reverb and echo). While the piano continues, the electric bass doubles its bass pitches, and a hi-hat-sounding synth-generated effect emerges. In contrast to the quieter vocals of the first part of the intro, here he dramatically raises his voice, which takes on a raspy quality. His dramatically sung lines approach a yell. For the verse's two final lines, he again lowers his voice. This gives a sense that the verse is ticking down to a completed thought (and for a moment, he sings the conclusion *a cappella*).

The prechorus marks a dramatic sonic change: it builds up energy to the refrain as the piano and hand claps continue; electric guitar, horns, and a synth string drone are added; the intro's vocables return; and the bass guitar becomes lower and gets more reverb applied to it. Williams uses elements of gospel singing here to create clipped, dramatic lines about power and freedom. In the first part of the refrain, he hits his highest vocal range, actually screaming the word "freedom!" three times. The most echo and reverb effects are applied to his vocals at this climax. In contrast, in the second part, he settles back into his quieter, softer vocal delivery to sing "freedom" a few more times (giving the sense that the song has reached a moment of pensiveness). As he repeats the word, the music changes sonically again, this time with all the accompaniment but the piano dropping out, which creates a sparse texture. As the end of the refrain becomes quiet, the piano's ostinato enters the foreground, against his singing and quiet grunts and gasps. Once he stops singing, the piano's ostinato turns into a vamp and becomes a bridge to verse 2.

As with the second part of the intro into verse 1, the piano continues into verse 2. The accompaniment is just like that of verse 1, with snaps introduced in the first part and claps replacing them in the second part. This time, however, congas are added. In the second part, the same electric instruments are used to add texture. Like verse 1, all the accompaniment drops out at the end of the second part as Williams concludes singing its last line. The prechorus repeats, with just modified lyrics. The refrain also repeats but is modified slightly by Williams as he indulges in some flourishes (for variation) and inserts an additional line, "breathe in," during its second part. Here, Williams uses the same dramatic contrast with his voice, moving from screams to concluding on quieter vocals that resemble those in the earlier refrain. The same bridge that features the piano vamp leads into verse 3.

Unlike verses 1 and 2, verse 3 is not bifurcated; it therefore sounds truncated. The piano, snaps, and ride cymbal accompany Williams and drop out when he reaches his final line (with some applied reverb). The female chorus's repeated "la" vocables reappear, now as accompaniment to Williams's singing. The final iteration of the prechorus is modified by different lyrics. The main difference is that it instead concludes the way verses 1 and 2 did: all the accompaniment drops off and Williams sings his concluding point. Here, he sings about how all that he mentions are made from the same things, how all life is connected. The final iteration of the refrain is also modified. Though it is the same as earlier iterations in the first part, the second part concludes with just Williams and the piano, punctuated by his "uhs" and gasps. Here, he sings "freedom" quietly in his lower range. After the fourth "freedom," the piano halts, and he sings the fifth "freedom" *a cappella*, therefore using the same dramatic device used in verses 1 and 2 as well as in the modified prechorus".

As a songwriter, Williams made his name by teaming with fellow Virginia Beach native Chad Hugo (Charles Edward Hugo, 1974–) to form the Grammy-winning production-songwriting duo The Neptunes (1992–). The duo was made famous by record producer and singer-songwriter Terry Riley (Edward Theodore Riley, 1967–), who is credited with creating new jack swing. As a member of The Neptunes, Williams co-founded the record label Star Trak Entertainment (2001–). Williams is a much-sought-after and accomplished singer, having been used as a guest vocalist on more than 70 songs. Williams continues producing, recording, performing, and collaborating with internationally known hip hop artists. As of 2021, he has won thirteen Grammy Awards.

CHAPTER 3

Impact on Popular Culture

When discussing the impact of hip hop (which, to reiterate, is usually considered synonymous with rap), it is always important to remember that rapping or MCing is only one element, despite the fact that its influence is far reaching, its elements and ethos making their way into various music genres. In fact, music is only one element of hip hop culture. For this reason, a book on hip hop should not focus solely on music, but rather include the ideological, social, historical, and artistic conventions that inform *all* of hip hop culture. In other words, hip hop is more than just an umbrella term for describing certain urban-based cultural phenomena such as music and dance; it is an aesthetic—a way of thinking—that has and will continue to influence cultures around the world.

From humble beginnings in the Bronx and Queens in the early 1970s, hip hop culture now influences almost every aspect of daily life: from the mean streets of New York and Los Angeles, it has utterly changed the American idea of lifestyle, permeating not only urban streets, but suburbia and rural America as well. Hip hop came into being because New York and Los Angeles-based African American and Puerto Rican communities needed a way to express themselves through art forms that they could call their own—and that were affordable to the average person. Today, no matter where one travels in the United States, evidence of DJing (turntablism), MCing (rapping), graffiti creating, and break dancing (called b-boying and b-girling by those involved in hip hop) is present, as are examples of hip hop-influenced fashion.

By the 1990s, many covers of *Rolling Stone* magazine exemplified the influence that hip hop has had on popular music, entertainment, and fashion. Other popular culture-oriented magazines less focused on music, such as *InStyle*, *GQ*, and *Ebony*, have focused on hip hop icons, introducing readers to an endless variety of interests, such as interior decorating, activism, acting and directing, and youth movements, to identify just a few. As part of a DIY (do-it-yourself) culture, hip hop is about creating with what one has at hand. For this reason, rap music can be considered a cousin of punk music, and like both punk and its more popular sister genre, new wave rock, hip hop exists to challenge rock and roll's dominating hold on listeners. Ultimately, hip hop assimilated into mainstream American culture, with LL Cool J, Will Smith, Ice Cube, Queen Latifah, and Ice-T becoming familiar faces in movies and television. Others paved the way for hip hop's acceptance in the mainstream in different ways, finding themselves marketing their goods through commercials and television shows such as *Oprah* or *Live* (especially on former versions of this show such as *Live with Regis and Kathy Lee* and *Live with Regis and Kelly*). For example, rapper Sean Jean Combs (known as Puff Daddy, P. Diddy, Puffy, or Diddy) became an award-winning menswear fashion designer, advertising his blazers on *Live with Regis and Kelly* and *Late Night with David Letterman*. Rapper Jay-Z became a successful label president, entrepreneur (clothing line and streaming music service), club owner, and marketing consultant, eventually advertising his subscription-based streaming music service TIDAL through television and Internet commercials. Their impact on mainstream America can be seen through the lens of hip hop's varied elements: music, dance, fashion, politics, and street/gang culture. Each of these is the focus of the following sections of this chapter.

MUSIC

For the past twenty years, hip hop has slowly overtaken classic rock and country music as the dominant popular commercial music genre in the mainstream in the United States. Hip hop music has not only surpassed rock and roll sales in the United States; in 1998, it topped country music, which was formerly the top-selling genre. One doesn't have to look hard to also find hip hop's impact on music worldwide, in countries as diverse as Canada, Ghana, Iceland, India, Korea (South Korea), Nigeria, and the United Kingdom. Early on, hip hop experienced success on the American Billboard 200 album charts, but it was its acceptance into mainstream (white American) culture that moved the needle and made hip hop into the commercial success that it became by the 1990s—and this despite the regional nature of rap, which by all expectations should have been a localized subgenre with limited audience appeal. But the emergence of gangsta rap as the hip hop music style of choice in suburban America caught many (especially parents and political leaders) by surprise. But, as of 2021, hip hop (both rap and hip hop-influenced dance music) had become, and currently remains, the most successfully marketed genre of music, not just in the United States but around the world, leading to extremely successful international hip hop debuts such as Canada's Drake, Korea's Psy and BTS, and India's Yo Yo Honey Singh and A. R. Rahman. In Poland and Russia, the sound also caught on, with acts such as Donatan (Poland) and Little Big (Russia).

This international success is likely due to hip hop's (especially rap's) concerns with themes that appeal to youth everywhere, especially immigrant youth: racism/prejudice, poverty, authoritarian brutality, and the need to combat all these evils with freedom and artistry (quite a lot of rap/hip hop takes the form of the braggadocio or bragging song). Hip hop's largest global impact has been a political one, as it has offered a venue for immigrants and ethnic minorities to protest injustice and challenge white privilege and anti-immigrant policies. For example, M.I.A., who was born in London to a Sri Lankan activist Tamil family, was once a graphic designer who became a chant rapper who wrote politically charged lyrics (so much so that she was placed on a United States travel ban list). But with lyrical concerns, instrumentation (traditional instruments), and music videos that were international in their scope, drawing inspiration from various countries and sources, she produced the immensely successful album *Kala* (2007), which led to her being listed as one of *Time* magazine's "100 Most Influential People."

In other words, hip hop's most immediate impact, both in the United States and abroad, was that it offered an alternative outlet, other than violence and/or drug dependency, for the desperation and anger that had led urban youth toward gang participation. Early on in hip hop history, New York musician and activist Afrika Bambaataa sought to recruit gang members into hip hop culture, encouraging them to replace fighting with b-boying (breakdancing) and krumping (aggressively dancing as part of a challenge to an opponent). In the late 1980s, hip hop music addressed police brutality, stop-and-frisk practices, and the targeting by police of Black youth. From 1986 to 1992 (nicknamed the golden era of hip hop), rap music was political, progressive, even radical; Malcolm X was sampled more often than Martin Luther King, and the Nation of Islam and Black Nationalism both became commercially successful hip hop ideologies.

Today, hip hop's influence on other music genres such as pop, R&B, electronica, and electronic dance music (EDM) is predominant. Popular boy bands such as the Backstreet Boys and NSYNC, as well as R&B and neo-soul acts such as Mary J. Blige and R. Kelly, drew heavily on hip hop styles and musical elements. This influence went far beyond the use of rap. As the Must-Hear Music entries in this book attest, frequently used rap music elements include hiccupped beats, turntablism (or synth-produced sounds that are reminiscent of turntablism), extended dance breaks, synth-produced keyboard ostinatos and stingers, heavy bass lines and sub-bass voices, and synth-produced sound effects. The influence of individual producers was also seen far and wide in the music industry. Dr. Dre, Jam Master Jay, Timbaland, Swizz Beatz, J Dilla, and The Neptunes moved their focus from rapping, singing, songwriting, and/or DJ-ing with turntablism, to production, mixing, and remix culture. Together, these producers, among others, have helped changed the general view of music producers as being backroom clerks in a technical role to becoming accepted as musicians who contribute heavily to recordings.

BLOCK PARTIES AND DJS

Hip hop found its beginnings in African and Latinx American communities' need for entertainment. The Jamaican-born DJ Kool Herc, who can legitimately be referred to as a sound pioneer, began organizing block parties in the Bronx. He found ways to put together musical equipment so that his sound was lively, clear, and loud. But more importantly, his musical events drew on one of the original concepts behind hip hop: community. He and other early DJs believed in organizing the community so that people could showcase their talent as dancers, fellow DJs, or rappers. While he was entertaining his fellow New Yorkers, DJ Kool Herc introduced two of the most essential elements of early hip hop, turntablism and breakbeats. Using two turntables and alternating between them mid-song, he extended percussive fragments of the music he was playing on vinyl albums to create a continuous drum and percussion beat. This beat allowed for song sections where dancers could either showcase their moves or square off in battle—or proto-MCs could find a spot to either toast or rap. Later, Grandmaster Flash isolated and extended the break beat, which b-boys could then use to showcase acrobatic moves. To do so, he pioneered the concept (and skill) of needle dropping, which prolonged short drum breakbeats: he played two copies of a record simultaneously and moved the needle on one turntable back to the start of the break while the other played. His mentee, Grand Wizzard Theodore, came up with the idea of scratching, or moving the record back and forth under a record player stylus. It is impossible to overestimate the importance of this discovery to early hip hop music.

Turntablism techniques now almost always involve moving an armed needle back and forth on one or two vinyl records or picking the needle up and setting it back down to play only certain parts of songs. The overall effect was the creation of the rap crew DJ. More skilled DJs were able to literally pick up a record player needle and then place it back in its original place while a vinyl album was turning, although the most skilled DJ often use stickers as markers on their vinyl albums. Armed with two vinyl records, a master DJ can shift quickly between two pieces of music by switching power from one turntable to another through a device called a crossfader (which can be a knob or a slider, or both). Basic techniques such as *baby scratches*, and *rubbing*, *looping*, and *drops* were mastered with and without the crossfader to create more advanced ones such as *flares*. Master turntablists combined these techniques in endless ways, and with multiple albums and turntables their routines included *beat juggling*. In addition, Grandmaster Flash came up with the quick-mix theory, sectioning off parts of albums on his turntables, creating what he called the *backspin* and the *double-back*. DJ Grand Mixer DXT furthered scratching by making it more rhythmic and using two turntables, playing at different velocities, in order to alter the pitch. Scratching entered the mainstream when DXT was used as a guest artist on jazz musician Herbie Hancock's hit song "Rockit" (1982), further discussed in our Must-Hear Music entries. Today, scratching, either via turntable, synth, DJ controller, or instrumental mimicry, is ubiquitous in hip hop music.

Turntablism, however, is only one aspect of music that was introduced by hip hop culture. Just as influential was the development of the 808 drum. This was a specific synthesizer drum sound that could be made to "hiccup" (an effect created by clipping the delay of the drum sound while repeating it many times), a core convention in hip hop music often used in transitional sections of songs. The concept of sampling—using identifiable parts of previously recorded songs in a new song—is also essential in hip hop. Sampling, however, not only quotes songs, but also involves modifying isolated pre-existing music (usually a musical phrase or two) and media sound bites to create what is called a loop or hiccup (for a discussion on an excellent example of a loop, see the Must-Hear Music entry on M.I.A.'s "P.O.W.A."). Early on, these techniques were executed through the use of two or more turntables. The two MCs of Run-D.M.C., Run and D.M.C., made their DJ famous by allowing him (Jam Master Jay) to showcase his sampling and remixing skills in both performances and recordings. Unfortunately, the role of the DJ was quickly downplayed because MCs and singers became the focus of rap crews and bands, and an increased use of computer software, tapes, and other studio techniques/software made the DJ's skills redundant.

RAPPERS (MCS)

Rapping can be traced back to various West African musical practices and the Jamaican style of rhythmic speech known as toasting. In the United States, its precursor was jazz poetry readings by the likes of Langston Hughes, Amiri Baraka, Gil Scott-Heron, and The Last Poets. Early rapping, as it is understood today, appeared in recordings by Isaac Hayes and George Clinton. But the first rap song hit was released in 1979, when an independent label in Englewood, New Jersey, Sugar Hill Records, released the Sugarhill Gang's "Rapper's Delight," a chart-topping phenomenon. In the mid-1980s, old-school rap (characterized by simple beats, a sing-song rap flow, and a predominance of end rhymes) gave way to new school, with rap crews such as Run-D.M.C., who recorded for Profile, one of several new labels that took advantage of the growing market for rap music. The trio fused rap with hard rock to create a new sound. In addition, it popularized the hip hop lifestyle through fashion statements such as "bling" (e.g., large gold chains and diamond rings) and street wear such as Kangol hats, running suits, starter jackets, unlaced Adidas tennis sneakers, and wool-felt fedoras. Meanwhile, Def Jam, another important record label, featured LL Cool J, Beastie Boys, and Public Enemy. Across the continent, Ruthless Records' premiere act, N.W.A., released its album, *Straight Outta Compton* (1988), which introduced graphically violent tales of the inner city—and caught fire in suburbia, where it sold millions of copies. Los Angeles's rival label, Death Row Records, built an empire around rap icons Dr. Dre, Snoop Dogg, and Tupac Shakur. Meanwhile, New York City's Bad Boy Records introduced Puff Daddy and the Notorious B.I.G. In the early 2000s, the South became the hip hop mecca, thanks to New Orleans-based Cash Money and No Limit Records and Atlanta-based LaFace Records.

But back to the beginning of our story. Though Grandmaster Flash and the Furious Five's Melle Mel was likely the first rapper to use the title "MC," it was MC Hammer who made the title internationally popular. The practice of MCing nevertheless traces back further, to the Jamaican practice of toasting, when a master of ceremonies, or emcee (shortened to MC), working in the dance halls, discovered that by lowering the sound of vocal tracks on an album and raising the volume on the beats and accompanying bass, he could talk or toast over the albums. These early MCs used rhymed introductions and announcements to engage the crowd before and after a dancer or a band performed. The MC could also call out for people to dance, shout, and clap, in addition to encouraging partygoers to have a good time while enjoying the unique sound of his studio system and music selections.

FASHION

Hip hop fashion has become a highly lucrative industry on its own, while at the same time it has become influential in pop culture. For urban youth, rappers and hip hop producers are not only survivors, but also entrepreneurial heroes, which has led to hip hop fashion's further popularization through emulation. Many hip hop producers created their own clothing lines. Def Jam's Russell Simmons and his ex-wife Kimora created the clothing lines Phat Farm and Baby Phat. Other clothing lines include 50 Cent's G-Unit; Puff Daddy's Sean John; Jay-Z's Akademics, Enyce, and Rocawear; Beyoncé's House of Dereon; and Nelly's Apple Bottom. Fashion lines like FUBU and Tommy Hilfiger33 are showcased through music videos, as well as in movies such as *Boyz N Da Hood* and television shows like *The Fresh Prince of Bel-Air*—or better yet, during their advertising breaks.

Just as pop culture fashion movements since the 1960s featured musicians who inspired the emulation of their hair and clothing fashions, 1970s hip hop acts, such as dance crews like The Lockers (a.k.a. The Campbell Lockers, discussed later in this chapter's section on dance) and the Electric Boogaloos, influenced hairstyles, clothing, and accessories. Although comical and somewhat absurdist, their large, colorful beret-style hats, colorful (and overly large) pants, large suspenders, striped socks, black hats, and white gloves influenced the predominant color combinations of West Coast funk fashion: black, white, and red. In addition, viewers tuned in to television series such as the dance showcase and variety show *Soul Train* and the sitcom *What's Happening!* (which included in its cast Fred Berry, one of the original Lockers), and they could not possibly miss the hip hop-influenced fashions. On the East Coast, b-boys and b-girls adopted more athletic apparel, in the form of tracksuits, brand-name tennis shoes (Nike and Adidas especially), and Kangol brand hats (made by the English clothing company famous for its headwear made of angora and wool and featuring the company's famous kangaroo logo; the hat was nicknamed "the Kangaroo hat").

Through the 1980s, the most popular color combination was red and black. Breakdancing crews and individual dancers donned leather jackets in both colors, usually adorned with zippers and chains. Hairstyles and fashion accessories evolved to become more noticeable. Hairstyles became more voluminous (a.k.a. big hair). Hip hop artists and fashion moguls also introduced the idea of ostentatiousness, especially in jewelry (which was a sign of both wealth and power). Their bling became increasingly more ostentatious (e.g., Flavor Flav's giant clock necklace). This took the form of oversized jewelry, chains, watches, and rings (on every finger) in particular. Women learned a fondness for gigantic hoop earrings, as well as shoulder-enhanced shirts and jackets. The small waist look emerged, along with its polar opposite, the very baggy "Harem" style pants (parachute pants, quickly nicknamed "M.C. Hammer pants," since he popularized them in his videos). As the decade came to a close, a cultural shift toward roots pride occurred, leading to the inclusion of traditional African prints and colors. For example, the band members of Public Enemy wore Rastafarian accessories and hairstyles. Many hip hop fans started sporting dreadlocks.

In the 1990s, rappers and DJs started wearing clothing that emphasized a softer look, with brighter, including neon, colors. At the time, young rappers such as The Fresh Prince and LL Cool J were popularizing this kind of fashion. The all-female trio TLC set the tone for many women's fashions. In 1993, the trio donned plain, utilitarian overalls (creating a loose-fit coverall silhouette), which the band had found in the men's department. They would then spray-paint the overalls or pin condoms to them. The effect was three very attractive young women dressed like boys, a style that was both cartoonish and *fly*. The trio also experimented with "luxe" (luxury), appearing at the Nickelodeon Kids' Choice Awards in 1995 in matching Tommy Hilfiger-branded crop top-and-boxer sets. Rappers also embraced designer clothing, namely Hilfiger and FUBU (originally an acronym for Four Urban Brothers United, it became For Us, By Us in 1992). Designers who embraced hip hop culture started to employ rappers for their runway shows. Sports jerseys (sometimes described as throwback jerseys) and sport team hats continued to be prominent. The emphasis on large and oversized clothing earned a nickname, "Balla," which included flashy gold and diamond jewelry and other expensive accessories. Women rappers, such as MC Lyte and Queen Latifah, embraced a more masculine fashion, but with the added touch of makeup to feminize themselves. Rappers like Lil' Kim and Foxy Brown popularized a sexier look that accented the female silhouette.

Eventually, mainstream fashion began to adopt a hip hop look, with the color scheme (achromatic variations of black, white, and gray) embraced by the hard core or gangsta rappers that were emerging in the 1990s as a way to preserve the street origins of hip hop. Youth in suburbia began to wear clothing that evolved toward the boxy look that resembled prison wear. As markets opened up, more hip hop artists, rappers, and producers branched into the fashion business, with labels and designs of their own. In 1998, Puff Daddy began his aforementioned clothing line Sean John, which was especially known for its tailored dress jackets. In 2002, Atlanta-based duo OutKast started their own short-lived clothing line, OutKast Clothing.

STREET CULTURE

Where rap differs most greatly from the other forms of hip hop music—most notably boy/girl band music (e.g., Destiny's Child, NSYNC, Tony! Toni! Toné!)—is in its ties to street culture. Rap is informed by "street cred" or authenticity. No other music style requires that its musicians come from a particular type of background, which includes geographic area, familial structure, and lifestyle; having either been abused in a drug-addicted, dysfunctional family (Eminem); having lived on the streets (Big Pun); having been a gang member (Snoop Dogg); or having engaged in violent criminal activity (N.W.A.). Rappers can achieve success without this background, but those who do (e.g., Drake) are rare, and when they do, they spend their careers trying to establish their street cred. As with male rappers, female rappers have to establish authenticity, in that they have to adopt the "b****" persona (e.g., Foxy Brown, Da Brat, Lil' Kim, Nicki Minaj, and Cardi B) and spend their careers engaging in diss battles with (mostly) other female rappers and "haters" (celebrity critics, including other rappers).

This is because hip hop culture placed competition above all. This worldview goes all the way back to early hip hop rap battling (this may be a chicken/egg issue, as according to some accounts, battling created rap). Battling could be found on the street corners of every major U.S. city. Battling as a concept existed in both rap music and hip hop dance (b-boying/b-girling) since the early years of both. In fact, the dance style krumping was created specifically as a way to turn b-boying into an aggressive, in-your-face contest that mimicked physical fighting. In music, rap freestyle battling was more a game of wits. It allowed rappers to showcase their improvisation skills. Matched against one another, two rappers would, while accompanied by a basic instrumental beat, a sample, or human beatboxing (or possibly delivered *a cappella* or unaccompanied), challenge each other's lyrical and flow skills. Raps would involve clever lyrics and wordplay, with the end goal of establishing dominance. These battles, both freestyle and with prepared lyrics, took place informally on street corners and formally on a concert or battle stage. In order to prove that a freestyle was being made up on the spot, rappers would refer to places and objects in their immediate setting, or would take suggestions on lyrics from the crowd.

The aforementioned beatboxing also developed as part of hip hop street culture. Beatboxing (not to be confused with Grandmaster Flash's idea of the beat box, a manually operated, custom-rigged synthesizer drum machine) gave poor urban youth a way to be musical without having to purchase expensive instruments. They were able to create a beat against which an MC could rap, despite the fact that absolutely no instrumentation was available. This was especially useful in informal street rap battling, as it allowed for a consistent rhythmic beat that established musical time. Simply defined, *beatboxing* is the practice of making drum and synthesizer sounds using mainly the mouth and nose. Some very skilled beatboxers literally beat on body parts as well, or they stomped. Master beatboxers like Doug E. Fresh—nicknamed the human beat box—created both a beat and a melodic line simultaneously, emulating the sounds of drum machines, tap dancing, various percussion instruments, and synthesizers. Incredibly, Doug E. Fresh did so using only his mouth, throat, and a microphone.

Beatboxing can also be viewed as an entry-level activity into the world of rapping: Biz Markie began as a beatboxer, working closely with his friend, rapper Big Daddy Kane. As a form of battling, beatboxing survives today. Whereas early beatbox battles were conducted on the streets and makeshift stages used by early rappers, today's beatboxers compete in a highly formal atmosphere. International competitions are currently held in Germany every three years. World beatboxing champions as of 2021 were Mael Gayaud of France and Kaila Mullady of the United States. The current crew (group) champion is Beatbox Collective, out of England.

GANG CULTURE

Gang activity has been highly influenced by rap music. Early efforts by rappers were to prevent localized street and area gangs, such as the Bloods and the Crips of Los Angeles, from uniting youth in criminal activity and gang warfare against perceived enemies. Afrika Bambaataa, for example, wanted to emulate gang culture's ability to offer protection (for members of a marginalized minority subculture) and unite youth into a common cause. Most importantly, this common cause would by its nature be anti-violence. Hip hop dance's origins in New York City during the late 1970s coincided with a significant peak in gang activity in poor and working-class minority areas. Afrika Bambaataa, through the Universal Zulu Nation, offered a replacement for gangs with the common cause of the pursuit of hip hop culture. Public Enemy rapped about organizing politically and independently of the gang scene. In 1990, several West Coast rappers, under the name West Coast Rap All-Stars, released the single "We're All in the Same Gang" to promote an anti-violence message. Missy Elliott also used her music to direct young people away from gangs.

Gangs and rap have had a reciprocal relationship. Rap music offered an alternative to the gangsta lifestyle, with the perks being a longer expected lifespan and a method for African Americans to make money by using capitalism in their favor (rather than becoming its economic victims). In turn, gang activity provided rappers with subject matter that led to the creation of gangsta and g-funk (Los Angeles), thug (New Orleans), mobb (New York), trap (Atlanta), and horrorcore (Detroit and Houston). Early rappers Schoolly D and the members of N.W.A. drew heavily on the gang scene for the stories they rapped in their songs, as well as the stage personas they crafted in order to do so. In his lyrics, Snoop Dogg drew on a gang-affiliated past; Geto Boys made marketable the graphic portrayal of the violence of gang life, though critics argued that the band depicted this violence in too loving a detail.

GRAFFITI

Since the early recordings of rap, musicians have used graffiti as cover art for their albums. Graffiti is now considered not vandalism but an art form: some private companies and city leaders have commissioned graffiti art (in San Antonio, for example, Latino artists are commissioned to beautify older buildings, in some cases including apartment housing). Large-scale murals are now a significant part of graffiti art; however, during hip hop's early years, uncommissioned graffiti, which was considered vandalism, could be found in almost any urban environment, usually on buildings, train cars, other means of public transportation, and public roadway overpasses and bridges. Graffiti normally takes the form of spray-painted symbols, words, and images. Today's graffiti art has multiple functions, from expressing the artist's individuality and skill, to protesting war, to calling attention to significant political issues in America and internationally. It can nevertheless be used to mark gang territory, serving as a warning to members of rival gangs. Gang-related "tagging" can commonly be found on highway overpasses, train cars, public concrete walls, and government buildings and grounds.

American graffiti artist and rapper Fab 5 Freddy was known for having introduced various elements of hip hop, street art, dancing, and rapping to the mainstream art world through his graffiti, as he is best known for his graffiti tagging (and as the original host of MTV's *Yo! MTV Raps*). Intimately involved in the early history of hip hop, he also produced the classic American break-dancing film *Wild Style* (1982) and was referenced in Blondie's No. 1 (on the Billboard Hot 100) song "Rapture," making an appearance in the song's official video. He also made hip hop international: in the early 1980s, he went on the first rap tour in Europe with Afrika Bambaataa, Grand Mixer DXT (as Grand Mixer D.ST), and The Rock Steady Crew, among others. In 1991, he served as associate producer for New Jack City (film studio), and he directed hip hop videos for Queen Latifah, Snoop Dogg, and Nas.

POLITICS AND ACTIVISM

The Black Power Movement of the mid-1960s and early 1970s inspired songs that expressed Black pride, such as James Brown's "Say It Loud (I'm Black and Proud)" (1969) and Gil Scott-Heron's spoken-word and jazz track "The Revolution Will Not Be Televised" (1971). Both songs were influential on what came to be known as politically and socially conscious rap. Socially conscious rap crews and rappers such as Public Enemy, Tupac Shakur, and later Kendrick Lamar all exhibit the influence of Scott-Heron and The Last Poets, in that they employed rap as a form of expression to make public their dissatisfaction with injustice and disenfranchisement. In other words, once it was socially conscious, hip hop allowed minority communities to fight against the marginality to which they are often relegated.

Arguably, rap is by nature a political music. Some of this is by choice, as socially conscious rappers decided to eschew the party, story, sex, and bling themes that informed many of rap-based hip hop's earliest songs, choosing instead to become musical activists who argued against racism, discrimination, and related economic issues. In addition, rap has a history of being repeatedly attacked and censored by politicians; rappers therefore needed to defend themselves, thus becoming political on two fronts, as they found themselves defending a culture and a lifestyle. During the 1990s, rap music was censored for both its violent and sexual content, which politicians tried to argue was the cause of the destruction of American values (just as they had when rock music started to become popular). In 1990, Florida governor Bob Martinez and Broward County sheriff Nick Navarro brought obscenity charges against 2 Live Crew for its album *As Nasty As They Wanna Be* (1989). These government officials pursued and threatened record store owners, arguing that if they sold copies of the album they might be prosecutable. In 1992, U.S. vice president Dan Quayle called on Interscope Records to withdraw Tupac Shakur's *2Pacalypse Now* (1991). It took decades for politicians to embrace the music, but in 2008, Barack Obama referenced Jay-Z by doing his "brush the dirt off your shoulder" (from *The Black Album*, 2003) motion in a rally.

Today, rap is *de rigueur* in politics and is actively used by the United States State Department for what is called hip hop diplomacy, the use of hip hop cultural practices to cultivate and encourage good will and diplomatic relationships between countries, especially between the United States and other nations. The State Department began to incorporate hip hop into its diplomacy programs beginning in the early 2000s. In 1961, the United States Congress had passed the Fulbright-Hayes Act, officially known as the Mutual Educational and Cultural Exchange Act, to create a cultural exchange between the United States and other countries, and, in 2005, the State Department began sending groups of hip hop artists, including rappers, DJs, and dancers, to parts of Europe, Africa, Asia, and the Middle East in an attempt to combat the radicalization of Muslim youth in those areas. Hip hop was considered the musical genre with which global youth, especially Muslim youth, could most easily identify, because of its roots as protest music in marginalized communities in the United States, as well as its international popularity with minority immigrant communities.

Domestically, rap has served another important political function, becoming a vehicle by which Black Nationalism was made popular. Black Nationalism argues for a global Black population as part of one coherent nation, and claims that Black people of African descent share fundamental common interests and should view their membership in the Black global nation as their primary basis for cultural identification. It embraced unification in nongeographic terms (a nation as an idea rather than a place could be traced to the theories of Frantz Fanon, Stokely Carmichael, Malcolm X, and Louis Farrakhan). Public Enemy's politically charged music and videos contained many elements of Black Nationalism; Afrika Bambaataa formed the Universal Zulu Nation, now found in France, Japan, South Africa, Australia, and South Korea; and the activist rap duo Dead Prez's self-identification with the nationalist Uhuru Movement and the International People's Democratic Uhuru

Movement led them to incorporate Black Nationalist colors into their album artwork and music videos.

The related Islamic Five-Percent Nation, also referred to as the Nation of Gods (men) and Earths (women), took its name from the belief that five percent of the world's population is comprised of those who know the truth and seek to educate and enlighten others. The Five-Percent Nation adheres to a spiritual responsibility to teach others the doctrine of their faith, which posits that God and the universe can be understood through science and mathematics and numerology. Artists such as Rakim and Chuck D used Five Percent teachings in their music, as did Brand Nubian, Wu-Tang Clan, Poor Righteous Teachers, Big Daddy Kane, Nas, Mos Def, Gang Starr, The Roots, and Erykah Badu.

DANCE

By the early 1970s, breakdancing, originally called b-boying (for break boy) and later b-girling, was beginning to flourish in New York. In addition to his influence on early rapping, James Brown influenced dance, as recordings of his dancing while singing the funk song "Get on the Good Foot" (1972) inspired some early hip hop moves, such as the boogaloo and the camel walk, which influenced the moon walk. The Lockers, a Los Angeles-based dance group established by dancers and choreographers Toni Basil and Don "Campbellock" Campbell, promoted street dance as an art form. They introduced some of the earliest hip hop dance styles, such as popping and locking. Popping and locking are American hip hop dance moves sometimes associated with a third move called dropping. Combined, the dance moves create the illusion of the body's motion being slowed or reversed, as in dubstep dancing. Popping consists of various techniques that cause it to differ greatly from most breakdancing techniques, as there is very little floor work (dance moves performed while lying down), positioning oneself upside down, or sitting down, in popping. Popping creates its illusions best when the dancer is standing.

Locking, today used extensively in hip hop, was originally a funk dance technique. Like popping, it is a dance technique designed to create a robotic illusion, achieved by starting with a fast, usually large-scale movement, and then immediately freezing and locking into a statuesque position. This freeze is typically held for a while, which makes locking different from popping, which is more consistently fluid. This influenced DJs (turntablists) because when performers took turns with solos, there was a need for break beats to allow them to set up a move. The Zulu Nation created some of the earliest breakdance crews, which led to more professional crews like Rock Steady Crew and The Electric Boogaloos. Breakdancing battles allowed rival crews to compete. Hip hop dance eventually evolved to include more floor work, influenced by gymnastics, acrobatics, and martial arts moves that showcased balance and agility. Freezes became conventional, and competitions began to focus on freezing, breaking, and power moves. Styles like gangsta (e.g., the Crip Walk and the Blood Bounce), jookin, turfing, jerkin', clowning, and krumping became popular, and significant changes to freestyle form led to counts (choreographing dance moves to coincide with beats and musical phrases), a technique credited to Basil, whose work on 1980s videos introduced a new way of structuring hip hop dancing.

Organizations like Hip Hop International have since created dance championships, competitions between all-male and all-female crews who battle and showcase power moves. American crews such as Jabbawockeez, Quest Crew, Poreotics, and Beat Freaks have competed internationally, and have influenced international crews, such as South Korea's Morning of Owl. Breakdancing battles can be solo or team-oriented, and, like rap battles, can happen informally on street corners or at staged competitions. B-boy and b-girl battles are a combination of prepared material and improvisation (although less improvisation is used than with rap battling, due to the nature of team dancing). These battles are social events, where teams interact with each other and with the judges and spectators, often incorporating humor in the form of subtle jabs at opposing teams' skills. The break beat continued to provide a rhythmic basis that let dancers display their improvisational skills within the duration of a break.

Hip hop music has also created dances such as jerkin,' a Los Angeles-based young adult and teen street dance that began gaining popularity on both the East and West coasts around 2009, after hip hop duo New Boyz released their single "You're a Jerk." The video featured the duo and its posse doing street dancing, using various versions of the jerk. That same year, another hip hop duo, Audio Push, released the single "Teach Me How to Jerk," which uses a hiccupped/repeated chorus similar to Cali Swag District's more famous Top 40 hit "Teach Me How to Dougie," also released in 2009. Jerkin' hip hop crews included The Rej3ctz, whose 2011 dance single "Cat Daddy" made it into the Billboard Hot 100.

CHAPTER 4

Legacy

The legacy of hip hop music cannot be overstated. It has become more popular than any other commercial music, with its elements (especially turntablism, rapping, and 808 or 808-sounding beats) finding their way into the soul, R&B, dance, rock, alternative, indie, and, surprisingly, country genres. This is nothing short of amazing given the hurdles that hip hop faced early on in its existence. The most obvious of these is hip hop's ethnic origin: initially a musical style that was largely confined to urban block parties, street corners where b-boys danced, and African American-affiliated radio stations, hip hop became the most popular genre among American youth. Equally amazing is the fact that its origins were humble, as is appropriate for a music produced by economically depressed cultures. What began as music to support freestyle rap and b-boy battling became a force that had to survive continuous attempts at censorship. It did not invent violence and misogyny, but it was often represented as doing so by the media and by members of Congress.

Unfortunately, hip hop's legacy was threatened early on through its association with the violence of gang culture. The East Coast-West Coast rivalry and the murders of Tupac Shakur and The Notorious B.I.G. fed into the fears of suburban parents—but these high-profile crimes did little to halt rap's acceptance in mainstream American culture. This is because rap music's roots were set solidly in the African oral tradition (such as that of the griot), as passed down through jazz poetry and spoken word. What began as the voice of marginalized and disenfranchised African American and Latinx American youth achieved astounding commercial success, so the music industry as a whole had no choice but accept it as the new norm. Like many other music genres, hip hop started out as a scapegoat for all that American political leaders found problematic in youth culture, including minority-on-minority crime. But consumer demand outweighed social concerns, and ultimately white suburban youth not only purchased but in fact appropriated hip hop (as it had other music genres). In essence, hip hop produced DIY (do-it-yourself) underground community music that became a marketable commodity—a story that had been seen before with a slightly earlier musical genre and artistic movement, punk.

Rappers, producers, and singers became urban heroes, having survived the poverty, drugs, and meanness of the inner city through hip hop music. Such heroic survival has influenced other marginalized cultures, who have also adopted hip hop musical elements because of it. For example, people with disabilities have begun to use rap music that addresses their experience for the purpose of activism and/or education. Like much rap, disability hip hop tracks are often protests against social and political conditions—in this case problems such as lack of access, affordability of care, and discrimination. Leroy F. Moore Jr., an African American poet, writer, and activist who has cerebral palsy, created the Krip Hop Nation, which highlighted deaf rappers such as Wawa, who uses sign language as a way to bridge hearing audience members into the deaf world to give the message that it is important to keep a sense of humor and stay positive.

FILM

Although hip hop music's legacy is most noticeable in the music industry (as this book attests), with both American and international music incorporating its aesthetics and musical elements, hip hop acts have influenced culture through fashion, movies, television, marketing, and changes to American slang. Hip hop's earliest influence was felt in the film industry, which was essential to getting hip hop's messages out to international audiences.

Filmmaking, both in the United States and around the globe, has been greatly influenced by rap music and hip hop culture—from soundtrack choices to story content, character development, and cinematic style. An example of the last is Darren Aronofsky's film π (a.k.a. *Pi*, 1998), in which he adopted a form of audiovisual editing he called "hip hop montage," which featured visual and sonic ruptures, fractures, and repetitions inspired by the back-spinning, punch phrasing, and scratching of turntablism. Hip hop and film, however, became strongly associated in the early 1980s when hip hop musicals became internationally famous. The association got its second wind in the 1990s with the influx of Hollywood-produced urban gangsta films.

The 1980s saw the popularization of American films such as *Wild Style* (1983), *Beat Street* (1984), and *Krush Groove* (1985), all of which got international attention because of their emphasis on b-boying and b-girling. These early 1980s films featured celebrities, including rappers, playing themselves. For example, *Krush Groove* featured Run-D.M.C., LL Cool J, and Beastie Boys. These films also introduced key hip hop concerns and themes, including not only rap celebrity, but also graffiti art, b-boying and b-girling, and fashion. Urban areas, such as the Bronx, became meaningful film locales. Spike Lee's *Do the Right Thing* (1989) explored racism in a single block of Brooklyn's Bed-Stuy (Bedford-Stuyvesant) neighborhood, and the character Radio Raheem's playing Public Enemy's "Fight the Power" on his boom box is one of the film's iconic music moments. This proved to other directors that the genre could be used to depict a wide array of emotions and perspectives.

Films such as *Do the Right Thing* provided a model for the burgeoning New Jack Cinema (a.k.a. New Black Realism), named after the highly successful *New Jack City* (1991). That film focused on young Black men in the inner city of Brooklyn or Los Angeles, typically would-be and burgeoning gangstas deeply involved in drug culture. These films tended to be violent and visually realistic, and they demonstrated that innocent women, children, and the elderly are often the victims of gang conflict. *Boyz n the Hood* (1991), *Straight out of Brooklyn* (1991), *Menace II Society* (1993), and *Above the Rim* (1994) portrayed real anxieties over rising unemployment in Black communities and its role in turning young Black men into criminals. Hip hop—more specifically, rap—was prominent in these works. Hollywood hip hop has broadened in genre and style, resulting in films such as *Dead Presidents* (1995), *Eve's Bayou* (1997), and *Love and Basketball* (2000), as well as parodies and satires such as *Fear of a Black Hat* (1993), *Don't Be a Menace to South Central While Drinking Your Juice in the Hood* (1996), *Tales from the Hood* (1995), and *Tales from the Hood 2* (2018). Since the 2000s, crossover films, including opera adaptations (e.g., 2001's *Carmen: A Hip Hopera*), have become popular. Documentary filming techniques have been employed more than ever in several popular rap musician biopics, as exemplified in *Straight Outta Compton* (about N.W.A., 2015) and *All Eyez on Me* (about Tupac Shakur, 2017).

DOCUMENTARIES

Beat This: A Hip Hop History was released in 1984, but there were predecessors that opened the door for such films. Early American hip hop documentaries included *Right On: Poetry on Film* (1971), which featured music by members of Harlem's The Last Poets. Often credited as the first hip hop documentary to achieve commercial success, *Style Wars* (1983), directed by Tony Silver, introduced audiences worldwide to hip hop culture, presenting graffiti as an art rather than as vandalism. The film included interviews with prominent New York City graffiti artists and featured b-boys Crazy Legs and Frosty Freeze, as well as a soundtrack of mostly old-school rap songs, such as The Sugarhill Gang's "8th Wonder" (1980), Grandmaster Flash and the Furious Five's "The Message" (1982), and Treacherous Three's "Feel the Heartbeat" (1981). Later documentaries that focused on breakdancing, such as *Wreckin' Shop from Brooklyn* (1992), were influenced by the British documentary *Electro Rock* (1985), which offered some of the earliest footage of non-American b-girls. *Big Fun in the Big Town* (1986), filmed in New York City, highlighted the New York rap scene, with interviews and performances by The Last Poets, Grandmaster Flash, Roxanne Shanté, Doug E. Fresh, Run-D.M.C., LL Cool J, and Schoolly D. Rusty Cundieff's aforementioned *Fear of a Black Hat* (1993) offered parody in the form of a mockumentary, with parodies of Public Enemy, The Fat Boys, and N.W.A.

Behind-the-scenes concert preparations and reunions continued into the new century, with documentaries like *Rock the Bells* (about the Wu-Tang Clan, 2006), *Notorious B.I.G.: Bigger Than Life* (2007), *2 Turntables and a Microphone: The Life and Death of Jam Master Jay* (2008), *The Wonder Year* (about producer 9th Wonder, 2011), and *Ruthless Memories: Preserving the Life and Legend of Eric (Eazy E) Wright* (2012). Other rap topics in documentaries include beatboxing, as in *Beatboxing: The Fifth Element of Hip Hop* (2011), and b-boying, as in *Bouncing Cats* (2010), *Bomb It* and *Bomb It 2* (2007 and 2010), and the British film *Turn It Loose!* (2009).

CROSSOVER MUSIC

Hip hop's legacy can best be seen in how it has infiltrated various styles of music to create crossover or hybrid subgenres. This has led to the emergence of Chicano rap, trip hop, Christian hip hop, hip house, glitch hop, and other new types of hip hop music. These new music styles differ from typical rap not only in message and thematic concerns, but also in instrumentation, vocalization, sampling, and flow.

Chicano artists such as Lalo Guerrero (big band and swing), Ritchie Valens, Carlos Santana, Linda Ronstadt, and Selena mixed Mexican, Tejano, and rock music or dance elements to one degree or another into their rock and pop music, which became popular among southwestern and midwestern Mexican Americans who often self-identify as Chicano (a.k.a. Chicana, Xicano, or Xicana). The Latin rhythms and rock beats they made popular would later be combined with hip hop beats and dance or gangsta rap lyrics to create Chicano rap, which produced acts such as Mellow Man Ace, Kid Frost (a.k.a. Frost), A.L.T. (and the project band Latin Alliance), Jonny Z, and Cypress Hill. Latin rhythms and rock beats would also be used by other Latinx hip hop dance musicians, such as Pitbull and The Welfare Poets.

Trip hop came into prominence in the early 1990s in Bristol, England, through the efforts of Massive Attack, Portishead, and Tricky. This hip hop subgenre fused some rap and R&B styles with many of the musical foundations of psychedelic rock, as well as electronica. From hip hop, it borrowed musical practices such as looped samples, turntablism, and sequencing, which it added to its atmospheric melodic instrumentation and ethereal lead singing (usually created in post-production through vocal distortion and backgrounding techniques). In trip hop, rapping often became secondary (with the exception of the band Massive Attack) to an atmospheric sound that focused on a groove. Trip hop musicians created their sound by employing laid-back tempos and an artful multilayering of real instruments and virtual ones; their sampling involved elaborately changing the original sound file, especially by slowing down the tempo and by moving voices that normally appear in the foreground into the background. Trip hop is highly influenced by technology, resulting in a studio (synthesizer and computer hookup) sound that was difficult to reproduce live, so success often relied more on record sales than revenues from live concerts. Trip hop did evolve to include greater clarity of instrumental sound, less vocal distortion, and more acoustic instruments; however, the bands who made these changes, such as Morcheeba, Sneaker Pimps, Lamb, Goldfrapp, and Thievery Corporation eventually moved away from hip hop and toward psychedelia.

Rap was combined with Christian music to create Christian hip hop (a.k.a. CHH or Christian rap), a form of old-school-style rap concerned with Christian values and biblical verses. CHH emerged in 1985 with Stephen Wiley's four-song EP *Bible Break*, released just six years after "Rapper's Delight" by the Sugarhill Gang. Like many of his contemporaries in the early CHH scene, Wiley was an African American youth minister who used rap to teach his students. In 1987, Michael Peace released his highly influential *RRRock It Right*, widely recognized as the first full-length commercially released CHH album. Other early CHH MCs and groups include D-Boy Rodriguez, Dynamic Twins, LPG (a.k.a.

Living Proof of Grace), P.I.D. (a.k.a. Preachers in Disguise or Preachas), and S.F.C. (a.k.a. Soldiers for Christ). Gangsta rap fully hit the CHH scene in the early 1990s with Christian groups such as Gospel Gangstaz. Other prominent CHH groups include the Cross Movement, KJ-52, Lecrae, MA$E, the New Breed (a.k.a. Israel Houghton and the New Breed), and T-Bone. Female CHH rappers such as Elle R.O.C. and Sister Souljah emerged after 1992. The success of RedCloud ushered in the representation of Native Americans and Hispanic Americans in CHH. Since the 1990s, several labels, including Reach Records and Cross Movement Records, have been devoted solely to CHH.

Industrial hip hop fuses hip hop beats and/or rap vocals with industrial music, which is typically experimental electronic music that draws on harsh, discordant, metallic-sounding beats, noise, and power chords. The two suit each other well, since both rap and industrial music generally are transgressive and provocative lyrically, and because industrial music is related to some styles of trip hop, dubstep, and digital hardcore. Early influences included Bristol, England-based vocalist Mark Stewart, London keyboardist and producer Adrian Sherwood, and New York City–based bassist and producer Bill Laswell. Guitarist, rapper-songwriter, and spoken-word artist Michael Franti co-founded the Beatn**s, a band which combined hardcore punk, industrial, jazz, and rap, on the American West Coast. Later industrial hip hop bands included Meat Beat Manifesto, Franti's the Disposable Heroes of Hiphoprisy, and MC 900 Ft. Jesus. Second-generation industrial rap acts included Antipop Consortium, Death Grips, and dälek.

Hip house (a.k.a. rap house or house rap) is a combination of house music, normally associated with dance-oriented nightclubs, and hip hop beats. It became popular in the late 1980s, appearing first in large urban areas such as New York and Chicago. One of the earliest bands to popularize hip house was the Beatmasters, who, working with the pop crossover female rap duo Cookie Crew, released the hit "Rok Da House" (1987). Other early recordings included that of Tyree and Kool Rock Steady, whose "Turn up the Bass" was released in 1988, and Vitamin-C's 1990 club hit "The Chicago Way." The two songs that made hip house ubiquitous with clubbing were by jazz and hip hop trio Jungle Brothers, with "I'll House You," and the duo of Rob Base and DJ E-Z Rock, with "It Takes Two." Since 2000, hip house has evolved into a sound called electro hop, which is hip house combined with electro-pop, a style of synth-pop featuring a harder sound. It became influential on iconic pop performers such as Lady Gaga. Artists who adopted this sound included LMFAO, Black Eyed Peas, Pitbull, Flo Rida, Azealia

Banks, and Diplo. Another style of hip house, Brick City club, became popular from 1995 to 2000 in the Newark, New Jersey, area. There DJs created tracks that bordered on house music but consisted of breakbeats and strung-together, repetitive sound bites (short looped vocal excerpts similar to those in trap and bounce) with musical phrases that emphasized high energy over lyrical content or musical complexity. Brick City used a pronounced kick drum in the programmed drum tracking, and samples were short ("chopped"). The style was renamed Jersey Club when DJs outside Newark became more involved with its production and popularity. Though it was influenced by rap, the style has in turn influenced rap artists such as Missy Elliott and Timbaland, particularly on the album *Miss E . . . So Addictive* (2001).

Hip hop merged with R&B, as well as funk and gospel, to create new jack swing. R&B and hip hop singer Teddy Riley introduced the sound at nightclubs in Harlem, but Babyface, Bernard Belle, Jimmy Jam, Terry Lewis, and L.A. Reid took the sound national. In addition, the American crime thriller film *New Jack City* (1991) guaranteed that the music would catch on with mainstream audiences. Notable early new jack examples included Janet Jackson's "Nasty" (1986), Club Nouveau's "Lean on Me" (1986), Keith Sweat's "I Want Her" (1987), and Bobby Brown's "Don't Be Cruel" (1988). New jack swing employs typical hip hop music instrumentation: drum machines, synthesizers, and turntables; a funky bass line played by either a synthesizer or a bass guitar; and sampled beats sometimes produced by a Roland TR-808. Looped beats are used, usually with kick drum on the first and third beats, as well as snare drum on the second and fourth beats for a syncopated swing sound. Sixteenth-note percussion on the first beats produces a shuffle effect, as in Paula Abdul's "Straight Up" (1988). Other well-known new jack swing artists included Bel Biv DeVoe, Boyz II Men, and Tony! Toni! Toné. New jack swing went international, with songs charting in Australia, Canada, New Zealand, Sweden, and the United Kingdom. The French group Tribal Jam recorded several new jack swing songs in French.

Perhaps surprisingly, hip hop found its way into laptop music with glitch hop, a subgenre of electronica. Glitch hop blends breakbeats, hip hop bass grooves, and rap samples with the sounds, techniques, and looping practices of glitch music, which is music that deliberately incorporates errors or glitches, such as audio malfunctions—skips, hums, distortion, noise, and incorrect bit rate use. Glitch and hip hop merged in the late 1990s with Push Button Objects. Its EP *Cash* (1997) was heavily influenced by hip hop, relying on a drum machine to create breakbeats, using the machine's looping and layering functions, and sampling pre-existing sounds and vocal passages, usually transforming them digitally to mimic scratching effects created on turntables. This approach is also found in the first album by Prefuse 73, *Vocal Studies + Uprock Narratives* (2001). Glitch hop's influence can be found in the two A$AP Rocky songs discussed in our Must-Hear Music list, and is popular internationally, with many artists originating not only from the United States, but also from Australia, Japan, New Zealand, and the United Kingdom.

INTERNATIONAL MUSIC

Hip hop and rap may have begun in the United States, but they spread quickly to many countries and cultures worldwide. During its formative years, exchanges between artists from the United States and artists who were either in other countries or part of the American immigrant experience resulted in the emergence of hip hop culture's basic elements: beat making, b-boying and b-girling, graffiti production, fashion, literature, activist education, filmmaking, and rapping. Harlem's The Last Poets, one of rap music's earliest influences, engaged in hip hop activities that were an exchange among West African cultures and music. Hip hop music quickly extended its reach globally, into countries where Americans had introduced sound recordings and films and were allowed to teach breakdancing. In Jamaica, American hip hop became popular at close to the same time as its emergence in the United States, as it also did in both American Samoa and Samoa, as well as in faraway New Zealand.

A second and much larger fertile ground for hip hop's reception was a set of countries that already had a music industry and were active in a global exchange of music, especially with hits. For example, the first commercial release of a rap song, the Sugarhill Gang's "Rapper's Delight" (1979), not only charted on the Billboard Hot 100 but also charted in Austria, Belgium, Canada, France, Germany, Israel, the Netherlands, Norway, South Africa, Sweden, Switzerland, and the United Kingdom. Its parent album, which went double platinum in the United States, attained platinum status in Canada, gold in Spain, and silver in the United Kingdom. In addition, Blondie's "Rapture" (1980) reached the Top 40 in every country where "Rapper's Delight" charted. MTV, which began in 1981 in the United States, was aired in most of the same countries where these songs were hits. The music videos for "Rapture" and Malcolm McLaren's "Buffalo Gals" predated the releases and international distribution of the first American full-length motion pictures featuring hip hop culture: *Wild Style* (1983), *Flashdance* (1983), *Beat Street* (1984), *Breakin'* (1984), and *Breakin' 2: Electric Boogaloo* (1984). Like audiocassettes, videocassettes were artifacts of hip hop that could be shipped, exchanged, bootlegged, pirated, and sold. The popularity of these films also helped hip hop spread to more countries in Africa, East Asia, India, Southeast Asia, and South America.

The spread of American hip hop and cultural exchanges are just part of the story of global hip hop. Rappers in some countries began rapping in American vernacular and adapting previously composed beats in their music. They also learned American breakdancing footwork and moves. Examples of hip hop activity could be found by the mid to late 1980s in countries such as Botswana, Brazil, Bulgaria, Ghana, Greece, India, Jamaica, Pakistan, South Africa, Vietnam, and former Yugoslavia. As influential as early American hip hop was to artists, the need to make the music local—using the home language of a nation or tribe—grew. Likewise, the desire to fuse hip hop with traditional native music or other kinds of local popular music allowed artists to give their version of hip hop an authentic, local feel. In countries like France and Portugal, the need to make hip hop local and part of an authentic cultural identity tied to regional dialect was particularly strong.

For this reason, French hip hop—in the French language—focused more on political and socially conscious lyrical content than did early American rap, which was more dance and party based. French rap therefore became more influential than American rap in French-speaking countries worldwide, many of which were dealing with volatile social issues. By 1983, French rap became popular in countries like Algeria, Belgium, Cameroon, Canada, Congo, Gabon, Guadeloupe, Lebanon, Martinique, the Netherlands, Nigeria, Senegal, and Vietnam. Likewise, Portuguese hip hop, known as hip hop tuga, became popular in Angola, Brazil, Cape Verde, Guinea-Bissau, and Mozambique, where Portuguese is the official language or a common language.

Of course, using a native language is not the only way countries make rap local. Many countries began to fuse hip hop beats with traditional or indigenous music, using authentic instrumentation. For example, Ghanaian hip hop (called GH rap), used American-inspired rap music beats but had a softer sound because of its fusion of reggae. By the early 1990s, Ghanaian hip hop acts had started to combine elements of rap with modernized Ghanaian highlife, an acoustic guitar musical style with roots tracing back to the 1920s. Highlife was itself a fusion of American swing jazz and rock with Jamaican ska and Congolese *soukous*. The result was called hiplife. Reggae's influence on hip hop has been especially strong in the Caribbean, Africa, parts of South America, and Oceania.

INTERNATIONAL IMMIGRANT COMMUNITIES

The need to remake hip hop as a local phenomenon with local themes and concerns was felt especially in marginalized immigrant and indigenous communities. For example, rap culture quickly became popular among urban indigenous populations living in Australia (in the urban areas of Melbourne and Sydney), where indigenous peoples self-identified with urban African American youth, embracing rap's Blackness. Rap became for them a tool for political discourse, a way for disenfranchised youth to criticize local living conditions and discrimination, as well as to confront social and economic inequality. Since the 1980s, indigenous hip hop—consisting of indigenous music and instrumentation—has had a strong presence in Australia and New Zealand, as well as Bolivia, Canada, Colombia, Ecuador, Finland, Mexico, Mongolia, and the United States.

Immigrants also found ways to make hip hop their own, as in Stockholm, Sweden, where immigrant communities took an early interest in recreating hip hop music as a unique, immigrant-based experience. By the early 1990s, Swedish rappers rapped in both Swedish and Rinkeby, a local pidgin dialect with American English, Arabic, Kurdish, Italian, Persian, Spanish, and Turkish slang. The Latin Kings, which had members of Chilean and Venezuelan descent, used this dialect. Germany is the home to most Turkish hip hop acts (and most early German rappers were Turkish immigrants); Belgium is home to many Congolese hip hop acts; Portugal is home to many Angolan hip hop acts. Romani hip hop acts can be found in Austria, the Czech Republic, Denmark, and Hungary, among other countries. In brief, contemporary hip hop is informed by global exchanges, and the incorporation of traditional music instruments in instrumentation creates a fusion of diverse world music styles.

Other than the United States and the U.K., the nations that have embraced hip hop most fully are Canada, India, Nigeria, and Ghana. The first commercially successful Canadian rapper was Maestro Fresh Wes, an old-school rapper comparable to the American rapper Big Daddy Kane. Toronto-based, Jamaican-born radio DJ Ron Nelson helped to popularize hip hop music in Canada by promoting early acts such as Main Source, Dream Warriors, Dan-e-o, Devon, and female rapper/actor Michie Mee. "Northern Touch" (1998), a rap collective song, served as the Canadian hip hop mission statement, and this brought

Vancouver-based rap group Rascalz (whose 1998 Juno award protest led to rap awards being held on stage, rather than off camera) into the public eye. Rap found its way into the mainstream in 2001 when radio station CFXJ (93.5) became the country's first urban music station. A second generation of Canadian hip hop artists, including Kardinal Offishall, Drake, and Somali Canadian K'naan emerged. Drake continued his musical career by rewriting the American Billboard Hot 100 record books in various categories.

As of 2021, producer, singer, and actor Yo Yo Honey Singh (a.k.a. Honey Singh) is the most popular hip hop artist in India. Like many countries, India was introduced to rap in the mid-1980s, and Indian youth started to create a hip hop culture that became extremely popular in India's major urban cities such as Mumbai, Delhi, Chennai, Bangalore, and Kolkata. Most striking was Kolkata because it was host to many aboveground hip hop dance workshops and academies that emerged by the late 1980s. In contrast, rap was a larger focus of development in Mumbai, Delhi, Bangalore, and Chennai. Baba Sehgal was India's first rapper, releasing his debut and second albums *Dilruba* and *Alibaba* in 1991; however, it was the Tamil film *Kadhalan* (1994) that caused hip hop to catch on, as it produced a hit song, "Pettai Rap," in a scene which featured a colorful, androgynous character who emulates Flavor Flav in his comic dress style and vocal choices. In addition, bhangra-beat, a hybrid music genre that combines hip hop and rap with the folk dance and music of Panjabi farmers, became popular first in Pakistan and India, and then the United States and Canada.

Nigeria saw reggae and hip hop emerge in the 1980s. By 2014, Nigeria had become Africa's largest economy, and it has one of the largest youth populations in the world, making it fertile ground for a proliferation of rap music infused with traditional folk and popular sounds, highly influenced by the country's various ethnic regions. Traditional instrumentation tends toward diversity, with the most common instruments being xylophones (balafons), marimbas, bells, scrapers (similar to guiros), shakers, drums, brass instruments, and woodwinds. Nigerian hip hop is named Naija hip hop, and Sound on Sound's *From Africa from Scratch* (1988) was an early Nigerian example of hip house (the band had connections to Sugar Hill Records). By the early 1990s, Nigerian youth were listening to not only American and French hip hop, but also African hip hop. In 1991, the trio Emphasis released *Big Deal*, often considered the earliest Naija hip hop album. Other early acts included Junior & Pretty, Fela Kuti, Eedris Abdulkareem, eLDee, and Naeto C. Hip hop continued to gain popularity, and the founding of Kennis Music, eLDee's Trybe

Records, Paybacktyme Records, and Dove Records officially established the rap recording industry. Recent notable acts include M.I., Jesse Jagz, Ice Prince, and Nikki Laoye (Nigeria's most popular female rapper).

In the 1980s, Ghanaian hip hop, or GH rap, emerged in the capital city, Accra, shortly after the arrival of American hip hop. Most GH Rap was in English with American vernacular, though pidgin English (combining English with Ghanaian dialects) was sometimes used. Ghana's first rap crew, Chief G and the Tribe, was started by a 10-year-old New York–born rapper and singer-songwriter, Jay Ghartey. Other pioneering artists such as Native Funk Lords (NFL), Talking Drums, and Nananom (Kings and Queens) began combining highlife (especially its heavy use of rhythm guitar) with American hip hop, creating the aforementioned subgenre hiplife. In 1993, Talking Drums released the first hiplife single, "Aden?" In 1999, the duo Obrafour's (The Executioner) *Pae mu ka* (*To Proclaim the Truth*) became the best-selling hiplife album in Ghana. Ghana's current most popular rapper is Sarkodie.

Despite rap's international appeal, it could not get a foothold in some countries, for either political, cultural, or economic reasons. For example, Afghanistan had no hip hop scene until 2002 as a result of the Taliban government's control of radio and the Internet—that is, until the new government under President Hamid Karzai allowed an Afghan popular music scene to emerge. It took until 2013 for hip hop to become part of the global music curriculum at Afghanistan's National Institute of Music, and for women rappers such as Sonita Alizadeh to emerge. As recently as 2018, some governments severely restricted hip hop activity, to the extent that underground performance was forbidden, censored, and/or punished. Censorship and exile were practiced, and rappers were sued, imprisoned, tortured, and/or killed.

Some countries had earlier hip hop activity—until new governments came into power. One gets a real sense of how controversial rap is and how geared it is toward activism by looking at a list of countries that limit rap activity (to various extents): Afghanistan, Albania, Algeria, Angola, Argentina, Armenia, Azerbaijan, Bahrain, Bangladesh, Belarus, Brunei, Burundi, Cambodia, Central African Republic, Chad, Chile, China, Comoros, Croatia, Cuba, Democratic Republic of the Congo, Djibouti, East Timor, Ecuador, Egypt, Equatorial Guinea, Eritrea, Ethiopia, The Gambia, Georgia, Guatemala, Guinea, Guinea-Bissau, Honduras, Indonesia, Iran, Iraq, Ivory Coast, Jordan, Kazakhstan, Kenya, Kyrgyzstan, Laos, Lebanon, Liberia, Libya, Malaysia, The Maldives, Mali, Morocco, Mozambique, Myanmar, North Korea, Oman, Pakistan, Palestine, Papua New Guinea, Paraguay, Peru, Qatar, Republic of Congo, Russia, Rwanda,

Saudi Arabia, Singapore, Somalia, South Sudan, Sudan, Swaziland, Syria, Tajikistan, Thailand, Tibet, Togo, Tunisia, Turkey, Turkmenistan, Uganda, Ukraine, United Arab Emirates, Uzbekistan, Venezuela, Vietnam, Yemen, and Zimbabwe.

Southeast Asian nations Brunei and Cambodia are simply too dangerous for rappers. Brunei, a Sunni nation ruled by Sharia law, exercises government control of all media. Its hip hop scene was nonexistent until recently, when businesses globalized and started hiring from other countries. Cambodia has a history marred by the Vietnam War–related U.S. bombing of Cambodia, the Khmer Rouge Genocide, and the Cambodian–Vietnamese War, events which stifled the country's musical growth. It had no hip hop culture until the late 1990s, when self-exiled Cambodians returned to their country from exile. The Democratic Republic of the Congo (a.k.a. DRC) is one of the poorest and most dangerous countries in the world, plagued by the First and Second Congo Wars, the neighboring Rwandan civil war, and its role in the Rwandan genocide. Limited media delayed access to hip hop.

Some countries are simply too poor to support a thriving hip hop music scene. East Timor, a sovereign island nation of more than one million people in Southeast Asia, had not seen a rap scene until 2013, when the Australian government began sending emissaries to teach East Timor youth breakdancing and hip hop culture through workshops and building makeshift music studios. As recently as 2019, East Timor was still suffering from ongoing terrorist attacks and third-world development issues, such as lack of access to clean running water and a disengaged youth culture that has resorted to rebellion and crime. Equatorial Guinea's capital city, Malabo, has hosted an International Hip Hop Festival since 2006 to promote tourism; however, the country, which is isolated geographically, rarely produces popular music, so musicians usually travel to neighboring Cameroon or to Europe to record. Haiti saw street rappers in the 1980s, but most of these musicians faded into obscurity, with the exception of the originator of Haitian hip hop music and culture, Master Dji, known for his 1982 rap song, "Vakans." Recent popular hip hop acts mainly come from Port-au-Prince: Barikad Crew, RockFam Lame-a, Dug G., and Jimmy O (one of the rappers killed during the Haitian earthquake of 2010).

As discussed here, as of 2021, hip hop music's legacy remains strong, yet often changing as new scenes emerge and new styles influence other countries' hip hop cultures. Adaptations of older styles have led to the creation of hip hop subgenres, such as reggaetón (originally from Panama) in Puerto Rico and genge in Kenya, as well as sister genres to hip hop, such as kwaito in South Africa. Hip hop fusion, exemplified by many recordings discussed in this book's Must-Hear Music entries, remains very much alive worldwide. These international hip hop musicians' creativity—from combining styles and playing with previously established song structures to introducing new ways to rap and innovative beats—continue to deserve close listening.

Further Reading

Adams, Kyle. 2015. "What Did Danger Mouse Do? The Grey Album and Musical Composition in Configurable Culture." *Music Theory Spectrum* 37, no. 1: 7–24.
Barrett, Clara. 2016. "'Formation' of the Female Author in the Hip Hop Visual Album: Beyoncé and FKA Twigs." *Soundtrack* 9, nos. 1–2: 41–57.
Boone, Mary. 2008. *Akon.* Hockessin, DE: Mitchell Lane.
Boutros, Alexandra. 2014. "'My Real'll Make Yours a Rental': Hip Hop and Canadian Copyright." In Rosemary J. Coombe, Darren Wershler, and Martin Zeilinger, eds., *Dynamic Fair Dealing: Creating Canadian Culture Online,* 317–326. Toronto: University of Toronto Press.
Bridgewater, Pamela D., André Douglas Pond Cummings, and Donald F. Tibbs, eds. 2015. *Hip Hop and the Law.* Durham, NC: Carolina Academic Press.
Bua, Justin. 2011. "QBert." *The Legends of Hip Hop.* New York: Harper Design.
Buskin, Richard. 2008. "Afrika Bambaataa & the Soulsonic Force: 'Planet Rock.'" Interview with Arthur Baker. *Sound on Sound,* November. https://www.soundonsound.com/people/afrika-bambaataa-soulsonic-force-planet-rock.
Chaney, Cassandra. 2014. "The Tears of Black Men: Black Masculinity, Sexuality, and Sensitivity in R&B and Hip Hop." In Brittany C. Slatton and Kamesha Spates, eds., *Hyper Sexual, Hyper Masculine? Gender, Race, and Sexuality in the Identities of Contemporary Black Men,* 103–132. New York: Routledge.
Chang, Jeff. 2005. "Soul Salvation: The Mystery and Faith of Afrika Bambaataa" and "Zulus on a Time Bomb: Hip Hop Meets the Rockers Downtown." *Can't Stop Won't Stop: A History of the Hip Hop Generation,* chs. 5 and 8. New York: Picador.
Chapman, Dale. 2008. "'That Ill, Tight Sound': Telepresence and Biopolitics in Post-Timbaland Rap Production." *Journal of the Society for American Music* 2, no. 2: 155–75.

Charnas, Dan. 2010. *The Big Payback: The History of the Business of Hip Hop*. New York: New American Library.
Christopher, Roy, ed. 2019. *Dead Precedents: How Hip Hop Defines the Future*. London: Repeater.
Clark, Msia Kibona. 2013. "Representing Africa! Trends in Contemporary African Hip Hop." *Journal of Pan African Studies* 6, no. 3: 1–4.
Coval, Kevin, Quraysh Ali Lansana, and Nate Marshall, eds. 2015. *The BreakBeat Poets: New American Poetry in the Age of Hip Hop*. Chicago: Haymarket Books.
Crowdus, Miranda L. 2019. *Hip Hop in Urban Borderlands: Music-making, Identity, and Intercultural Dynamics on the Margins of the Jewish State*. Berlin: Peter Lang.
Daniel, Jeff. 1995. "A True Reggae Toastmaster Shaggy Takes the Music Back to Its Melodic Roots." *St. Louis Post-Dispatch*, October 26, 15.
Devitt, Rachel. 2008. "Lost in Translation: Filipino Diaspora(s), Postcolonial Hip Hop, and the Problems of Keeping It Real for the 'Contentless' Black Eyed Peas." *Asian Music* 39, no. 1: 108–34.
Djupvik, Marita B. 2017. "Naturalizing Male Authority and the Power of the Producer." *Popular Music and Society* 40, no. 2: 181–200.
Durden, E. Moncell. 2019. *Beginning Hip Hop Dance*. Champaign, IL: Human Kinetics.
Dyson, Michael Eric, and Everett Dyson. 2019. *Jay-Z: Made in America*. New York: St. Martin's.
Edgers, Geoff. 2019. *Walk This Way: Run-DMC, Aerosmith, and the Song that Changed American Music Forever*. New York: Blue Rider Press.
Farrugia, Rebekah. 2009. "Building a Women-Centered DJ Collective." *Feminist Media Studies* 9, no. 3: 335–51.
Farrugia, Rebekah, Kellie D. Hay, and Piper Carter. 2020. *Women Rapping Revolution: Hip Hop and Community Building in Detroit*. Oakland, CA: University of California Press.
Fink, Robert. 2005. "The Story of ORCH5, or, the Classical Ghost in the Hip Hop Machine." *Popular Music* 24, no. 3: 339–56.
Fleetwood, Nicole R. 2012. "The Case of Rihanna: Erotic Violence and Black Female Desire." *African American Review* 45, no. 3: 419–35.
Flores, Juan. 2000. *From Bomba to Hip Hop: Puerto Rican Culture and Latino Identity*. New York: Columbia University Press.
Fonseca, Anthony J. *Listen to Rap! Exploring a Musical Genre*. Exploring Musical Genres series. Santa Barbara, CA: Greenwood, 2019.
Forman, Murray. 2004. "Media Form and Cultural Space: Negotiating Rap 'Fanzines.'" *Journal of Popular Culture* 29, no. 2: 171–88.
Fricke, Jim, and Charlie Ahearn. 2002. *Yes Yes Y'all: The Experience Music Project Oral History of Hip Hop's First Decade*. Cambridge, MA: Da Capo Press.

Gault, Erika, and Travis Harris. 2020. *Beyond Christian Hip Hop: A Move Toward Christians and Hip Hop*. New York: Routledge.

George, Nelson. 2014. *The Hippest Trip in America: Soul Train and the Evolution of Culture and Style*. New York: William Morrow.

Gill, Jon Ivan. 2020. *Underground Rap as Religion: A Theopoetic Examination of a Process Aesthetic*. New York: Routledge.

Goldsmith, Melissa Ursula Dawn. 2020. *Listen to Classic Rock! Exploring a Musical Genre*. Exploring Musical Genres series. Santa Barbara, CA: Greenwood.

Goldsmith, Melissa Ursula Dawn, and Anthony J. Fonseca, eds. 2019. *Hip Hop around the World: An Encyclopedia*. 2 vols. Santa Barbara, CA: Greenwood.

Grem, Darren E. 2006. "'The South Got Something to Say': Atlanta's Dirty South and the Southernization of Hip Hop America." *Southern Cultures* 12, no. 4: 55–73.

Hancock, Herbie, and Lisa Dickey. 2014. *Possibilities*. New York: Viking.

Hancox, Dan. 2019. *Inner City Pressure: The Story of Grime*. London: William Collins.

Hardy, Ernest. 2003. "Fugees: *The Score*; Wyclef Jean: *The Carnival*; Lauryn Hill: *The Miseducation of Lauryn Hill*." In Oliver Wang, ed., *Classical Material: The Hip Hop Album Guide*, 74–77. Toronto: ECW Press.

Haupt, Adam, Quentin Williams, H. Samy Alim, and Emile Jansen. 2019. *Neva Again: Hip Hop Art, Activism and Education in Post-apartheid South Africa*. Cape Town, South Africa: HSRC Press.

Hazzan, Dave. 2016. "K-pop Chords of Sexism." *Herizons* 30, no. 2: 44–48.

Hernandez-Reguant, Ariana. 2004. "Blackness with a Cuban Beat." *NACLA Report on the Americas* 38, no. 2: 31–36.

Hess, Mickey, ed. 2009. *Hip Hop in America: A Regional Guide*. 2 vols. Santa Barbara, CA: Greenwood Press.

Hilburn, Robert. 1997. "Cover Story: Crown Prince of Pop: At 38, Babyface Has Won Six Grammys and Is Nominated for Another Dozen, But Does He Mind His Work Being Tagged 'Commercial'? Not One Bit." *Los Angeles Times*, February 23, 5.

Huntington, Carla Stalling. 2007. *Hip Hop Dance: Meanings and Messages*. Jefferson, NC: McFarland.

Iandoli, Kathy. 2019. *God Save the Queens: The Essential History of Women in Hip Hop*. New York: William Morrow.

Istodor, Luca. 2017. "Ana Tijoux's Radical Crossing of Borders." *Revista: Harvard Review of Latin America* 16, no. 2: 65–66.

Jones, Esther. 2013. "On the Real: Agency, Abuse, and Sexualized Violence in Rihanna's 'Russian Roulette.'" *African American Review* 46, no. 1: 71–86.

Katz, Mark. 2006. "Men, Women, and Turntables: Gender and the DJ Battle." *The Musical Quarterly* 89, no. 4: 580–99.

Katz, Mark. 2010. "The Turntable as Weapon: Understanding the Hip Hop DJ Battle." In *Capturing Sound: How Technology Has Changed Music*, rev. ed., 124–45. Berkeley: University of California Press.

Katz, Mark. 2012. *Groove Music: The Art and Culture of the Hip Hop DJ*. New York: Oxford University Press.

Katz, Mark. 2019. *Build: The Power of Hip Hop Diplomacy in a Divided World*. New York: Oxford University Press.

Khabeer, Su'ad Abdul. 2016. *Muslim Cool: Race, Religion, and Hip Hop in the United States*. New York: New York University Press.

Kim, Bora, Karin Kuroda, and Samantha Y. Shao. 2018. "How to Make a K-Pop Boy Band." *Journal of American Studies* 52, no. 4: 943–68.

K'naan. 2011. "A Son Returns to the Agony of Somalia." *New York Times*, September 25, SR5 ("Sunday Review" section).

Koreman, Rian. 2014. "Legitimating Local Music: Volksmuziek, Hip Hop/Rap and Dance Music in Dutch Elite Newspapers." *Cultural Sociology* 8, no. 4: 501–19.

Krims, Adam. 2000. *Rap Music and the Poetics of Identity*. Cambridge, UK: Cambridge University Press.

Lamotte, Martin. 2014. "Rebels without a Pause: Hip Hop and Resistance in the City." *International Journal of Urban and Regional Research* 38, no. 2: 686–94.

Lara, Francisco, and Diana Ruggiero. 2016. "Highland Afro-Ecuadorian Bomba and Identity along the Black Pacific at the Turn of the Twenty-First Century." *Revista de Música Latinoamericana* 37, no. 2: 135–64.

LaVoulle, Crystal. 2019. *Read, Write, Rhyme Institute: Educators, Entertainers, and Entrepreneurs Engaging in Hip Hop Discourse*. New York: Peter Lang.

Lee, Shayne. 2010. "Sultry Divas of Pop and Soul: Janet, Beyoncé, and Jill." In *Erotic Revolutionaries: Black Women, Sexuality, and Popular Culture*, 1022. Lanham, MD: Hamilton Books.

Lester, Paul. 2015. *In Search of Pharrell Williams*. London: Omnibus Press.

Leung, Ambrose, and Cheryl Kier. 2010. "Music Preferences and Young People's Attitudes Towards Spending and Saving." *Journal of Youth Studies* 13, no. 6: 681–98.

Lindholm, Susan. 2017. "Hip Hop Practice as Identity and Memory Work in and in-between Chile and Sweden." *Suomen Antropologi: Journal of the Finnish Anthropological Society* 42, no. 2: 60–74.

Lipsitz, George. 2006. "Breaking the Silence: The Fugees and *The Score*." *Journal of Haitian Studies* 12, no. 1: 4–23.

Locilento, Micah. 2002. *Shaggy: Dogamuffin Style*. Toronto: ECW Press.

Madden, David. 2012. "Cross-Dressing Backbeats: The Status of the Electroclash Producer and the Politics of Electronic Music." *Dancecult: Journal of Electronic Dance Music Culture* 4, no. 2: 27–47.

Malone, Christopher, and George Martinez, Jr., eds. 2015. *The Organic Globalizer: Hip Hop, Political Development, and Movement Culture*. New York: Bloomsbury Academic.

Marx, Hannelie, and Viola Candice Milton. 2011. "Bastardized Whiteness: 'Zef'-Culture, Die Antwoord and the Reconfiguration of Contemporary Afrikaans Identities." *Social Identities* 17, no. 6: 723–45.
Masquelier, Adeline Marie. 2019. *Fada: Boredom and Belonging in Niger*. Chicago: The University of Chicago Press.
Maxwell, Ian. 2003. *Phat Beats, Dope Rhymes: Hip Hop Down Under Comin Upper*. Middletown, CT: Wesleyan University Press.
Mays, Kyle T. 2018. *Hip Hop Beats, Indigenous Rhymes: Modernity and Hip Hop in Indigenous North America*. Albany: State University of New York Press.
McEwen, Jérémie. 2019. *Philosophie du Hip Hop: Des Origines à Lauryn Hill*. Montreal: XYZ.
McLeod, Kembrew. 2005. "Confessions of an Intellectual (Property): Danger Mouse, Mickey Mouse, Sonny Bono, and My Long and Winding Path as a Copyright Activist-Academic." *Popular Music and Society* 28, no. 1: 79–93.
Miller, Monica R., Anthony B. Pinn, and Bernard Freeman, eds. 2015. *Religion in Hip Hop: Mapping the New Terrain in the U.S*. New York: Bloomsbury Academic.
Miszczynski, Milosz, and Adriana Helbig, eds. 2017. *Hip Hop at Europe's Edge: Music, Agency, and Social Change*. Bloomington: Indiana University Press.
Miszczynski, Milosz, and Przemyslaw Tomaszewski. 2014. "'Spitting Lines-Spitting Brands': A Critical Analysis of Brand Usage in Polish Rap." *European Journal of Cultural Studies* 17, no. 6: 736–52.
Miszczynski, Milosz, and Przemyslaw Tomaszewski. 2017. "Wearing Nikes for a Reason: A Critical Analysis of Brand Usage in Polish Rap." In Milosz Miszczynski and Adriana Helbig, eds., *Hip Hop at Europe's Edge: Music, Agency, and Social Change*. Bloomington: Indiana University Press.
Mitchell, Tony, ed. 2001. *Global Noise: Rap and Hip Hop Outside the USA*. Middletown, CT: Wesleyan University Press.
Monteyne, Kimberley. 2013. *Hip Hop on Film: Performance Culture, Urban Space, and Genre Transformation in the 1980s*. Jackson: University Press of Mississippi.
Neal, Mark Anthony, and Murray Forman, eds. 2004. *That's the Joint: The Hip Hop Studies Reader*. New York: Routledge.
Newman, Michael. 2005. "Rap as Literacy: A Genre Analysis of Hip Hop Ciphers." *Text* 25, no. 3: 399–436.
Norris, Chris. 2010. "The Black Eyed Peas." *Rolling Stone* no. 1103, April 29, 48–56.
Olusegun-Joseph, Yomi. 2014. "Transethnic Allegory: The Yoruba World, Hip Hop, and the Rhetoric of Generational Difference." *Third Text* 28, no. 6: 517–28.
Orlando, Valerie. 2003. "From Rap to Raï in the Mixing Bowl: Beur Hip Hop Culture and Banlieue Cinema in Urban France." *Journal of Popular Culture* 36, no. 3: 395–416.

Oswald, Vanessa. 2019. *Hip-Hop: A Cultural and Musical Revolution.* New York: Lucent Press.
Perkins, William Eric, ed. 1996. *Droppin' Science: Critical Essays on Rap Music and Hip Hop Culture.* Philadelphia: Temple University Press.
Pfadenhauer, Michaela. 2009. "The Lord of the Loops. Observations at the Club Culture DJ-Desk." *Qualitative Social Research* 10, no. 3: 1–17.
Planas, Melissa Castillo, and Jason Nichols, eds. 2016. *La Verdad: An International Dialogue on Hip Hop Latinidades.* Columbus: The Ohio State University Press.
Porfilio, Bradley J., and Michael J. Viola, eds. 2012. *The Cultural Practice and Critical Pedagogy of International Hip Hop.* New York: Peter Lang.
Price, Emmett G. III. 2006. *Hip Hop Culture.* Santa Barbara, CA: ABC-CLIO.
Price, Emmett G. III, Tammy L. Kernodle, and Horace J. Maxile, Jr. 2010. *Encyclopedia of African American Music.* 3 vols. Santa Barbara, CA: Greenwood.
Rajakumar, Mohanalakshmi. 2012. *Hip Hop Dance.* Santa Barbara, CA: Greenwood.
Rakim, and Bakari Kitwana. 2019. *Sweat the Technique: Revelations on Creativity from the Lyrical Genius.* New York: HarperCollins.
Ramsey, Guthrie P., Jr. 2003. *Race Music: Black Cultures from Bebop to Hip Hop.* Berkeley: University of California Press.
Rawls, Jason D., and John Robinson. 2019. *Youth Culture Power: A #HipHopEd Guide to Building Teacher-Student Relationships and Increasing Student Engagement.* New York: Peter Lang.
Rodier, Kristin, and Michelle Meagher. 2014. "In Her Own Time: Rihanna, Post-Feminism, and Domestic Violence." *Women* 25, no. 2: 176–93.
Rollefson, J. Griffith. 2017. *Flip the Script: European Hip Hop and the Politics of Postcoloniality.* Chicago: The University of Chicago Press.
Ross, Rick, and Neil Martinez-Belkin. 2019. *Hurricanes: A Memoir.* Toronto, Ontario, Canada.
Saucier, P. Khalil, and Kumarini Silva. 2004. "Keeping It Real in the Global South: Hip Hop Comes to Sri Lanka." *Critical Sociology* 40, no. 2: 296–300.
Saunders, Tanya L. 2015. *Cuban Underground Hip Hop: Black Thoughts, Black Revolution, Black Modernity.* Austin: University of Texas Press.
Scarface (Brad Jordan), and Benjamin Meadows-Ingram. 2015. *Diary of a Madman: The Geto Boys, Life, Death, and the Roots of Southern Rap.* New York: HarperCollins.
Schloss, Joseph Glenn. 2009. *Foundation: B-Boys, B-Girls, and Hip Hop Culture in New York.* Oxford, U.K.: Oxford University Press.
Schmidt, Bryan. 2014. "'Fatty Boom Boom' and the Transnationality of Blackface in Die Antwoord's Racial Project." *TDR: The Drama Review* 58, no. 2: 132–48.

Sciullo, Nick J. 2019. *Communicating Hip-Hop: How Hip-Hop Culture Shapes Popular Culture*. Santa Barbara, CA: Praeger.

Shipley, Jesse Weaver. 2017. "Parody after Identity: Digital Music and the Politics of Uncertainty in West Africa." *American Ethnologist* 44, no. 2: 249–62.

Shiu, Anthony Sze-Fai. 2007. "Styl(us): Asian North America, Turntablism, Relation." *CR: The New Centennial Review* 7, no. 1: 81–106.

Smith, Emily. 2013. *The Akon Handbook: Everything You Need to Know about Akon*. Aspley, Australia: Emereo.

Sobral, Ana. 2013. "The Survivor's Odyssey: K'naan's 'The Dusty Foot Philosopher' as Modern Epic." *African American Review* 46, no. 1: 21–36.

Song, Myong-son. 2019. *Hanguk Hip Hop: Global Rap in South Korea*. Cham, Switzerland: Palgrave Macmillan.

Tan, Marcus. 2015. "K-Contagion: Sound, Speed, and Space in 'Gangnam Style.'" *TDR: The Drama Review* 59, no. 1: 83–96.

Tingen, Paul. 2007. "Inside Track: Justin Timberlake's "SexyBack.'" Interview with Jimmy Douglass. *Sound on Sound*, July. https://www.soundonsound.com/Techniques/secrets-mix-engineers-jimmy-douglass.

Tiongson, Antonio T., Jr. 2013. *Filipinos Represent: DJs, Racial Authenticity, and the Hip Hop Nation*. Minneapolis: University of Minnesota Press.

Tobak, Vikki. 2018. *Contact High: A Visual History of Hip-Hop*. New York: Random House-Crown.

Toltz, Joseph. 2011. "'Dragged into the Dance'—the Role of Kraftwerk in the Development of Electro-Funk." In Sean Albiez and David Pattie, eds., *Kraftwerk: Music Non-Stop*, 181–93. New York: Continuum.

Toth, Lucille. 2017. "Praising Twerk: Why Aren't We All Shaking Our Butt?" *French Cultural Studies* 28, no. 3: 291–302.

Travis, Raphael, Jr. 2016. *The Healing Power of Hip Hop*. Santa Barbara, CA: Praeger.

Tricky, and Andrew Perry. 2019. *Hell Is Round the Corner*. London: Blink Publishing.

Viator, Felicia Angeja. 2020. *To Live and Defy in L.A.: How Gangsta Rap Changed America*. Cambridge, MA: Harvard University Press.

Vito, Christopher. 2019. *The Values of Independent Hip Hop in the Post-Golden Era: Hip Hop's Rebels*. Cham, Switzerland: Palgrave Macmillan.

Wang, Oliver. 2015. *Legions of Boom: Filipino American Mobile DJ Crews in the San Francisco Bay Area*. Durham, NC: Duke University Press.

Weems, Lisa. 2014. "Refuting 'Refugee Chic': Transnational Girl(hood)s and the Guerilla Pedagogy of M.I.A." *Feminist Formations* 26, no. 1: 115–42.

Wells, Alan. 1990. "Popular Music: Emotional Use and Management." *Journal of Popular Culture* 24, no. 1: 105–17.

Westhoff, Ben. 2016. *Original Gangstas: The Untold Story of Dr. Dre, Eazy-E, Ice Cube, Tupac Shakur, and the Birth of West Coast Rap*. New York: Hachette Books.

Williams, Justin A. 2013. *Rhymin' and Stealin': Musical Borrowing in Hip Hop Music*. Ann Arbor: University of Michigan Press.

Williams, Justin A., ed. 2015. *The Cambridge Companion to Hip Hop*. Cambridge, U.K.: Cambridge University Press.

Williams, Pharrell, Buzz Aldrin, Ian Luna, and Lauren A. Gould. 2012. *Pharrell: Places and Spaces I've Been*. New York: Rizzoli.

Wong, Ketty. 2012. *Whose National Music? Identity, Mestizaje, and Migration in Ecuador. Studies of Latin American and Caribbean Music*. Philadelphia: Temple University Press.

Index

Aaliyah, 13–17, 19
Abdul, Paula, 19–22, 43, 118, 237
Afrika Bambaataa, 9, 24–30, 111, 197–203, 217, 227. *See also* Time Zone
Afrika Bambaataa & the Soulsonic Force, 24–30
Afroman, 30–33
"Ageispolis," 37–38
Akon, 33–36, 129
The Alabama Washboard Stompers. *See* Washboard Rhythm Kings
Antibalas, 172
Aphex Twin, 37
A$AP Rocky, 39–42
Atlanta (TV Series), 68–69
"Atomic Dog," 76–81
Attitude, 187, 188, 189
Auto-tuning, 8, 26

Babyface, 43–46, 54
Backstreet Boys. *See* NKOTBSB
Baker, Arthur, 24–26
"Balle," 179–183
"Bang," 119–122
Baran, Jaroslaw, 86
Battling, 223–224, 228
B-boying. *See* Breakdancing
Beatboxing, 7, 10–11, 224

"Beautiful," 33–36
"Because I Got High," 30–33
"Beggar Dude," 104–106
Beinhorn, Michael, 110, 111
Bell Biv Devoe. *See* Bivins, Michael
Bellatrix, 11
Belmonte, Francesca, 203–205
"Better That Way," 206–209
Beyoncé, 46–51, 153, 157, 221
B-girling. *See* Breakdancing
Bhangra-beat, 81–82, 241
Bhasker, Jeff, 171
Bivins, Michael, 54, 56
Black Eyed Peas, 51–54, 87, 130, 236
Black Nationalism, 227–228. *See also* Politics
BlackOut, 147
"Blue Moon," 137–139
"Boom Pow," 51–54
"Borders," 136, 141
Boyz II Men, 43, 54–57, 237
Breakdancing, 228–229
Brett Domino, 57–61
Brick City Club, 237
Brown, James, 10, 23, 79, 173, 174, 175
Bruce Waynne. *See* MIDI Mafia

Bruno Mars, 170–175
BTS, 61–65, 125, 150

Cabello, Camila. *See* Fifth Harmony
Calvin the Second, 70
Canada, 240–241
Capi, 94
Carbo, Kevin, 94
Carrasco, Nicolás, 182
"Carry Out," 187, 189–191
Cass Browne, 102
Cee-Lo Green, 65–68
Chani, Charanjit, 166–167
Channel Orange (album), 156–157
Cheshire Cat, 179–183
Chicano rap, 234–235
Childish Gambino, 68–73, 129, 177
Chinese Man, 73–76, 206–210
Christian rap, 235–236
Clarke, Stanley, 14, 17
Cleo, 85–89
"Clint Eastwood," 101–103
Clinton, George, 15, 25, 76–81, 173, 174. *See also* Funkadelic; Parliament
"Come Back in One Piece," 14–17
Cooleyhighharmony (album), 54
"Cosmic Assassins," 141–145

"Dame esta noche." *See* "Worth It"
Dan the Automator, 101
Danger Mouse, 40, 65
Danja, 187, 188, 192
The Dap-Kings, 172
DAW. *See* Digital audio workstation
Del tha Funky Homosapien, 101, 102
Demon Days (album), 101, 103
Die Antwoord, 36–39, 132
Digital audio workstation, 8
Diplo, 133
Dirty Swift. *See* MIDI Mafia
DJ APS, 81–85
DJ Danger Mouse. *See* Danger Mouse
DJ Hollywood, 2

DJ Kool Herc, 9, 218
DJ Qbert, 5, 141–145
DJing. *See* Turntablism
DMX, 13, 15–17
"Don't Turn Out the Lights (D.T.O.T.L.)," 149–152
Donatan, 85–89
Doug E. Fresh, 10–11, 234
Douglass, Jimmy, 66, 192

808 drums, 6, 8–9, 21, 219
Elliot, Missy, 13, 82, 137, 186, 192, 193–194, 225, 237
The E.N.D. (album), 51–52
Eriksen, Mikkel S. *See* Stargate

Fab 5 Freddy, 10, 111, 142, 226
"Feels Good," 19–20, 22–23
Fifth Harmony, 89–93, 172
Fike, Dominic, 93–97
Five-Percent Nation, 228. *See also* Politics
4 (album), 47–48
"Freedom," 210–214
From Russia with Love (film), 184–185, 186
Fugees, 97–100. *See also* Jean, Wyclef
Funkadelic, 76–77, 81. *See also* Clinton, George; Parliament
Furtado, Nelly, 187–189, 191

"Gangnam Style," 161–165, 169
Gangsta rap, 3–4, 225
The Gap Band, 171–172, 174
Ghana, 242
"Ghetto Stars," 203–205
"Give It to Me," 187–189, 190
Glitch hop, 237–238
Göransson, Rickard, 120
Gorillaz, 101–103
Graffiti, 225–226
Grand Mixer D.ST. *See* GrandMixer DXT

Grande, Ariana, 119–122, 137, 140
Grandmaster Flash, 9, 218, 219, 234
Grandmaster Flash and the Furious Five, 6, 220, 234
GrandMixer DXT, 110, 111, 219
Great Big Sea, 104–106

Hamilton: An American Musical (cast), 106–109
Hancock, Herbie, 109–114, 142, 145, 198–199, 219
Harrell, Kuk, 120
Headfridge, 30
Héctor Delgado, 40
Hermansen, Tor Erik. *See* Stargate
Herrera, Eduardo, 183
Highlife, 70, 71, 239
Hip hop music
  activism (*see* Politics)
  authenticity, 223
  fashion, 221–223
  film, 232–234
  gang culture, 224–225
  international censorship, 242–243
  international impact, 216–217, 238–244
  legacy, 231–244
  other music genres, 217–218, 234–238
Hip house, 236–237
Holloway, Anthony. *See* DJ Hollywood
The Hooligans, 172
How to Make a Hit Pop Song (Youtube video), 57–58, 60–61
The Human Beat Box. *See* Robinson, Darren
"Hummin' to Myself (I've Got That Tune)," 73, 74, 75

"I Don't Believe You Want to Get Up and Dance (Oops!)," 171–172, 174

"Idol," 61–65, 150
"I'll Be Around," 65–68
India, 241
Industrial hip hop, 236
Irv Gotti, 14
"Istanbul (Not Constantinople)," 207–208
"It Wasn't Me," 175–179
"It's No Crime," 43–45
"I've Got That Tune," 73–76
Ivis Flies, 123, 126

"Jaan Punjabi," 165–167
Jackson, Janet, 19, 113, 114–119
Jam Master Jay, 9, 219
Jay-Z, 13, 17–19, 153, 221, 227
Jazz poetry, 2, 220
Jean, Wyclef, 33, 36, 97–100. *See also* Fugees
Jerkin', 229
Jessie J, 119–122
Jimmy Jam and Terry Lewis, 56, 114, 115, 116
Joe "Fingers" Carr. *See* "Istanbul (Not Constantinople)"
Johnny Rotten. *See* Lydon, John
J-Roc, 189
Junior Dan, 102

Kakkar, 168, 169
Kala (album), 133, 137
Kardinal Offishall, 33, 35
Kaur, Ranjit, 83–85
Kayo, 43, 44
Kid Ink, 89–92
Kid Kamillion, 137
Kid Koala, 101
"Kids Turned Out Fine," 39, 41–42
Kingman, Mateo, 122–126
Kiriakou, Eman, 150
K'Naan, 126–130
Knowles, Beyoncé. *See* Beyoncé
K-Pop, 62

Kraftwerk, 25, 26, 28
Kuk Harrell, 17

"La Di Da Di," 11
La Materialista, 191, 194–197
L.A. Reid, 43, 46
The Last Poets, 2, 220, 234
Laswell, Bill, 110, 111, 113, 198–200, 202
Lil Rob, 14
Little Big, 130–132, 163
The Lockers, 221, 228
"Los Pantaloncitos," 191, 194–197
Lubim, 131
Lydon, John, 197–202

M.I.A., 132–141
"Makhna," 167–169
The Marcels, 137, 138–139
Martha Zolanski (Nicki Minaj persona), 147
Martin, Max, 120
Martinez, Anthony Ramos, 108–109
Mcing. *See* Rapping
MIDI Mafia, 153
Millennial Yodel, 64
Miranda, Lin-Manuel, 106–109
"Mitran da Tabba," 82, 83
Mix Master Mike, 5, 9, 141–145
Mixing and mastering. *See* Production (music)
Mixolydian mode, 176–177
"Motownphilly," 54–57
"My Słowianie," 85–89

"Nappy Heads (Remix)," 97–100
The Neptunes, 45, 214, 218. *See also* Williams, Pharrell
New jack swing, 19, 20–21, 23–24, 237
New Kids on the Block. *See* NKOTBSB
Nicki Minaj, 65, 119, 121–122, 145–149, 223

Nigeria, 241–242
"1977," 183–186
1977 (album), 183
NKOTBSB, 149–152
Nostalgia, Ultra (album), 153

Ocean, Frank, 93, 94, 152–157
Odom, Leslie, Jr., 108–109
O'Donis, Colby, 33, 35
Offlicence, 166–167

"Paper Planes," 132–136
Parliament, 14–15, 76–77, 81. *See also* Clinton, George; Funkadelic
PBN. *See* Punjabi by Nature
"Pinocchio," 57–61
"Planet Rock," 24–30, 111, 197, 198
Plastician, 157–161
Politics, 226–228, 231–232, 240–244
"Pon de Floor," 48, 50
Ponce, Daniel, 111
Popping and locking, 228
"P.O.W.A.," 136–141
Production (music), 7–8
Psy, 161–165, 169
Punjabi by Nature, 165–167

Ramenofsky, Tim. *See* Headfridge
Ramos, Anthony. *See* Martinez, Anthony Ramos
Rapping, 7, 220–221
"Rhythm Nation 1814," 114–119
Rihanna, 13, 17–19, 137, 140
Rikrok, 175–178
Roberson, Kevin. *See* Kayo
Robie, John, 24–26
Robinson, Darren, 10
"Rockit," 109–113, 145, 199, 219
Roland TR-808 Rhythm Composer. *See* 808 drums
"Roman Holiday," 145, 147–149
Roman Zolanski (Nicki Minaj persona), 147–149

Index **257**

Romeo Must Die (film), 14
Ronson, Mark, 170–175
Rua, Jonathan, 108–109
"Run the World (Girls)," 46–51
Rustan, Hallgeir. *See* Stargate

Salmanzadeh, Ilya, 120
Sampling, 7, 9–10
The Score (album), 97, 100
Scott-Heron, Gil, 2, 220, 226
"Sendero Del Monte," 122–126
"Sexyback," 191–194
7/27 (album), 89–90
Shaggy, 175–179
Shea, 48
Shider, Garry, 77, 79
Shin Donghyuk. *See* Supreme Boi
Siddiq, Mohammed "Mohd," 83–85
Singhsta, 167, 168, 169
"Sir Nose D'Voidoffunk," 14–15
"Skibidi," 130–132, 163
Smith, Ben, 74–75
Smith, Jaden, 42
Sparks, Clinton, 36
Spradley, David, 77, 79
Stargate, 90
Sting International, 176
Sting Ray Davis, 78, 79. *See also* Parliament
Stogie T. *See* Tumi
"Straight to Hell," 133–134, 136
"Straight Up," 19–22
Strummer, Joe. *See* "Straight to Hell"
The Sugarhill Gang, 6, 220, 234, 238
Sukshinder Shinda, 179–183
"Sundress," 39–41
Supreme Boi, 62
"Swim Good," 93, 94, 152–157
Switch, 48
Syk Sense, 40

"Tabba," 81–85
"Tainted," 157, 159–161
Taiwan MC, 73, 76, 206, 208–209
"Take a Minute," 126–130
Tame Impala, 40
Taylor, David James Andrew. *See* Switch
Taylor, Robert. *See* Shea
Tayurskaya, Sonya. *See* Little Big
TDO, 167, 168, 169
"Ten Duel Commandments," 106–109
Tenashus, 179, 181–182
Terry Lewis. *See* Jimmy Jam and Terry Lewis
The-Dream, 17, 48
Theme and variations, 158–159
"There She Goes," 43, 45–46
They Might Be Giants. *See* "Istanbul (Not Constantinople)"
"This Is America," 68–73, 129, 177
"3 Nights," 93–97
Tijoux, Ana, 183–186
Timbaland, 8, 13, 14, 65–68, 187–191, 191–194, 218, 237
Timberlake, Justin, 187–191, 191–194
Time Zone, 197–203
Toasting, 3, 220–221
Tony! Toni! Toné!, 19–20, 22–23, 223, 237
Trans-Europa Express (album), 25, 26, 28
Tricky, 203–206, 235
Tricky Stewart, 17
Trinidad Jame$, 171–172
Trip hop, 235
Tumi, 206–210
Turntablism, 7, 9, 218–220
Tyler, the Creator, 153, 155–156, 157

"Ugly Boy," 36–39
"Umbrella," 14, 17–19

"Uptown Funk," 170–175
Urban Desi. *See* Bhangra-beat

Vocal processing. *See* Auto-tuning
Vocoder. *See* Auto-tuning

Washboard Rhythm Kings, 73, 74, 75
Washington, Steve, 73, 74, 75
"Wavin' Flag," 125, 126, 130
will.i.am, 192. *See also* Black Eyed Peas
Williams, Pharrell, 45–46, 157, 210–214. *See also* The Neptunes
"Windwalker," 157–159
Wolff, Elliott, 21
"World Destruction," 197–202
Worrell, Bernie, 15, 78, 198, 201. *See also* Parliament
"Worth It," 89–93, 172

Yo Yo Honey Singh, 167–169, 241
Yoo Gun-hyung, 162
Young Thug, 70, 72

About the Authors

ANTHONY J. FONSECA is library director and adjunct associate professor of humanities at Elms College in Massachusetts, where he teaches rap music and rap lyrics as text, rock-and-roll history and literature, first-year seminar, and serves as the college's interim archivist and rare books librarian. He specializes in popular music (vampire-related music and hip hop) and film music (horror film). Fonseca's previous book in the Exploring Musical Genres Series is *Listen to Rap! Exploring a Musical Genre* (Greenwood, 2019). His books on horror, with June Michele Pulliam, include *Ghosts in Popular Culture and Legend* (Greenwood, 2016), *Richard Matheson's Monsters: Gender in the Stories, Scripts, Novels, and Twilight Zone Episodes* (2016), *Encyclopedia of the Zombie* (Greenwood, 2014), *Hooked on Horror III: A Guide to Reading Interests* (Libraries Unlimited, 2009), *Hooked on Horror: A Guide to Reading Interests in Horror Fiction* (Libraries Unlimited, 2003), and *Read On . . . Horror Fiction* (Libraries Unlimited, 2006).

MELISSA URSULA DAWN GOLDSMITH, a musicologist, is a lecturer in the Department of Music and a visiting associate professor in the College of Graduate and Continuing Studies at Westfield State University in Massachusetts. Her courses there include jazz history, world music, music appreciation, and a seminar in music in the baroque and classical eras. Also an adjunct lecturer at Elms College, she has taught rock-and-roll history and literature, history of the English language, and a music-oriented rhetoric course. Prior to moving to Massachusetts, Goldsmith taught film music analysis, music criticism, and music research at Nicholls State University in Thibodaux, Louisiana, where she was director of a grant-funded music learning center and early music ensemble (Collegium musicum). Her previous book in the Exploring Musical Genres Series is *Listen to Classic Rock! Exploring a Musical Genre* (Greenwood, 2020).

Together, Fonseca and Goldsmith's books include *Hip Hop around the World: An Encyclopedia* (Greenwood, 2019), *The Encyclopedia of Musicians and Bands on Film* (2016, coauthored with Paige A. Willson), and *Proactive Marketing for the New and Experienced Library Director* (2014). Both own and work as composers, singer-songwriters, music engineers, and multi-instrumentalists for their music production company, Dapper Kitty Music, which releases indie, progressive, hard rock, electronica, jazz, traditional covers, incidental music, spoken-word, and poetry with music sound recordings.

www.ingramcontent.com/pod-product-compliance
Lightning Source LLC
Chambersburg PA
CBHW060946230426
43665CB00015B/2079